THE CAMPGROUND GUIDE

Oregon/Washington Edition

THE
CAMPGROUND GUIDE

Oregon/Washington
Edition

By KiKi Canniff

Ki² Books
1214 Wallace Rd. NW #165
Salem, OR 97304

ISBN 0-941361-51-9

TABLE OF CONTENTS

INTRODUCTION

There are 2,074 rv parks and campgrounds in Oregon and Washington. These range from deluxe resorts with sewer, electrical and water hookups, modern bath houses, swimming pools, hot tubs and cable tv, to primitive camps offering little more than picnic tables, fire rings and pit toilets. Nearly 500 of these campgrounds are cost-free.

You may already be aware of some State Park and National Forest campgrounds, but this is the only book available that includes all of these, plus every private park, city, county, BLM, Dept. of Natural Resources, Recreation Area, and other public campground. It provides an easy way to compare campgrounds, is written by a Pacific Northwest resident, and published locally.

Because individual campers and rv'ers are not all looking for the same experience, the campgrounds are not given ratings. After reading this introduction you will be able to tell if a park is right for your needs based on the type of operator, location, and facilities available.

Every effort has been made to insure that the information is accurate. If you visit a campground and find the facilities differ, please let us know. You can send update information to the author c/o Ki^2 Enterprises, 1214 Wallace Rd. NW #165, Salem, Oregon 97304.

HOW THE BOOK IS LAID OUT

Both states have been divided into four sections: Coast, I-5 Corridor, Central and East. These divisions are shown on the state map found at the beginning of each state's listings. See pages 15 and 165.

There is also a map at the beginning of each section. It includes page numbers down one side so that you can quickly find the cities in the area you will be visiting. These maps are not intended for navigation. You can get a free full-size highway map by contacting the state's tourism office.

Within each section, the cities are listed north to south. Each city's campgrounds appear alphabetically, and include the operating agency. Next, you will find a brief, but complete, listing of facilities. Most campgrounds have

7

picnic tables and firepits at each site; all campgrounds have toilet facilities and drinking water unless otherwise noted.

If flush toilets are not mentioned, assume that the campground has pit or vault toilets. It is noted if restrooms are handicap accessible. Established operating seasons and elevations for campgrounds over 500' have been included. Overnight charges and driving directions complete the listing.

An alphabetical listing of each state's campgrounds can be found in the index at the back of the book, providing a quick way to locate campgrounds you know by name. The index is also a good way to locate areas that offer desirable facilities such as group or horse camps, and also contains an alphabetical list of each state's cities.

DIRECTIONS AND ABBREVIATIONS

The final block of information in each campground listing consists of simply stated directions. **FSR** has been substituted for Forest Service Road and **CR** for County Road. When exploring unpopulated lands, such as those managed by the Forest Service or BLM, it is helpful to have a detailed map of the area.

OVERNIGHT FEES

The cost of an overnight stay in a Pacific Northwest campground ranges from less than $5.00 to over $30.00. Nearly all campgrounds charge an additional $5.00 for extra vehicles, and a $2.00 per person fee for parties with more than two people in them is the norm for privately operated parks.

Taxes are generally not included in the overnight rate. Oregon has no state sales tax, but Washington does. Some areas also levy a hotel tax on privately-operated campgrounds.

When a listing shows a range of prices, the lowest fee is for a tent site. A higher fee is generally charged for hookups, or a premium site that overlooks the ocean or lake.

Exact fees are given for group campsites, unless the charge is determined by the size of the group. In that case you will need to call the number listed for rates.

The region's 471 free campgrounds do not have hookups, showers or other luxuries, but many have excellent hiking trails, great fishing, and terrific scenery.

THE LOWDOWN ON CAMPGROUND OPERATORS

Campground operators come in two varieties – government and privately owned. Each operating entity has its own standard type of facilities and rules. The following information will show you what to expect.

Private Campgrounds & RV Parks

Private parks are operated by individuals, families and businesses. They are perfect for those who want hookups, and the security of on-site caretakers. Some have swimming pools, hot tubs, saunas, game rooms, cable tv and laundry facilities; others cater to boaters, people who fish, bicyclists and other activity-orientated campers. Most have paved or gravel lanes for rvs, but many also have separate grassy areas just for tents.

The majority of private campgrounds are open year round, have no restrictions on how long you can stay, and take reservations. Because these campgrounds are less publicized than government owned sites, many are half empty, even during peak vacation seasons.

National Forest Service Camps

There are 19 National Forests in Oregon and Washington. No matter where you go, there will probably be at least one within a two-hour drive. National Forests provide prime space for camping, hiking, boating, fishing, swimming, mountain climbing, skiing and other outdoor fun.

There is currently no fee to enter our National Forests. A stop at the ranger station will yield maps, information on local trails, impending weather conditions, and directions to special places you'll want to check out. The Forest Service's regional office is at 333 SW First Ave., in Portland.

Most NF campgrounds have water, picnic tables, firepits, toilets, and a maximum stay limit of 14 days. Many are accessible to the physically challenged, and some offer group campsites. Services are reduced during the winter.

National Park Campgrounds

The National Park Service provides campgrounds at Washington's Mount Rainier, Olympic and North Cascades National Parks, as well as Oregon's Crater Lake.

Entrance fees are charged at most National Parks. Golden Eagle and Golden Age Passports are available, providing discounted fees to disabled visitors, and those over the age of 62. These can be obtained at any National Park location.

Improved NP campgrounds offer drinking water, flush toilets, picnic tables, firepits, and have a 14 day limit. some National Parks prohibit firearms, and pets and motorized vehicles are not allowed on many trails. Pack and saddle horses, however, are allowed on most trails.

BLM Sites

The Bureau of Land Management has nearly 16 million acres in Oregon. Several white water rivers flow through this land, including the Deschutes, John Day, Grande Ronde, Owyhee and Rogue Rivers. The BLM also provides areas for off-road vehicle recreation, see index.

Unless posted otherwise, the maximum stay in BLM campgrounds is 14 days. Facilities generally include drinking water, picnic tables, toilets, and firepits. National Park Golden Eagle and Golden Age Passport holders receive a discount on overnight fees.

The gathering of rocks, minerals, gemstones, berries, nuts and flowers on BLM land for personal use is allowed; permits are required for large collections. They also have laws prohibiting the disturbance or removal of historic artifacts. The region's BLM headquarters is located at 1515 SW Fifth, in Portland – (503)952-6001.

Oregon State Parks

Most of Oregon's Pacific Ocean beaches are state owned. Some of this land is restricted to day-use, but other State Parks include large campgrounds. You will also find State campgrounds near many of Oregon's most spectacular rivers, lakes, scenic and natural attractions.

Many State Park campgrounds are open all year; others only from mid April to late October. Most offer flush toilets, showers, picnic tables and firepits; many have utilities, group areas, sites for the disabled, and other amenities.

Reservations are booked months in advance for some of the State's high-use campgrounds. A toll-free number has been included within each listing. The Oregon Parks and Recreation headquarters is at 1115 Commercial St. NE in Salem – (503)378-6305.

Washington State Parks

Washington State Parks also offer camping. Most have flush toilets, showers, picnic tables, firepits, hookups, and have a 10 day maximum stay. Parks with picnic areas have piped water, fireplace stoves and shelters. Many Washington Parks have interpretive displays focusing on the area's historical or geological events.

A great number of Washington State Park campgrounds are open year round; the rest April thru September. Most offer facilities that meet barrier-free guidelines for accessibility, and some have group areas.

Campers who come from states where a surcharge is levied on out-of-state visitors are required to pay that same fee on top of the regular overnight charge. For further information on this, call Washington State Parks at (800)233-0321. Washington State Parks where reservations are taken have a toll-free number listed.

Other Operators

Other campground operators in Oregon and Washington include the Corps of Engineers, National Recreation Areas, the Dept. of Natural Resources, various Indian tribes, timber and power companies, and county and city parks departments. Although most only operate campgrounds in one or two areas, they are an important piece to the complete campground picture.

RV CAMPING

When the RV symbol appears after a campground name, that campground includes sites with a fairly level parking space for a camper, trailer or rv. Hookup availability is explained within the listing, along with information on pull thrus and maximum lengths.

Whenever the term full hookups is used, you can expect to find appropriate fittings for water, electricity and sewer. Some of the mobile home and rv parks also offer cable tv and telephone hookups.

Many of the parks that provide trailer waste disposal do so without additional charge to their guests. Most will also pump out non-guest holding tanks for a small fee.

The maximum site and trailer length are given when available to help you to determine whether or not you will be able to comfortably park your rv or trailer. When no maximum length is given, it is best to assume it was designed for a pickup camper or small trailer.

If your vehicle is too long for most spots, or you require a pull-thru site, call the number listed for further information.

TENT CAMPING

When the tent symbol appears after a campground name, that campground has non-paved, non-gravel sites where tents can be pitched. These are generally the same units available to rvs, unless otherwise stated.

Tent camps are plentiful in Oregon and Washington. Most of them include a parking space for your vehicle. If the term walk-in is used, expect to be far enough away from your car to have to carry all of your equipment to your tent site, but near enough to run back for overlooked items.

A hike-in campsite can mean anything from a 30 minute walk to a couple of hour hike. The approximate distance is included at the end of the driving directions. A good rule of thumb for hike-in campsites is that unless you can carry all of your supplies in one trip, you won't want to choose a hike-in campground.

BICYCLE, HORSE AND BOAT CAMPS

Many state parks, and other campgrounds, have special areas set aside for campers traveling by bicycle. Most offer shared facilities, providing lone bicyclists with an opportunity to meet others. The charge is generally small, and based on the number of people in your group.

There are also dozens of horse camps with corrals, hitchracks, loading ramps and watering facilities. Check the index, under horse trails or facilities, for a list of page numbers where these can be found. When taking your horse into a Wilderness Area, or National Park, call the

12

ranger station to acquaint yourself with any pre-trip feeding or other restrictions.

Lots of our best campgrounds are located at lakes, and beside rivers. Many include boat ramps. Every effort has been made to include any boating restrictions on campground lakes. If motors are not allowed, or there is a speed limit, this information has been included to help motor boaters, water skiers and canoeists select a site where they can enjoy their sport. The index also has a listing for boat-in campgrounds.

Reservoirs often have predictable periodic fluctuations in water levels. However, changes in water level are not always predictable, so if the season has been drier than usual, or you are unsure of the norm, call the operating agency and ask about the water level.

ACCESSIBILITY FOR DISABLED CAMPERS

Wheelchair accessible restrooms are found at many Pacific Northwest campgrounds. A few even offer rv sites with modified hookups. If your limitations require more than barrier-free restrooms, call the campground operator and discuss your needs. We have taken each operators word on accessibility; so please let us know if you encounter problems.

Sites that have been modified for people with accessibility limitations can usually be reserved, even when all other sites are on a first-come basis. The phone number has been included within the campground listing.

The National Forest Service maintains a TTD/TDD phone number for campground reservations for those with hearing impairments. It is (800) 879-4496.

PLANNING A GROUP CAMPOUT

Hundreds of group campsites are available in Oregon and Washington. A few are strictly for tents, but most can accommodate rvs and trailers as well. Check the index for a list of page numbers where group facilities can be found.

Most group areas are available only by reservation. Call the phone number included in the listing for complete details on group facilities, fees and reservations.

CAMPING WITH PETS

Pets are welcome in most Pacific Northwest campgrounds, as long as you follow three simple rules of courtesy.

1) Dogs should never be allowed to disturb others by barking or running loose.

2) Pets should not be permitted to chase wildlife or destroy the setting.

3) Your pet's feces should be picked up and properly disposed of when on trails and in camp.

Private campground operators may have additional rules. If there is a restriction on size or type of pets allowed or an extra charge, it is noted within the listing.

When tying your dog up in camp, be sure the rope or chain will not damage the site or plant life. Dogs are permitted on nearly all National Forest trails, but banned from some Wilderness and National Park trails. You will find this fact posted on signs at the trailhead, or you can call ahead and ask the operating agency. Dogs are not allowed on some public swimming beaches.

In short, responsible pet owners are welcome, neglectful ones are not. If your pet is allowed to cause problems, the next pet owner may well be turned away.

OREGON'S CAMPGROUNDS

Whether you're looking for a quiet place to pitch your tent or a deluxe rv park, you'll find an abundance of campgrounds to choose from in Oregon. The following map shows the four sections used in organizing the state's 1,118 campgrounds. Each section has many unique camping experiences.

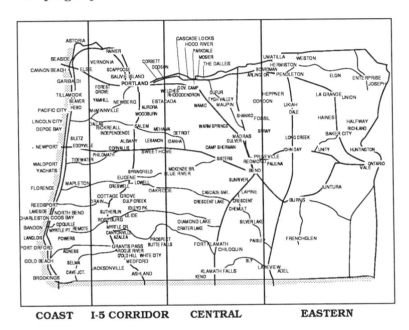

| COAST | I-5 CORRIDOR | CENTRAL | EASTERN |

THE OREGON COAST

Most of Oregon's 360 miles of Pacific Ocean coastline is state-owned, providing an unparalleled opportunity for every visitor to find his or her own quiet spot on the beach.

Along the southern coast you'll encounter the state's "banana belt", the wild and scenic Rogue River, and one of the world's largest coastal dune areas. The northern portion has historic lighthouses, wildlife refuges, protected estuaries, Indian shell mounds, and spouting horns.

OREGON'S I-5 CORRIDOR

The I-5 corridor is extremely popular with travelers in a hurry, yet just off its path a myriad of experiences beckon.

Most of Oregon's four dozen covered bridges are within this area, the scenery is gorgeous, wildlife is abundant, and historic sights are easy to view.

The land surrounding the southern I-5 corridor holds Crater Lake National Park, Oregon Caves National Monument, the Oregon Vortex, historic Jacksonville, and lots of great fishing streams. In the northern portion you'll discover pristine wilderness areas, towering Mt. Hood, the scenic Columbia River Gorge, and the state's largest cities.

CENTRAL OREGON

The eastern side of the Cascade Mountain Range, and Central Oregon, offer plenty of sunshine. The sheer height of these mountains snags most rain clouds, making it the perfect place to go when the western side of the state is too wet for camping.

The largest collection of volcanic remains in the continental U.S. can be found in the southern half of central Oregon. Ice caves, lava cast forests, obsidian flows, giant cracks in the ground, and Newberry Crater are all fun to visit. The John Day Fossil Beds, Smith Rock, numerous ghost towns, and the Deschutes, Metolius, Crooked and Columbia Rivers are all found to the north.

EASTERN OREGON

Cross Oregon to its very eastern edge, and you'll find a variety of unusual landscapes. In the northeast corner you'll encounter what residents refer to as the Little Switzerland of America. Hell's Canyon, the world's deepest gorge, guards its eastern border. National Forests protect much of this land, making it a great place for campers.

The southeast corner of the state shelters colorful Leslie Gulch, the spectacular Steens Mountains, and a 30 mile long, 4 mile wide, lava flow where obsidian, agate and petrified wood are easy to find.

OREGON COAST
CAMPGROUNDS

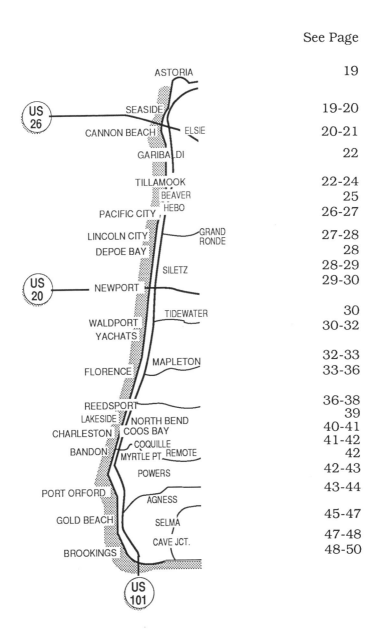

US 26

US 20

US 101

ASTORIA

ASTORIA/SEASIDE KOA (Private) ⚠️ RV
310 campsites - 142 w/full hookups, 87 w/water & elec., plus tent sites & cabins, reservations (800)KOA-8506, showers, handicap access, fire rings, laundry, groceries, swimming pool, spa, satellite tv, playground, pets okay, $23-27/night.
Located 10 miles west of Astoria, across from Fort Stevens.

FORT STEVENS (Oregon State Park) ⚠️ RV
605 campsites - 213 w/hookups for water/elec./sewer, 128 w/ elec., plus 253 tent units & yurts, reservations (503)861-1671, maximum site 69', group campsites, wheelchair access, picnic area, historical museum, self-guided walking tour, remains of Civil War era fort, showers, trailer waste disposal, boat launch, swimming, fishing, ocean beach access, beachcombing, bicycle trail, hiking trails, open year round, $11-20/night.
Located 10 miles west of Astoria, near Warrenton - follow signs.

KAMPERS WEST KAMPGROUND (Private) ⚠️ RV
250 campsites - 137 w/hookups for water/elec./cable tv, 50 w/water & elec., plus tent sites, reservations (800)880-5267, showers, laundry, ice, trailer waste disposal, river, fishing, pets okay, $15-20/night.
Located 10 miles west of Astoria. Follow Warrenton/Fort Stevens signs - located at 1140 NW Warrenton Dr.

ROGERS RV PARK (Private) ⚠️ RV
25 units - 15 w/full hookups plus 10 tent sites w/fire rings, showers, on North Fork Claskanie River, playground, $10-15/night.
On State 202, southwest of town, at milepost marker 11.2.

SUNSET LAKE RESORT (Private) ⚠️ RV
50 units - 15 w/full hookups plus 35 w/water/elec./cable tv, tents okay, reservations (503)861-1760, showers, laundry, on Neacoxie Lake, fishing, swimming, hiking, boat launch & rentals, walk to ocean, pets okay, open year round, $16-20/night.
Take US 101 south 9 miles, Sunset Beach Drive west .3 mile.

SEASIDE

CIRCLE CREEK CAMPGROUND (Private) ⚠️ RV
30 units w/full hookups, 14 w/water & elec., plus 18 tent sites, reservations (503)738-6070, showers, laundry, $17-20/night.
Take US 101 south 1 mile.

PINE COVE TRAILER COURT (Private) ⚠️ RV
8 units w/full hookups plus 3 w/elec./water/cable only, grassy tent area - no fire rings, reservations (503)738-5243, showers, laundry, pets okay, open year round, $8-12/night.
Located just beyond north end of town at 2481 US 101 North.

TRUCKE'S RV PARK (Private)
15 units w/hookups for elec./cable tv, tents okay, reservations (503)738-8863, trailers to 38', restrooms, store, tackle & bait, gas, diesel, near lake, fishing, pets okay, $15/night.
Located 1 block past first light - at 1921 S. Holladay Dr.

VENICE RV PARK (Private)
31 units w/full hookups, no tents, reservations (503)738-8851, picnic facilities, showers, laundry, picnic area, river, fishing, $20/night.
Near south end of Newana River bridge at 1032 24th Ave.

CANNON BEACH

BUD'S CAMPGROUND/RV PARK (Private)
35 units - 24 w/full hookups plus 11 tent sites, reservations (503)738-6855, showers, laundry, handicap access, groceries, ocean fishing, crabbing, clamming, pets okay, $13-18/night.
Take US 101 north 11 miles - located just past Gearhart.

ECOLA (Oregon State Park)
Hike-in camping, fire pits, creek, fishing, hiking, $10/night.
Leave US 101 at Cannon Beach's north exit, follow signs to park and hike Lewis & Clark Trail to Indian Creek and campground.

FOREST LAKE RESORT (Private)
16 units w/full hookups, 17 w/water/elec./cable tv, 19 w/water & elec., plus 28 tent sites, reservations (503)738-6779, showers, laundry, river, pond swimming, fishing, pets okay, $15-25/night.
Follow US 101 north 7 miles.

NEHALEM BAY (Oregon State Park)
284 sites w/hookups for elec., 17 site horse camp w/corrals, 9 yurts, reservations (800)551-6949, showers, wheelchair access, picnic area, trailer waste disposal, boat launch, fishing, ocean access, bicycle & horse trails, open year round, $14-19/night.
Take US 101 south 17 miles; is 3 miles past Manzanita junction.

NEHALEM BAY TRAILER PARK (Private)
37 units w/full hookups, no tents, reservations (503)368-5180, showers, laundry, groceries, ocean & river fishing, crabbing, clamming, small pets okay, $19/night.
Follow US 101 south 14 miles.

NEHALEM FALLS (Tillamook State Forest)
14 campsites plus 4 walk-in tent sites & group area, hiking, fishing in nearby Nehalem River, open mid-May thru Oct., camp hosts, $5-10/night.
Take US 101 south about 14 miles to intersection with State 53, head east 1.3 miles, take Miami Foley Rd. for 1 mile, and go east on Foss Rd. 7 miles to campground.

NEHALEM SHORES RV PARK (Private)
25 trailer sites w/full hookups, cable tv, no tents, reservations (503)368-6670, showers, laundry, fire pits, on Nehalem River, fishing, boat moorage, small pets okay, $20/night.
Take US 101 south 15 miles to Nehalem, 7th St. north .2 mile, and North Fork Rd. .6 mile east to park.

OSWALD WEST (Oregon State Park)
36 hike-in campsites, picnic area, hiking, fishing, situated in a rain forest of massive spruce & cedar trees, $14/night.
Take US 101 south 10 miles and follow trail to campground.

RV RESORT @ CANNON BEACH (Private)
100 units w/full hookups, no tents, reservations (503)436-2231, showers, laundry, wheelchair access, game room, playfield, playground, swimming & therapy pools, groceries, propane, gasoline, river, fishing, hiking, pets okay, $33-55/night.
Located just off the Cannon Beach exit ramp, .6 mile past milepost 29, at 345 Elk Creek Rd.

SADDLE MOUNTAIN (Oregon State Park)
10 primitive campsites, picnic area, hiking, $10/night.
Take US 101 north 5 miles, US 26 east approximately 16 miles.

SEA RANCH RESORT (Private)
71 units - 25 w/hookups for water/elec./sewer, 13 w/water & elec., plus 33 tent sites, reservations (503)436-2815, showers, trailer waste disposal, nearby ocean access, swimming, fishing, hiking, summer horseback riding, pets okay, $19-22/night.
Located 6 blocks north of city center, at 415 N. Hemlock St.

WRIGHT'S FOR CAMPING (Private)
19 campsites, reservations (503)436-2347, showers, laundry, wheelchair access., near beach, pets okay, open Mem. Day thru Sept., $17/night.
Take 2nd Cannon Beach exit to just east of the viaduct, campground is at 334 Reservoir Rd.

ELSIE

SPRUCE RUN (Clatsop County)
33 sites, trailers to 35', information (503)325-9306, flush toilets & drinking water in summer, on Nehalem River, swimming, fishing, rafting, bicycling, open mid-May thru mid-Sept., $12/night.
Located 5.2 miles south of Elsie on US 26.

GARIBALDI

BARVIEW JETTY (Tillamook County) [A] [RV]
60 sites w/full hookups plus 200 tent sites, information (503)322-3477, showers, handicap facilities, playground, trailer waste disposal, ocean access, fishing, hiking, pets okay, $14-18/night.
US 101 north 2 miles, Cedar Ave. west to jetty and park.

HARBOR VIEW INN (Private) [RV]
2 sites w/elec. plus 23 dry sites, no tents, reservations (503)322-3251, marina, on bay, pets okay, open year round, $9-14/night.
Located at marina - 302 S. 7th St.

MIAMI COVE RV PARK (Private) [RV]
14 units w/full hookups, no tents, reservations (503)322-3300, trailers to 56', pull thrus, showers, laundry, pets okay, open year round, $18/night.
Take US 101 to Garibaldi Ave. - at 503 E. Garibaldi Ave.

TILLAMOOK

BAY CITY RV PARK (Private) [A] [RV]
18 pull thrus - 12 w/full hookups plus grassy tent area, reservations (503)377-2124, trailers to 40', showers, laundry, pets okay, open year round, $15-21/night.
Follow US 101 3 miles north of Tillamook Cheese Factory - located at 7930 Alderbrook Rd.

BAY SHORE RV PARK (Private) [RV]
52 units w/hookups for water/elec./sewer, no tents, trailers to 40', reservations (503)842-7774, showers, laundry, ice, meeting room, ocean access, boat launch & rental, fishing, $19-21/night.
Take Netarts Hwy. west 6 miles, and Bilyeu Ave. .3 mile to #2260.

BIG BARN MARINA & RV PARK (Private) [A] [RV]
26 units w/water/elec./cable tv, grassy tent area, reservations (503)842-8596, trailers to 40', showers, laundry, wheelchair access, trailer waste disposal, on Tillamook River, boat ramp & dock, fishing, hiking, pets okay, open year round, $10-16/night.
Follow Netarts Highway west 1 mile - located at 85 3rd St.

BIG SPRUCE RV PARK (Private) [RV]
23 units w/hookups for water/elec./sewer/cable, trailers to 45', information (503)842-7443, showers, laundry, creek, $18/night.
Take Netarts Hwy. west 6.5 miles.

BROWNS CAMP (Tillamook State Forest) [A] [RV]
29 units, fire pits, picnic tables, off-road vehicle staging area, trails to Rogers Camp & University Falls, open March thru Nov., camp hosts, $10/night.
State 6 northeast 30 miles, Scoggins Creek Rd. south 1 mile.

CAPE LOOKOUT (Oregon State Park) 🏕️ RV
250 units - 53 w/water/elec./sewer, 197 tent sites, group areas & yurts, maximum site 60', reservations (503)842-4981, showers, wheelchair access, picnic area, trailer waste disposal, ocean, hiking, fishing, $16-20/night.
Take Netarts Hwy. west to Cape Lookout Rd.; go south 8 miles.

DIAMOND MILL (Tillamook State Forest) 🏕️ RV
20 campsites, advanced staging area for off road vehicles, FREE.
State 6 northeast 21 miles, North Fork Rd northwest 2.5 miles.

ELK CREEK (Tillamook State Forest) 🏕️
15 walk-in tent sites, at Elk Creek & Wilson River, trailheads to Kings Mtn./Elk Mtn./Old Wilson River Wagon Rd., nearby fishing, open mid-May thru Oct., $5/night.
Follow State 6 northeast 27 miles.

GALES CREEK (Tillamook State Forest) 🏕️ RV
23 units - 19 standard plus 4 walk-in tent sites, picnic area, trailhead to Gales Creek trails, camp host, open mid-May thru Oct., $5-10/night.
State 6 northeast 34 miles, Rigers Rd. north .7 mile.

HAPPY CAMP (Private) RV
10 units - 1 w/full hookups plus 9 w/water/ elec., no tents, reservations (503)842-4012, showers, trailer waste disposal, beachfront, ocean access, fishing, $20/night.
Take Netarts Hwy. west 7 miles.

JETTY FISHERY (Private) 🏕️ RV
30 units - 15 w/hookups for water & elec. plus 15 tent sites, reservations (503)368-5746, groceries, ocean access, river, boat launch & rental, swimming, fishing, $13-18/night.
Take US 101 north 18 miles.

JONES CREEK (Tillamook State Forest) 🏕️ RV
38 units - 28 tent/trailer units, 9 walk-in tent sites, plus group area, picnic area, group reservations (503)842-2545, maximum site 50', hiking, nearby swimming/kayakking/fishing, open mid-May thru Oct., camp hosts, $5-10/night.
Follow State 6 northeast 21 miles.

JORDAN CREEK (Tillamook State Forest) 🏕️ RV
6 campsites, off road vehicle trails, open late-May thru November, $10/night.
Follow State 6 northeast 18 miles, and Jordan Creek Rd. 2.2 miles to campground.

KILCHIS RIVER PARK (Tillamook County) 🏕️ RV
34 units, 2 group areas, information (503)842-6694, playground, trailer waste disposal, river, boat ramp, swimming, fishing, hiking, open May to Oct., $10/night - groups $20-30/night.

Follow US 101 .5 mile north of Tillamook Cheese Factory, then Kilchis River Rd. northeast 7 miles to park.

PACIFIC CAMPGROUND & RV PARK (Private)
67 units - 29 w/full hookups, 4 w/water & elec., 5 w/elec. only, plus 30 grassy tent sites, reservations (503)842-5201, showers, ice, cold drinks, $10-19/night.
Take US 101 north 2 miles.

PLEASANT VALLEY RV PARK (Private)
85 units - 15 w/full hookups, 60 w/water & elec., plus 10 tent sites, reservations (503)842-4779, showers, laundry, playground, groceries, propane, trailer waste disposal, river, fishing, hiking, pets okay, $14-20/night.
Take US 101 south 6 miles.

SHOREWOOD TRAVEL TRAILER VILLAGE (Private)
13 units w/hookups for water/elec./sewer, no tents, reservations (503)355-2278, showers, laundry, ice, playground, trailer waste disposal, ocean access, fishing, pets okay, $21/night.
Take US 101 north 12.7 miles, and go southwest 3 blocks at the Shorewood sign.

STAGECOACH HORSE CAMP (Tillamook State Forest)
10 campsites w/hitching post, picnic table & firepit, corrals, no drinking water - horse water only, picnic shelter, two loop trails, $5/night.
State 6 northeast 29 miles, University Falls Rd. 5 miles.

TRASK PARK (Tillamook County)
60 units, trailers to 60', reservations (503)842-4559, picnic area, trailer waste disposal, on Trask River, swimming, fishing, hiking, pets okay, open May thru Sept., $10/night.
Follow Trask River Rd. east 11.8 miles.

TRASK RIVER MOBILE HOME PARK (Private)
4 trailer sites w/hookups for water & elec., reservations (503)842-6142, showers, laundry, river, fishing, $15/night.
Located at 3370 Geinger Rd.

WILSON RIVER RV/FISHERMAN PARK (Private)
69 units - 59 w/full hookups, 10 w/water/elec./cable, reservations (503)842-2750, trailers to 40', showers, laundry, playground, game room, trailer waste disposal, on Wilson River, fishing, hiking, pets okay, open year round, $16-18/night.
Take State 6 east to milepost 5.

BEAVER

ADLER GLEN (BLM) 🏕 RV
10 units, handicap access, fishing, swimming, elev. 700',
$6/night.
Follow the Nestucca River Rd. east 18 miles.

CAMPER COVE RV PARK (Private) 🏕 RV
24 campsites - 12 w/hookups for water/elec./sewer, 4 dry RV
sites, plus 8 tent units, trailers to 40', reservation information -
(503)398-5334, showers, laundry, trailer waste disposal, river,
fishing, enclosed cooking area, hiking, pets okay, $18/night.
Located 2.5 miles north of town on US 101.

DOVRE (BLM) 🏕 RV
9 units, group shelter, fishing, swimming, elev. 1500', $6/night.
Follow the Nestucca River Rd. east 21 miles.

ELK BEND (BLM) 🏕 RV
3 units, drinking water, elev. 950', $6/night.
Follow the Nestucca River Rd. east 21 miles.

FAN CREEK (BLM) 🏕 RV
11 units, handicap accessible, fishing, swimming, elev. 1200',
$6/night.
Follow the Nestucca River Rd. east 24 miles.

ROCKY BEND (Siuslaw NF) 🏕 RV
6 units, picnic area, no drinking water, fishing, FREE.
Follow the Nestucca River Rd. east 15 miles.

HEBO

CASTLE ROCK (Siuslaw NF) 🏕
4 tent units, well, stream, fishing, elev. 200', FREE.
Take State Hwy. 22 southeast 4.2 miles.

HEBO LAKE (Siuslaw NF) 🏕 RV
15 units, trailers to 18', picnic shelter, lake - no motors, swimming, fishing, hiking, barrier-free trail around lake, elev. 1600',
$6/night.
Take US 101 north .1 mile, State 22 southeast .3 mile, and FSR
14 east 5 miles.

MT. HEBO (Siuslaw NF) 🏕
4 tent sites on top of Mt. Hebo, elev. 3000', $3/night.
Take State Hwy 22 southeast .3 mile, FSR 14 east 9.6 miles, and
FSR 14115 east .1 mile to campground.

PACIFIC CITY

CAPE KIWANDA RV PARK (Private) 🔺 RV
158 units - 109 w/full hookups, 19 w/water & elec., plus 30 tent sites, reservations (503)965-6230, showers, laundry, trailer waste disposal, groceries, ocean access, pets okay, $15-21/night. Follow Cape Dr. northwest 1.2 miles.

PACIFIC CITY TRAILER PARK (Private) RV
20 trailer sites w/full hookups, adults only, reservations (503)965-6820, showers, laundry, trailer waste disposal, walk to river, fishing, pets okay, $17/night. Located on Pacific Ave., 1 block east of city center.

RAINES RESORT (Private) 🔺 RV
14 units - 12 w/hookups for water/elec./sewer plus 2 tent sites, reservations (503)965-6371, showers, laundry, river, fishing, boat launch & rental, $12-20/night. Follow Cape Dr. northwest 1 mile to just past the bridge, and take Ferry St. west .1 mile to resort.

RIVERVIEW LODGE CAMPGROUND (Private) 🔺 RV
12 units w/hookups for water & elec. plus grassy tent area, reservations (503)965-6000, showers, laundry, river, fishing, boat rental, $15/night. Take US 101 exit off US 101 and go west 1 mile.

SAND BEACH (Siuslaw NF) 🔺 RV
101 campsites plus two overflow lots for additional 140 units, trailers to 40', reservations (800)280-CAMP, flush toilets, handicap access, trailer waste disposal, atv, ocean & sand dunes access, boating, fishing, ORV area, pets okay, reservations (800)280-2267 mid-March thru Sept., $6-12/night. Follow Cape Dr. and Sandlake Rd. northwest 9.6 miles and FSR S3001 southwest .5 mile.

TOMICHI VILLAGE (Private) 🔺 RV
36 units - 32 w/full hookups plus 4 w/water & elec., tents okay, reservations (503)965-7006, showers, deli-store, laundry, on ocean - @ Cape Kiwanda, pets okay, $15-19/night. Located at 33145 Webb Park Rd.

WEBB PARK (Tillamook County) 🔺 RV
30 sites, trailer waste disposal, reservations (503)965-5001, sport fishing camp, ocean access, dory launch, $10/night. Follow Cape Dr. northwest 2.2 miles.

WHALIN ISLAND PARK (Tillamook County) 🔺 RV
30 campsites, trailer waste disposal, ocean access, pond, boat launch, swimming, fishing, estuary, birdwatching, pets okay, $10/night.

Follow Cape Dr. northwest to Sandlake Rd. - park is 4.4 miles
north of Cape Kiwanda on Three Capes Scenic Loop.

WOODS PARK (Tillamook County)
7 units - 3 w/water/elec./sewer plus 4 tent sites, trailers to 40',
Nehalem River, fishing, hiking, pets okay, $10-12/night.
Follow Cape Dr. northwest 1.2 miles.

LINCOLN CITY

CHINOOK BEND RV PARK (Private) [RV]
73 sites w/full hookups plus 14 w/water/elec./cable, showers,
laundry, clubhouse, on Siletz River, boat launch & moorage, fishing, pets okay, open to public mid-Oct. thru mid-May, $16/night.
US 101 south 1.5 miles, State 229 east 3 miles to #2980.

COYOTE ROCK RV PARK (Private) [RV]
45 sites w/full hookups plus 14 w/water/elec./cable, reservations (541)996-6824, showers, ball courts, on Siletz River, boat
launch & rental, fishing, propane, bait, pets okay, $16-25/night
US 101 south 1.5 miles, State 229 east 1 mile.

DEVIL'S LAKE (Oregon State Park) [A] [RV]
100 units - 32 w/hookups for water/elec./sewer, 68 tent sites
plus group area, reservations (800)452-5687, maximum site 62',
showers, wheelchair access, on East Devil's Lake, boat launch,
fishing, swimming, open year round, $13-20/night.
Located just off US 101 - well marked by signs.

EVERGREEN PARK (Private) [A] [RV]
32 units - 25 w/hookups for water/elec./sewer plus 7 tent sites,
reservations (541)994-3116, showers, trailer waste disposal,
propane, river, fishing, hiking, $12/night.
US 101 north 5 miles, State 18 east 6 miles.

H. B. VanDUZER FOREST (Oregon State Park) [A]
Hiker/biker tent camping, no trailers, fishing, $10/night.
US 101 north 5 miles, State 18 east 15 miles.

LINCOLN CITY KOA (Private) [A] [RV]
85 units - 23 w/full hookups, 29 w/water & elec., plus 32 tent
sites, reservations - (541)994-2961, showers, laundry, playground, gam & rec room w/kitchen, groceries, propane, trailer
waste disposal, pets okay, $19-24/night.
US 101 north 4 miles, East Devils Lake Rd. southeast 1 mile.

SPORTSMAN'S LANDING (Private) [RV]
30 trailer sites w/full hookups, no tents, reservations(541)996-
4225, showers, laundry, river, fishing, boat launch & rental,
restaurant, pets okay, $16/night.
US 101 south 1.5 miles, State 229 east 3.9 miles.

SUNSET LANDING (Private) 🔺 RV
20 units w/full hookups, 21 w/water & elec., plus tent area, reservations (541)996-2060, handicap access, trailer waste disposal, boat ramp/docks/rentals, open May thru Oct., $10/night. US 101 south 1.5 miles, State 229 east 4 miles to #4274.

GRAND RONDE

WANDERING SPIRIT RV PARK (Private) 🔺 RV
79 sites w/full hookups, tents okay, pull thrus, trailers to 50', reservations (800)390-6980, showers, laundry, store, $12-20/night. Located at 28800 Hwy. 18; 1 mile west of Spirit Mtn. Casino.

DEPOE BAY

FOGARTY CREEK RV PARK (Private) RV
53 units w/full hookups, no tents, reservation information - (541)764-2228, showers, laundry, trailer waste disposal, propane, pets okay, $21/night. Follow US 101 north 2 miles.

MARTIN'S TRAILER HARBOR (Private) RV
15 units w/hookups for water/elec./sewer, no tents, reservations (541)765-2601, showers, laundry, pets okay, $20/night. US 101 just north of bridge to Collins St. - park is 2 blocks.

PIRATE'S COVE RV RESORT (Private) RV
100 sites w/full hookups - some w/ocean view, no tents, reservations - (541)765-2302, showers, laundry, groceries, fishing, pets okay - fee, $23-35/night. Follow US 101 north 1 mile.

SEA & SAND RV PARK (Private) RV
95 units w/full hookups, no tents, reservations (541)764-2313, trailers to 35', showers, laundry, wheelchair access, trailer waste disposal, ocean access, swimming, fishing, pets okay, $21/night. Follow US 101 north 3.5 miles.

SILETZ

A. W. JACK MORGAN PARK (Lincoln County) 🔺 RV
6 primitive sites, no running water, handicap access, some trailers, on Lower Siletz River, drift boat launch, fishing, FREE. Located 7.5 miles north of Siletz just off State 229.

MOONSHINE PARK (Lincoln County) 🏕️ RV
36 units, trailers okay, information (541)444-1326, flush toilets, wheelchair accessible, picnic tables, playground, on Siletz River, drift boat ramp, open April thru Oct., pets okay, $10/night.
Take Upper Siletz Rd. east 6 miles to Logsden, and follow Upper Farm Rd. northeast 3.5 miles to campground.

NEWPORT

AGATE BEACH TRAILER & RV PARK (Private) RV
32 units - 27 w/full hookups plus 9 w/water/elec./cable tv, no tents, reservations - (541)265-7670, showers, laundry, lounge, trailer waste disposal, near ocean beaches, $23/night.
Follow US 101 north 3 miles.

BEVERLY BEACH (Oregon State Park) 🏕️ RV
279 units - 53 w/hookups for water/elec./sewer, 76 w/elec., 136 tent sites, plus group area, reservations (800)452-5687, showers, wheelchair access, picnic area, trailer waste disposal, fishing, ocean access, hiking, open year round, $11-20/night.
Follow US 101 north 7 miles.

CITY CENTER TRAILER PARK (Private) RV
3 trailer sites w/full hookups, no tents, reservations (541)265-5731, trailers to 40', cable tv, showers, laundry, 3 blocks from ocean, pets okay, open year round, $22-24/night.
Located at 721 N. US 101.

ELK CITY PARK (Lincoln County) 🏕️ RV
11 campsites, flush toilets, on Yaquina River, boat launch & docks, pets okay, open April thru Oct., $10/night
Take US 20 east 6 miles to Toledo, and follow Elk City Rd. southeast 8 miles.

HARBOR VILLAGE TRAILER PARK (Private) RV
140 units w/full hookups, no tents, reservations (541)265-5088, showers, laundry, ocean access, pets okay, $15/night.
Take US 20 east .5 mile, SW Moore Dr. south .5 mile, and SE Bay Blvd. east 1 block.

NEWPORT MARINA/RV PARK (Port of Newport) RV
114 units w/full hookups, no tents, reservations (541)867-3321, cable tv, showers, laundry, wheelchair access, groceries, trailer waste disposal, river, fishing, boat launch, $22/night.
At the south end of the Yaquina Bay Bridge, take the Marine Science Center exit off US 101 - park is .5 mile east.

PACIFIC SHORES RV RESORT (Private) RV
287 paved units w/full hookups, no tents, reservations (800)666-6313, trailers to 55', showers, laundry, wheelchair access, play-

ground, swimming pool, sauna, hot tub, game room, 2 mile path to beach, pets extra, open year round, $25-40/night.
Located at north end of town - 6225 US 101.

SAWYER'S LANDING RV PARK (Private) ⚠ RV
50 units w/water/elec./tv, 12 w/sewers, plus grassy tent area w/firepits, reservations (541)265-3907, showers, conv. store, on Yaquina River, boat launch & moorage, fishing, $18-24/night.
Leave US 101 heading thru old town and follow yaquina Bay Rd. 4 miles to marina and RV park.

SOUTH BEACH (Oregon State Park) ⚠ RV
244 units w/hookups for elec. plus group campsites, reservations (541)867-4715, showers, handicap access, trailer waste disposal, at ocean, fishing, hiking, $13-20/night.
Follow US 101 south 2 miles.

SPORTSMAN'S TRAILER PARK (Private) RV
60 trailer sites w/hookups for water/eléc./sewer, no tents, reservation information - (541)867-3330, ocean access, river, fishing, boat launch & rental, $25/night.
At the south end of the Yaquina Bay Bridge, take the Marine Science Center exit off US 101 - park is 1 block.

WANDAMERE CAMPGROUND (Private) ⚠ RV
3 sites w/full hookups, 8 w/water & elec., plus 9 tent sites, reservations (541)867-4825, showers, near ocean, pets okay, open year round - restrooms open March thru Oct., $14-17/night.
Follow US 101 south 2 miles, and turn left on 148th Dr.

TIDEWATER

BLACKBERRY (Siuslaw NF) ⚠ RV
32 units, trailers to 25', flush toilets, picnic area, on Alsea River, boat launch, swimming, fishing, hiking, $8/night.
Take State 34 southeast 6 miles.

RIVEREDGE (Siuslaw NF) ⚠ RV
Group shelter, reservations required - (541)563-3211, wheelchair access inc. trail, stream, boat launch, swimming, fishing, hiking, open May thru Sept., $50/night.
Take State 34 southeast 11 miles.

WALDPORT

BEACHSIDE (Oregon State Park) ⚠ RV
82 units - 32 w/hookups for elec. plus 50 tent sites, reservations (800)452-5687, maximum site 30', showers, picnic area, ocean access, fishing, open year round, $13-20/night.
Take US 101 south 4 miles.

CANAL CREEK (Siuslaw NF)   ⚠ RV

11 units, trailers to 22', picnic area, narrow roads, $7/night.
State 34 southeast 7 miles, FSR 3462 south 4.1 miles.

CHINOOK RV PARK (Private)   ⚠ RV

44 units - 22 w/hookups for water/elec./sewer, 12 w/water &
elec., plus 10 tent sites, reservations (541)563-3485, fire pits,
showers, laundry, Alsea River, fishing, pets okay, $12-16/night.
State 34 east 3.3 miles.

DRIFT CREEK LANDING (Private)   RV

60 units - 52 w/hookups for water/elec./sewer plus 8 w/water &
elec., no tents, reservations - (541)563-3610, showers, laundry,
river, boat launch & rental, fishing, pets okay, $18-20/night.
State 34 east 3.7 miles.

FISHIN' HOLE PARK & MARINA (Private)   ⚠ RV

21 units - 10 w/full hookups plus 11 w/water & elec., tents okay,
reservations (541)563-3401, showers, laundry, river, boat launch
& rental, fishing, crabbing, $13-15/night.
State 34 east 3.8 miles.

HANDY HAVEN RV PARK/CAR WASH (Private)   RV

11 units w/full hookups, no tents, reservations - (541)563-4286,
showers, laundry, groceries, trailer waste disposal, $20/night.
Located near city center - just east of US 101.

HAPPY LANDING RV PARK/MARINA (Private)   RV

29 units - 17 w/hookups for water/elec./sewer plus 12 w/water
& elec., no tents, reservations (541)528-3300, showers, laundry,
river, boat launch & rental, fishing, $16-20/night.
State 34 east 7 miles, on Risley Creek Rd.

KING SILVER RV PARK (Private)   ⚠ RV

33 units - 27 w/hookups for water/elec./sewer plus 5 tent sites,
reservations - (541)563-3502, trailers to 35', showers, laundry,
ice, tackle/RV/marine supplies, river, fishing, covered moorage,
boat launch & rental, $12-18/night.
State 34 east 3.6 miles.

KOZY KOVE MARINA & RV PARK (Private)   ⚠ RV

22 units w/full hookups plus grassy tent area, reservations
(541)528-3251, showers, laundry, groceries, restaurant, trailer
waste disposal, river, boat launch & rental, fishing, $18-20/night.
State 34 east 9.5 miles.

McKINLEY'S MARINA & RV PARK (Private)   ⚠ RV

15 units w/hookups for elec. & cable tv plus 20 dry sites, tents
okay, reservations (541)563-4656, trailers to 50', on bay, crabbing, clamming, boat launch & rentals, moorage, fishing, pets
okay, open year round, $12-14/night.
Located about 1 mile east of the stop light - follow signs.

31

SEAL ROCKS TRAILER COVE (Private) [A] [RV]

44 units - 30 w/hookups for water/elec./sewer plus 14 w/elec. only, tents okay, trailers to 35', reservations (541)563-3955, showers, trailer waste disposal, fishing, clamming, $18-26/night. Take US 101 north 4.8 miles - located near Seal Rock.

TAYLORS LANDING (Private) [A] [RV]

27 units - 21 w/hookups for water/elec./sewer plus 6 w/water & elec., reservations (541)528-3388, showers, laundry, restaurant, river, boat moorage & rental, fishing, hiking, $11-19/night. State 34 east 7.2 miles.

TILLICUM BEACH (Siuslaw NF) [A] [RV]

57 units - some w/ocean view, trailers to 36', flush toilets, fishing, pets okay, $12/night. Take US 101 south 4.7 miles.

WALDPORT/NEWPORT KOA (Private) [A] [RV]

70 sites w/full hookups, reservations (541)563-2250, showers, river, fishing, hiking, sea lion watching, $18-23/night. On US 101 - at north end of bridge.

YACHATS

CAPE PERPETUA (Siuslaw NF) [A] [RV]

37 units, group area - reservations 541)563-3211, trailers to 36', flush toilets, trailer waste disposal, stream, ocean access, fishing, hiking, pets okay, open late May thru Sept, $12/night. Follow US 101 south 2.7 miles.

ROCK CREEK (Siuslaw NF) [A] [RV]

16 units, trailers to 22', flush toilets, ocean access, fishing, open late May thru Sept., $12/night. Follow US 101 south 10 miles.

SEA PERCH RV PARK/CAMPGROUND (Private) [A] [RV]

48 units - 21 w/full hookups, 27 w/ water/elec., plus 4 tents sites, reservations (541)547-3505, showers, laundry, groceries, ocean access, swimming, fishing, pets okay, $19-23/night. Follow US 101 south 6.5 miles.

TEN MILE CREEK (Siuslaw NF) [A] [RV]

6 units, trailers to 18', no water, nature trail, elev. 400', FREE. Follow US 101 south 10 miles.

MAPLETON

ARCHIE KNOWLES (Siuslaw NF) [A] [RV]

9 units, trailers to 32', flush toilets May thru Sept., $10/night. Take State 126 east 3 miles.

C & D DOCK RV (Private) 📇 RV
56 units - 37 w/full hookups, 19 w/elec., some tents. reservations (541)268-9950, showers, trailer waste disposal, on Siuslaw River, fishing, boat moorage, $12-15/night.
Take State 126 east 10 miles to #9634.

CLAY CREEK (BLM) 📇 RV
21 units, trailers okay, wheelchair access, on river, boating, swimming, fishing, hiking, open mid-May thru Nov., $8/night.
State 126 east 12.5 miles; Siuslaw River Rd. south 16 miles.

MAPLE-LANE TRAILER PARK & MARINA (Private) 📇 RV
46 units w/water/elec./sewer plus 2 tent sites, reservations (541)268-4822, showers, river, fishing, boat launch, $9-14/night.
Located on State 126 at milepost #14.

WHITTAKER CREEK (BLM) 📇 RV
31 units, trailers okay, wheelchair accessible toilets, picnic area, non-motorized boating only, swimming, fishing, $8/night.
Take State 126 southeast 14 miles, and follow Whittaker Creek Rd. to campground.

FLORENCE

ADA FISHING RESORT (Private) 📇 RV
40 units w/full hookups, tents okay, reservations (541)997-2342, trailers to 38', showers, laundry, on Lake Siltcoos, boat launch & rental, bait shop, pets okay, open year round, $16-20/night.
Take US 101 south 2 miles, and Canary Rd. east 13 miles.

ALDER DUNE LAKE (Siuslaw NF) 📇 RV
39 units, trailers to 36', flush toilets, lake - no motors, swimming, fishing, hiking, open May thru Sept., $12/night.
Follow US 101 north 7 miles.

BUCK LAKE MOBILE HOME & RV PARK (Private) 📇 RV
19 units - 12 w/hookups for water/elec./sewer plus 4 tent sites, reservations - (541)997-2840, showers, laundry, swimming, fishing, pets okay, $12-15/night.
Follow US 101 north 7 miles.

CARL G. WASHBURNE (Oregon State Park) 📇 RV
66 units - 58 w/hookups for water/elec./sewer plus 8 tent sites, maximum site 45', showers, picnic area, ocean access, fishing, swimming, hiking, open year round, $13-19/night.
Follow US 101 north 14 miles.

CARTER LAKE (Siuslaw NF) 📇 RV
22 units, trailers to 32', information - (800)280-2267, flush toilets, lake, boat launch, swimming, fishing, hiking, $13/night.
Take US 101 south 8.5 miles, and FSR 1084 west .1 mile.

CUSHMAN RV & MARINA (Private) `RV`

10 sites w/hookups for water/elec./sewer, no tents, reservations (541)997-2169, showers, laundry, groceries, gas, on Siuslaw River, boat launch, marina, fishing, pets okay, $13/night.
Take State 126 east 4 miles.

DARLINGS RESORT (Private) `RV`

15 units w/hookups for water/elec./cable, reservations (541)997-2841, showers, laundry, groceries, lounge, on Siltcoos Lake, motor & paddle boat rentals, fishing, pets okay, $18/night.
Take US 101 south 5 miles and follow Darling Loop to resort.

DRIFTWOOD II (Siuslaw NF) `A` `RV`

70 units, reservations required (800)280-2267, trailers to 50', flush toilets, wheelchair access, ocean fishing, hiking, ORV, pets okay, $13/night.
Take US 101 south 7 miles, and FSR 1078 west 1.4 miles.

FISH MILL LODGES (Private) `RV`

11 units w/water/elec./sewer/cable, no tents, reservations (541)997-2511, showers, trailer waste disposal, on Siltcoos Lake, boat launch & rental, tackle shop, $17/night.
Take US 101 south 6 miles.

HAPPY PLACE RV PARK & STORAGE (Private) `A` `RV`

52 units w/full hookups, trailers to 50', reservations (541)997-1434, showers, laundry, wheelchair accessible, propane, nearby fishing & hiking, pets okay, $25/night.
Located at 4044 US 101.

HARBOR VISTA CAMPGROUND (Lane County) `A` `RV`

38 units - 31 w/hookups for water/elec. plus 7 tent sites, reservations (541)997-5987, showers, playground, trailer waste disposal, beach access, hiking, pets okay, $11-15/night.
Leave US 101 on Heceta Beach Rd. and follow to Harbor Vista Dr. - campground is 3 miles north of Florence.

HECETA BEACH RV PARK (Private) `A` `RV`

38 units - 23 w/hookups for water/elec./sewer, 9 w/water & elec., plus 6 tent sites, reservations - (541)997-7664, pull-thrus, showers, laundry, trailer waste disposal, pets okay, $16-23/night.
US 101 to Heceta Beach Rd. - located at 04636 Heceta Beach Rd.

JESSIE M. HONEYMAN (Oregon State Park) `A` `RV`

378 units - 50 w/hookups for water/elec./sewer, 91 w/elec., 237 tent sites, plus group areas, reservations (800)452-5687, maximum site 55', showers, wheelchair access, picnic area, trailer waste disposal, lakes, boat launch, fishing, swimming, trails, sand dunes, open year round, $13-20/night.
Take US 101 south 3 miles.

LAGOON (SILTCOOS) (Siuslaw NF)
40 units, reservations required (800)280-2267, trailers to 32',
flush toilets, river, swimming, fishing, hiking, ocean access, ORV,
$13/night.
Take US 101 south 7 miles, and FSR 1076 west 1.3 miles.

LAKE'S EDGE RV PARK (Private)
13 units w/full hookups, no tents, adult park, trailers to 40',
reservations - (541)997-6056, showers, laundry, fishing, boat
dock, pets okay, $20/night.
Take US 101 south 6 miles, Pacific Ave. east .5 mile, and Laurel
St. east 1 mile.

LAKESHORE RV PARK (Private)
20 units w/full hookups, tents okay, reservations (541)997-2741,
showers, laundry, on Woahink Lake, swimming, fishing, pets
okay, $18/night.
Take US 101 south 4.5 miles - located near milepost #195.

MERCER LAKE RESORT (Private)
RV sites w/water & elec., some w/sewer, no tents, reservations
(800)355-3633, store, tackle & bait, private beach & dock, boat
ramp, boat & motor rental, moorage, fishing, secluded, cabins,
$15-19/night.
Leave US 101 5 miles north of town on Mercer Lake Rd. and turn
left after .7 mile on Bayberry Lane.

NIGHTINGALE'S FISHING CAMP (Private)
35 units w/hookups for water & elec. plus tent area, reservations
(541)997-2892, trailers to 30', showers, laundry, wheelchair
access, trailer waste disposal, on Siltcoos Lake, boat launch,
moorage, boat gas, fishing, hiking, pets okay, $13-15/night.
Take US 101 2 miles south of the bridge to Canary Rd., go east 9
miles and follow signs.

NORTH FORK SIUSLAW (Siuslaw NF))
5 tent units, on river, fishing, primitive, elev. 100', $5/night.
Take State Hwy. 36 east 1 mile, CR 5070 northeast 13.5 miles,
and FSR 715 east .1 mile.

PORT SIUSLAW RV PARK & MARINA (Port)
84 units - 60 w/full hookups plus 24 w/water & elec., tents okay,
reservations (541)997-3040, showers, laundry, trailer waste disposal, river, boat launch, crabbing, fishing, $16-18/night.
Leave US 101 3 blocks north of bridge on Maple, head 2 blocks
southeast to 1st St, then 3 blocks east to park.

RHODODENDRON TRAILER PARK (Private)
18 units w/full hookups, no tents, reservations - (541)997-2206,
showers, laundry, pets okay, $17/night.
Take US 101 north 3 miles.

SILTCOOS LAKE RESORT (Private)
12 RV sites w/hookups for water/elec./sewer, trailers to 32', reservations (541)997-3741, showers, playground, lake, boat launch & rental, 8 unit motel, swimming, fishing, bait/tackle shop, hiking, pets okay, $18/night.
Take US 101 south 6 miles, Pacific Ave. 3 miles.

SIUSLAW MARINA (Private)
24 units w/full hookups, some tent spaces, reservations (541)997-3254, showers, laundry, on Siuslaw River, boat rental, fishing, pets okay, $10-15/night.
Located at 6516 State Hwy. 126.

SUTTON CAMPGROUND (Siuslaw NF)
80 units plus 2 group sites, group reservations - (541)268-4473, trailers to 40', flush toilets, picnic area, trail to ocean, fishing, pets okay, group site $40-100/night - individuals $12/night.
Follow US 101 north 6 miles, and FSR 794 northwest 1.6 miles - bicycles can take access route off US 101.

TYEE (Siuslaw NF)
16 units, trailers to 28', boat launch, swimming, fishing, open May thru Nov., $13/night.
Take US 101 south 6 miles, and FSR 1068 southeast .1 mile.

WAXMYRTLE (SILTCOOS) (Siuslaw NF)
56 units, trailers to 30', reservations (800)280-2267, flush toilets, ocean/dune access, river, fishing, hiking, ORV, open mid-May thru mid-Oct., $13/night.
Take US 101 south 7 miles, and FSR 1078 west 1.4 miles.

WAYSIDE RV & MOBILE PARK (Private)
22 units w/full hookups, no tents, reservations (541)997-6451, showers, laundry, lounge, small dogs okay, $18/night.
Take US 101 north 1.7 miles.

WOAHINK LAKE RV RESORT (Private)
78 units w/full hookups, no tents, reservations (541)997-6454, showers, laundry, game room, lake access, atv dune access - no dune buggies, fishing, hiking, pets w/prior approval, $20/night.
Take US 101 south 4.5 miles.

REEDSPORT

COHO MARINA & RV PARK (Private)
49 units w/hookups for water/elec./sewers, no tents, trailers to 40', reservations (541)271-5411, showers, Umpqua River, fishing, boat launch, pets okay, $13/night.
Located in town, on US 101 at 16th St.

DISCOVERY POINT RESORT (Private)
60 units - 50 w/hookups for water/elec./sewer plus 10 tent sites, reservations (541)271-3443, showers, laundry, groceries, propane, ocean access, fishing, ATV dune access & rentals, $$-$13-18/night.
US 101 southwest 4 miles, Salmon Harbor Dr. west 1 mile.

EAST SHORE RECREATION SITE (BLM)
8 tent units, picnic facilities, boating, fishing dock, swimming, $6/night.
Follow US 101 south - located near Siskiyou Nat'l Forest.

EEL CREEK (Siuslaw NF)
52 units, trailers to 20', flush toilets, stream, hiking, $13/night.
Take US 101 south 12.1 miles.

FAWN CREEK (BLM)
2 primitive sites @ confluence w/Smith River, no drinking water, boat ramp, fishing, FREE.
Leave US 101 north of town heading east on Smith River Rd for 25 miles. Watch for old road along river - no sign.

LOON LAKE (BLM)
61 units, trailers okay, reservations (800)242-4256, picnic area, showers, trailer waste disposal, boat launch, fishing, swimming, hiking, geology & nature study, elev. 700', open late May thru Sept., $10-25/night.
Take State 38 east 12.5 miles, and Loon Lake Rd. south 7 miles.

LOON LAKE LODGE RESORT (Private)
115 units - 37 w/hookups for water & elec. plus 78 dry sites, tents okay, reservations (541)599-2244, groceries, restaurant, lake, boat launch & rental, swimming, fishing, hiking, pets okay, $15-18/night.
Take State 38 east 12.5 miles, and Loon Lake Rd. south 8 miles.

OREGON DUNES KOA (Private)
Large campsite area w/full hookups, tents okay, reservations (541)756-4851, pull-thrus, kitchen, propane, firewood, 50 amp service, atv access to ODRA, near ocean, casino, atv rentals & tours, cabins, $17-23/night.
US 101 south 19 miles at milepost marker #229.

SALMON HARBOR MARINA/RESORT (Private)
336 sites - 56 w/water/elec./sewer/cable plus 280 dry sites, no tents, reservations (541)271-3407, showers, laundry, groceries, play area, boat moorage & gas, two boat launches, $7-17/night.
Take US 101 southwest 4 miles to Salmon Harbor Drive and follow signs.

SALMON HARBOR RV PARK (Private) [RV]
66 units w/full hookups, no tents, reservations (541)271-2791, showers, laundry, rec room, propane, cable available, near beach, crabbing & fishing, pets okay, $14/night.
Located at 75325 US 101, about 2 miles south of town.

SMITH RIVER FALLS (BLM) [A] [RV]
8 units, picnic area, berry picking, fishing, elev. 100', FREE.
Northeast of Reedsport. Take US 101 1.5 miles north of Gardiner and follow Smith River Road east 44 miles.

SURFWOOD CAMPGROUND (Private) [A] [RV]
100 sites w/full hookups, 41 w/water & elec.. plus 22 tent sites, reservation (541)271-4020, showers, laundry, pool, playground, tennis, groceries, trailer waste disposal, pets okay, $12-16/night.
Follow US 101 south 2 miles.

TAHKENITCH CAMPGROUND (Siuslaw NF) [A] [RV]
34 campsites, trailers to 22', flush toilets, hiking, $13/night.
Take US 101 north 7 miles, and FSR 1090 west .1 mile.

TAHKENITCH LANDING (Siuslaw NF) [A] [RV]
26 campsites, trailers to 22', no drinking water, boat launch, fishing, elev. 100', $12/night.
Take US 101 north 8 miles.

UMPQUA LIGHTHOUSE (Oregon State Park) [A] [RV]
64 units - 22 w/full hookups plus 42 tent sites, reservations (800)452-5687, maximum site 45', showers, picnic area, boat launch, fishing, dunes, hiking trails, $10-17/night.
Take US 101 south 6 miles.

VINCENT CREEK (BLM) [A] [RV]
6 units, picnic area, fire rings, fishing, FREE.
Leave US 101 north of town heading east on Smith River Rd. for 35 miles.

WILLIAM M. TUGMAN (Oregon State Park) [A] [RV]
115 units w/hookups for elec., maximum site 50', reservations (541)888-4902, showers, wheelchair access, picnic area, trailer waste disposal, boat launch, fishing, swimming, $15/night.
Take US 101 south 8 miles.

WINDY COVE COUNTY PARK (Douglas County) [A] [RV]
96 units in 2 areas - 63 w/full hookups plus 33 tent sites, information (541)271-4138, showers, wheelchair access, bay fishing, $12-15/night.
US 101 southwest 4 miles, Salmon Harbor Dr. west .3 mile.

LAKESIDE

NORTH LAKE RESORT & MARINA (Private) [A] [RV]
100 units - 20 w/water/elec./sewer, 14 w/water & elec., plus 66 tent sites, reservations (541)759-3515, showers, groceries, lake, boat gas/launch/rental, swimming, fishing, $16-22/night.
Take North Lake Ave. 1 mile east to 2090 North Lake Ave.

OSPREY POINT RESORT (Private) [A] [RV]
132 sites w/full hookups plus grassy tent area, reservations (541)759-2801, fire pits, showers, laundry, pub/pizza, boat moorage/docks/ramp, Ten Mile Lake, fishing, cabins, $16-28/night.
Follow signs to Ten Mile Lake Recreation Area - located at 1505 North Lake Rd.

SUNLAKE MARINA RV (Private) [RV]
17 units - some w/elec., reservations (541)759-3869, picnic area, showers, small store, play area, in Big Creek area of North Ten Mile Lake, swimming, fishing, bait, boat & paddleboat rentals, boat launch & moorage, remote, 2 cabins, pets okay, $12/night.
Take North Lake Rd. to end of pavement and take this steep and narrow road and turn left - watch for signs.

NORTH BEND

BLUEBILL CAMPGROUND (Siuslaw NF) [A] [RV]
19 units plus group area, reservations (800)280-2267, trailers to 22', flush toilets, lake, fishing, hiking, ocean/dune access, open May thru Oct., $13/night.
Take US 101 north 4 miles and Horsefall Dunes Rd. 3.1 miles.

FIRS TRAILER PARK (Private) [RV]
6 trailer sites w/full hookups, pull thrus, reservations (541)756-6274, showers, laundry, $15/night.
Follow US 101 north 7 miles, and Wildwood Dr. east 1.1 miles.

HORSEFALL CAMPGROUND (Siuslaw NF) [A] [RV]
70 units plus additional 35 parking lot dry sites, reservations (800)280-2267, showers, ORV access to sand dunes, $13/night.
Follow US 101 north 4 miles, and Horsefall Dunes Rd. to camp.

SPINREEL (Siuslaw NF) [A] [RV]
37 sites, trailers to 32', ORV access to dunes, trail, $13/night.
Take US 101 north 8 miles.

WILD MARE HORSE CAMP (Siuslaw NF) [A] [RV]
12 units, reservations (800)280-2267, trailers to 36', handicap access, hiking, horse corrals, no ORV, $12/night.
Follow US 101 north 4 miles, and Horsefall Dunes Rd. to camp.

COOS BAY

ARBE'S RV PARK (Private)   `RV`
15 sites w/full hookups inc. cable, no tents, reservations (541)267-3030, showers, handicap access, laundry, small pets okay, $15/night.
Leave US 101 and travel one block on Commercial and Central to Ocean Blvd., follow this to 2625 Ocean Blvd. SE.

DRIFTWOOD RV PARK (Private)   `RV`
30 sites w/full hookups, reservations (541)888-6103, showers, laundry, bay access, fishing, small pets okay, $15/night.
Take Cape Arago Highway west 7 miles.

KELLEY'S RV PARK (Private)   `RV`
38 units w/full hookups, no tents, reservations (541)888-6531, showers, laundry, $16/night.
Take Cape Arago Highway west 4.5 miles; park is at 412 Driftwood Lane.

LUCKY LOGGERS RV PARK (Private)   `RV`
78 units w/full hookups, no tents, reservations (541)267-6003, pull thrus, rest rooms, laundry, game room, small pets okay, walk to downtown & bay, $22-24/night.
Leave US 101 at Fred Meyers and head east; park is behind the Safeway at 250 E. Johnson Ave.

NESIKA PARK (Coos County)   `△` `RV`
20 campsites, picnic facilities, on Millicoma River, boating, fishing, swimming, hiking, $5/night.
Follow Coos River Hwy. 21 miles east - is 5 miles past Allegheny.

PLAINVIEW MOTEL & RV PARK (Private)   `RV`
39 units w/full hookups, cable tv, reservations (541)888-5166, showers, laundry, ocean access, lake, fishing, pets okay, $16/night.
Take Cape Arago Highway west 7.5 miles to #2760.

ROOKE-HIGGINS PARK (Coos County)   `△` `RV`
18 campsites, on Millicoma River, boat ramp, boating, fishing, hiking, rockhounding, $5/night.
Follow Coos River Hwy. 10 miles east.

SAND BAR MOBILE & RV PARK (Private)   `RV`
42 units w/full hookups - 7 pull-thrus, reservations (541)888-3179, laundry, bay fishing, crabbing, clamming, small pets okay, $15/night.
Take Cape Arago Highway west 5.5 miles.

SUNSET BAY (Oregon State Park)   `△` `RV`
139 units - 29 w/hookups for water/elec./sewer, 34 w/water & elec., 72 tent sites, plus group campsites, reservations (800)452-

6587, maximum site 47', showers, wheelchair access, picnic area, swimming, fishing, hiking trail, $16-19/night.
Take Cape Arago Highway west to Sunset Bay.

CHARLESTON

BASTENDORFF BEACH PARK (Coos County)
81 units - 56 w/hookups for water & elec. plus 25 tent sites, trailers to 70', information (541)888-5353, flush toilets, showers, picnic area, playground, trailer waste disposal, ocean access, fishing, hiking, pets okay, open year round, $15-17/night.
Take Cape Arago Highway south 2 miles.

CHARLESTON MARINA/RV PARK (Port)
119 units - 110 w/full hookups plus 9 tent sites, reservation (541)888-9512, showers, laundry, cooking facilities, playground, trailer waste disposal, propane, ocean access, river, boat launch, fishing, pets okay, $14/night.
Take Boat Basin Dr. north 2 blocks, Kingfisher Dr. east 1 block.

SEA PORT RV PARK (Private) <img RV>
26 RV sites w/full hookups, information - (541)888-3122, RVs to 40', laundry, near ocean, fishing, clamming, crabbing, $15/night.
Cross the Charleston Bridge and take Boat Basin Dr. to park.

COQUILLE

HAM BUNCH CHERRY CREEK (Coos County)
15 units, community kitchen, stream, fishing, hiking, $5/night.
Take State 42 southeast 9 miles, and Dora Rd. east 7 miles.

LAVERNE PARK (Coos County)
84 units - 20 w/hookups for water & elec. plus 64 w/out hookups, flush toilets, showers, community kitchen, playfield, playground, trailer waste disposal, fish ladder, swimming, hiking, rockhounding, $9-13/night.
Follow the Coquille/Fairview Rd. northeast 15 miles.

PARK CREEK (BLM)
15 units, well water, fire rings, picnic area, old growth, FREE.
Take State 42 southeast 9 miles, and Dora Rd. east 7 miles.

BANDON

BANDON RV PARK (Private)
46 trailer sites w/full hookups, no tents, reservations (800)393-4122, showers, laundry, pets okay, $19/night.
Located 1 block west of US 101/State 42 junction at 935 E. 2nd.

BULLARDS BEACH (Oregon State Park) 🔺 RV

192 units - 92 w/hookups for water/elec./sewer plus 99 w/elec., reservations (800)452-5687, maximum 64', showers, wheelchair access, trailer waste disposal., boat launch, fishing, horse trails & corrals, bike trails, 1896 lighthouse, $13-19/night.
Take US 101 north 1 mile to campground.

REMOTE

BEAR CREEK (BLM) 🔺 RV

9 units, no water, fire rings, picnic area, elev. 700', FREE.
Take State 42 southeast 9 miles, and Dora Rd. east 7 miles.

GULLS @ SLEEPY HOLLOW RV PARK (Private) 🔺 RV

15 units - 11 w/hookups for water/elec./sewer plus 4 tent sites, reservations (541)572-2141, showers - $2.50, laundry, play area, Middle Fork Coquille River, swimming, fishing, $7-13/night.
Take State 42 west 8.5 miles -to just east of the bridge.

REMOTE OUTPOST RV PARK (Private) 🔺 RV

25 units w/full hookups, tents okay, trailers to 40', reservations (541)572-5105 or (888)816-1530, showers, laundry, Middle Fork Coquille River, swimming, fishing, pets on approval, $17/night.
Follow State 42 east 1 mile.

MYRTLE POINT

BENNETT PARK (Coos County) 🔺 RV

18 units, picnic area, fishing, hiking, rockhounding, $5/night.
Take Dora-Sitkum Hwy. northeast 8 miles - campground is near Gravel Ford.

FRONA PARK (Coos County) 🔺 RV

17 units, picnic facilities, fishing, $5/night.
Take the Dora-Sitkum Hwy. northeast 18 miles.

POWERS

DAPHNE GROVE (Siskiyou NF) 🔺 RV

14 units plus small group site, trailers to 30', picnic area, handicap access, on Coquille River, swimming, fishing, hiking, petroglyphs, elev. 800', $3/night.
Powers South Rd. south 4.2 miles, and FSR 33 south 10.4 miles.

MYRTLE GROVE (Siskiyou NF) 🔺

4 tent units, along S. Fork Coquille River, swimming, fishing, hiking, primitive, elev. 500', FREE.
Take CR 90 southeast 4.2 miles and FSR 33 south 4.5 miles.

POWERS COUNTY PARK (Coos County)
70 units - 40 w/water & elec. plus 30 tent sites, information (541)439-2791, flush toilets, showers, trailer waste disposal, lake - no motors, fishing, swimming, hiking, $9-12/night. Located 1 mile north of town on Gaylord Rd.

SQUAW LAKE (Siskiyou NF)
7 units, lake - no floating devices, picnic area, swimming, fishing, trails, primitive, elev. 2200', FREE. Take CR 90 southeast 4.2 miles, FSR 33 south 12.6 miles, FSR 321 southeast 4.6 miles, and FSR 3342 east 1 mile.

ROCK CREEK (Siskiyou NF)
7 tent units, swimming, fishing, trails, elev. 1200', $3/night. Take the Powers South Rd. south 4.2 miles, FSR 33 south 13 miles, and FSR 3347 southwest 1.3 miles. Located near Azalea Lake Trail.

PORT ORFORD

AGATE BEACH TRAILER PARK (Private)
22 units w/hookups for water/elec./sewer/cable plus 3 tent sites, reservations (541)332-3031, shower, laundry, ocean access, lake, agate hunting, surf fishing, $14/night. Follow US 101 to 12th St. and go west .7 mile.

BANDON-PORT ORFORD KOA (Private)
16 sites w/full hookups, 24 w/water & elec., plus 34 tent sites, reservations (541)348-2358, showers, laundry, playground, groceries, propane, trailer waste disposal, pets okay, $17-22/night. Follow US 101 north 10 miles.

BUTLER BAR (Siskiyou NF)
16 units, trailers to 18' river, swimming, fishing, hiking, access to Wild & Scenic Elk River, elev. 800', FREE. Follow US 101 to 9th St. and go west 2 blocks.

CAMP BLANCO RV PARK (Private)
25 units w/full hookups, tents okay - no fire pits, reservations (541)332-6175, handicap access, showers, rec room, pets okay, walk to restaurant & laundry, $14-17/night. Located on US 101 at 2011 Oregon Street.

CAPE BLANCO (Oregon State Park)
58 campsites w/elec., reservations (800)452-5682, maximum site 65', showers, picnic area, trailer waste disposal, black sand beach, fishing, hiking, historic Hughes House, $13-18/night. Take US 101 north 4 miles, and follow park road west 5 miles.

EDSON CREEK (BLM) △ RV

25 campsites, group camp - reservations (541-751-4418, picnic facilities, small boat ramp, swimming, fishing, @ Sixes River, $5/night - call for group rates.
Take US 101 north 5 miles, Sixes River Rd. east 4 miles, and turn left before bridge.

ELK RIVER RV CAMPGROUND (Private) △ RV

50 units w/full hookups, tents okay, information (541)332-2255, pull thrus, showers, laundry, trailer waste disposal, on Elk River, fishing, $10-14/night.
US 101 north 3 miles, Elk River Rd. southeast 1.7 miles.

EVERGREEN PARK (Private) △ RV

15 units - 13 w/hookups for water/elec./sewer plus 2 tent sites, reservations (541)332-5942, showers, laundry, trailer waste disposal, $16/night.
Follow US 101 to 9th St. and go west 2 blocks.

HUMBUG MOUNTAIN (Oregon State Park) △ RV

108 units - 30 w/water/elec./sewer plus 78 tent sites, reservations (800)452-5687, maximum site 55', showers, wheelchair access, picnic area, trailer waste disposal, ocean fishing, Oregon Coast Trail, $16-18/night.
Follow US 101 south 6 miles.

MADRONA 101 RV PARK (Private) RV

15 units w/full hookups inc. cable, no tents, reservations (541)332-4025, showers, laundry, telephone & rec room, pets okay, walk to restaurant, $14/night.
Located on US 101 at Madrona, in north part of town.

PORT ORFORD RV TRAILER VILLAGE (Private) △ RV

49 units - 36 w/full hookups, 9 w/water/elec./tv, plus 6 tent sites, reservations (541)332-1041, showers, laundry, public kitchen, rec room, trailer waste disposal, $17/night.
Leave US 101 at the north end of town on Madrona Ave., go east 1 block, and follow Port Orford Loop .5 mile north.

SIXES RIVER (BLM) △ RV

19 units, no water, fishing, trails, gold panning, $5/night.
Go to Sixes, 5 miles north of Port Orford on US 101 and head east along river for 11 miles.

AGNESS

ILLAHE (Siskiyou NF) △ RV

14 campsites, trailers to 22', information - (541)247-6651, accessible flush toilets, picnic area, located on Rogue River, fishing, closed in winter, elev. 900', FREE.
Take the Agness/Illahe Rd. north 4.9 miles.

GOLD BEACH

AGNESS RV PARK (Private) 🏕 RV
84 units - 53 w/hookups for water/elec./sewer plus 31 w/elec. only, tents okay - no fire pits, reservations (541)247-2813, showers, laundry, trailer waste disposal, on rogue River, boat launch, fishing, hiking, pets okay, $17/night.
Follow Jerry's Flat Rd. east 28 miles.

ARIZONA BEACH RV PARK (Private) 🏕 RV
127 units - 11 w/hookups for water/elec./sewer, 85 w/water & elec., plus 31 tent sites, reservations (541)332-6491, showers, laundry, playfield, trailer waste disposal, groceries, ocean access, stream, swimming, fishing, pets okay, $18 and up/night.
Take US 101 north 14 miles.

FOUR SEASONS RV RESORT (Private) RV
45 sites w/full hookups, reservations (800)248-4503 or (541)247-4503, showers, laundry, playfield, trailer waste disposal, groceries, river, boat launch, fishing, hiking, $25 and up/night.
Take the North Bank Rogue River Rd. east 6.5 miles.

GOLD BEACH TRAVEL PARK (Private) RV
12 units w/full hookups inc. cable tv, trailers to 35', reservations (541)247-5512, showers, laundry, walk to restaurants, pets okay, $12/night
Take US 101 south .8 mile, and follow Hunter Creek Loop west .8 mile.

HONEY BEAR CAMPGROUND (Private) 🏕 RV
150 units - 55 w/full hookups, 18 w/water & elec., plus 77 tent sites, reservations (541)247-2765, showers, laundry, wheelchair access, playground, trailer waste disposal, groceries, ocean access, swimming, fishing, hiking, pets okay, $14-17/night.
Take US 101 north 7 miles, and Ophir Rd. north 2 miles.

HUNTER CREEK MOBILE & RV PARK (Private) 🏕 RV
60 units w/full hookups, tents okay, reservations (541)247-2322, showers, laundry, rec room, fishing, $20/night.
Take US 101 south .8 mile, and Hunter Creek Loop west .8 mile.

INDIAN CREEK RECREATION PARK (Private) 🏕 RV
125 units - 100 w/full hookups plus 25 tent sites, reservations (541)247-7704, showers, laundry, wheelchair access, playfield, playground, groceries, river, fishing, pets okay, $18 and up/night.
Follow Jerry's Flat Rd. east .5 mile.

IRELAND'S OCEAN VIEW RV PARK (Private) 🏕 RV
33 units w/full hookups inc. cable, tents okay, reservations (541)247-0148, handicap access, showers, laundry, rv supplies, on ocean, walk to restaurants & shops, pets okay, $22/night.
Located at 29272 Ellensburg Ave. (US 101), at south end of town.

KIMBALL CREEK BEND RV RESORT (Private) ⚠ RV

79 units - 66 w/full hookups plus 13 tent sites, reservations (888)814-0633 or (541)247-7580, showers, laundry, trailer waste disposal, river, boat launch, fishing, hiking, $17-26/night.
Take the North Bank Rogue River Rd. east 8 miles.

LOBSTER CREEK (Siskiyou NF) ⚠ RV

7 units plus open camping on gravel bar, trailers to 28', flush toilets, wheelchair accessible, picnic area, on Rogue River, boat ramp, fishing, hiking, pets okay, elev. 100', $5/night.
Follow Jerry's Flat Rd. east 8.5 miles.

LUCKY LODGE RV PARK (Private) RV

32 units w/hookups for water/elec./sewer plus 4 sites w/water & elec., trailers to 35', reservations (541)247-7618, showers, laundry, trailer waste disposal, Rogue River, fishing, $18/night.
Take the North Bank Rogue River Rd. east 8 miles.

NESIKA BEACH RV PARK CAMPGROUND (Private) ⚠ RV

37 units - 17 w/full hookups, 10 w/water & elec., plus 10 tent sites, trailers to 40', reservations (541)247-6077, some pull thrus, showers, laundry, groceries, $14-19/night.
Take US 101 north 7 miles, and Nesika Rd. southwest .7 mile.

OCEANSIDE RV CAMP (Private) RV

95 units - 35 w/full hookups plus 60 w/water/elec./cable tv, no tents, reservations (541)247-2301, showers, tackle shop, ocean access, river, boat launch, fishing, $20/night.
Leave US 101 at Port of Gold Beach exit and head west .5 mile to the South Jetty and campground.

QUOSATANA (Siskiyou NF) ⚠ RV

43 units plus group area, trailers to 32', information (541)247-6651, flush toilets, wheelchair access - inc. trail, trailer waste disposal, on recreational section of Rogue River, boat launch, fishing, paved trail thru myrtlewood grove, $7/night.
Follow Jerry's Flat Rd. east 14.2 miles.

ROGUE LANDING RIVERVIEW CAMP (Private) RV

13 units w/full hookups inc. cable, 6 w/water/elec./sewer, no tents, reservations (541)247-2711, showers, laundry, restaurant, lounge, on Rogue River, boat docks, fishing, pets okay, small motel, $15-18/night.
Follow Jerry's Flat Rd. east 1.5 miles east.

SECRET CAMP (Private) ⚠ RV

25 units - 10 w/water & elec. - some w/sewer, 9 tent sites - w/firepits, reservations (888)239-8365, handicap access, showers, play area, community firepit, walk to Rogue River - fishing, swimming, $16-20/night.
Follow Jerry's Flat Rd. east 2.6 miles east.

SELMA

GRANTS PASS/REDWOOD HWY KOA (Private) [A] [RV]
41 units - 26 w/hookups for water & elec. plus 15 w/water only, tents okay, reservations (541)476-6508, showers, laundry, playfield, playground, rec. room, groceries, propane, trailer waste disposal, stream, $17-22/night.
Take US 199 northeast 7 miles - is between mileposts 14 and 15.

LAKE SELMAC (Josephine County) [A] [RV]
96 units, 31 w/full hookups, trailers to 40', information (541)474-5285, showers, playfield, playground, trailer waste disposal, on lake, boat launch, swimming, fishing, hiking, $12-17/night.
Take US 199 to Lake Selmac Junction, and Lake Shore Dr. east.

CAVE JUNCTION

BOLAN LAKE (Siskiyou NF) [A] [RV]
12 units, trailers to 18', boat launch, lake - no motors, fishing, swimming, hiking, elev. 5400', FREE.
Take State 199 south 7.0 miles to O'Brien, Cr 5560 east 4.0 miles, CR 5828 for 2.0 miles, FSR 48 for 6.0 miles, FSR 4812 for 3.0 miles, FSR 4812.040 for 1 mile to campground.

CAVES CREEK (Siskiyou NF) [A] [RV]
18 campsites, trailers okay, hiking, elev. 2500', $8/night.
Take State 46 east 16 miles, and FSR 4032 south 1 mile; is near Oregon Caves National Monument.

COUNTRY HILLS RESORT (Private) [A] [RV]
25 wooded units - 12 w/elec., 2 w/water & elec., 1 w/full hookups plus 10 waterfront tent sites w/fire rings, reservations (541)592-3406, pull-thrus, handicap access, showers, laundry, store, trailer waste disposal, swimming, pets okay, $12-18/night.
Take State 46 east 8 miles.

DEWITT'S TOWN & COUNTRY RV PARK (Private) [A] [RV]
51 units - 39 w/hookups for water/elec./sewer/cable plus tent area, trailers to 50', reservations (541)592-2656, showers, laundry, on Illinois River, pets okay, open year round, $16/night.
Follow US 199 south 2 miles.

GRAYBACK (Siskiyou NF) [A] [RV]
36 units plus 2 handicap sites, nearby group sites - reservations (541)592-3400, trailers to 45', picnic area, flush toilets, handicap access - includes trail, picnic shelter, stream, swimming, fishing, inter. trail, elev. 1800', $12-15/night.
Take State 46 east 12 miles.

KERBY TRAILER PARK (Private)   🔺 RV

14 units - 5 w/hookups for water/elec./sewer, 9 w/water & elec., tent area, reservations - (541)592-2897, showers, laundry, pets okay, $11/night.
Follow US 199 north 2.8 miles to Kerby.

SHADY ACRES RV PARK (Private)   🔺 RV

29 units - 25 w/hookups for water/elec./sewer plus 4 tent sites, reservations (541)592-3702, showers, cable access, laundry, meeting room, propane, pets okay, $12-14/night.
Follow US 199 south 1 mile.

TRAILS END CAMPGROUND (Private)   🔺 RV

100 units - 40 w/hookups for water/elec./sewer, 40 w/water & elec., plus 20 tent sites, reservations (541)592-3354, showers, trailer waste disposal, river, swimming, pets okay, $10-15/night.
Follow US 199 south 2.5 miles, and take Burch Dr. southwest .1 mile to campground.

BROOKINGS

AT RIVERS EDGE RV RESORT (Private)   🔺 RV

112 units w/hookups for water/elec./sewer plus tent area, trailers to 40', reservations recommended (541)469-3356, showers, laundry, rec hall, propane, trailer waste disposal, on Chetco River, small boat ramp, pets okay, $20-25/night.
Take Southbank Chetco River Rd. east 1.5 miles.

BEACH FRONT RV PARK (Private)   🔺 RV

184 units - 48 w/full hookups, 56 w/water & elec., plus 75 dry sites, tents okay, reservations (800)441-0856, trailers to 40', showers, wheelchair access, laundry, trailer waste disposal, river, boat launch/dock/marina, fishing, swimming, restaurant, open year round, small pets okay, $9-18/night.
Leave US 101 on Lower Harbor Rd. - located at intersection of Lower Harbor Rd. and Benham Ln.

CHETCO RV PARK (Private)   RV

120 trailer sites w/full hookups - 80 are pull-thrus, adult park, no tents, reservations (541)469-3863, showers, laundry, ice, trailer waste disposal, small pets okay, $17/night.
Located 1 mile south of the Chetco River Bridge, on US 101 .

DRIFTWOOD RV PARK (Private)   RV

108 campsites - 100 w/full hookups plus 8 w/water/elec., no tents, reservations (541)469-3213, showers, laundry, ocean access, fishing, nearby boat launch, pets okay, $16-20/night.
Leave US 101 on Lower Harbor Rd. - located .7 mile west.

HARRIS BEACH (Oregon State Park)　　　▲ RV

152 units - 34 w/hookups for water/elec./sewer, 52 w/elec. only, 66 tent sites, plus group campsites, reservations (800)452-5687, maximum site 50', showers, wheelchair access, picnic area, trailer waste disposal, ocean access, fishing, hiking trails, open year round, $16-19/night.
Take US 101 north 2 miles.

LITTLE REDWOOD (Siskiyou NF)　　　▲ RV

12 units, trailers to 18', picnic area, on Chetco River, boating, swimming, fishing, elev. 200', $5/night.
Take Northbank Chetco River Rd. northeast 7.5 miles, and FSR 376 northeast 6 miles to campground.

LOEB (Oregon State Park)　　　▲ RV

53 units w/hookups for elec., reservations (800)452-5687, maximum site 50', showers, wheelchair accessible, picnic area, fishing, swimming, hiking, open year round, $16/night.
Take Northbank Chetco River Rd. northeast 10 miles.

LUDLUM PLACE (Siskiyou NF)　　　▲ RV

Group area/shelter, reservations only (541)469-2196, trailers to 32', no water, on river, fishing, swimming.
Follow US 101 southeast 5.7 miles, Winchuck River Rd. northeast 6.3 miles, FSR 3907 east 1 mile, and FSR 4029 north 1.5 miles.

PORTSIDE RV PARK (Private)　　　RV

104 units w/full hookups, no tents, trailers to 60', reservations (541)469-6616, pull thrus, showers, laundry, rec room, propane, pets okay, $20/night.
Located on Lower Harbor Rd.

RIVER BEND TERRACES (Private)　　　RV

35 units w/full hookups inc. cable, no tents, reservations (541-469-9369, handicap access, showers, laundry, small pets okay, $14/night.
Leave US 101 on South Bank Rd. heading east 2 blocks before turning right onto Payne. Park is at 97864 Payne Rd.

RIVERSIDE RV PARK (Private)　　　▲ RV

25 units w/full hookups inc. cable plus grassy tent area w/ grills & tables, reservations (541)469-4799, some pull thrus, handicap access, showers, club house w/pool table & piano, picnic tables, boat ramp, tepees w/cots, pets okay, $14-22/night.
Follow US 199 south 1 mile.

SEA BIRD RV PARK (Private)　　　RV

60 trailer sites w/hookups for water/elec./sewer/cable, senior park, no tents, reservations (541)469-3512, handicap access, showers, laundry, ocean fishing, trailer waste disposal, pets okay, $16/night.
Located on US 101, just south of the Chetco River Bridge.

WHALESHEAD BEACH RESORT (Private)   🅰 🆁🆅

109 units - 100 w/full hookups, 4 w/water & elec., plus 5 tent sites, reservations (541)469-7446, showers, laundry, beach access, hiking, pets okay, $16-25/night.
Take US 101 north 7 miles to Whaleshead Rd. - located at 19936 Whaleshead Rd.

WINCHUCK (Siskiyou NF)   🅰 🆁🆅

13 units, trailers to 18', on river, swimming, fishing, $5/night.
Follow US 101 southeast 5.7 miles, Winchuck River Rd. northeast 6.3 miles, and FSR 3907 east 1.1 miles.

OREGON I-5 CORRIDOR CAMPGROUNDS

See Page

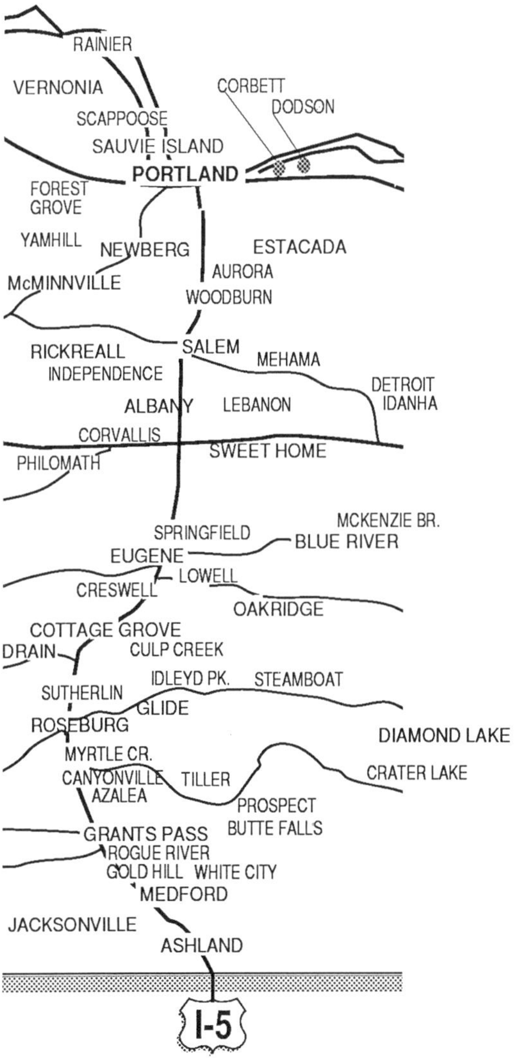

RAINIER

HUDSON/PARCHER PARK (Columbia County) [A] [RV]
15 sites w/hookups for water & elec. plus tent area, reservations (503)556-9050, flush toilets, showers, playfield, playground, picnic tables, grills, boating, fishing, windsurfing, $11-14/night - bicyclists $2/person.
Take State 30 west to Larson Rd., and follow .4 mile.

SCIPIO'S GOBLE LANDING (Private) [RV]
40 units w/full hookups plus 12 w/water & elec., reservations (503)556-6510, trailers to 40', showers, store, trailer waste disposal, on Columbia River, boat launch/rental/dock/moorage, boat gas & diesel, pets okay, $20/night.
Located on State 30 - between mileposts 40 & 41.

VERNONIA

BIG EDDY (Columbia County) [A] [RV]
23 sites w/hookups for water & elec., 5 w/water/elec.,/sewer, plus tent sites, information (503)429-6982, showers, picnic tables, grills, playground, trailer waste disposal, on Nehalem River, boat launch, fishing, $11-14/night - bicyclists $2/person.
Follow State 47 north 7 miles.

CAMP WILKERSON (Columbia County) [A] [RV]
7 primitive units plus large group camp, reservations required - (503556-3536, flush toilets, picnic shelter, day lodge, play areas, hiking trails, $7-9/night - bicyclists $2/person.
Take State 47 north 8 miles, turn onto Apiary Rd. and go 6 miles to park.

SCAPPOOSE

SCAPONIA PARK (Columbia County) [A] [RV]
7 campsites, water, stream, elev. 600', $7-9/night.
Park is 13 miles west of Scappoose along the road to Vernonia.

SCAPPOOSE/AIRPORT PARK (Columbia County) [A] [RV]
17 units - 6 w/hookups for water/elec./sewer plus tent area, playground, adjacent to airport, $7-9/night.
Leave State 30 just north of Scappoose, go east on West Lane Rd, and follow Honeyman Rd. to park.

SAUVIE ISLAND

REEDER BEACH RV PARK (Private) [A] [RV]
47 units - 39 w/hookups for water/elec./sewer plus 9 w/water & elec., tents okay, reservations advised (503)621-3098, showers,

laundry, groceries, trailer waste disposal, on Columbia River, fishing, ice, $17-20/night.
Located on the Columbia River side of the island, at 26048 NW Reeder Beach Rd.

PORTLAND

AINSWORTH (Oregon State Park) [A] [RV]
45 sites w/full hookups plus walk-in tent sites, maximum site 60', showers, picnic area, trailer waste disposal, hiking, access to Columbia Gorge Trail, campground host March-Nov., $12-18/night
Take US 30 east 37 miles - is near I-84/US 30 junction.

BELLACRES MOBILE ESTATE (Private) [RV]
12 trailer sites w/hookups for water/elec./sewer, no tents, trailers to 35', information (503)665-4774, showers, laundry, rec. room, pets okay, monthly only.
Leave I-84 on the Wood Village exit and follow NE 238th Dr. south 2.6 miles (road becomes 242nd then Hogan Dr.), turn east on Division St. and go .6 mile to park at #2980.

COLUMBIA GORGE RV VILLAGE (Private) [RV]
105 units w/full hookups, no tents or tent trailers, reservations (503)665-6722, trailers to 54', showers, laundry, wheelchair access., on Sandy River, fishing, hiking, small pets okay, $22/night.
Leave I-84 on Troutdale exit - located in Troutdale, around the corner from city hall, at 633 E. Historic Columbia River Hwy.

FIR GROVE-EL RANCHO TRAILER PARK (Private) [RV]
6 units w/full hookups, no tents, reservations (503)252-9993, trailers to 40', showers, laundry, wheelchair accessible, pets okay, open year round, $22-25/night.
Leave I-205 at exit #23B and take Columbia Blvd. west to 72nd St. - located at 5541 N.E. 72nd.

JANTZEN BEACH RV PARK (Private) [RV]
169 units w/hookups for water/elec./sewer, no tents, reservations (800)443-7248 or (503)289-7626, showers, laundry, seasonal pool, playground, rec room, nearby shops, $23/night.
Take I-5 to exit #308 and follow North Hayden Island Dr. west .5 mile.

LEROSE RV PARK (Private) [RV]
Sites w/full hookups, no tents, reservations (503)639-1501, trailers to 40', pull thrus, showers, laundry, small pets okay, open year round, monthly only.
Leave I-5 at exit #290 and go 5 blocks to 18040 SW Lower Boones Ferry Rd.

OXBOW REGIONAL PARK (State) ⚠ RV

45 campsites, no hookups, trailers to 30', information - (503)663-4708, wheelchair access, pit toilets, fire pits, playfield, playground, river, boat launch, fishing, hiking, no pets, maximum stay 5 days, gates locked sunset to 6:30 a.m., $10-13/night.
Follow Division St. east - located 8 miles east of Gresham.

PHEASANT RIDGE RV PARK (Private) RV

130 units w/full hookups, no tents, reservations (800)532-7829 or (503)682-7829, trailers to 42', pull thrus, showers, laundry, wheelchair accessible, pond, fishing, hiking, pets on approval only, open year round, $26/night.
Leave I-5 on Wilsonville exit #286 and go east .5 mile to 8275 SW Elligsen Rd.

PORTLAND-FAIRVIEW RV PARK (Private) RV

407 units w/full hookups, reservations (503)661-1047, showers, laundry, pool, rec room, horseshoes, exercise room, walk to river - fishing, pets okay, $25/night.
Leave I-84 on the Parkrose exit and follow Sandy Blvd. east 2 miles to 21401 NE Sandy Blvd.

PORTLAND MEADOWS RV PARK (Private) RV

32 units w/hookups for water/elec./sewer, no tents, reservations (503)285-1617, trailers to 50', showers, laundry, wheelchair accessible, pets to 20 lbs. okay, open year round, $18/night.
Leave I-5 on the Columbia Blvd exit, go east 2 blocks to Martin Luther King Blvd, north 1 mile to Gertz Rd., and west to park.

ROAMER'S REST RV PARK (Private) RV

93 units w/full hookups, no tents, reservations (503)692-6350, trailers to 40', pull thrus, showers, laundry, wheelchair accessible, Tualatin River, fishing, pets okay, open year round, $23/night.
Leave I-5 at Tualatin exit #289, go right on State 212, then right on State 99 to 17585 S.W. Pacific Hwy.

ROLLING HILLS MOBILE TERRACE (Private) RV

101 rv sites w/full hookups, no tents, reservations (503)666-7282, trailers to 40', basic cable, pull thrus, showers, laundry, wheelchair access, swimming pool, game room, small pets okay, $22/night.
Leave I-84 westbound on Sandy Blvd. exit - park is west .7 mile at 20145 NE Sandy Blvd.

RV/TRAILER PARK OF PORTLAND (Private) RV

120 units - 100 w/full hookups plus 20 w/water & elec., no tents, reservations (503)692-0225, showers, laundry, play area, groceries, river, fishing, $19-22/night.
Leave I-5 on Tualatin exit #289, and take State 212 east .2 mile to park at 6645 Sw Nyberg Rd.

TOWN & COUNTRY RV PARK (Private)   RV
66 sites w/full hookups, no tents, information (503)771-1040, showers, wheelchair access, laundry, rec room, $16-21/night. Leave I-205 on Foster Ave. exit, go west to 82nd Ave., and south to 9911 SE 82nd Ave.

CORBETT

CROWN POINT RV PARK (Private)   ⚠ RV
20 trailer sites w/hookups for water/elec./sewer plus a few tent sites, reservations (800)291-4520 or (503)695-5207, showers, laundry, trailer waste disposal, store, pets okay, $15-20/night. Take the Scenic Loop Highway .2 mile east of Corbett to milepost #9 and campground.

DODSON

FISHERY - COVERTS LANDING (Private)   ⚠ RV
15 sites w/hookups for elec., tents okay, reservations - (541)374-8577, showers, wheelchair access, trailer waste disposal, ice, gas, boat launch & moorage, fishing, pets okay, $10-14/night. Leave I-84 at exit #35 and follow signs.

FOREST GROVE

ROSE GROVE RV PARK (Private)   RV
19 units w/hookups for water/elec./sewer, no tents, reservations (503)357-7817, trailers to 40', showers, laundry, small pets okay, $21-25/night. Located at 3839 Pacific Ave.

SID'S FERNWOOD RV PARK (Private)   ⚠ RV
12 large wooded creekside units w/full hookups plus 2 tent sites, information (503)357-9494, showers, store, $25/night. Take State 8 northwest 9 miles, and State 6 northwest 1 mile - located at 57625 NW Wilson River Hwy.

YAMHILL

FLYING "M" RANCH (Private)   ⚠ RV
100 campsites - self-contained rvs okay, reservation information - (503)662-3222, showers, restaurant, lounge, pond, river, fishing, cabins, horse rental, $12/night. Located at 23029 Flying "M" Rd. call for directions, or head to Yamhill and follow signs.

NEWBERG

CHAMPOEG (Oregon State Park)
54 units - 48 w/hookups for elec., 6 walk-in tent sites, plus group area, reservations (800)452-5687, maximum site 50', showers, wheelchair access, trailer waste disposal, boating, fishing, bicycle & hiking trails, interpretive center/OR's first government., open year round, $11-19/night.
Follow State 99W to State 219 - park is about 7 miles southeast of town. (Also accessible via exit #278 off I-5.)

ESTACADA

ALDER FLAT (Mt. Hood NF)
6 hike-in tent sites, no drinking water, picnic area, on Clackamas River, fishing, hiking trails, elev. 1300', FREE.
Take State 224 southeast 25.8 miles and Trail #574 .7 mile.

ARMSTRONG (Mt. Hood NF)
12 units - some barrier-free sites by reservation (800)280-2267, trailers to 16', on Clackamas River, fishing, elev. 900', $5/night.
Take State 224 southeast 15.4 miles.

BARTON PARK (Clackamas County)
91 campsites - 88 w/hookups for water & elec. plus 3 w/water only, tents okay, reservations (503)650-3484, showers, handicap facilities, playground, trailer waste disposal, river, boat launch, swimming, fishing, open May thru Sept., $10-14/night.
Follow State 224 northwest 9 miles to park road.

BREITENBUSH LAKE (Mt. Hood NF)
20 campsites, no drinking water, lake - no motors, boating, swimming, fishing, trails, elev. 5500', FREE.
Take State 224 southeast 26.7 miles, FSR 46 south 28.6 miles, FSR 4220 south 8.4 miles. Access road is rough.

CAMP TEN (Mt. Hood NF)
10 campsites, trailers to 16', no drinking water, lake - no motors, boating, fishing, trails, elev. 5000', $6/night.
Take State 224 southeast 26.7 miles, FSR 46 south 28.6 miles, FSR 4220 south 6.1 miles.

CARTER BRIDGE (Mt. Hood NF)
15 units, trailers to 28', wheelchair access, on Clackamas River, fishing, elev. 800', $8-11/night.
Take State 224 southeast 15 miles.

FISH CREEK (Mt. Hood NF)
24 units, trailers to 16', reservations (800)280-CAMP, barrier free, on Clackamas River, fishing, hiking, elev. 900', $10-12/night.
Take State 224 southeast 15.6 miles.

FRAZIER TURN AROUND (Mt. Hood NF)

8 tent units, trailhead to Rock Lakes, elev. 4700', $3/night.
Take State 224 southeast 27.0 miles, FSR 57 east 7.5 miles, FSR 58 northeast 7.6 miles, FSR S457/4610 northeast 2.2 miles, FSR S456/4610240 west 4.2 miles. Primitive road.

HIGH ROCK SPRING (Mt. Hood NF)

6 tent units, elev. 4400', FREE.
Take State 224 southeast 27.0 miles, FSR 57 east 7.5 miles, and FSR 58 northeast 10.5 miles.

HORSESHOE LAKE (Mt. Hood NF)

6 tent units, no drinking water, lake - no motors, boating, swimming, fishing, elev. 5200', FREE.
Take State 224 southeast 26.7 miles, FSR 46 south 28.6 miles, and FSR 4220 south 8.3 miles.

INDIAN HENRY (Mt. Hood NF)

86 units - some barrier-free sites by reservation (800)280-2267, trailers to 22', flush toilets, trailer waste disposal, on Clackamas River, fishing, hiking, elev. 1200', $10-12/night - groups $32.
Take State 224 southeast 23 miles, FSR 53 southeast .5 mile.

KINGFISHER (Mt. Hood NF)

23 sites, trailers to 16', reservations (800)280-CAMP, on Hot Springs Fork of Collawash River, fishing, elev. 1300', $10-12/night.
Take State 224 southeast 26.5 miles, FSR 46 south 3.5 miles, FSR 63 south 3 miles, and FSR 70 southwest 2 miles.

LAKE HARRIET (Mt. Hood NF)

13 units, trailers to 30', wheelchair access, lake - no motors, boat launch, fishing, elev. 2100', $10-12/night
Take State 224 southeast 26.5 miles, and FSR 57 east 4 miles.

LAZY BEND (Mt. Hood NF)

21 units - some barrier-free sites by reservation (800)280-CAMP, trailers to 16', flush toilets, on Clackamas River, swimming, fishing, hiking, elev. 800', $10-12/night.
Take State 224 southeast 10.7 miles.

LITTLE FAN CREEK (Mt. Hood NF)

3 units, no drinking water, stream, fishing, hiking, @ mouth of Hot Springs Fork of Collawash River, elev. 1600', FREE.
Take State 224 southeast 26.7 miles, FSR 46 south 3.7 miles, and FSR 63 for 4.6 miles.

LOCKABY (Mt. Hood NF)

30 units - some barrier-free sites by reservation (800)280-CAMP, trailers to 16', on Clackamas River, fishing, elev. 900', $10-12/night.
Take State 224 southeast 15.3 miles.

LOWER LAKE (Mt. Hood NF)　　　　　　　　　　▲ RV
8 units, no water, trailers to 18', trails, elev. 4600', FREE.
Take State 224 southeast 26.7 miles, FSR 46 south 28.6 miles, and FSR 4220 south 4.5 miles.

METZLER (Clackamas County)　　　　　　　　▲ RV
70 units - 46 w/hookups for water & elec. plus 24 tent sites, reservations (503)650-3484, showers, handicap facilities, picnic area, playground, basketball court, $10-14/night.
Follow State 211 south 4 miles, Tucker Rd. west .5 mile, and Metzler Park Rd. 1.6 miles to campground.

MILO McIVER (Oregon State Park)　　　　　　▲ RV
45 sites w/hookups for elec. plus group area, reservations (503)452-5687, maximum site 50', showers, wheelchair access, picnic area, trailer waste disposal, boat launch, fishing, horse/bicycle & hiking trails, $10-16/night.
Leave State 211 at Estacada and follow signs - is 5 miles west.

OLALLIE MEADOW (Mt. Hood NF)　　　　　　　▲ RV
7 units, trailers to 16', no water, trails, elev. 4500', $6/night.
Take State 224 southeast 26.7 miles, FSR 46 south 28.6 miles, and FSR 4220 south 1.4 miles.

PANSY LAKE (Mt. Hood NF)　　　　　　　　　　▲
3 tent units, hike-in only, lake, elev. 4000', $3/night.
Take State 224 southeast 26.7 miles, FSR 46 south 3.7 miles, FSR 63 south 5.4 miles, FSR 708/6340 southwest 8.0 miles, and Trail #551 for 1.0 mile.

PAUL DENNIS (Mt. Hood NF)　　　　　　　　　▲ RV
17 units, trailers to 16', information (503)557-1010, lake - no motors, groceries, gas, ice, boat launch & rental, swimming, fishing, hiking trails, elev. 5000', $9/night.
Take State 224 southeast 27 miles, FSR 46 south 21.8 miles, FSR 4690 southeast 8.2 miles, and FSR 4220 south 6.3 miles.

PENINSULA (Mt. Hood NF)　　　　　　　　　　▲ RV
35 units, trailers to 24', wheelchair access includes trails and fishing, lake - no motors, boat launch, swimming, fishing, hiking, elev. 4900', $6-12/night.
Take State 224 southeast 27 miles, FSR 46 south 21.8 miles, FSR 4690 southeast 8.2 miles, and FSR 4220 south 6.6 miles.

PROMONTORY (PGE)　　　　　　　　　　　　　▲ RV
58 sites, trailers to 20', reservation information - (503)630-5152, showers, playground, groceries, lake, fishing, boat launch & rental, hiking, open Memorial Day weekend thru Oct., $15/night.
Take State 224 southeast 7 mile.

RAAB (Mt. Hood NF)　　　　　　　　　　　　　▲ RV
27 units, trailers to 22', river, fishing, elev. 1500', $10-12/night.

Take State 224 southeast 26.7 miles, FSR 46 southeast 3.7 miles, and FSR 63 southeast 1.0 mile.

RAINBOW (Mt. Hood NF) ▲ RV
17 units, barrier-free sites by reservation (800)280-CAMP, trailers to 16', swimming, fishing, hiking, elev. 1400', $10-12/night.
Take State 224 southeast 27 miles, and FSR 46 south .1 mile.

RIPPLEBROOK (Mt. Hood NF) ▲ RV
13 units - some barrier-free sites by reservation (800)280-CAMP, trailers to 16', stream, fishing, hiking, elev. 1500', $10-12/night.
Take State 224 southeast 26.5 miles.

RIVERFORD (Mt. Hood NF) ▲ RV
10 units, trailers to 18', river, swimming, fishing, trails, elev. 1500', $8/night.
Take State 224 southeast 26.7 miles and FSR 46 south 3.5 miles.

RIVERSIDE (Mt. Hood NF) ▲ RV
16 units - some barrier-free sites by reservation (800)280-CAMP, trailers to 30', river, fishing, hiking, elev. 1400', $10-12/night.
Take State 224 southeast 27 miles, and FSR 46 south 2.7 miles.

ROARING RIVER & GROUP CAMP (Mt. Hood NF) ▲ RV
19 units - some barrier-free sites plus group camp by reservation (800)280-CAMP, trailers to 16', at junction of Roaring & Clackamas Rivers, fishing, hiking, elev. 1000', $10-12/night.
Take State 224 southeast 18.2 miles.

ROUND LAKE (Mt. Hood NF) ▲
6 tent units, hike-in only, no water, lake - no motors, swimming, fishing, elev. 3200', FREE.
Take State 224 southeast 26.7 miles, FSR 46 south 3.7 miles, FSR 63 southeast 12.4 miles, FSR 6370 southeast 6.7 miles, and hike-in .3 mile.

SHELLROCK CREEK (Mt. Hood NF) ▲ RV
10 units, fishing, elev. 2300', $8/night.
Take State 224 southeast 27.0 miles, FSR 57 east 7.5 miles, and FSR 58 north .4 mile.

SILVER FOX RV PARK (Private) RV
70 units w/full hookups, no tents, reservations (503)630-7000, showers, handicap access, laundry, walk to Clackamas River, fishing, swimming, pets - fee, $22/night.
Take State 224 southeast 8.6 miles.

SUNSTRIP (Mt. Hood NF) ▲ RV
9 units - some barrier-free sites by reservation (800)280-CAMP, trailers to 18', trailer waste disposal, on Clackamas River, fishing, elev. 1000', $10-12/night.
Take State 224 southeast 18.6 miles.

TRIANGLE LAKE HORSE CAMP (Mt. Hood NF)
8 units, trailers to 30', handicap access, horse facilities, elev. 4600', FREE.
Take State 224 southeast 26.7 miles, FSR 46 south 23.6 miles, and FSR 4690 southwest 7 miles.

AURORA

ISEBERG PARK RV (Private)
130 campsites w/hookups for water/elec./sewer, tents okay, reservations - (503)678-2646, showers, laundry, groceries, rec room, hiking, pets okay, $24/night.
Leave I-5 at exit #278 and follow signs east toward Aurora.

McMINNVILLE

FLAMINGO MOBILE & RV PARK (Private)
2 sites - 1 w/water/elec./sewer and 1 w/elec., no tents, information (503)472-7728, no restrooms, open year round, $20/night.
Located at 849 N. Hwy 99W.

MULKEY RV PARK (Private)
71 units w/hookups for water/elec./sewer, plus grassy tent area, reservations (503)472-2475, pull thrus, showers, laundry, walnut orchard, near landfill, river, fishing, pets okay, $15-19/night.
Located on State 18, 4 miles southwest of town.

OLDE STONE VILLAGE MOBILE/RV PARK (Private)
70 units w/full hookups, no tents, reservations (503)472-4315, trailers to 60', pull thrus, showers, laundry, wheelchair accessible, swimming pool, rec room, small pets okay, $20/night.
Located on State 18 - across from the airport.

WOODBURN

FEYRER PARK (Clackamas County)
19 w/hookups for water/elec. tents okay, reservations (503)650-3484, showers, wheelchair access, picnic facilities, play area, volleyball, horseshoes, trailer waste disposal, on Molalla River, boat launch, fishing, $10-14/night.
Leave I-5 on exit #271, take State 211 east 16 miles, go thru Molalla to Feyrer Park Rd., and head southeast 1.9 miles to park.

WOODBURN I-5 RV PARK (Private)
148 units w/full hookups, reservations (503)981-0002, paved pull thrus, showers, wheelchair access, laundry, heated pool in summer, playground, rec room, open year round, $22/night.
Take exit #271 off I-5 - located on west side of freeway.

RICKREALL

POLK COUNTY FAIRGROUNDS (County)   🅰 RV
40 units w/water & elec., tents okay, information - (503)623-3048, showers, trailer waste disposal, pets okay, $10/night.
Follow State 99 west to the fairgrounds.

SALEM

ELKHORN (BLM)   🅰 RV
Campsites on N. Fork Santiam River, no drinking water, secluded fishing, swimming, hiking, FREE.
Follow State 22 east 34 miles and take N. Fork Rd. into the Little N. Fork Recreation Area.

ELKHORN VALLEY (BLM)   🅰 RV
22 units, trailers okay, fishing, swimming, hiking trails, open mid May thru Sept., elev. 1000', $8/night.
Follow State 22 east 24 miles and Elkhorn Rd. north 10 miles to campground.

FOREST GLEN RV RESORT (Private)   🅰 RV
83 units w/hookups for water/elec./sewer, tents okay, reservations (503)363-7616, showers, laundry, miniature golf, therapy pool, game room, hiking, $20/night.
Leave I-5 5 miles south of Salem on exit #248, go east over freeway, and follow Enchanted Way south .5 mile to the campground.

SALEM CAMPGROUND & RV (Private)   🅰 RV
195 units - 135 w/hookups for water/elec./sewer, 40 w/water & elec., plus 30 tent sites, reservations (800)826-9604 or (503)581-6736, pull thrus, trailers to 65', showers, laundry, playground, game room, groceries, trailer waste disposal, $15-20/night.
Leave I-5 on exit #253, take State 22 southeast .2 mile, and Lancaster Dr., south .5 mile to park - behind Home Depot.

SALEM RV PARK (Private)   RV
158 units w/full hookups, no tents, reservations (800)837-4166, (503)364-5490, trailers to 60', showers, laundry, wheelchair access, swimming pool, lounge, store, pets okay, open year round, $21/night.
Leave I-5 on the Market St. exit, go east .5 mile to 45th St. and north to Silverton Rd. - located at 4490 Silverton Rd. N.E.

SILVER FALLS (Oregon State Park)   🅰 RV
104 units - 53 w/hookups for elec., 51 tent sites, plus group areas, reservations (800)452-5687, maximum site 60', showers, wheelchair access, picnic facilities, trailer waste disposal, bike trails, hiking trails, waterfalls, swimming, fishing, horse camp, $13-20/night.

Follow State 214 east 26 miles. The route is well marked by signs. This park is also accessible from Silverton.

TRAILER PARK VILLAGE (Private)   RV
22 units w/hookups for water/elec./sewer, adults only, no tents, information - (503)393-7424, showers, laundry, ice, no pets, nearby groceries & restaurant, $21/night.
Leave I-5 on exit #258 and take State 99E north .5 mile.

MEHAMA

FISHERMEN'S BEND (BLM)   A RV
37 units - 21 w/hookups for water, 16 tent sites, plus group area, group reservations (503)375-5646, flush toilets, showers, basketball/volleyball/baseball facilities, trailer waste disposal, on North Santiam River, boat launch, fishing, elev. 750', $10-14/night.
Follow State 22 east of town 8.5 miles - located west of Mill City.

JOHN NEAL MEMORIAL PARK (Linn County)   A RV
40 units, trailers to 22', playground, playfield, river, boat launch, fishing, hiking, pets okay, $8/night.
Go south 1 mile to Lyons, east 1.5 miles to Memorial Park Rd., and north to the park.

SHADY COVE (Willamette NF)   A RV
9 units, some trailers, on Little North Santiam River, fishing, hiking, elev. 1400', $5/night.
Take State 22 east .9 mile, CR 967 east 15.3 miles, FSR S80 east 1.1 miles, and FSR 581 east 2.1 miles.

INDEPENDENCE

ASH CREEK MOBILE PARK (Private)   RV
77 units w/full hookups, no tents, trailers to 40', reservations (503)838-4552, showers, laundry, wheelchair accessible, nearby store, propane, on Ash Creek, hiking, small pets okay, open year round, $18/night.
Located at 141 S. 17th St.

DETROIT

BREITENBUSH (Willamette NF)   A RV
30 units plus group camp, trailers to 18', wheelchair access, groceries, gas, river, fishing, elev. 2200', $10/night.
Take FSR 46 northeast 9.8 miles.

CLEATOR BEND (Willamette NF)   A RV
9 units, trailers to 18', river, fishing, elev. 2200', $10/night.
Take FSR 46 northeast 9.6 miles.

COVE CREEK (Willamette NF)

63 units, group area - reservations (503)854-3366, trailers okay, handicap access, boating fishing, swimming, elev. 1600', $16/night.
Take State 22 southeast 2.9 miles, and FSR 10 west 3.8 miles.

DETROIT LAKE (Oregon State Park)

311 campsites - 107 w/full hookups, 70 w/elec. only, 134 tent sites, plus group area, reservations (800)452-5687, maximum site 60', showers, picnic area, boat launch, fishing, swimming, $13-20/night.
Follow State 22 west 2 miles to park.

ELK LAKE (Willamette NF)

12 units, no trailers, stream, primitive boat launch, rough road, fishing, swimming, hiking, elev. 3700', FREE.
Take FSR 46 northeast 4.6 miles, FSR 4696 north 7.1 miles, FSR 2209 northwest 9.5 miles, and FSR 360 southwest .4 mile.

HOOVER (Willamette NF)

37 units, trailers to 22', reservations (800)280-CAMP, flush toilets, wheelchair access, on Detroit Lake, boat launch, swimming, fishing, water skiing, interpretive services, elev. 1600', $10/night.
Take State 22 southeast 2.9 miles, and FSR 10 west .8 mile.

HOOVER GROUP CAMP (Willamette NF)

Group camp - 70 people max., reservations required - (800)280-CAMP, trailers to 18', picnic shelter, playfield, boating, swimming, fishing, water skiing, elev. 1600.
Take State 22 southeast 2.9 miles, and FSR 10 west .8 mile.

HUMBUG (Willamette NF)

22 units, trailers to 22', on Breitenbush River, fishing, hiking, elev. 1800', $10/night.
Take FSR 46 northeast 4.8 miles.

KANE'S HIDEAWAY MARINA & RV PARK (Private)

19 units w/hookups for water & elec., no tents, reservations - (503)854-3362, showers, tavern, trailer waste disposal, groceries, gas, on Detroit Lake, fishing, boating, pets okay, $20/night.
Leave State 22 on Clester Rd. and follow the signs.

PIETY ISLAND (Willamette NF)

12 tent units, boat-in only, on Detroit Lake, swimming, fishing, water skiing, primitive, elev. 1600', FREE.
Southwest of Detroit by boat 1.1 miles on lake.

SOUTH SHORE (Willamette NF)

30 units, trailers to 22', picnic area, wheelchair access, on Detroit Lake, boat launch, swimming, fishing, water skiing, elev. 1600', $10/night.
Take State 22 southeast 2.9 miles, and FSR 10 west 3.5 miles.

UPPER ARM (Willamette NF)
5 tent units, lake, boating, swimming, fishing, elev. 1600', FREE.
Take FSR 46 northeast 1.1 mile - located on Breitenbush Arm of
Detroit Lake.

IDANHA

BIG MEADOWS HORSE CAMP (Willamette NF)
9 campsites - each w/4 stall corral, trailers to 36', disabled
mount/dismount ramp, fishing, hiking, $8/night.
Take State 22 east 20 miles, FSR 2267 west 1 mile, and FSR 2257
north .5 mile.

MARION FORKS (Willamette NF)
15 units, trailers to 22', stream, swimming, fishing, hiking, nearby salmon hatchery, elev. 2500', $8/night.
Take State 22 southeast 12 miles, and FSR 502 south .1 mile.

MOUNTAIN VIEW MOBILE PARK (Private) 🅰 RV
28 units - 14 w/full hookups plus 14 tent sites, reservation information - (503)854-3774, showers, laundry, Santiam River, fishing, hiking, water sports, $14-18/night.
Leave State 22 on Church St., go 2 blocks south to Willow St., 2
blocks east to Mountain Ave., and 1 block to park.

RIVERSIDE (Willamette NF) 🅰 RV
37 units, trailers to 22', on North Santiam River, fishing, hiking,
elev. 2400', $8/night.
Take State 22 southeast 9.6 miles.

WHISPERING FALLS (Willamette NF) 🅰 RV
16 units, trailers to 22', flush toilets, on North Santiam River,
waterfalls across river, fishing, elev. 1900', $8/night.
Take State 22 east 4.1 miles.

LEBANON

TWIN CEDARS MOBILE PARK (Private) RV
5 sites w/full hookups, no tents, reservations (541)451-1029,
showers, laundry, walk to restaurants, no pets, $20/night.
Located at 2796 S. Main Rd.

WATERLOO CAMPGROUND (Linn County) 🅰 RV
60 units - 50 w/hookups for water & elec. plus 10 w/out
hookups, tents okay, showers, handicap accessible, covered picnic area, trailer waste disposal, South Santiam River, boat dock,
fishing, swimming, hiking, $12-14/night.
Follow US 20 southeast of town 4 miles - located in Waterloo.

WOODS TRAILER/RV PARK (Private)   `RV`
14 sites w/full hookups, no tents, reservations (541)451-1569,
laundry, nearby restaurant, small pets okay, $18/night.
Leave State 22 on Church St., go 2 blocks south to Willow St., 2
blocks east to Mountain Ave., and 1 block to park.

ALBANY

ALBANY/CORVALLIS KOA (Private)   `A` `RV`
105 sites - 60 w/full hookups, 14 pull-thrus w/elec., plus 14 tent
sites, reservations (541)967-8521, showers, groceries, tv, laundry,
playground, mini golf, heated pool, pets okay, $17-24/night.
Take exit #228 off I-5, drive 5 miles west on State 34 to Oakville
Rd., and head south to campground.

BLUE OX RV PARK (Private)   `RV`
100 trailer sites w/hookups for water/elec./sewer, no tents,
reservations (541)926-2886, showers, laundry, rec hall & meeting
room, groceries, pets okay, $22/night.
Leave I-5 on exit #233 and head east to Price Rd. - campground
is located at 4000 Blue Ox Dr.

KNOX BUTTE RV PARK (Private)   `A` `RV`
53 sites w/full hookups, tents okay, reservations (541)928-9033,
showers, laundry, across from fairgrounds, can walk to groceries
& restaurants, $10-23/night.
Leave I-5 on fairgrounds exit #234A and follow to 125 Expo Pkwy.

CORVALLIS

BENTON COUNTY FAIRGROUNDS (County)   `A` `RV`
Lots of paved RV sites w/hookups for water & elec. plus
tent area, group reservations (541)757-1521, seasonal flush toilets & showers, wheelchair accessible, horse corrals, hiking &
horse trails, pets okay, closed in winter, $12-14/night.
Leave I-5 on State 34 and take a right on 53rd St. - fairgrounds
are 2 miles.

WILLAMETTE PARK (Benton County)   `A` `RV`
15 sites, group reservations - (541)753-3119, trailers to 30', open
April thru mid-Oct., $8/night.
South of Corvallis leave State 99W to head east on SE Goodnight.

SWEET HOME

CASCADIA (Oregon State Park)   `A` `RV`
26 primitive units, maximum site 35', wheelchair access, picnic
area, fishing, hiking trails, $12/night.
Follow US 20 east 14 miles.

FERNVIEW (Willamette NF) 🔺 RV
11 units, trailers to 18', river, swimming, fishing, elev. 1400', $8/night.
Follow US 20 east 23.5 miles.

HOUSE ROCK (Willamette NF) 🔺
17 tent units in virgin old growth douglas fir, picnic area, river, swimming, fishing, hiking, elev. 1600', $8/night.
Follow US 20 east 26.5 miles, and FSR 2044 southeast .1 mile.

LOST PRAIRIE (Willamette NF) 🔺 RV
4 units, trailers to 22', wheelchair access, stream, hiking, historic site, elev. 3300', $8/night.
Follow US 20 east 39.2 miles.

SUNNYSIDE PARK (Linn County) 🔺 RV
165 units - 131 w/hookups for water/elec. plus 34 tent sites, reservations (541)967-3917, picnic shelter, showers, handicap access, trailer waste disposal, on Foster Res., boat launch, hiking, fishing, swimming, pets okay, open April-Sept., $12-14/night.
Take US 20 east 5 miles to Quartzville Dr. and go north 1 mile.

SWEET HOME/FOSTER LAKE KOA (Private) 🔺 RV
Sites w/full hookups and tent sites, pull thrus reservations (800)KOA-0367 or (541)367-5629, 50 amp, mini golf, pool - May-Sept., firewood, fishing, $16-22/night.
Take US 20 east toward Foster Lake - located at 6191 US 20.

TROUT CREEK (Willamette NF) 🔺 RV
24 units, trailers to 22', wheelchair access, swimming, fishing, near wilderness trailhead, elev. 1300', $8/night.
Follow US 20 east 18.7 miles.

WHITCOMB CREEK (Linn County) 🔺 RV
39 units, picnic area, on Green Peter Lake, boat launch, swimming, fishing, hiking, open May-Sept., $9/night.
Take US 20 east 5 miles to Quartzville Dr. and head northeast 9 miles to campground.

YELLOWBOTTOM (BLM) 🔺 RV
21 units, trailers okay, picnic area, swimming, fishing, nature study, open mid May thru Sept., elev. 1500', $8/night.
Take US 20 east 5 miles to Quartzville Dr. and head northeast 26 miles - camp is beyond reservoir.

YUKWAH (Willamette NF) 🔺 RV
20 units, trailers to 32', wheelchair access, river, swimming, fishing, nature trail, elev. 1300', $8/night.
Follow US 20 east 19.3 miles.

PHILOMATH

ALSEA FALLS (Benton County)
16 campsites, trailers okay, handicap accessible restrooms, picnic area, fishing, hiking, nature study, open mid May thru Sept., elev. 800', $6/night.
Take State 34 southwest 19 miles. Just west of Alsea take the S. Fork Alsea Rd. southeast to waterfalls and campground.

MARYS PEAK (Benton County)
6 units, trailers to 18', picnic area, handicap access, hiking, elev. 3500', open mid-May thru mid-Oct., $5-7/night.
Take State 34 southwest 9.1 miles and follow Marys Peak Rd. northwest 9.2 miles to campground.

SALMONBERRY PARK (Benton County)
19 sites, trailers to 50', wilderness access, $7/night.
Take State 34 20 miles west - located 6 miles past Alsea.

McKENZIE BRIDGE

ALDER SPRINGS (Willamette NF)
7 units, no trailers, no drinking water, stream, trail to Linton Lake, elev. 3600'.
Take State 126 east 4.3 miles and State 242 east 8.2 miles.

BELKNAP SPRINGS RESORT (Private)
25 sites w/hookups for water/elec./sewer, 17 w/water & elec. plus tent area, reservations (541)822-3512, showers, laundry, cabins & lodge rooms, trailer waste disposal, natural hot springs, river, fishing, hiking, $12-18/night.
East 5 miles on State 126, north .3 mile on Belknap Springs Rd.

COLDWATER COVE (Willamette NF)
35 units plus 2 group sites, trailers to 22', reservations - (800)280-2267, wheelchair access includes trails, on Clear Lake - no motors, boat launch & rental, fishing, hiking, snack bar, groceries, open May to Oct., elev. 3100', $10/night.
State 126 northeast 14.2 miles, FSR 1372 southeast .1 mile.

FISH LAKE (Willamette NF)
8 units, trailers to 22', lake - no motors - is low in summer, swimming, fishing, near lava beds, elev. 3200', $6/night.
State 126 northeast 22.4 miles, FSR 1374 west .1 mile.

ICE CAP CREEK (Willamette NF)
22 units, trailers to 18', flush toilets, near Carmen Res./Koosah & Sahalie Falls, open May to Oct., elev. 3000', $6/night.
State 126 northeast 19.2 miles, FSR 14071 northeast .1 mile.

LAKE'S END (Willamette NF)
17 tent units, boat-in only, on Smith Reservoir - speed limits, boating, fishing, swimming, elev. 3000', FREE.
Take State 126 northwest 13.2 miles, FSR 1477 northwest 3.3 miles and boat 1.8 miles north on Smith Reservoir.

LIMBERLOST (Willamette NF)
12 units, trailers okay, picnic area, creek, fishing, elev. 1800', $6/night.
Take State 126 east 4.3 miles and State 242 east .5 mile to camp.

McKENZIE BRIDGE (Willamette NF)
20 units, trailers to 22', reservations - (800)280-2267, on McKenzie River, boating, fishing, hiking, open May to Oct., elev. 1400', $10/night.
Take State 126 west 1 mile.

OLALLIE (Willamette NF)
17 units, trailers to 22', at confluence of McKenzie River & Olallie Creek, boating, fishing, elev. 2000', $6/night.
State 126 northeast 11.1 miles.

PARADISE (Willamette NF)
64 units, trailers to 22', reservations (800)280-CAMP, flush toilets, picnic area, on McKenzie River, fishing, hiking, open May to Oct., elev. 1600', $10/night.
Take State 126 east 3.5 miles.

SCOTT LAKE (Willamette NF)
20 tent sites, fishing, hiking, FREE.
Take State 126 east 4.3 miles and State 242 east 13.2 miles.

TRAIL BRIDGE (Willamette NF)
26 units, trailers to 32', on reservoir. - speed limits, boat ramp, fishing, hiking, open April to Nov., elev. 2000', $6/night.
Take State 126 northeast 13.2 miles and FSR 1477 southwest .2 mile to campground.

BLUE RIVER

BOX CANYON HORSE CAMP (Willamette NF)
14 units, trailers to 22', stream, trails, elev. 3700', FREE
Take State 126 east 3.5 miles and FSR 19 south 27.0 miles around reservoir to campground.

CAMP YALE (Private)
11 sites w/full hookups, 5 w/water & elec., plus 6 tent sites, reservations (541)822-3961, showers, laundry, trout pond, $10-14/night.
Take State 126 15 miles east and State 242 .5 mile.

COUGAR REC. AREA (Willamette NF) [A] [RV]
Two camp areas - Sunnyside & Cougar Crossing at south end of
Cougar Reservoir, $5/night.
Take State 126 east 3.5 miles and FSR 19 south 9 miles.

DELTA (Willamette NF) [A] [RV]
38 sites, trailers to 22', wheelchair access, picnic area, on
McKenzie River, fishing, old growth trail, elev. 1200', $5/night.
Take State 126 east 3.5 miles, FSR 19 south .3 mile, and FSR 194
west .7 mile.

FRENCH PETE (Willamette NF) [A] [RV]
17 units, trailers to 18', river, boating, swimming, fishing, water
skiing, hiking, elev. 2000', $5/night.
Take State 126 east 3.5 miles and FSR 19 south 11 miles.

FRISSELL CROSSING (Willamette NF) [A] [RV]
12 units, trailers to 18', river, fishing, hiking, elev. 2600',
$5/night.
Follow State 126 east for 3.5 miles and FSR 19 south 23 miles.

HOMESTEAD (Willamette NF) [A] [RV]
7 units, river, fishing, primitive, elev. 2200', FREE.
Take State 126 east 3.5 miles, FSR 19 south .3 mile, and FSR 194
west .7 mile.

HORSE CREEK GROUP CAMP (Willamette NF) [A] [RV]
20 group units - reservations required (800)280-CAMP, trailers to
22', fishing, open May thru Oct. , elev. 1400', $50/night.
Take State 126 east .2 mile, and CR 161 southeast 5.1 miles.

LAZY DAZE MOBILE/RV PARK (Private) [RV]
16 trailer sites w/full hookups, reservations (541)822-3889,
showers, laundry, propane, McKenzie River, fishing, $23/night.
Follow State 126 east 1.5 miles.

LOOKOUT (Willamette NF) [A] [RV]
55 units, handicap access, fishing, $4/night
Take State 126 east 3.5 miles, FSR 15 northeast .5 mile.

MONA (Willamette NF) [A] [RV]
23 units, trailers to 22', flush toilets, wheelchair access, on Blue
River Res., boat launch, swimming, fishing, water skiing, elev.
1400', $10/night.
Take State 126 east 2 miles, FSR 15 northeast 3.9 miles, and FSR
15120 south .3 mile.

PATIO RV PARK (Private) [RV]
60 RV sites w/full hookups, no tents, reservations (541)822-3596,
showers, laundry, trailer waste disposal, playfield, on McKenzie
River, fishing, hiking, $23/night.
State 126 east 6 miles, McKenzie River Dr. east 2.5 miles.

RAINBOW MOBILE/RV PARK (Private) ▲ RV
Units w/full hookups inc. cable, partial hookups and grassy tent sites, reservations (541)822-3928, showers, laundry, pool table, quiet, across from covered bridge, $13-16/night.
Take Unity Rd. north 1.8 miles, Place Rd. east .4 mile, Big Fall Creek Rd. east 9.5 miles, and FSR 18 east 6.5 miles.

SLIDE CREEK (Willamette NF) ▲ RV
16 units, trailers okay, picnic area, lake, boating, swimming, fishing, water skiing, elev. 1700', $5/night.
Take State 126 east 3.5 miles, FSR 19 south 11.6 miles, and FSR 195 north 1.5 miles.

SPRINGFIELD

CHALET VILLAGE (Private) RV
24 units w/hookups for water/elec./sewer, no tents, reservation information - (541)747-8311, showers, $22/night.
Leave I-5 on exit #194 and follow Main St. to 4th St. and park.

COBURG HILLS RV RESORT (Private) RV
215 campsites w/full hookups, reservations (541)686-3152, pullthrus, showers, laundry, fishing, restaurant, $22/night.
Take I-5 north to exit #199 - park is in Coburg, at 33100 Van Duyn Rd.

EUGENE KAMPING WORLD (Private) ▲ RV
144 units - 70 w/full hookups, 25 w/water & elec., 7 w/out hookups, plus 30 tent sites, reservations (800)343-3008 or (541)343-4832, showers, laundry, playground, mini-golf, trailer waste disposal, groceries, pets okay, $15-21/night.
Take I-5 north to exit #199 - campground is .3 mile west, at 90932 S. Stuart St.

EUGENE

EUGENE MOBILE VILLAGE (Private) RV
30 units w/full hookups, no tents, reservations (541)747-2257, showers, laundry, playground, trailer waste disposal, groceries, pets okay, $17/night.
Leave I-5 on exit #189, go east over highway, and take the Frontage Rd. 1 mile north.

FERN RIDGE SHORES (Private) RV
61 units w/full hookups, no tents, information (541)935-2335, showers, laundry, shade trees, picnic facilities, ice, boat ramp & moorage, fishing, swimming, pets okay, $22/night.
Take State 126 west 7.3 miles to Ellmaker Rd., and go north to Jeans Rd. - campground is at 29652 Jeans Rd.

HULT POND (BLM)   [△] [RV]
Unimproved camp area, picnic area, no motors on pond, fishing, swimming, nearby boat ramp, elev. 800', FREE.
Take State 36 northwest 28 miles.

RICHARDSON PARK (Lane County)   [△] [RV]
50 units w/water & elec. - 2 barrier free, tents okay, trailers to 60', reservations (541)935-2005, showers, laundry, picnic area, volleyball court, trailer dump station, on Fern Ridge Res., boat ramp/docks, open mid-April thru mid-Oct., $15/night.
Take State 126 west 8.5 miles, and Territorial Rd. north 4 miles.

SHAMROCK VILLAGE MOBILE/RV PARK (Private)   [RV]
101 units 30 w/full hookups plus 8 w/water & elec., no tents, trailers to 50', reservations (541)747-7473, pull thrus, showers, laundry, trailer waste disposal, river, fishing, $22/night.
Leave I-5 on exit #191, take Glenwood Blvd. north .7 mile, and Franklin Blvd. southeast 1 mile.

CRESWELL

EUGENE/CRESWELL KOA (Private)   [△] [RV]
125 units w/full hookups, 5 w/water only, plus 10 tent sites, reservations (541)895-4110, showers, laundry, swimming & therapy pool, playground, trailer waste disposal, store, $17-22/night.
Leave I-5 at exit #182 and go .1 mile.

TAYLOR'S TRAVEL PARK (Private)   [△] [RV]
39 units - 17 w/full hookups, 7 w/water & elec., 15 w/water only, plus grassy tent area, reservations (541)895-4715, showers, trailer waste disposal, $12/night.
Leave I-5 at exit #182, head west to Highway 99S, go south 1.3 miles to Davisson Rd., then south .4 mile to park.

LOWELL

BEDROCK (Willamette NF)   [△] [RV]
19 campsites, trailers to 22', handicap accessible, picnic area, creek, swimming, fishing, hiking, elev. 1100', $8/night.
Take Unity Rd. north 1.8 miles, Place Rd. east .4 mile, Big Fall Creek Rd. east 9.5 miles, and FSR 18 east 4.8 miles.

BIG POOL (Willamette NF)   [△] [RV]
5 campsites, trailers to 24', no drinking water, handicap accessible, creek, fishing, hiking, elev. 1000', $8/night.
Take Unity Rd. north 1.8 miles, Place Rd. east .4 mile, Big Fall Creek Rd. east 9.5 miles, and FSR 18 east 1.7 miles.

BROKEN BOWL (Willamette NF) ▲ RV
16 units, trailers to 24', flush toilets, wheelchair accessible, creek, fishing, swimming, hiking, elev. 1000', $8/night.
Take Unity Rd. north 1.8 miles, Place Rd. east .4 mile, Big Fall Creek Rd. east 9.5 miles, and FSR 18 east .9 mile.

CASCARA (Corps) ▲ RV
60 campsites, trailers okay, fire pits, on Fall Creek Res., boat ramp & dock, open mid May to mid Sept., $8-12/night.
Take Unity Rd. north 1.8 miles, Place Rd. east .4 mile, Winberry Creek Rd. southeast 4 miles, and Peninsula Rd. north 7 miles.

CLARK CREEK ORG. CAMP (Willamette NF) ▲ RV
Group camp for 80 people, handicap access, kitchen, ball fields, 1000' elev., contact (541)782-4730 for rates and reservations.
Take Unity Rd. north 1.8 miles, Place Rd. east .4 mile, Big Fall Creek Rd. east 9.5 miles, and FSR 18 east 2.3 miles.

DEXTER SHORES MOBILE/RV PARK (Private) ▲ RV
56 units w/full hookups plus tent area, reservations (541)937-3711, showers, laundry, wheelchair access, play area, trailer waste disposal, pets okay, open year round, $15-22/night.
Head southwest to the town of Dexter - at 39140 Dexter Rd.

DOLLY VARDEN (Willamette NF) ▲
6 tent sites, stream, fishing, hiking, elev. 1000', $7/night.
Take Unity Rd. north 1.8 miles, Place Rd. east .4 mile, and Big Fall Creek Rd. east 7 miles.

FISHERMAN'S POINT GROUP AREA (Corps) ▲ RV
1 group site - reservations (541)937-2131 ext. 53, trailers okay, fire pits, on Fall Creek Reservoir, open mid May to mid Sept., $30-80/night.
Take Unity Rd. north for 1.8 miles, Place Rd. east .4 mile, Winberry Creek Rd. southeast 4 miles, and Peninsula Rd. north 7.1 miles.

PUMA (Willamette NF) ▲ RV
11 units, trailers to 24', handicap accessible, creek, swimming, fishing, hiking, elev. 1100', $8/night.
Take Unity Rd. north 1.8 miles, Place Rd. east .4 mile, Big Fall Creek Rd. east 9.5 miles, and FSR 18 east 6.5 miles.

WINBERRY (Willamette NF) ▲ RV
7 units, trailers okay, picnic area, fishing, hiking, elev. 1900', $6/night.
Take Unity Rd. north 1.8 miles, Place Rd. east .4 mile, Winberry Creek Rd. southeast 8 miles.

OAKRIDGE

BLACK CANYON (Willamette NF)　　　　　▲ RV
72 units, trailers to 22', picnic area, wheelchair access includes trails & fishing, river, at head of Lookout Point Res. - speed limit, boat launch, fishing, swimming, hiking, elev. 1000', $8/night. Take State 58 northwest 8.5 miles.

BLAIR LAKE (Willamette NF)　　　　　　　▲
7 tent units - some hike-in sites, lake - no motors, fishing, swimming, hiking, elev. 4800', $4/night.
Salmon Creek Rd. east 3 miles, FSR 24 northeast 8 miles, FSR 1934 northeast 7.4 miles, and FSR 733 east 1.5 miles.

BLUE POOL (Willamette NF)　　　　　　　▲ RV
25 units, trailers to 18', no water, picnic area, river, fishing, swimming, near McCredie Hot Springs, elev. 1900', $8/night. Take State 58 southeast 8.8 miles.

CAMPERS FLAT (Willamette NF)　　　　　▲ RV
5 units, trailers to 24', reservations (800)283-2267, picnic area, fishing, hiking, elev. 2000', $8/night.
Take State 58 southeast 2.2 miles, Hills Creek Res. Rd. south .5 mile, and FSR 21 south 20 miles.

GOLD LAKE (Willamette NF)　　　　　　　▲ RV
25 units, trailers to 18', picnic area, lake - no motors, boat ramp, fly fishing, swimming, hiking, elev. 4800', $8/night.
Take State 58 southeast 25.6 miles, and FSR 500 northeast 2.2 miles.

HAMPTON (Willamette NF)　　　　　　　　▲ RV
4 units, trailers to 32', on Lookout Point Res., boat launch, swimming, fishing, water skiing, elev. 1100', $8/night.
Take State 58 northwest 10 miles.

HARRALSON HORSE CAMP (Willamette NF)　　　▲ RV
6 units, trailers to 18', boat ramp, boating, swimming, fishing, access to Waldo Lake Recreation Area, elev. 5500', FREE.
Take State 58 southeast 23.1 miles, FSR 5897 northeast 10.5 miles, and FSR 5898 northwest 1.3 miles.

INDIGO LAKE (Willamette NF)　　　　　　　▲
5 units, hike-in only, lake, swimming, fishing, dispersed camping, elev. 5900', FREE.
Take State 58 southeast 2.2 miles, CR 360 southeast .5 mile, FSR 21 southeast 38.4 miles, FSR 2154 south 3.2 miles, and Trail #3649 south 2.0 miles.

INDIGO SPRINGS (Willamette NF)　　　　　▲ RV
3 units, trailers to 18', creek, elev. 2800', FREE.

Take State 58 southeast 2.2 miles, CR 360 southeast .5 mile, and FSR 21 southeast 28.8 miles.

ISLET (Willamette NF)
55 units, trailers okay, picnic area, fishing, swimming, boating, hiking, $10-12/night.
Take State 58 southeast 23.1 miles, FSR 5897 northeast 10.5 miles, and FSR 5898 northwest 2.6 miles.

KIAHANIE (Willamette NF)
19 units, trailers okay, handicap access, picnic facilities, boating, fishing, hiking, $8/night.
Head north to Westfir and follow FSR 19 northeast 16 mile.

OPAL LAKE (Willamette NF)
1 walk-in tent unit, lake - no motors, carry-in boating, fishing, nearby trails, elev. 5400', FREE.
Take State 58 southeast 2.2 miles, CR 360 southeast .5 mile, FSR 21 southeast 38.4 miles, FSR 2154 south 2.1 miles, and hike in .2 mile.

NORTH WALDO (Willamette NF)
58 units, picnic area, swimming, fishing, boating, hiking, $10-12/night.
Take State 58 southeast 23.1 miles, FSR 5897 northeast 10.5 miles, and FSR 5898 northwest 1.6 miles.

PACKARD CREEK (Willamette NF)
33 units, trailers to 32', reservations (800)280-CAMP, wheelchair access includes trails, picnic area, on Hills Creek Reservoir, boat launch, swimming, water skiing, fishing, hiking, elev. 1600', $8/night.
Take State 58 southeast 2.2 miles, Hills Creek Res. Rd. south .5 mile, and FSR 21 south 5.2 miles.

SACANDAGA (Willamette NF)
17 units, trailers okay, fishing, hiking, elev. 2400', FREE.
State 58 southeast 2.2 miles, CR 360 southeast .5 mile, and FSR 21 southeast 23.3 miles.

SALMON CREEK FALLS (Willamette NF)
15 units, trailers to 18', picnic area, fishing, swimming, kayakking, elev. 1500', $8/night.
Take Salmon Creek Rd. east 3 miles, and FSR 24 northeast 3.7 miles.

SAND PRAIRIE (Willamette NF)
21 campsites, trailers to 32', reservations (800)280-CAMP, flush toilets, wheelchair access includes trails, near head of Hills Creek Res., swimming, fishing, elev. 1600', $8/night.
Take State 58 southeast 2.2 miles, Hills Creek Res. Rd. south .5 mile, and FSR 21 south 11.6 miles.

SKOOKUM CREEK (Willamette NF)   🅰

8 tent units, well, trails to high country lakes, horse facilities, elev. 4500', $4/night.
Head north to Westfir and follow FSR 19 northeast 31.4 miles and FSR 1957 southeast 3.7 miles.

SECRET (Willamette NF)   🅰 RV

6 units, trailers to 18', river, fishing, elev. 2000', $6/night.
Take State Highway 58 southeast 2.2 miles, CR 360 southeast .5 mile, and FSR 21 south 18.3 miles.

SHADOW BAY Willamette NF)   🅰 RV

92 units, trailers okay, group area, swimming, fishing, hiking, elev. 5400', $10-12/night
Take State 58 southeast 23.1 miles, FSR 5897 northeast 6 miles and FSR 5896 to Waldo Lake and campground.

SHADY DELL (Willamette NF)   🅰 RV

9 units, trailers to 18', on N. Fork Willamette River, fishing, elev. 1000', $8/night.
Take State 58 northwest 7 miles.

TIMPANOGAS LAKE (Willamette NF)   🅰 RV

10 units, trailers to 22', lake - no motors, swimming, fishing, trails, elev. 5200', $6/night.
Take State 58 southeast 2.2 miles, Hills Creek Reservoir Rd. south .5 mile, FSR 21 southeast 38.4 miles, and FSR 2154 south 3 miles.

COTTAGE GROVE

BAKER BAY (Lane County)   🅰 RV

49 campsites plus 2 group sites - reservations (541)942-7669, trailers to 40', showers, picnic area, trailer waste disposal, located on Dorena Res., boat dock & launch, fishing, $11/night - groups $40.
Leave I-5 at exit #174, take Row River Rd. east 4 miles and Government Rd. southeast 3 miles.

COTTAGE GROVE LAKE PRIMITIVE (Corps)   🅰 RV

18 campsites, group reservations (541)942-8657, on lake, fishing, $6-10/night - groups $30.
Leave I-5 at exit #170, take London Rd. south 3.5 miles, and Reservoir Rd. east 1 mile.

PASS CREEK (Douglas County)   🅰 RV

30 campsites w/hookups for water/elec./sewer, picnic area, showers, wheelchair access, picnic pavilion, playground, stream, $11-14/night.
Leave I-5 at exit #163 - campground is 10 miles south of Cottage Grove, in the town of Curtin.

PINE MEADOWS (Corps)

92 campsites, flush toilets, showers, playground, trailer waste disposal, on Cottage Grove Lake, swimming, fishing, open May thru Sept., $12/night.
Leave I-5 at exit #170, take London Rd. south 3.5 miles, and Reservoir Rd. east .5 mile.

SCHWARZ PARK/DORENA LAKE (Corps)

72 units plus 6 group sites, group reservations (541)942-1418, flush toilets, showers, wheelchair access, trailer waste disposal, lake, boat ramp, on Row River, fishing, open April thru Sept., $10-14/night - groups $50-95.
Leave I-5 at exit #174, take Row River Rd. east 4 miles and Government Rd. southeast 1 mile.

VILLAGE GREEN RV PARK (Private)

42 trailer sites w/hookups for water/elec./sewer, no tents, information (541)942-2491, trailers to 50', pull thrus, wheelchair accessible, laundry, swimming pool, spa, game room, coffee shop & lounge, playground, trailer waste disposal, pets okay, $28/night.
Leave I-5 at exit #174 and follow Row River Rd. east .1 mile to 725 Row River Rd.

CULP CREEK

CEDAR CREEK (Umpqua NF)

8 units, trailers to 18', no drinking water, handicap access, picnic area, stream, fishing, nearby hiking, elev. 1600', FREE.
Take Row River Road southeast 4.3 miles, and CR 2470 southeast 4.0 miles along Brice Creek.

HOBO CAMP (Umpqua NF)

2 units, no drinking water, trailers to 16', stream, fishing, hiking, elev. 1800', FREE.
Take Row River Rd. east 4 miles, and FSR 17 northeast 2 miles.

LUND PARK (Umpqua NF)

5 units, trailers to 16', no drinking water, handicap access, picnic facilities, stream, fishing, hiking, elev. 1700', FREE.
Take Row River Road southeast 4.3 miles, and CR 2470 southeast 6.9 miles along Brice Creek.

MINERAL CAMP (Umpqua NF)

2 tent units, no drinking water, picnic facilities, stream, fishing, hiking, elev. 1800', FREE.
Take Row River Road southeast .8 mile and CR 2460 south 12.3 miles to camp.

RUJADA (Umpqua NF)   🔺 RV

8 units plus 2 group sites, trailers to 22', flush toilets, picnic area,
play field, stream, fishing, hiking, elev. 1200', $4/night.
Take Row River Rd. east 4 miles, and FSR 17 northeast 2 miles.

SHARPS CREEK (BLM)   🔺 RV

10 units, trailers to 30', handicap access, well, creek, gold panning, fishing, elev. 1200', open mid-May thru mid-Oct., $5/night.
Follow Row River Rd. east .5 mile and take Sharps Creek Rd.
south 4 miles to campground.

DRAIN

ELKTON RV PARK (Private)   🔺 RV

43 sites w/full hookups plus 10 for drift boat tents, reservations
(541)584-2832, cable tv, walk to store, river, fishing, $20/night.
Take State 38 west of Drain 14 miles to Elkton, go 2 blocks west
of bridge and turn onto 2nd St. - park is 1 block.

IDLEYLD PARK

BOGUS CREEK (Umpqua NF)   🔺 RV

15 campsites, trailers to 35', flush toilets, fire pits, whitewater
boating, fly fishing, hiking, elev. 1100', $7/night.
Take State 138 east 14 miles.

CANTON CREEK (Umpqua NF)   🔺 RV

5 units, trailers to 24', flush toilets, picnic shelter, on Steamboat
Creek - no fishing, swimming, hiking, elev. 1200', $7/night.
Follow State 138 east 18 miles to Steamboat, and take FSR 38
northeast .4 mile.

EAGLE ROCK (Umpqua NF)   🔺 RV

25 units, trailers to 30', fire pits, access to North Umpqua River,
white water boating, hiking, fly fishing, next to Boulder Creek
Wilderness, elev. 1676', $7/night.
Take State 138 east 30 miles.

HORSESHOE BEND (Umpqua NF)   🔺 RV

24 units plus group area, group reservations (541)496-3532, trail-
ers to 35', flush toilets, wheelchair access, picnic facilities, on
North Umpqua River, boat launch, fly fishing, hiking, elev. 1300',
$10/night - groups $40.
Follow State 138 east 25.6 miles, FSR 4750 south .1 mile, and
FSR 4750-001 southwest .3 mile.

MILLPOND (BLM)   🔺 RV

12 units, trailers okay, picnic area w/shelter, flush toilets, handicap access, ball field, playground, swimming, fishing, nature

study, elev. 1100', open mid-May thru mid-Oct., pets okay, $8/night.
Take State 138 east .5 mile, and Rock Creek Rd. north 5 miles.

MOUNTAIN COUNTRY RV PARK (Private)
25 units w/full hookups, tents okay, reservations (541)498-2454, showers, laundry, on North Umpqua River, $17/night.
Located at 117 Elk Ridge Lane, in Idleyld Park.

ROCK CREEK (BLM)
17 units, trailers okay, picnic area, swimming, fishing, nature study, elev. 1200', open mid-May thru mid-Oct., pets okay, $7/night.
Take State 138 east .5 mile, and Rock Creek Rd. north 8 miles.

SUSAN CREEK (BLM)
31 units, trailers okay, showers, handicap access, North Umpqua River, fly fishing, swimming, hiking, birdwatching, $10/night.
Take State 138 east 2 miles.

TIMBER RIVER RV PARK (Private)
17 units w/hookups for water/elec./sewer/cable, tents okay, information (541)496-0114, trailers to 50', pull thrus, showers, laundry, nearby store, on Umpqua River, fishing, hiking, $15/night.
Located in town, at 22113 N. Umpqua Hwy.

WILLIAMS CREEK (Umpqua NF)
3 units, picnic facilities, no drinking water, stream, fly fishing, swimming, hiking, elev. 1100', FREE.
Take State 138 southeast 8.0 miles, FSR 4710 northeast 3.5 miles, and FSR 480 northeast 5.3 miles.

STEAMBOAT

APPLE CREEK (Umpqua NF)
8 units, trailers to 22', on N. Umpqua River, no drinking water, fly fishing, hiking, elev. 1400', $5/night.
Take State 138 east 4.9 miles.

BOULDER FLAT (Umpqua NF)
11 units plus group site, trailers to 22', on N. Umpqua River, no drinking water, picnic facilities, white water rafting, fly fishing, hiking, located near Boulder Creek Wilderness, elev. 1600', $5/night.
Take State 138 east 14.1 miles.

CLEARWATER FALLS (Umpqua NF)
12 units, trailers to 25', picnic facilities, no drinking water, waterfall, fishing, elev. 4200', $5/night.
Take State 138 east 28.2 miles.

ISLAND (Umpqua NF) [A] [RV]
7 units, trailers to 22', picnic facilities, no drinking water, on N. Umpqua River, fly fishing, hiking, white water rafting, elev. 1200', $5/night.
Take State 138 east 1.3 miles.

SCARED MAN (Umpqua NF) [A] [RV]
9 units, well, on Canton Creek, swimming, elev. 1300', FREE.
Take Canton County Road 4 miles to campground.

STEAMBOAT FALLS (Umpqua NF) [A] [RV]
10 units, trailers to 24', no drinking water, hiking, elev. 1400', $5/night.
Take CR 38 northeast 5.5 miles and FSR 3810 southeast .6 mile.

TOKETEE LAKE (Umpqua NF) [A] [RV]
33 units, trailers to 30', picnic facilities, no drinking water, river, boat ramp, fishing, water skiing, on lake, elev. 2400', $5/night.
Take State 138 east 17.2 miles and FSR 34 northeast 1.4 miles.

WHITEHORSE FALLS (Umpqua NF) [A] [RV]
5 units, trailers to 25', no drinking water, picnic area, stream, waterfall, fishing, next to Clearwater River, elev. 3800', $5/night.
Take State 138 east 24.4 miles.

SUTHERLIN

HI-WAY HAVEN RV PARK (Private) [A] [RV]
97 sites w/full hookups inc. cable, 2 w/water & elec. plus tent area, reservations (541)459-4557, showers, laundry, wheelchair access, groceries, trailer waste disposal, fishing, $20-21/night.
Leave I-5 at exit #136 and go southwest to 609 Fort McKay Rd.

TREES OF OREGON RV PARK B&B (Private) [A] [RV]
28 sites w/full hookups, 14 w/water/elec./cable, tent area, reservations (541)849-2181, trailers to 50', cont. breakfast avail. - $3, showers, laundry, wheelchair access, game room, trailer waste disposal, pets okay, $18/night.
Take State 99 north 2 miles.

TYEE (BLM) [A] [RV]
15 units, picnic shelter, handicap access, on Umpqua River, swimming, fishing, elev. 200', $7/night.
Take State 138 northwest 12 miles, cross bridge and turn right.

GLIDE

BOULDER FLAT (Umpqua NF) [A] [RV]
11 sites - 3 trailers, stream, fishing, hiking, elev. 1600', $5/night.
Take State 138 east 34 miles.

CAVITT CREEK (BLM) [A] [RV]
8 units, trailers okay, picnic area, waterfall, swimming, fishing, nature study, elev. 1100', open mid-May thru mid-Oct., pets okay, $7/night.
Follow Little River Rd. south 6 miles and Cavitt Creek Rd. south 2 miles to campground.

COOLWATER CAMP (Umpqua NF) [A] [RV]
7 units, trailers to 24', picnic facilities, well, river, fishing, nearby hiking trails, swimming, elev. 1300', $5/night.
Take Little River Rd. southeast 15.5 miles.

HEMLOCK LAKE (Umpqua NF) [A] [RV]
13 units, trailers to 35', picnic facilities, no drinking water, lake - no motors, nearby boat ramp, swimming, fishing, loop trail, elev. 4400', $5/night.
Take Little River Road southeast 32 miles.

LAKE IN THE WOODS (Umpqua NF) [A] [RV]
11 units plus shelter, trailers to 35', flush toilets, fire pits, picnic area, lake - no motors, fishing, hiking trails to Hemlock & Yakso Waterfalls plus Hemlock Lake, elev. 3200', $7/night.
Take Little River Rd. southeast 20 miles, and FSR 27 north 7 miles.

WHITE CREEK (Umpqua NF) [A]
4 walk-in sites, well, river, fishing, trails, elev. 1600', $5/night.
Follow Little River Road southeast 16.8 miles and FSR 2792 east .5 mile.

WOLF CREEK (Umpqua NF) [A] [RV]
8 units plus 3 group sites, group reservations (541)496-3532, trailers to 30', flush toilets, picnic facilities, swimming, fishing, hiking, elev. 1100', $7/night - groups $45.
Take Little River Rd. southeast 12.4 miles; campground is 1 mile past Job Corp Center.

WOLF CREEK PARK (Josephine County) [A] [RV]
28 units - 19 w/water & elec, picnic area, playground, trailer waste disposal, disc golf, ball field, creek, swimming, fishing, hiking, pets okay, open April thru Sept., $12-15/night.
Take Wolf Creek exit #76 off I-5; located at end of Main St.

ROSEBURG

ALAMEDA AVE. TRAILER COURT (Private) [RV]
35 units w/full hookups, no tents, reservations (541)672-2348, trailers to 40', cable avail., showers, laundry, wheelchair accessible, store, trailer waste disposal, small pets okay, $15/night.
Leave I-5 on exit #125, go east to N.E. Stevens and turn left, follow to Alameda Ave. - located at 581 N.E. Alameda Ave.

AMACHER PARK (Douglas County) [A] [RV]

30 units - 20 w/full hookups plus 10 tent sites, information (541)672-4901, picnic area, showers, wheelchair access, playground, river, fishing, boat launch, $11-14/night.
Take I-5 north to exit #129, and follow old Highway 99 south .3 mile to the park.

MT. NEBO RV PARK (Private) [RV]

25 sites w/full hookups, no tents, reservations (541)673-4108, trailers to 45', pull thrus, showers, laundry, ice, trailer waste disposal, $18/night.
Leave I-5 on exit #125 and take Garden Valley Rd. east .8 mile, and State 99 north .7 mile.

RISING RIVER RV PARK (Private) [RV]

41 units w/full hookups inc. cable, no tents, reservations (541)679-7256, on South Umpqua River, pets okay, nearby restaurant & groceries, $18/night.
Located at 5579 Sw Grange Rd.

TWIN RIVERS VACATION PARK (Private) [A] [RV]

85 units w/full hookups plus grassy tent area, reservations (541)673-3811, showers, laundry, playground, groceries, swimming, fishing, $15/21/night.
Leave I-5 at exit #125 and, take Garden Valley Rd. west 5 miles, and Old Garden Valley Rd. west an additional 1.5 miles.

UMPQUA SAFARI RV PARK (Private) [RV]

30 units w/full hookups plus 2 w/water/elec./cable tv, reservations (541)679-6328, trailers to 60', pull thrus, showers, wheelchair accessible, trailer waste disposal, pets okay, open year round, $18/night.
Leave I-5 south at exit #119 and take State 99 west 2.5 miles to the town of Winston - located at 511 NE Main.

WHISTLER'S BEND (Douglas County) [A] [RV]

23 rustic sites plus group area, information (541)673-4863, flush toilets, showers, handicap access, playground, wildlife reserve, river, fishing, boat launch, $8/night.
Take State 138 northeast 12 miles, and Whistler's Bend Rd. west 2 miles.

WILDLIFE SAFARI RV PARK (Private) [A] [RV]

Space for 20 self-contained units - 2 w/elec., pull thrus, tents okay, open March thru Sept., $8-10/night.
Leave I-5 south at exit #119 and take State 99 west 2.5 miles to the town of Winston - located at the park, on Safari Rd.

MYRTLE CREEK

MILLSITE PARK & RV PARK (City) [A] [RV]
11 units w/hookups for water & elec. plus tent area, information (541)863-3171, showers, wheelchair access, playground, trailer waste disposal, on S. Umpqua River, fishing, hiking, $3-10/night. Located at 441 4th St.

ON THE RIVER RV & GOLF (Private) [A] [RV]
25 units w/full hookups plus tent area, reservations (541)679-3505, showers, laundry, handicap access, playground, 6-hole par 3 golf course, on S. Umpqua River, fishing, swimming, floating, pets okay, $10-17/night.
Leave I-5 at exit #113 and follow signs; it's about 2 miles.

RIVERS WEST RV PARK (Private) [A] [RV]
52 units w/full hookups plus 68 w/water & elec., tents okay, reservations (541)863-7601, showers, laundry, on South Umpqua River, boat ramp, kayak rental, fishing, restaurant, $12-20/night.
Leave I-5 at exit #110/112 and follow signs a short distance.

DIAMOND LAKE

BROKEN ARROW (Umpqua NF) [A] [RV]
148 campsites, trailers to 35', reservations (800)283-CAMP, flush toilets, wheelchair access, picnic facilities, trailer waste disp., on Diamond Lake - speed limits, boat ramp, fishing, hiking, $9/night - groups $45-110.
Take State 138 north .2 mile, and FSR 4795 west and south 3.8 miles to campground.

BUNKER HILL (Umpqua NF) [A] [RV]
8 units, trailers to 22', on Lemolo Lake, boating, no drinking water, picnic facilities, swimming, fishing, water skiing, elev. 4200', $5/night.
Follow State 138 north 6 miles, Lemolo Lake Rd. north 5.4 miles, cross dam and turn right onto FSR 2610/999, follow .5 mile - is on north shore of lake.

DIAMOND LAKE (Umpqua NF) [A] [RV]
238 units, trailers to 35', reservations (800)280-CAMP, flush toilets, picnic facilities, trailer waste disposal, on Diamond Lake - speed limits, boat launch, swimming, fishing, hiking, bicycle path, interpretive services, elev. 5200', $10-15/night.
Take State 138 north .2 mile, and FSR 4795, west 2.5 miles.

DIAMOND LAKE RV PARK (Private) [RV]
120 units w/hookups for water/elec./sewer, reservations (541)793-3318, showers, laundry, wheelchair access, trailer waste disposal, groceries, on Diamond Lake - speed limits, boat

launch, swimming, fishing, hiking, 11 mile bike path around lake, elev. 5300', $20/night.
Go south to Diamond Lake South Shore Rd., then north 1 mile.

EAST LEMOLO (Umpqua NF)　　　　　　　　　　【△】【RV】
10 sites in primitive fishing camp, trailers to 22', no drinking water, picnic facilities, at Lemolo Lake, boating, swimming, water skiing, elev. 4200', $5/night.
Follow State 138 north 6 miles, Lemolo Lake Rd. north 3.2 miles, and FSR 400 northeast 2.3 miles.

INLET (Umpqua NF)　　　　　　　　　　　　　　【△】【RV】
14 units, no drinking water, trailers to 22', picnic facilities, river, elev. 4200', $5/night.
Follow State 138 north 6 miles, Lemolo Lake Rd. north 3.2 miles, and FSR 400 northeast 2.7 miles. Is on Lemolo Lake at confluence of North Umpqua River.

KELSAY VALLEY HORSE CAMP (Umpqua NF)　　【△】【RV】
10 units, trailers to 18', primitive, no drinking water, picnic facilities, stream, fishing, horse facilities, trails, elev. 4300', $5/night.
Follow State 138 north 6 miles, Cascade Lakes Hwy. northeast 4.7 miles, and Kelsay Valley Rd. east .3 mile; is located near Lemolo Lake.

LEMOLO LAKE RESORT (Private)　　　　　　　　【△】【RV】
29 pull thrus w/full hookups, 5 w/water & elec., plus 31 tent sites, reservations (541)793-3300, trailers to 45', showers, laundry, wheelchair access, groceries, restaurant, lounge, cabins, gas, on lake, boat rentals & moorage, pets okay, $10-17/night..
Go north 6 miles on State 138 and 5 miles on Lemolo Lake Rd.

POOLE CREEK (Umpqua NF)　　　　　　　　　　【△】【RV】
59 units, trailers to 35', reservations - (800)283-CAMP, on Lemolo Lake, boat launch, swimming, fishing, water skiing, elev. 4200', $9-12/night - groups $45.
Go north 6 miles on State 138 and 4.2 miles on Lemolo Lake Rd.

THIELSEN VIEW (Umpqua NF)　　　　　　　　　　【△】【RV】
60 units, trailers to 35', handicap access, picnic facilities, on Diamond Lake - speed limits, boat launch, swimming, fishing, hiking, elev. 5200', $9/night.
Take State 138 north .2 mile, and FSR 4795, west and south 3.1 miles to campground.

CRATER LAKE

LOST CREEK (Crater Lake NP)　　　　　　　　　　　　　【△】
16 tent sites, open July thru mid-Sept., elev. 6000', $5/night.
Located in southern portion of Crater Lake National Park - follow signs to Pinnacles Rd. and campground.

MAZAMA (Crater Lake NP)   [A] [RV]
200 campsites, trailers okay,showers, wheelchair access, trailer waste disposal, groceries, lake, fishing, hiking, open June thru Sept., elev. 6000', $11/night.
Located in southern portion of Crater Lake National Park, .5 mile east of the Annie Spring entrance.

CANYONVILLE

CHARLES V. STANTON PARK (Douglas County)   [A] [RV]
20 units w/full hookups plus 27 tent sites, information (541)839-4483, showers, wheelchair access, playground, pavilion, public dump station, river, fishing, $11-14/night.
Leave I-5 north at exit #99 and head north 1 mile to park. From I-5 south you must take exit #101 and head east to park.

COW CREEK GAMING CENTER RV PARK (Private)   [RV]
38 rv sites w/hookups for water/elec./sewer, no tents, pull thrus, information (541)839-1111, trailers to 50', restrooms are in casino - no showers, restaurant, pets okay, $14-16/night.
Leave I-5 at exit #99 and follow signs.

TILLER

BOULDER CREEK (Umpqua NF)   [A] [RV]
12 units, trailers to 18', no drinking water, creek, hiking, elev. 1400', FREE.
Take State 227 southeast .3 mile and S. Umpqua Road northeast 14 miles.

CAMP COMFORT (Umpqua NF)   [A] [RV]
5 units plus shelter, trailers to 18', no drinking water, picnic facilities, stream, fishing, trails, elev. 2000', FREE.
Take State 227 southeast .3 mile and S. Umpqua Rd. northeast 26 miles.

COVER (Umpqua NF)   [A] [RV]
7 units, trailers to 18', no drinking water, stream, fishing, hiking, elev. 1700', FREE.
Take State 227 southeast .3 mile, S. Umpqua Rd northeast 5 miles, and Jackson Creek Road east 13 miles.

DUMONT CREEK (Umpqua NF)   [A] [RV]
5 units, trailers to 18', no drinking water, picnic facilities, stream, fishing, elev. 1300', FREE.
Take State 227 southeast .3 mile and S. Umpqua Rd. northeast 11 miles.

THREEHORN (Umpqua NF) 🔺 RV
5 units, trailers to 22', no drinking water, picnic facilities, hiking, elev. 2600', FREE.
Take Tiller Trail Hwy. south 13 miles.

AZALEA

DEVILS FLAT (Umpqua NF) 🔺 RV
3 campsites, no drinking water, picnic facilities, nearby historic cabin, Cow Creek Falls Trail, fishing, hiking, elev. 2200', FREE.
Take Upper Cow Creek Rd. 17 miles east.

TUCKER FLAT (Umpqua NF) 🔺 RV
8 units, no drinking water, picnic facilities, on Rogue River, boating, swimming, fishing, hiking, elev. 650', FREE.
Located at the town of Marial. Leave I-5 at exit #80 about 10 miles south of Azalea, follow Glendale/Cow Creek Rd. 16 miles west, Dutch Henry Rd. 15 miles southwest, and Marial Rd. 15 miles southwest.

PROSPECT

ABBOTT CREEK (Rogue River NF) 🔺 RV
23 units, trailers to 22', fishing, elev. 3100', $8/night.
Take State 62 north 6.8 miles, and FSR 68 northwest 3.4 miles.

FAREWELL BEND (Rogue River NF) 🔺 RV
61 units, trailers to 22', reservations (800)416-6992, flush toilets, on Rogue River, fishing, elev. 3400', $10/night.
Take State 62 north 11.6 miles; near Union Creek Resort.

HAMAKER (Rogue River NF) 🔺
10 tent sites, river, fishing, hiking, elev. 4000', $8/night.
Follow State 62 north 12 miles, State 230 north 11 miles, FSR 6530 southeast .6 mile, and FSR 900 south .6 mile.

HUCKLEBERRY MTN. (Rogue River NF) 🔺 RV
25 sites, trailers to 22', well, berry picking, elev. 5400', FREE.
Take State 62 east 17.4 miles and FSR 60 south 4.1 miles.

JOSEPH P. STEWART (Oregon State Park) 🔺 RV
201 units - 151 w/hookups for elec., plus 50 tent sites, group area, maximum site 80', wheelchair access, trailer waste disposal, boat launch, fishing, swimming, hiking/bike trails, access to Upper Rogue River & Pacific Crest Trails, $10-15/night.
Take State 62 southwest 10 miles.

MILL CREEK (Rogue River NF) 🔺 RV
8 units, trailers to 22', fishing, elev. 2800', FREE.
Take State 62 north 2 miles and FSR 30 east 1 mile.

MT. HOME MOBILE VILLAGE (Private)　　　　🔺 RV
7 units w/full hookups, tents okay, reservation (541)560-3504, trailers to 36', showers, laundry, play area, nearby fishing, pets okay, open year round, $12/night.
Take 1st St. to Mill Creek Dr. - located at 51 Mill Creek Dr.

NATURAL BRIDGE (Rogue River NF)　　　　🔺 RV
16 units, trailers to 22', river, fishing, trails, river flows underground at this point, elev. 3200', FREE.
Take State 62 north 9.9 miles and FSR 30 west 1 mile.

RIVER BRIDGE (Rogue River NF)　　　　🔺 RV
6 units, trailers to 22', river, fishing, hiking, elev. 2900', FREE.
Take State 62 north 4 miles and FSR 6210 north 1 mile.

UNION CREEK (Rogue River NF)　　　　🔺 RV
78 units, trailers to 18', reservations (800)416-6992, fishing, hiking, elev. 3200', $8/night.
Take State 62 north 10.8 miles, and FSR 3136 west .2 mile.

BUTTE FALLS

BIG BEN (Rogue River NF)　　　　🔺
2 tent units, stream, fishing, hiking, elev. 4000', FREE.
Take the Butte Falls-Fish Lake Rd. southeast 14.1 miles, FSR 34 northeast 8.2 miles, and FSR 37 southeast .8 mile.

FOURBIT FORD (Rogue River NF)　　　　🔺
7 tent units, stream, fishing, elev. 3200', $8/night.
Take the Butte Falls-Fish Lake Rd. southeast 6 miles, FSR 30 east 2 miles, and FSR 37 northeast .8 mile.

IMNAHA (Rogue River NF)　　　　🔺
4 tent sites, stream, fishing, remote, elev. 3800', FREE.
Take the Butte Falls-Fish Lake Rd. southeast 2.7 miles and FSR 37 northeast 8 miles.

PARKER MEADOWS (Rogue River NF)　　　　🔺
8 tent units, picnic area, hiking, elev. 5000', $3/night.
Take the Butte Falls-Fish Lake Rd. southeast 6 miles, FSR 30 east 2 miles, and FSR 37 northeast 11 miles.

SNOWSHOE (Rogue River NF)　　　　🔺
5 tent sites, well, elev. 4000', FREE.
Take the Butte Falls-Fish Lake Rd. southeast 9.3 miles and FSR 3065 northeast 4.8 miles.

SOUTH FORK (Rogue River NF)　　　　🔺 RV
6 units, trailers to 18', fishing, hiking, elev. 4000', $3/night.
Take Butte Falls-Prospect Rd. northeast 11.1 miles, and Lodgepole Rd. northeast 7.7 miles.

WHISKEY SPRINGS (Rogue River NF) △ RV
35 units, trailers to 18', reservations (800)416-6992, picnic area, hiking, elev. 3200', $8/night.
Take the Butte Falls-Fish Lake Rd. southeast 6 miles, FSR 30 east 2 miles, and FSR 37 east .3 mile.

WILLOW LAKE RESORT (Jackson County) △ RV
25 sites w/full hookups, 20 w/water & elec., plus 28 tent sites, reservations (541)865-3229, showers, trailer waste disposal, groceries, restaurant/lounge, swimming, fishing, boat launch & rental, hiking, elev. 3000', $12-16/night.
Take the Butte Falls-Fish Lake Rd. southeast 6 miles, and follow Willow Lake Rd. 2 miles southwest to resort.

GRANTS PASS

ALAMEDA PARK (Josephine County) △ RV
25 primitive sites plus group area, trailers okay, trailer waste disposal, river, boat ramp, fishing, rafting, host in summer, pets okay, open April thru Sept., $12/night.
Leave I-5 at exit #61 and take the Merlin-Galice Rd. 19 miles west.

BEND O' THE RIVER CAMPGROUND (Private) △ RV
26 units w/hookups for water/elec./sewer plus grassy tent area, reservations (541)479-2547, showers, laundry, playground, on Rogue River, swimming, fishing, $10-16/night.
Follow G St. 7.5 miles west - becomes Upper & Lower River Rds.

BIG PINE (Siskiyou NF) △ RV
13 units, trailers to 22', wheelchair access - includes trails, picnic area, fishing, world's tallest Ponderosa pine, sightless interpretive trail, elev. 2400', $5/night.
Leave I-5 north of town on exit #61, take the Merlin-Galice Rd. northwest 12.4 miles, and FSR 25 southwest 12.8 miles.

DIXON GREENVALLEY CAMPERS (Private) RV
31 sites w/full hookups, showers, $12/night.
Leave I-5 at Grants Pass/Coast Highway exit. Located about 2.5 miles from freeway, just beyond fairgrounds.

GRANTS PASS OVER-NITERS (Private) △ RV
29 units w/hookups for water/elec./sewer, 11 w/water & elec., plus grassy tent area, reservations (541)479-7289, showers, laundry, swimming pool, propane, $13-18/night.
Leave I-5 at exit #61, turn east, take Frontage Rd. north .5 mile.

GRANTS PASS/SUNNY VALLEY KOA (Private) △ RV
88 units - 11 w/hookups for water/elec./sewer, 61 w/water & elec., plus 16 tent sites, reservations - (541)479-0209, showers,

laundry, swimming pool, playground, game room, groceries, trailer waste disposal, petting zoo, $12-17/night.
Take I-5 north to the Sunny Valley exit #71 and campground.

GRIFFIN PARK (Josephine County)
18 units - 14 w/hookups for water/elec./sewer plus 4 tent sites, reservations - (541)474-5285, showers, playfield, playground, trailer waste disposal, river, rafting, boat launch, swimming, fishing, hiking, $12-17/night.
Take US 199 west 4 miles, Riverbanks Rd. 2.5 miles to park.

INDIAN MARY PARK (Josephine County)
42 units w/hookups for water/elec./sewer plus 60 tent sites, trailers to 35', reservations (541)474-5285, showers, playfield, playground, volleyball, disc golf course, river, boat launch, swimming, fishing, hiking, $12-17/night.
Leave I-5 at exit #61, and take the Merlin-Galice Rd. 7.6 miles west.

JOE CREEK WATERFALLS RV PARK (Private)
36 sites w/full hookups plus 15 tent sites, reservations (541)479-7974, restrooms, handicap access, laundry, mini-mart & videos, on Jumpoff Joe Creek - swimming hole, small pets okay, $15-18/night.
Leave I-5 at exit #66 and go north .3 mile - park is 10 miles north of Grants Pass.

RIVERPARK RV RESORT (Private)
47 units w/full hookups plus 3 tent sites, reservations - (800)677-8857, trailers to 50', showers, laundry, trailer waste disposal, on Rogue River, fishing, hiking, pets okay, open year round, $16-20/night.
Leave I-5 on exit #55, turn left on Parkdale, left on State 99, and go south 2 miles to 2956 Rogue River Hwy.

ROGUE VALLEY OVERNIGHTERS (Private)
110 trailer sites w/full hookups, no tents, reservations - (541)479-2208, showers, laundry, trailer waste disposal, $21/night.
Leave I-5 at exit #58 and go south 1 block to NW 6th St. - located at 1806 NW 6th St.

SAM BROWN (Siskiyou NF)
33 units, trailers okay, wheelchair access, picnic shelters, solar showers, amphitheater, creek, fishing, swimming, hiking trails, elev. 2300', $2/night.
Leave I-5 north of town on exit #61, take the Merlin-Galice Rd. northwest 12.4 miles, FSR 25 southwest 13.4 miles, and FSR 2512 west .6 mile.

SAM BROWN HORSE CAMP (Siskiyou NF)
7 campsites - each w/corral, trailers to 22', wheelchair access, fire rings, picnic tables, exercise corral, trails, elev. 2300', $5/night.

Leave I-5 north of town on exit #61, take the Merlin-Galice Rd. northwest 12.4 miles, FSR 25 southwest 13.4 miles, and FSR 2512 west .6 mile.

SCHROEDER (Josephine County)   🅰️ RV
31 campsites - 29 w/hookups for water/elec./sewer, tents okay, trailers to 35', showers, tennis, basketball, playfield, playground, river, handicap fishing dock, boat launch, fishing, $12-17/night.
Follow G St. 4 miles west - becomes Upper River Rd.

SPAULDING POND (Siskiyou NF)   🅰️ RV
3 campsites, wheelchair accessible, picnic tables, 3 acre stocked lake, 2 fishing docks, historic mill site, May-Oct., elev. 3000', $5/night.
Take US 199 southwest 15 miles, FSR 25 northwest 6 miles, and FSR 2524 west 3.5 miles.

TIN CAN (Siskiyou NF)   🅰️ RV
5 campsites, wheelchair access, creek, fishing, hiking, FREE.
Leave I-5 north of town on exit #61, take the Merlin-Galice Rd. northwest 12.4 miles, and FSR 25 southwest 5.1 miles.

WHITE HORSE (Josephine County)   🅰️ RV
8 units w/hookups for water/elec./sewer, 2 w/elec., plus 29 tent sites, trailers to 35', information - (541)474-5285, showers, playground, river, boat launch, fishing, hiking, $12-17/night.
Follow G St. 6 miles west - becomes Upper River Rd.

ROGUE RIVER

CIRCLE W RV PARK (Private)   RV
25 units - 17 w/full hookups plus 8 w/water/elec./cable tv, reservations (541)582-1686, showers, laundry, playground, store, ice, propane, trailer waste disposal, river, swimming, fishing, paddle boat rentals, $16-20/night.
Leave I-5 at exit #48 and take State 99 west 1 mile.

CYPRESS GROVE RV PARK (Private)   RV
45 units w/full hookups, no tents, reservations (800)758-0719, trailers to 50', pull thrus, showers, laundry, wheelchair access, propane, pets okay, open year round, $21/night.
Leave I-5 south of town on exit #45 and follow signs.

ELDERBERRY FLAT (BLM)   🅰️ RV
10 campsites, no drinking water, picnic facilities, atv, elev. 2000', FREE.
Take the road to Wimer and after 19 miles you'll find the campground on the left.

HAVE-A-NICE DAY CAMPGROUND (Private)   ▲ RV
20 units w/water & elec., reservations (541)582-1421, showers, laundry, playground, trailer waste disposal, river, fishing, boat launch, $17/night.
Leave I-5 at exit #48 and take State 99 west 1.5 miles.

RIVERFRONT RV TRAILER PARK (Private)   ▲ RV
27 units - 19 w/full hookups, 2 w/water/elec./cable tv, plus 6 tent sites, reservations (541)582-0985, showers, laundry, ice, trailer waste disposal, river, boat launch, swimming, fishing, $20/night.
Leave I-5 at exit #48 and take State 99 west 2 miles.

VALLEY OF THE ROGUE (Oregon State Park)   ▲ RV
173 units - 97 w/hookups for water/elec./sewer, 55 w/elec. only, 21 tent sites, plus group area, reservations (800)452-5687, maximum site 75', showers, wheelchair access, picnic facilities, trailer waste disposal, boat launch, fishing, hiking, open year round, $11-18/night.
Leave I-5 south of town on exit #45.

GOLD HILL

GOLD'N ROGUE KOA (Private)   ▲ RV
90 units - 20 w/full hookups, 54 w/water & elec., plus 16 tent sites, reservations - (541)855-7710, showers, laundry, pool, playground, trailer waste disposal, groceries, propane, $18-22/night.
Leave I-5 at exit #40, north .3 mile, Blackwell Rd. east .2 mile.

LAZY ACRES MOTEL & RV PARK (Private)   ▲ RV
75 units - 60 w/hookups for water/elec./sewer plus 15 w/out hookups, tents okay, reservations (541)855-7000, showers, laundry, playfield, playground, on Rogue River, swimming, fishing, $8-15/night.
Leave I-5 at exit #40, north .3 mile, State 99 west 1.5 miles.

WHITE CITY

BEAR MOUNTAIN RV PARK (Private)   ▲ RV
37 units - 30 w/hookups for water/elec./sewer plus 7 w/water & elec., tents okay, reservations (800)586-2327 or (541)878-2400, showers, laundry, wheelchair access, playfield, playground, on Rogue River, fishing, hiking, pets okay, $12-16/night.
Take State 62 northeast 19 miles.

BEAVER DAM (Rogue River NF)   ▲ RV
4 sites, creek, fishing, hiking, biking, elev. 4500', FREE.
Take State 140 northeast 29.7 miles and FSR 37 south 6.5 miles - campground is south of Fish Lake.

DALEY CREEK (Rogue River NF) ⚠️ RV
7 units, creek, fishing, elev. 4500', FREE.
Take State 140 northeast 29.7 miles and FSR 37 south 6 miles - campground is south of Fish Lake.

DOE POINT (Rogue River NF) ⚠️ RV
25 units, trailers to 22', reservations (800)416-6992, flush toilets, on Fish Lake - speed limits, swimming, fishing, hiking, bicycling, elev. 4600', $10-12/night.
Take State 140 east 28.2 miles.

FISH LAKE (Rogue River NF) ⚠️ RV
17 units, trailers to 22', reservations (800)416-6992, flush toilets, on Fish Lake - speed limits, boat launch, swimming, fishing, hiking, elev. 4600', $10/night.
Take State 140 east 29.7 miles.

FISH LAKE RESORT (Private) ⚠️ RV
45 sites w/hookups for water/elec./sewer, 6 w/elec., 3 w/out hookups, tents okay, reservations (541)949-8500, showers, laundry, game room, groceries, fishing supplies, cafe, trailer waste disposal, lake, boat launch & rental, swimming, fishing, hiking, open May to Nov., elev. 4600', $11-19/night.
Take State 140 east 30 miles.

FLYCASTERS RV PARK (Private) RV
30 units w/hookups for water/elec./sewer, no tents, reservations (541)878-2749, showers, laundry, restaurant, lounge, on Rogue River, swimming, fishing, pets okay, $19-28/night.
Take State 62 northeast 13 miles.

MEDFORD OAKS CAMPARK (Private) ⚠️ RV
19 sites w/hookups for water/elec./sewer, 29 w/water & elec., plus tent area, trailers to 50', pull thrus, reservation (541)826-5103, showers, laundry, pool, playground, rec room, picnic pavilion, dance floor, groceries, trailer waste disposal, pond, fishing, $12-23/night.
Take State 140 east 6.8 miles.

NORTH FORK (Rogue River NF) ⚠️ RV
9 units, trailers to 18', stream, fishing, biking, elev. 4500', FREE.
Take State 140 northeast 28.1 miles and FSR 3706 south 1 mile.

ROGUE ELK CAMPGROUND (Jackson County) ⚠️ RV
37 campsites, trailers okay, reservation information - (541)776-7001, showers, playground, trailer waste disposal, river, boat ramp, fishing, rafting, swimming, hiking, pets okay, open mid-April thru mid-Oct., $14-15/night.
Take State 62 northeast 18 miles.

ROGUE RIVER RV PARK (Private)

65 sites w/full hookups, 5 w/water & elec., reservations (800)775-0367 or (541)878-2404, trailers to 40', pull thrus, showers, laundry, fishing, pets to 35 lb., $16-25/night.
Take State 62 northeast 20 miles.

SHADY TRAILS RV PARK (Private)

50 units - 20 w/full hookups, 30 w/water/elec./cable tv, plus tent area, reservations (541)878-2206, showers, playground, trailer waste disposal, river, boat launch, fishing, $12-20/night.
Take State 62 northeast 16 miles.

WILLOW PRAIRIE HORSE CAMP (Rogue River NF)

9 tent units - horse campers only, reservations (541)865-2700, elev. 4400', $6/night.
Take State 140 east 28 miles, FSR 37 north 1.6 miles, and FSR 3738 west 1.5 miles.

MEDFORD

HOLIDAY RV PARK (Private)

110 units w/hookups for water/elec./sewer/cable, no tents, reservations (541)535-2183, showers, wheelchair access, laundry, groceries, swimming pool, basketball court, covered bbq area, walk to outlet mall, pets okay, $21/night.
Take I-5 south to exit #24 - located on west side.

PEAR TREE CENTER (Private)

31 units w/full hookups, no tents, reservations (541)535-4445, showers, laundry, wheelchair access, pool, spa, playground, mini mart, restaurant, gas & propane, pets okay, $24/night.
Take I-5 south to exit #24 - located on east side.

JACKSONVILLE

BEAVER SULPHER (Rogue River NF)

10 tent sites, picnic area, stream, elev. 2100', $8/night.
Take State 238 southwest 8 miles, Applegate Rd. south 9 miles, and FSR 20 east 3 miles.

CANTRALL-BUCKLEY PARK (Jackson County)

42 units - 30 RV sites w/out hookups, 12 tent sites, plus group area, group reservations (541)776-7001, trailers to 25', showers, playground, stream, swimming, fishing, hiking, pets okay, open May thru mid-Oct., $10/night - group $65.
Take State 238 southwest 13 miles.

CARBERRY (Rogue River NF)

10 walk-in tent sites, wheelchair accessible, on Applegate Lake - 10 mph, fishing, hiking, mtn. biking, elev. 2000', $8/night.

Take State 238 southwest 8 miles, and Applegate Rd. south 10 miles to Carberry.

FLUMET FLAT (Rogue River NF) 🅰 RV
27 units, group site, trailers to 22', reservations (800)416-6992, flush toilets, wheelchair access, river, fishing, interpretive historic trail, elev. 1700', $8/night.
Take State 238 southwest 8 miles, Applegate Rd. south 9.9 miles, and FSR 1090 1.2 miles to camp.

FRENCH GULCH CAMP (Rogue River NF) 🅰 RV
9 units, trailers to 18', wheelchair access, lake, hiking, elev. 2000', $8/night.
Take State 238 southwest 8 miles, Applegate Rd. southwest 14 miles, FSR 1075 east 1.5 miles.

HART-TISH PARK (Rogue River NF) 🅰 RV
4 units, group site, trailers okay, reservations (800)416-6992, wheelchair accessible, lake - 10 mph, boat launch, swimming, fishing, hiking, elev. 2000, $10/night.
Take State 238 southwest 8 miles, and Applegate Rd. southwest 15 miles.

HARR POINT CAMP (Rogue River NF) 🅰
5 tent units, boat-in/walk-in only, boating, swimming, fishing, trails, elev. 2100', FREE.
Take State 238 southwest 8 miles, Applegate Rd. southwest 16 miles and walk to campsites from here - or boat in.

JACKSON (Rogue River NF) 🅰 RV
Campsites, piped water, handicap access, fishing, swimming, hiking, elev. 1700', $8/night.
Take State 238 southwest 8 miles, Applegate Rd. south 10 miles.

LATGAWA COVE CAMP (Rogue River NF) 🅰
5 tent units, boat-in/walk-in only, boating, swimming, fishing, trails, elev. 2100', FREE/
Take State 238 southwest 8 miles, Applegate Rd. southwest 14 miles, FSR 1075 east 1 mile, and walk to campsites - or boat in..

SQUAW LAKES (Rogue River NF) 🅰
17 tent units, group sites, remote, lake - no motors, swimming, fishing, hiking, elev. 3000', $8/night.
Take State 238 southwest 8 miles, Applegate Rd. southwest 14 miles, and FSR 1075 southeast 8 miles.

STRINGTOWN (Rogue River NF) 🅰
7 walk-in tent sites, on Applegate Lake - 10 mph, fishing, hiking, elev. 2000, $8/night.
Take State 238 southwest 8 miles, Applegate Rd. southwest 14 miles, and FSR 1075 southeast 3 miles.

TIPSU TYEE CAMP (Rogue River NF) ▲
5 tent sites, boat-in/walk-in only, lake, boating, swimming, fishing, trails, elev. 2000', FREE.
Take State 238 southwest 8 miles, and Applegate Rd. southwest 14 miles and walk to campsites - or boat in.

WATKINS (Rogue River NF) ▲
14 walk-in tent sites, handicap access, on Applegate Lake - 10 mph, fishing, hiking, elev. 2000', $8/night.
Take State 238 southwest 8 miles, and Applegate Rd. southwest 17 miles.

WRANGLE (Rogue River NF) ▲ RV
5 units, trailers to 18', picnic area w/community kitchen, swimming, hiking, elev. 6400', FREE.
Take State 238 southwest 8 miles, and Applegate Rd. southwest 10 miles, FSR 20 east 25 miles, and FSR 2030 northwest 1 mile.

ASHLAND

ASHLAND REGENCY RV PARK (Private) RV
12 pull thrus w/full hookups inc. cable, reservations (800)482-4701, hotel, pool, pets okay, $17/night.
Just off freeway - watch for hotel.

CAMPERS COVE RESORT (Private) RV
25 trailer units w/hookups for water/elec./sewer, reservations (541)482-1201, showers, restaurant, ice, on Hyatt Lake, fishing, boat launch, hiking, pets okay, elev. 5000', $14/night.
Take State 66 east 18 miles, Hyatt Lake Rd. northeast 3 miles, and Hyatt Prairie Rd. north 1.5 miles.

EMIGRANT LAKE CAMP (Jackson County) ▲ RV
42 campsites plus 2 group sites, reservation (541)776-7001, showers, waterslide, trailer waste disposal, lake, fishing, boat launch, swimming, playground, hiking, pets okay, $14/night - groups $100.
Take State 66 east 5 miles - at 7979 Hyatt Prairie Rd.

GLENYAN (Private) ▲ RV
68 campsites - 11 w/hookups for water/elec./sewer, 35 w/water & elec., plus 22 tent units, reservations (541)482-4138, showers, laundry, groceries, trailer waste disposal, swimming pool, pond, fishing, playground, pets okay, $18-22/night.
Take State 66 east 3.5 miles.

GRIZZLY CAMPGROUND (Jackson County) ▲ RV
20 campsites, trailers to 25', lake, fishing, boat launch, hiking, pets okay, elev. 4500', $12/night.
Take State 66 south 1 mile, Dead Indian Rd. east 20 miles, and Hyatt Prairie Rd. south 2 miles.

HOWARD PRAIRIE LAKE RESORT (Private) [A] [RV]

60 units w/full hookups, 90 w/water & elec., plus 150 tent units, information (541)482-1979, showers, laundry, wheelchair access, restaurant, groceries, trailer waste disposal, swimming, fishing, boat launch & rental, hiking, pets okay, elev. 4500', open mid April thru Oct., $12-17/night.
Take State 66 south 1 mile, Dead Indian Rd. east 20 miles, and Hyatt Prairie Rd. south 3.5 miles.

HYATT LAKE (BLM) [A] [RV]

48 units plus 2 group tent areas, group reservations (541)770-2200, trailers okay, pull thrus, picnic shelter, showers, basketball, volleyball, horse area, boat launch, fishing, swimming, hiking, open mid-May thru Oct., elev. 5000', $6-10/night.
Take State 66 east 16 miles, E. Hyatt Lake Rd. north 4 miles.

HYATT LAKE RESORT (Private) [A] [RV]

25 sites w/full hookups plus 11 tent sites, reservations (541)482-3331, showers, trailer waste disposal, fishing, boat launch, canoe & paddleboat rental, restaurant, hiking, pets okay, $12-18/night.
Take State 66 east 18 miles, Hyatt Lake Rd. northeast 3 miles, and Hyatt Prairie Rd. north 1 mile.

KLUM LANDING (Jackson County) [A] [RV]

30 units, lake, boat ramp, fishing, swimming, water skiing, hiking, pets okay, open mid April thru Oct., $12/night.
Take State 66 south 1 mile, Dead Indian Rd. east 20 miles, Hyatt Prairie Rd. south to Dam Rd., turn left - campground is 3 miles.

LILY GLEN (Jackson County) [A] [RV]

15 units plus group area, reservations (541)776-7001, horse barn /corral, lake, fishing, hiking, pets okay, $12/night - groups $125.
Take State 66 south 1 mile, and Dead Indian Rd. east 21 miles.

SUGAR PINE (Jackson County) [A] [RV]

1 group campsite, reservations (541)776-7001, lake, swimming, fishing, boat launch, hiking, horse trails, pets okay - $1, elev. 4500', $100/night.
Take State 66 south 1 mile, Dead Indian Rd. east 20 miles, and Hyatt Prairie Rd. south 2 miles.

WELL SPRINGS (Private) [A] [RV]

25 sites w/hookups for water/elec./sewer, plus large tent area, information (541)482-3776, showers, laundry, vegetarian cafe, ice, mineral pool & baths, pets - fee, $12-18/night.
I-5 north to exit #19, South Valley View Rd. .5 mile southwest.

WILLOW POINT (Jackson County) [A] [RV]

40 units, information (541)776-7001, lake, swimming, fishing, boat launch, hiking, pets okay - $1, elev. 5000', $12/night.
Take State 66 south 1 mile, Dead Indian Rd. east 20 miles, and Hyatt Prairie Rd. south 5 miles.

CENTRAL OREGON
CAMPGROUNDS

See Page

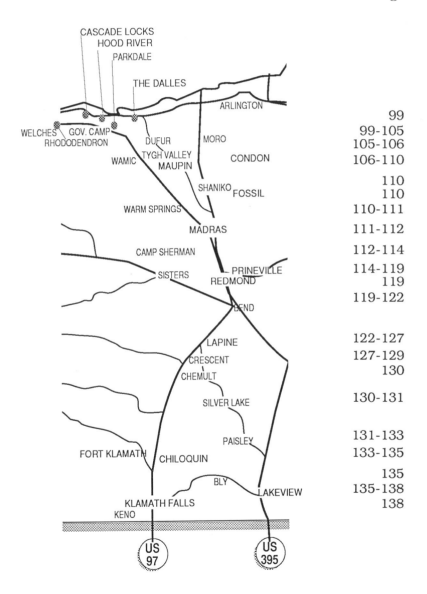

CASCADE LOCKS

BRIDGE OF THE GODS RV PARK (Private)　　　RV
15 sites w/full hookups, no tents, trailers to 35', reservations (541)374-8628, showers, laundry, motel, fishing, small pets okay, $15/night.
Located right on US 30, just before you cross the bridge.

CASCADE LOCKS KOA (Private)　　　A RV
78 units - 40 w/full hookups plus 38 w/water & elec., tents okay, reservations (541)374-8668, showers, laundry, groceries, swimming pool, trailer waste disposal, pets okay, $18-23/night.
At the east end of town take Forest Ln. 1 mile southeast.

CASCADE LOCKS MARINE PARK (Port)　　　A RV
45 sites - no hookups, trailers to 35', tents okay, reservations (541)374-8619, showers, wheelchair access, museum, playground, trailer waste disposal, river, boat launch, fishing, wind surfing, $8/night.
Located 3 blocks north of I-84's Cascade Locks exit.

EAGLE CREEK (CRGNSA)　　　A RV
19 units, trailers to 22', group area - reservations (541)668-1440, flush toilets, dis. access, bicycling, fishing, hiking, elev. 200', pets okay, $8/night.
Take I-84 west 4.5 miles, then go east on I-84 for 2 miles, and take FSR 240 southeast .1 mile to campground.

HERMAN CREEK HORSE CAMP (Mt. Hood NF)　　　A RV
7 units, trailers to 24', wheelchair access, swimming, fishing, hiking, horse trails/corrals/hitch posts, bicycling, $6/night.
Take the Herman Creek exit off I-84 and follow the road that parallels I-84 east 1.6 miles.

WYETH (Mt. Hood NF)　　　A RV
20 units plus group areas, flush toilets, fishing, hiking, $8/night.
Follow I-84 east 7 miles to exit #51 and campground.

HOOD RIVER

COLUMBIA RIVER GORGE RESORT (Private)　　　A RV
250 units w/hookups for water & elec. plus 100 tent sites, (541)478-3750, picnic area, showers, laundry, wheelchair access, trailer waste disposal, pond fishing, pool, spa, par 3 golf, sport courts, hiking, $14-18/night.
I-84 east 6 miles to exit #69 - in Mosier, at 2350 Carroll Rd.

KINGSLEY RESERVOIR (Hood River County)　　　A
20 tent sites, no water, information (541)386-6323, fishing, boat ramp & dock, hiking, mountain biking, $5/night.
Take Kingsley Road southwest to FSR N205 and reservoir.

ROUTSON PARK (Hood River County) ▲

20 tent sites, information (541)386-6323, flush toilets, on Hood River, fishing, pets okay, elev. 2500', $5/night.
Follow State 35 south 7 miles.

TUCKER PARK (Hood River County) ▲ RV

18 units w/hookups for water & elec. plus 28 dry sites, trailers to 30', reservations (541)386-4477, showers, handicap access, picnic shelter, play field, pets okay, $13-14/night.
Take Tucker Rd. out of Hood River and head south 6 miles.

VIENTO (Oregon State Park) ▲ RV

58 units w/elec. plus 17 tent sites, max. site 30', showers, wheelchair access, picnic area, open March thru Nov., $13-16/night.
Take I-84 west 8 miles to exit #56 and campground.

PARKDALE

CLOUD CAP SADDLE (Mt. Hood NF) ▲

3 tent units, piped water, starting point for climbing Mt. Hood or hiking Timberline Trail, historic area, elev. 5900', $3/night.
Take State 35 south 8 miles and FSR 3512 west 11.7 miles.

GIBSON PRAIRIE HORSE CAMP (Mt. Hood NF) ▲ RV

4 units, no drinking water, trailers to 16', horse/hiking trails, elev. 3900', FREE.
Take State 35 north 3 miles and FSR 17 southeast 15 miles.

HOOD RIVER MEADOWS TRAILHEAD (Mt. Hood NF) ▲

3 tent sites, stream, fishing, trailhead to Mt. Hood Wilderness, elev. 4400', $3/night.
Take State 35 southeast 25 miles.

INDIAN SPRINGS (Mt. Hood NF) ▲

4 tent units, stream, trails, access to Pacific Crest Trail, elev. 4200', $3/night.
Follow State 281 north 6 miles, CR 422 southwest 5 miles, FSR 13 west 5 miles, and FSR 1310 northwest 10.5 miles.

KINNIKINNICK LAURANCE LAKE (Mt. Hood NF) ▲ RV

20 campsites, trailers to 16', no water, lake - no gas motors, fishing, boating, $10/night.
Take Clear Creek Rd. 10 miles to Laurance Lake.

LOST LAKE (Mt. Hood NF) ▲ RV

125 units plus group camp, reservations (800)280-CAMP, trailers to 32', showers, wheelchair access, lake - no motors, boat launch & rental, swimming, fishing, hiking, bicycling, elev. 3200', $15-20/night.
Follow Hood River Highway north 6 miles, CR 501 southwest 5 miles, and FSR 13 southwest 9 miles.

RAINY LAKE (Mt. Hood NF)

4 tent units, no drinking water, located .1 mile from lake, boating, swimming, fishing, trails, elev. 4100', FREE.
Follow State 281 north 6 miles, FSR 18 west 2 miles, FSR 2820 northwest 5 miles, and FSR 28206 west 3 miles.

ROBINHOOD (Mt. Hood NF)

24 units, trailers to 18', picnic area, river, swimming, fishing, hiking, elev. 3600', $10-12/night.
Take State 35 south 12 miles.

SHERWOOD (Mt. Hood NF)

14 sites, trailers to 16', river, fishing, hiking, elev. 3000', $10/night.
Take State 35 south 8 miles.

TILLY JANE (Mt. Hood NF)

14 hike-in campsites, no drinking water, stream, trails, historic area, elev. 5700', $3/night.
Take State 35 south 8 miles and FSR 3512 west 11.7 miles.

TOLL BRIDGE PARK (Hood River County)

20 units w/full hookups, 44 w/water & elec., plus 16 tent sites, reservations (541)352-5522, showers, handicap access, trailer waste disposal, playfield, playground, on Hood River, fishing, hiking, pets okay, $13-14/night.
Take Base Line Dr. 1 mile east - campground is west of State 35 .

WAHTUM LAKE (Mt. Hood NF)

8 hike-in units, no water, fishing, rough roads, elev. 3700', FREE.
Follow Hood River Highway north 6 miles, CR 501 southwest 5 miles, FSR 13 west 5 miles (bearing right at the Y), FSR 1310 northwest 8 miles to Wahtum Lake, and hike .3 mile to camp.

THE DALLES

BOB'S BUDGET RV & TRAILER PARK (Private)

26 sites w/full hookups plus 10 tent sites, reservations (541)739-2272, pull thrus to 60', showers, laundry, wheelchair access, pets okay, $10-15/night.
Take I-84 east 24 miles to Rufus exit #109, Old Highway 30 west .5 mile, and Wallace St. south .2 mile.

DESCHUTES RIVER (Oregon State Park)

89 primitive sites plus 4 group areas, trailers to 30', reservations information (541)739-2322, fishing, boating, hiking trails, bicycle trails, wildlife viewing area, Oregon Trail display, $13-15/night.
Take I-84 east 17 miles.

LEPAGE PARK (Corps) [A] [RV]

20 sites w/water & elec., some pull-thrus, tents okay, information (541)296-1181, showers, trailer waste disposal, John Day River, boat launch, fishing, swimming area, pets okay, $10-14/night.
Take I-84 east 28 miles to exit #104, and follow the signs .2 mile to park.

LONE PINE RV PARK/MOTEL (Private) [RV]

22 RV sites w/full hookups, no tents, reservations (800)955-9626, showers, laundry, playground, fishing, pets okay, $20/night.
Leave I-84 on exit #87 - located near north end of overpass.

MEMALOOSE (Oregon State Park) [A] [RV]

43 sites w/full hookups, 67 tent sites, max. 60', reservations (541)478-3008, showers, dis. access, trailer waste disp., Mr.-Nov., $11-19/night.
Take I-84 west 11 miles - this campground is not accessible from I-84 eastbound.

WELCHES

LOST CREEK (Mt. Hood NF) [A] [RV]

16 units, reservations (800)280-CAMP, disabled access., fishing, hiking, $10-12/night.
Take US 26 east 1 mile, LoLo Pass Rd. northeast 4.8 miles, and FSR 1825 east 4 miles.

McNEIL (Mt. Hood NF) [A] [RV]

34 units, trailers to 22', fishing, hiking, elev. 2000', $8/night
Take US 26 east 1 mile, LoLo Pass Rd. northeast 4.8 miles, and FSR 1825 east to campground.

MT. HOOD RV VILLAGE (Private) [A] [RV]

420 units w/full hookups inc. cable, tents okay, reservations - (503)622-4011, showers, wheelchair access, indoor pool/hot tub, weight room, laundry, groceries, restaurant, propane, fishing, golf, $28/night.
Take US 26 west 2 miles.

RILEY HORSE CAMP (Mt. Hood NF) [A] [RV]

14 sites, trailers to 16', reservations (800)280-CAMP, stream, horse loading/hitchracks, trails, fishing, elev. 2100', $10/night.
Take US 26 east 1 mile, LoLo Pass Rd. northeast 4.8 miles, FSR 1825 east 1.2 miles, and FSR 382 southeast .1 mile.

GOVERNMENT CAMP

ALPINE (Mt. Hood NF) [A] [RV]

16 units, trailers to 18', no water, elev. 5400', $7/night.
Take US 26 east .8 mile, and Timberline Rd. northeast 4.6 miles.

BARLOW CREEK (Mt. Hood NF)　　　　　　　　🔺 RV
3 units, trailers to 18', no water, fishing, elev. 3100', FREE.
Take State 35 north 4.5 miles and FSR 3530 southeast 4.2 miles.

BARLOW CROSSING (Mt. Hood NF)　　　　　　🔺 RV
6 units, no water, trailers to 18', stream, fishing, elev. 3100',
FREE.
Take State 35 north 4.5 miles and FSR 3530 southeast 5.2 miles.

CLACKAMAS LAKE (Mt. Hood NF)　　　　　　🔺 RV
46 units, trailers to 32', reservations (800)280-CAMP, lake - speed
limit, fishing, hiking, elev. 3400', $10/night.
Follow US 26 southeast 15 miles, FSR 42 south 8 miles, and FSR
4270 east .5 mile.

CLEAR LAKE (Mt. Hood NF)　　　　　　　　🔺 RV
28 units, trailers to 32', reservations (800)280-CAMP, handicap
access, lake - 10 mph, swimming, fishing, hiking, elev. 3600',
$10-12/night.
Follow US 26 southeast 9 miles, FSR 2630 south 1 mile, and FSR
220 south 1 mile.

DEVILS HALF ACRE (Mt. Hood NF)　　　　　🔺 RV
2 units, no drinking water, trailers to 18', stream, fishing, elev.
3600', FREE.
Take State 35 north 4.5 miles and FSR 3530 east 1 mile.

FROG LAKE (Mt. Hood NF)　　　　　　　　　🔺 RV
33 units, trailers to 22', reservations (800)280-CAMP, handicap
access, lake - no motors, boat ramp, swimming, fishing, elev.
3800', $10-12/night.
Follow US 26 southeast 7 miles, FSR 2610 southeast 1 mile, and
FSR 230 south .5 mile.

GONE CREEK (Mt. Hood NF)　　　　　　　　🔺 RV
50 units, trailers to 32', reservations (800)280-CAMP, handicap
access, lake - 10 mph, boat ramp, swimming, fishing, hiking, elev.
3200', $10-12/night.
Follow US 26 southeast 15 miles, FSR 42 south 8 miles, and FSR
57 west 3.5 miles.

GRINDSTONE (Mt. Hood NF)　　　　　　　　🔺 RV
3 units, trailers to 18', stream, elev. 3400', FREE.
Take State 35 north 4.5 miles and FSR 3530 east 3 miles.

HOODVIEW (Mt. Hood NF)　　　　　　　　　🔺 RV
40 units, trailers to 32', reservation information - (800)280-CAMP,
handicap access, on Timothy Lake - 10 mph, boat ramp, swimming, fishing, hiking, elev. 3200', $10-12/night.
Follow US 26 southeast 15 miles, FSR 42 south 8 miles, and FSR
57 west 4 miles.

JOE GRAHAM HORSE CAMP (Mt. Hood NF) 🔺 RV
14 units, trailers to 27', reservations advised - (800)280-CAMP, fishing, hiking, elev. 3400', $10/night.
Take US 26 southeast 15 miles, and FSR 42 south 8 miles.

KINZEL LAKE (Mt. Hood NF) 🔺
5 tent sites - not maintained, primitive road, creek, swimming, trails, elev. 4400', FREE.
Take US 26 east 1 mile and FSR 32/2623 southwest 10.6 miles.

LITTLE CRATER LAKE (Mt. Hood NF) 🔺 RV
16 units, reservations (800)280-CAMP, hiking, elev. 3200', $10-12/night.
Follow US 26 southeast 15 miles, FSR 42 south 6 miles, FSR 58 west 2.7 miles, and FSR 230 west .3 mile.

MEDITATION POINT (Mt. Hood NF) 🔺
5 tent sites, boat-in or hike-in only, no drinking water, on Timothy Lake - speed limits, swimming, fishing, elev. 3200', FREE.
Follow US 26 southeast 15 miles, FSR 42 south 8 miles, FSR 57 west 6 miles, and boat or hike 1 mile north.

OAK FORK (Mt. Hood NF) 🔺 RV
47 units, reservations (800)280-CAMP, trailers to 32', on Timothy Lake - speed limit, boat ramp, swimming, fishing, hiking, elev. 3200', $10-12/night.
Follow US 26 southeast 15 miles, FSR 42 south 8 miles, FSR 57 west 3 miles, and FSR 170 north .5 mile.

PINE POINT (Mt. Hood NF) 🔺 RV
25 units, trailers to 32', reservations (800)280-2267, handicap access, on Timothy Lake - speed limit, boat launch, fishing, swimming, hiking trail, elev. 3200', $10-12/night - groups $20-30.
Follow US 26 southeast 15 miles, FSR 42 south 8 miles, and FSR 57 west 5 miles.

STILL CREEK (Mt. Hood NF) 🔺 RV
27 units, trailers to 18', reservations (800)280-CAMP, handicap access, fishing, elev. 3700', $10-12/night.
Take US 26 southeast 1.2 miles, and FSR 2650 south .5 mile.

SUMMIT LAKE (Mt. Hood NF) 🔺
5 tent units, no drinking water, no motors on lake, swimming, elev. 4000', FREE.
Follow US 26 southeast 15 miles, FSR 42 south 13 miles, and FSR 141 southeast 1 mile.

TRILLIUM LAKE (Mt. Hood NF) 🔺 RV
39 units, trailers to 22', reservations (800)280-CAMP, wheelchair access, lake - no motors, boat launch, swimming, fishing, bicycling, elev. 3600', $10-12/night.
Take US 26 southeast 2.2 miles, and FSR 2656 south 1.3 miles.

WHITE RIVER STATION (Mt. Hood NF)
5 units, no drinking water, trailers to 18', stream, fishing, elev. 2800', FREE.
Follow State 35 north 4.5 miles and FSR 3530 east 7.2 miles.

RHODODENDRON

CAMP CREEK (Mt. Hood NF)
24 units, trailers to 22', flush toilets - barrier free, reservations (800)280-CAMP, fishing, hiking, elev. 2200', $10-12/night.
US 26 southeast 2.9 miles, Camp Creek Rd. south .1 mile.

TOLLGATE (Mt. Hood NF)
15 units, trailers to 16', reservations (800)280-CAMP, stream, fishing, hiking, elev. 1700', $10-12/night.
Take US 26 southeast .5 mile.

MORO

COUNTY RV CORRAL (Sherman County)
33 units w/full hookups, reservations (541)565-3510, showers, playground, pets & horses okay, nearby wilderness access, $5-15/night.
Located in town, at county fairgrounds.

DUFUR

DUFUR CITY PARK (City)
15 sites w/full hookups, tents okay, information (541) 467-2832, showers, swimming pool, trailer waste disposal, $6-12/night.
Located in the town of Dufur - follow signs.

DUFUR RV PARK (Private)
26 units w/full hookups, no tents, trailers to 60', information (541)467-2449, showers, pets okay, $14/night.
Located at First & South Aikin Sts.

EIGHTMILE CROSSING (Mt. Hood NF)
21 units, trailers to 30', no drinking water, picnic area, stream, fishing, elev. 4200', $3/night.
Take Dufur Valley Rd. southwest 12 miles, FSR 44 west 4.2 miles, and FSR 4430 north .6 mile.

FIFTEEN MILE (Mt. Hood NF)
3 units, no water, trailers to 16', stream, elev. 4600', FREE.
Take Dufur Valley Rd. southwest 12 miles, FSR 44 west 6 miles, and FSR 2730 south 3.5 miles.

KNEBAL SPRINGS (Mt. Hood NF)　　　　　　　△ RV
8 units, no drinking water, trailers to 22/, elev. 4000', $3/night.
Take Dufur Valley Rd. southwest 12 miles, FSR 44 west 4.3 miles,
FSR 4430 north 4 miles, and FSR 1720 southwest 1 mile.

LOWER CROSSING (Mt. Hood NF)　　　　　　△ RV
3 units, no drinking water, trailers to 16', picnic area, stream,
fishing, elev. 3800', FREE.
Take Dufur Valley Rd. southwest 12 miles, FSR 44 west 4 miles,
and FSR 4440 north 1 mile.

PEBBLE FORD (Mt. Hood NF)　　　　　　　　△ RV
3 units, no water, trailers to 16', stream, elev. 4000', FREE.
Take Dufur Valley Rd. southwest 12 miles, FSR 44 west 5 miles,
and FSR 131 south .5 mile..

TYGH VALLEY

BEAVERTAIL (BLM)　　　　　　　　　　　　△ RV
20 units, trailers okay, on Deschutes River, rough road, $3/night.
Take State 216 east 5 miles to Sherar's Bridge, and follow
Deschutes River Rd. north 12 miles.

COUNTY FAIRGROUNDS (Wasco County)　　　△ RV
150 sites w/water & elec., reservations (541)483-2288, showers,
wheelchair access, kitchens, playground, trailer waste disposal,
stream, fishing, horse stalls avail., pets okay, $12/night.
Follow US 197 west 2 miles - located on Fairground Rd.

GET CANYON (BLM)　　　　　　　　　　　　△ RV
4 units, no water, on Deschutes River, rough road, $3/night.
Take State 216 east 5 miles to Sherar's Bridge, and follow
Deschutes River Rd. north 6.3 miles.

JONES CANYON (BLM)　　　　　　　　　　　△ RV
7 units, no water, on Deschutes River, rough road, $3/night.
Take State 216 east 5 miles to Sherar's Bridge, and follow
Deschutes River Rd. north 6 miles.

LITTLE BADGER (Mt. Hood NF)　　　　　　△ RV
3 units, no drinking water, trailers to 18', stream, fishing, elev.
2200', FREE.
Take Fairground Rd. west 3 miles, Badger Creek Rd. west 4.5
miles, FSR 27 west 2 miles, FSR 2710 west .5 mile, and FSR 130
west .2 mile.

MACKS CANYON (BLM)　　　　　　　　　　　△ RV
18 units, boat launch, hiking, fishing, rough road, $3/night.
Take State 216 east 5 miles to Sherar's Bridge, and follow
Deschutes River Rd. north 15 miles.

OAK BROOK (BLM)
4 units, no drinking water, on Deschutes River, rough road, $3/night.
Take State 216 east 5 miles to Sherar's Bridge, and Deschutes River Rd. north 5.5 miles.

RATTLESNAKE (BLM)
8 units, no drinking water, on Deschutes River, rough road, $3/night.
Take State 216 east 5 miles to Sherar's Bridge, and follow Deschutes River Rd. north 8 miles.

WAMIC

BADGER LAKE (Mt. Hood NF)
4 tent sites, no drinking water, lake - no motors, boating, swimming, fishing, elev. 4400', FREE.
Take Rock Creek Rd. west 6 miles, FSR 48 southwest 10 miles, FSR 4860 northwest 7 miles, and FSR 140 northwest 5 miles.

BONNEY CROSSING (Mt. Hood NF)
8 units, no drinking water, trailers to 16', stream, boating, fishing, elev. 2200', $3/night.
Take Rock Creek Rd. west 6 miles, FSR 48 southwest 1 mile, FSR 4810 west 2 miles, FSR 4811 northwest 1.2 miles, and FSR 2710 northwest 1.7 miles.

BONNEY MEADOWS (Mt. Hood NF)
6 units, no drinking water, trailers to 22', stream, fishing, elev. 4800', FREE.
Take Rock Creek Rd. west 6 miles, FSR 48 southwest 14 miles, FSR 4890 north 2 miles, and FSR 4891 north 4 miles.

BOULDER LAKE (Mt. Hood NF)
10 tent units, hike-in only, no drinking water, lake - no motors, boating, swimming, fishing, elev. 4600', $3/night.
Take Rock Creek Rd. west 6 miles, FSR 48 southwest 11.5 miles, FSR 4880 north 6 miles, and Trail #463 west .5 mile.

CAMP WINDY (Mt. Hood NF)
3 tent units, no drinking water, fishing, elev. 4800', FREE.
Take Rock Creek Rd. west 6 miles, FSR 48 southwest 10 miles, and FSR 4860 northwest 9.2 miles.

FOREST CREEK (Mt. Hood NF)
6 units, no drinking water, trailers to 16', fishing, elev. 3000', FREE.
Take Rock Creek Rd. west 6 miles, FSR 48 southwest 12.6 miles, FSR 4885 southeast 1 mile, and FSR 3530 south .2 mile.

JEAN LAKE (Mt. Hood NF) 🅰
3 tent units, lake - no motors, boating, swimming, fishing, elev. 4800', FREE.
Take Rock Creek Rd. west 6 miles, FSR 48 southwest 10 miles, FSR 4860 northwest 9.2 miles, and FSR 3550 northeast 2 miles.

PINE HOLLOW LAKESIDE RESORT (Private) 🅰 RV
62 units w/hookups for water & elec. plus 20 tent sites, reservations (541)544-2271, showers, laundry, restaurant, lounge, groceries, trailer waste disposal, boat launch & rental, swimming, fishing, pets okay, $15-17/night.
Take Pine Hollow Reservoir Rd. northwest 3.5 miles.

POST CAMP (Mt. Hood NF) 🅰 RV
4 units, no drinking water, trailers to 22', picnic area, fishing, elev. 4000', FREE.
Take Rock Creek Rd. west 6 miles, FSR 48 southwest 10 miles, FSR 4860 northwest 1.7 miles, FSR 240 east .5 mile, and FSR 4813 northwest .7 mile.

ROCK CREEK RESERVOIR (Mt. Hood NF) 🅰 RV
33 units, trailers to 18', reservations (800)280-CAMP, wheelchair access, lake - no motors, boat ramp, fishing, elev. 2200', $10-12/night.
Take Rock Creek Rd. west 6 miles, FSR 48 southwest 1.2 miles, FSR 4820 west .2 mile, and FSR 120 north .2 mile.

CONDON

BURNS PARK (Private) 🅰 RV
18 sites w/water & elec., showers, picnic shelter, pets & horses okay, $7/night.
Located on State 19 at fairgrounds.

CONDON MOBILE HOME & RV PARK (Private) RV
17 trailer sites w/full hookups, reservations (541)384-5666, showers, laundry, playground, $17/night.
Park is on State 206, at west city limits.

MAUPIN

BEAR SPRINGS (Mt. Hood NF) 🅰 RV
21 units, trailers to 32', handicap access, reservations (800)280-CAMP, fishing, elev. 3200', $9/night.
Follow State 216 west 25 miles.

BLUE HOLE (BLM) 🅰 RV
5 units, no water, wheelchair access includes fishing, reservations for accessible sites (541)395-2270, on Deschutes River, $3/night.
Take Deschutes River Rd. north 3.5 miles.

CLEAR CREEK CROSSING (BLM)
7 units, no water, trailers to 18', fishing, elev. 3000', FREE.
Take State 216 west 28 miles, FSR 2130 north 3 miles, and FSR 260 east .5 mile.

DEVIL'S CANYON (BLM)
5 units, no drinking water, on Deschutes River, narrow road, $3/night.
US 197 southwest 1 mile, Deschutes River Rd. south 4.2 miles.

HARPHAM FLAT (BLM)
20 units, no drinking water, on Deschutes River, narrow road, $3/night.
US 197 southwest 1 mile, Deschutes River Rd. south 2.4 miles.

KEEPS MILL (BLM)
5 tent units, no drinking water, stream, fishing, elev. 2600', FREE.
Take State 216 west 24 miles and FSR 2120 north 3 miles.

LONGBEND (BLM)
10 units, no drinking water, on Deschutes River, narrow road, $3/night.
US 197 southwest 1 mile, Deschutes River Rd. south 4 miles.

MAUPIN CITY PARK (City) [A] [RV]
20 units w/hookups, 25 tent sites and 2 group areas, reservations (541)395-2252, trailers to 24', trailer waste disposal, on Deschutes River, fishing, boat launch, open April thru Sept., $10-16/night.
Located in downtown Maupin.

McCUBBINS GULCH (BLM) [A] [RV]
5 units, no drinking water, trailers to 18', stream, fishing, primitive, elev., 3000', FREE.
Take State 216 west 24.5 miles, FSR 2110 east 1 mile, and FSR 230 northeast .5 mile.

NENA CREEK (BLM) [A] [RV]
5 units, no drinking water, on Deschutes River, narrow road, $3/night.
US 197 southwest 1 mile, Deschutes River Rd. south 6 miles.

OAK SPRINGS (BLM) [A] [RV]
5 units, no drinking water, on Deschutes River, narrow road, $3/night.
US 197 southwest 1 mile, Deschutes River Rd. south 4 miles.

OASIS FLAT (BLM) [A] [RV]
12 units, no water, on Deschutes River, narrow road, $3/night.
Take Deschutes River Rd. north 1 mile.

WAPINITIA (BLM)

5 units, no drinking water, on Deschutes River, narrow road, $3/night.
US 197 southwest 1 mile, Deschutes River Rd. south 2 miles.

WHITE RIVER (BLM)

10 units, no drinking water, on Deschutes River, narrow road, $3/night.
Take Deschutes River Rd. north 5 miles.

SHANIKO

SHANIKO CORRAL & RV PARK (Private)

65 units - 10 w/water/elec./sewer plus 55 dry sites, tents okay, res. (541)489-3441, trailers to 40', showers, laundry, wheelchair access, trailer waste disposal, pets okay, $11-17/night.
In Shaniko. Located at 2nd & E Sts.

FOSSIL

BEAR HOLLOW PARK (Wheeler County)

18 units, no potable water, information (541)763-2911, pets & horses okay, $5/night.
Take State 19 southeast 7 miles.

COUNTY FAIRGROUNDS (Wheeler County)

12 units w/full hookups, information (541)763-4560, showers, pets & horses okay, $15/night.
Fairgrounds are located on east 4th St.

FOSSIL MOTEL & TRAILER PARK (Private)

12 trailer sites w/water/elec./sewer plus tent area, res. (541)763-4075, motel, pets okay, $5-12/night.
Located on State 19 at Fossil Junction.

SHELTON (State)

36 primitive campsites, trailers to 30', picnic area, hiking, $7/night.
Take State 19 southeast 10 miles to park.

WARM SPRINGS

KAH-NEE-TA (Private)

48 units w/full hookups, 12 dry sites, no tents, reservations (800)554-4786, showers, laundry, ice, swimming & therapy pool, tennis, lodge, golf, mini golf, trailer waste disposal, fishing, boat & horse rental, hiking, $30-38/night.
Take Kah-Nee-Ta Rd. north 11 miles.

MECCA FLAT (BLM)　　　　　　　　　　　⚠ RV

10 units, boat-in or take rough road, no drinking water, on Lower Deschutes River, $3/night.
Located 2 miles northeast of US 26.

MADRAS

COUNTY FAIRGROUNDS (Jefferson County)　　⚠ RV

65 units w/full hookups plus grassy tent area, reservations (541)475-4460, trailers to 60', pull thrus, showers, wheelchair accessible, trailer waste disposal, pets okay, $15/night.
Take the Fairgrounds Rd. exit off US 97 and go 1 block.

COVE PALISADES (Oregon State Park)　　　⚠ RV

87 units w/full hookups, 91 w/elec., 94 tent sites plus group area, reservations (800)452-5687, trailers to 60', showers, wheelchair access, picnic area, trailer waste disposal, on river, marina, boat launch, fishing, swimming, hiking, $13-20/night.
Leave US 97 just south of Madras and follow park signs - it's about 15 miles.

CYRUS HORSE CAMP (Ochoco NF)　　　　　⚠ RV

5 units, no drinking water, picnic area, 4 corrals, elev. 2900', FREE.
Take US 97 south 9.3 miles, King Ln. southeast 3.3 miles, FSR 7130 south/east 4.5 miles, Cyrus Springs Rd. to campground.

DESCHUTES RIVER RESORT (Private)　　　⚠ RV

32 units - 26 w/full hookups plus 6 tent sites, information - (541)553-1011, pull thrus, trailers to 60', showers, laundry, playground, store, trailer waste disposal, on Deschutes River, fishing, rafting, pets okay, open year round, $10-17/night.
Take US 26 southwest 10 miles to 7228 NW Highway 26.

HAYSTACK RESERVOIR (Ochoco NF)　　　　⚠ RV

24 units, trailers to 32', flush toilets, lake, boat launch, swimming, fishing, water skiing, elev. 2900', $7/night.
Take US 97 south 9.3 miles, King Ln. southeast 3.3 miles, and FSR 68 north .6 mile.

MADRAS/CULVER KOA (Private)　　　　　⚠ RV

Large campground w/hookups, information (541)546-3046, pull thrus, seasonal pool, cabins, propane, $16-21/night.
Go 9 miles south of town on US 97 and turn east on Jericho Lane.

MONTY (Deschutes NF)　　　　　　　　　⚠ RV

20 units, trailers to 22', piped water, on Metolius River, fishing, elev., 2000', $5/night.
Follow the signs to Cove Palisades State Park, cross the bridge, and take FSR 63 and FSR 64 for 16 mile to campground.

PERRY SOUTH (Deschutes NF) 🔺 RV

63 units, trailers to 22', wheelchair accessible, on Lake Billy Chinook, boat launch, swimming, fishing, water skiing, elev. 2000', $9-12/night.
Follow the signs to Cove Palisades State Park, cross Lake Billy Chinook bridge, and take FSR 63 and 64 northwest 12 miles - located on the Metolius Arm of Lake Billy Chinook.

SOUTH JUNCTION (BLM) 🔺 RV

18 units, no drinking water, on Lower Deschutes River, $3/night.
Take US 97 northeast 25 miles to its junction with US 197, and follow South Junction Rd. southwest 11 miles.

TRAILS WEST RV PARK (Private) RV

30 units w/full hookups, no tents, reservations (541)475-6062, pull thrus, cable avail., showers, laundry, wheelchair accessible, nearby store, trailer waste disposal, pets extra, open year round, $15/night.
Located near south end of town - at 159 SW Bard Ln.

TROUT CREEK (BLM) 🔺 RV

15 units, 3 group sites, no drinking water, on Lower Deschutes River, boat ramp, hiking, $3-15/night.
Take US 97 northeast 3 miles, follow Clark Dr. north 9 miles to Gateway, and take Coleman Rd. 5 miles to campground.

CAMP SHERMAN

ABBOTT CREEK (Deschutes NF) 🔺 RV

4 units, trailers to 18', secluded, fishing, elev. 3100', FREE.
Take FSR 14 north 3 miles, FSR 1419 northwest 2 miles to junction of FSR 1420, and go 5 miles north.

ALLEN SPRINGS (Deschutes NF) 🔺 RV

17 units, group site, trailers okay, on Metolius River, fly fishing, hiking, elev. 2800', $10/night.
Take FSR 14 north 5 miles.

ALLINGHAM (Deschutes NF) 🔺 RV

10 units, group site, trailers okay, on Metolius River, fly fishing, hiking, elev. 2900', $10/night.
Take FSR 14 north 1 mile.

BLACK BUTTE RESORT (Private) RV

19 sites w/full hookups plus 9 w/water & elec., reservations (541)595-6514, showers, laundry, trailer waste disposal, motel, walk to river, fishing, playfield, playground, hiking, $19-21/night.
Located in town, on Camp Sherman Rd.

CAMP SHERMAN (Deschutes NF) 🔺 RV
15 units, 2 group sites, trailers to 22', picnic shelter, on Metolius River, fly fishing, hiking, elev. 3000', $10/night.
Take FSR 14 north .2 mile.

CANDLE CREEK (Deschutes NF) 🔺 RV
4 units, trailers to 18', fly fishing, hiking, elev. 2600', FREE.
Take FSR 14 north 7 miles and FSR 980 north 1.5 miles.

CANYON CREEK (Deschutes NF) 🔺 RV
4 units, fly fishing, trails, elev. 2900', FREE.
Take FSR 14 north 3 miles, FSR 1419 northwest 2 miles, and FSR 1420 for 3.4 miles.

COLD SPRINGS RESORT & RV PARK (Private) 🔺 RV
45 units w/full hookups, tents okay, trailers to 45', reservations (541)595-6271, showers, laundry, trailer waste disposal, river, fly fishing, hiking, pets okay, elev. 3000', $17-20/night.
Follow Camp Sherman Rd. north to Cold Springs Resort Ln.

GORGE (Deschutes NF) 🔺 RV
18 units, 6 group sites, piped water, trailers to 22', on Metolius River, fly fishing, hiking, elev. 2900', $10/night.
Take FSR 14 north 2 miles.

JACK CREEK (Deschutes NF) 🔺 RV
11 units, trailers to 16', fishing, hiking, elev. 3100', FREE.
Follow State 20 to FSR 12 and head northwest 4.5 miles, at FSR 1230 go .2 mile to campground.

JACK LAKE (Deschutes NF) 🔺
2 tent units, lake - no motors, boating swimming, fishing, horse facilities, trailhead into Mt. Jefferson Wilderness, elev. 5100', $3/night.
Follow State 20 to FSR 12 and head northwest 4.5 miles, at FSR 1230 go north .2 mile.

LOWER BRIDGE (Deschutes NF) 🔺 RV
12 units, group site, trailers to 22', on Metolius River, fly fishing, hiking, elev. 2800', $10/night.
Take FSR 14 north 7 miles.

PINE REST (Deschutes NF) 🔺
8 tent sites, picnic shelter, on Metolius River, fly fishing, hiking, elev. 2900', $10/night
Take FSR 14 north 1.5 miles.

PIONEER FORD (Deschutes NF) 🔺 RV
20 units, trailers to 22', wheelchair access, on Metolius River, fly fishing, hiking, elev. 2800', $10/night.
Take FSR 14 north 7 miles.

RIVERSIDE (Deschutes NF) △

Walk-in tent sites, fly fishing, trails, well, stream, elev. 3000', $6/night.
Take FSR 14 south 2 miles; located 2 miles south of Camp Sherman Store.

SHEEP SPRINGS HORSE CAMP (Deschutes NF) △ RV

10 campsites and 40 box stalls, well, by reservation only - (541)822-3799, horse trails, elev. 3200', $9/night.
Take FSR 14 north 1 mile, FSR 1217 west 1 mile, FSR 1420 north 2 miles, FSR 400 and campground road north 3 miles.

SMILING RIVER (Deschutes NF) △ RV

38 units, trailers to 22', wheelchair accessible, on Metolius River, fly fishing, hiking, elev. 2900', $10/night.
Take FSR 14 north 1.3 miles.

SISTERS

BIG LAKE (Willamette NF) △ RV

49 units, trailers to 18', flush toilets, reservations (800)280-2267, lake, boat launch, swimming, fishing, water skiing, near wilderness trailheads, open June thru Sept., elev. 4600', $10/night.
Take US 20 west 21.7 miles, and FSR 2690 south 3.4 miles.

BIG LAKE WEST (Willamette NF) △

11 tent units plus walk-in sites, reservations (800)280-2267, on Big Lake, boating, swimming, fishing, open June thru Oct., $10/night.
Take US 20 west 21.7 miles, and FSR 2690 south 4.3 miles.

BLACK PINE SPRINGS (Deschutes NF) △ RV

4 units, trailers to 18', hiking, elev. 4300', FREE.
Take FSR 16 south 8 miles.

BLUE BAY (Deschutes NF) △ RV

25 units, group sites, res. (800)280-CAMP, trailers to 22', Suttle Lake, boat launch, swimming, fishing, hiking, elev. 3400', $10/night.
Take US 20 west 13 miles, and FSR 2070 south 1 mile.

CIRCLE 5 TRAILER PARK (Private) △ RV

30 units w/hookups for water/elec./sewer, tents okay, reservations 10 days ahead - (541)549-3861, showers, laundry, trailer waste disposal, elev. 3200', $10-19/night.
Take US 20 southeast .7 mile.

COLD SPRINGS (Deschutes NF) △ RV

23 units, trailers to 22', well, stream, birdwatching, elev. 3400', $10/night.
Follow State 242 west 5 miles and turn on campground road.

COW CAMP HORSE CAMP (Deschutes NF) ▲ RV
5 units, trailers okay, water & corrals for horses, trails, elev. 3400', FREE.
Take State 242 west 1.7 miles and turn on campground road.

DRIFTWOOD (Deschutes NF) ▲ RV
17 units, trailers to 18', on Three Creek Lake - no motors, boating, swimming, fishing, trails, elev. 6600', $6/night.
Take FSR 16 south 16.9 miles.

GRAHAM CORRAL (Deschutes NF) ▲ RV
13 units, trailers to 18', piped water, horse corrals, trails, elev. 3400', $6/night.
Follow US 20 northwest 4.5 miles, FSR 1012 southwest 1 mile, FSR 300 northwest .8 mile, and FSR 340 northwest 1 mile.

INDIAN FORD (Deschutes NF) ▲ RV
25 units plus 10 group sites, trailers to 22', well, stream, fishing, birdwatching, elev. 3200', $10/night.
Take US 20 northwest 5 miles, and FSR 11 east .1 mile.

LAVA CAMP LAKE (Deschutes NF) ▲ RV
10 units, trailers to 22', swimming, fishing, trails, elev. 5300', FREE.
Take State 242 west 14.6 miles; located .2 mile off highway.

LINK CREEK (Deschutes NF) ▲ RV
23 units, group sites, res. (800)280-CAMP, trailers to 22', Suttle Lake, swimming, fishing, water skiing, hiking, elev. 3400', $11-13/night.
Take US 20 northwest 13 miles, and FSR 2070 south 2 miles.

MOUNTAIN SHADOW RV PARK (Private) RV
106 units w/full hookups, no tents, reservations (541)549-7275, trailers to 50', pull thrus, showers, laundry, wheelchair accessible, swimming pool, hot tub, pets okay, $27/night.
Located in Sisters, at 540 US 20.

ROUND LAKE (Deschutes NF) ▲
5 tent units, lake - no motors, boat ramp, swimming, fishing, trails, elev. 4300', FREE.
Take US 20 northwest 12 miles, FSR 12 north 1 mile, and FSR 1210 northwest 5.5 miles.

SCOUT LAKE GROUP CAMP (Deschutes NF) ▲
Open campsites, trailers to 22', res. (800)280-CAMP, lake - no motors, volleyball. swimming, hiking, elev. 3700', $8-22/night.
Take US 20 northwest 13 miles, FSR 2070 southwest 1 mile, and FSR 2066 south .5 mile.

SISTERS KOA (Private)   [A] [RV]
100 units - 60 w/full hookups plus 30 tent sites, reservations - (541)549-3021, showers, laundry, spa, mini golf, playground, restaurant, video rental, groceries, propane, gas, trailer waste disposal, pond, swimming, fishing, elev. 3200', $20-24/night.
Take US 20 southeast 4 miles.

SOUTH SHORE (Deschutes NF)   [A] [RV]
39 units, group sites, res. (800)280-CAMP, trailers to 22', Suttle Lake, boat ramp, wind surfing, swimming, fishing, hiking, elev. 3400', $11-13/night.
Take US 20 northwest 13 miles, and FSR 2070 south 1.5 miles.

SUTTLE LAKE RESORT/MARINA/CAMP (Private)   [A] [RV]
21 campsites - no hookups, tents okay, reservations (541)595-6662, trailers to 50', showers, store, restaurant, on lake, boat launch & rentals, fishing, hiking, pets okay, open May thru Oct., $13/night.
Take US 20 northwest 13.5 miles.

THREE CREEK LAKE (Deschutes NF)   [A] [RV]
10 units, trailers to 18', lake - no motors, boating, swimming, fishing, trails, elev. 6400', $6/night.
Take FSR 16 south 17 miles.

THREE CREEK MEADOW (Deschutes NF)   [A] [RV]
20 units - 9 horse sites w/box stalls, trailers to 18', creek, trails, elev. 6300', $6/night.
Take CR 16 south 15 miles; north of lake.

WHISPERING PINES HORSE CAMP (Deschutes NF)   [A] [RV]
9 units - w/4-horse box stalls, trailers to 22', creek, fishing, elev. 4400', $6/night.
Take State 242 west 5.5 miles and FSR 1018 south 4.3 miles.

PRINEVILLE

ANTELOPE FLAT RESERVOIR (Ochoco NF)   [A] [RV]
24 units, trailers to 32', no drinking water, picnic area, lake, boat launch, swimming, fishing, hiking, elev. 4600', $8/night.
Paulina Hwy. southeast 29 miles, FSR 17 south 11.3 miles.

BIGGS CAMPGROUND (Ochoco NF)   [A] [RV]
3 campsites, no drinking water, elev. 4800', FREE.
Take US 26 east 16.7 miles, Ochoco Creek Rd. northeast 8.5 miles, FSR 42 southeast 14.5 miles, FSR 4215 2.4 miles, and FSR 4215-150 .5 mile..

CASTLE ROCK (BLM)   [A] [RV]
5 units, no drinking water, on Crooked River, boating, $3/night.
Follow State 27 south 12 miles.

CHIMNEY ROCK RECREATION SITE (BLM)　△ RV
20 units plus group area, trailers to 30', picnic facilities, on Crooked River, boating, fishing elev. 1500', $3/night.
Follow State 27 south 15.6 miles.

COBBLE ROCK (BLM)　△ RV
15 units, no drinking water, on Crooked River, boating, $3/night.
Follow State 27 south 16.4 miles.

CROOK COUNTY RV PARK (Crook County)　△ RV
81 units w/full hookups plus 9 tent sites, reservations suggested (541)447-2599, showers, wheelchair access, trailer waste disposal, pets okay, $9-17/night.
Located next to the fairgrounds.

CRYSTAL CORRAL PARK (Private)　△ RV
16 sites w/full hookup, 7 w/water & elec., plus 20 tent sites, reservations (541)447-5932, showers, laundry, groceries, cabins, lake, swimming, fishing, boat ramp & docks, elev. 3200', pets okay, $8-16/night.
Take US 26 east 6.5 miles.

DEEP CREEK (Ochoco NF)　△ RV
6 units, no water, trailers to 22', fishing, elev. 4200', FREE.
Take US 26 east 16.7 miles, Ochoco Creek Rd. northeast 8.5 miles, FSR 42 southeast 23.6 miles, and FSR 460 south .1 mile.

DRY CREEK HORSE CAMP (Ochoco NF)　△ RV
5 units w/18 corrals, no drinking water, elev. 3900', FREE.
Take US 26 east 9 miles, Mill Creek Rd. north 5 miles, and FSR 3370 2.5 miles to campground road.

ELKHORN (Ochoco NF)　△ RV
4 units, no water, trailers to 32', primitive, elev. 4500', FREE.
Take Paulina Hwy. southeast 34.0 miles and FSR 16 southeast 4.3 miles.

LAKESHORE RV PARK & STORE (Private)　△ RV
43 units w/full hookups, 11 pull thrus, 10 tent sites, reservations (541)447-6059, showers, laundry, groceries, playground, trailer waste disposal, on Ochoco Lake, swimming, fishing, boat launch & rental, elev. 3100', $12-18/night.
Take US 26 east 7 miles.

LONE PINE (BLM)　△ RV
8 units, no water, Crooked River, boating, elev. 1500', $3/night.
Follow State 27 south 14.4 miles.

LOWER PALISADES (BLM)　△ RV
15 units plus group area, no water, Crooked River, boating, $3/night.
Follow State 27 south 14.8 miles.

117

OCHOCO LAKE (Crook County) △ RV
22 primitive units, maximum site 30', picnic area, boat launch, fishing, hiking trails, $12/night.
Take US 26 east 7 miles.

OCHOCO DIVIDE (Ochoco NF) △ RV
28 units, walk-in tent sites, trailers to 32', at Ochoco Pass summit, elev. 4700', $8/night.
Follow US 26 east/northeast 30.8 miles to campground.

OCHOCO FOREST CAMP (Ochoco NF) △ RV
6 units, picnic area, creek, hiking trails, elev. 4000', $8/night.
Take US 26 east 17 miles, and Ochoco Creek Rd. northeast 8.5 miles - campground is adjacent to ranger station.

POISON BUTTE (BLM) △ RV
6 units, group area, no water, Crooked River, boating, $3/night.
Follow State 27 south 17.4 miles.

POST PILE (BLM) △ RV
10 units, no drinking water, on Crooked River, boating, $3/night.
Follow State 27 south 16.9 miles.

PRINEVILLE RESERVOIR (Oregon State Park) △ RV
22 units w/full hookups plus 48 tent sites, reservations (800)452-5687, maximum 40', showers, picnic area, boat launch & dock, fishing, swimming, $7-20/night.
Take Paulina Hwy. south 1.7 miles, and Juniper Canyon Rd. southeast 15 miles.

PRINEVILLE RESERVOIR RESORT (Private) △ RV
71 units w/water & elec., tents okay, reservations (541)447-7468, trailers to 40', showers, groceries, trailer waste disposal, lake, swimming, fishing, boat launch & rental, water sports, elev. 3200', open April thru Oct., pets - fee, $17/night.
Take Paulina Hwy. south 1.7 miles, and Juniper Canyon Rd. southeast 17 miles.

STILLWATER (BLM) △ RV
10 units plus group area, no drinking water, on Crooked River, boating, $3/night.
Follow State 27 south 12.8 miles.

WALTON LAKE (Ochoco NF) △ RV
30 units, group site, trailers to 32', picnic area, lake - elec. motors, boating, fishing, swimming, hiking, elev. 5000', $8/night - groups $27.
Take US 26 east 17 miles, Ochoco Creek Rd. northeast 8.5 miles, FSR 22 northeast 6.2 miles, and FSR 2220 .3 mile.

WILDCAT (Ochoco NF) 🔺 RV
17 units, trailers to 22', picnic area, stream, fishing, hiking, adjacent to Mill Creek Wilderness, elev. 3700', $8/night.
Take US 26 east 9.2 miles, and Mill Creek Rd. northeast 11.9 miles to campground.

WILDWOOD (Ochoco NF) 🔺 RV
5 units, no water, trailers to 22', primitive, elev. 4800', FREE.
Take US 26 east 27 miles, FSR 2630 east 3 miles, and FSR 2210 north 3 miles.

WILEY FLAT (Ochoco NF) 🔺 RV
5 units, trailers to 32', piped water, primitive, elev. 5000', FREE.
Take Paulina Hwy. southeast 34 miles, FSR 16 southeast 9.8 miles, and FSR 16 west 1 mile.

REDMOND

CROOKED RIVER RANCH RV PARK (Private) 🔺 RV
61 sites w/full hookups, 30 w/water & elec., plus 26 tent sites, reservations (541)923-1441, showers, laundry, swimming pool, playground, restaurant, lounge, golf course, trailer waste disposal, river, fishing, hiking, elev. 2600', $12-19/night.
US 97 north 6 miles; Lower Bridge Rd. northwest 7 miles.

DESERT TERRACE (Private) 🔺 RV
20 units w/full hookups plus 5 tent sites, reservations (541)548-2546, showers, laundry, pets okay, elev. 3000', $10-20/night.
Follow US 97 south 3 miles.

GREEN ACRES (Private) 🔺 RV
45 units w/full hookups, 5 w/water/elec./cable tv, plus tent area, reservations (541)923-0868, trailers to 40', showers, laundry, wheelchair access, propane, trailer waste disposal, pets okay, $12-20/night.
Follow US 97 south 2 miles.

SMITH ROCK (Oregon State Park) 🔺
Walk-in camp on river, fishing, hiking, rock climbing, $10/night.
Take US 97 north 5 miles, Smith Rock Rd. northeast 4 miles.

BEND

BEND KAMPGROUND (Private) 🔺 RV
31 sites w/full hookups, 30 w/water & elec., plus 30 grassy tent sites, reservations (800)713-5333 or (541)382-7738, pull thrus, modem-friendly, showers, laundry, swimming pool, playground, groceries, gas, propane, pond fishing, $18-22/night.
Take US 97 north 2 miles.

119

BEND KEYSTONE RV PARK (Private) [RV]
29 units w/full hookups, no tents, reservations (541)382-2335, trailers to 36', showers, laundry, no dogs, $16/night.
Located in town, at 305 NE Burnside Ave.

BIG RIVER (Deschutes NF) [A] [RV]
13 units, trailers to 22', on Deschutes River, boat ramp, fishing, elev. 4200', $5/night.
Take US 97 south 22 miles and CR 42 southwest 5 miles.

CROWN VILLA RV PARK (Private) [A] [RV]
105 units w/full hookups inc. cable, plus 26 w/elec. & water, reservations (541)388-1131, showers, laundry, ice, pond, playground, wheelchair access, $28/night.
Follow US 97 south, just past the city limits, and go 2 miles southeast on Brosterhaus Rd.

DEVILS LAKE (Deschutes NF) [A]
9 walk-in units, lake - no motors, horse facilities, swimming, fishing, access to Three Sisters Wilderness, elev. 5500', $3/night.
Leave US 97 in town heading southwest on Century Drive Hwy. for 29 miles.

ELK LAKE (Deschutes NF) [A] [RV]
23 units, trailers to 22', picnic area, lake - speed limits, boating, swimming, fishing, hiking, elev . 4900', $9-18/night.
Leave US 97 in town heading southwest on Century Drive Hwy. for 31.5 miles to Elk Lake and campground.

IRISH & TAYLOR (Deschutes NF) [A]
12 tent sites - no tables, rough road, lake - no motors, boating, fishing, trails to Three Sisters Wilderness, elev. 5600', FREE.
Leave US 97 in town heading southwest on Century Drive Hwy. for 43.6 miles, FSR 4635 for .8 mile, FSR 4630 southwest 1.7 miles, and FSR 4636 west 4 miles.

LITTLE CULTUS (Deschutes NF) [A] [RV]
10 units, trailers to 22', well, lake - speed limit, boat ramp, fishing, swimming, hiking, elev. 4800', $5/night.
Leave US 97 in town heading southwest on Century Drive Hwy. for 43.6 miles, FSR 4635 southwest .8 mile, FSR 4630 south 1.7 miles, and FSR 4636 west 1 mile.

LITTLE FAWN (Deschutes NF) [A] [RV]
20 units plus 12 group sites - group reservations (541)382-9443, trailers to 22', Elk Lake - speed limit, boat launch, wind surfing, swimming, fishing, elev. 4900', $8/15/night - groups $70.
Leave US 97 in town heading southwest on Century Drive Hwy. for 34 miles, and take FSR 4625 southeast 2.1 miles.

LITTLE LAVA LAKE (Deschutes NF)   🔺 RV
10 units, trailers to 22', lake - speed limits, boat ramp, fishing, boating, hiking, elev. 4800', $5/night.
Leave US 97 in town heading southwest on Century Drive Hwy. for 38 miles and FSR 500 northeast .7 mile to campground road.

MALLARD MARSH (Deschutes NF)   🔺 RV
15 units, trailers to 22', well, on Hosmer lake - speed limit, fishing, hiking, elev. 4900', $5/night.
Leave US 97 in town heading southwest on Century Drive Hwy. for 34 miles and FSR 4625 southeast 1.3 miles.

McKAY CROSSING (Deschutes NF)   🔺 RV
10 units, trailers to 22', stream, fishing, elev. 4400', $8/night.
Leave US 97 in town heading southwest on Century Drive Hwy. for 23 miles, CR 21 east 3.2 miles, and FSR 2120 north 2.7 miles.

NORTH TWIN LAKE (Deschutes NF)   🔺 RV
10 units, trailers to 22', lake - no motors, small boat ramp, fishing, swimming, elev. 4300', $5/night.
Leave US 97 in town heading southwest on Century Drive Hwy. for 33 miles to campground.

PINE MOUNTAIN (Deschutes NF)   🔺 RV
3 campsites @ Pine Mountain Observatory, birdwatching, elev. 6200', FREE.
Take US 20 east 25.1 miles, and FSR 2017 south 7.7 miles.

POINT (Deschutes NF)   🔺 RV
10 units, trailers to 22', on Elk Lake - speed limits, boat ramp, swimming, fishing, elev. 4900', $9-18/night.
Leave US 97 in town heading southwest on Century Drive Hwy. for 33 miles to campground.

QUINN MEADOW HORSE CAMP (Deschutes NF)   🔺 RV
24 reservable sites w/corrals (541)382-9433, trailers to 18', horse trails to Three Sisters Wilderness, elev. 5100', $10-24/night.
Leave US 97 in town heading southwest on Century Drive Hwy. for 30 miles, and take FSR 450 southeast .3 mile.

SAND SPRINGS (Deschutes NF)   🔺 RV
3 units, trailers to 22', group sites, no water, elev. 5000', FREE.
Take US 20 east 21 miles and CR 23 southeast 18.8 miles.

SCANDIA RV & MOBILE PARK (Private)   RV
35 units w/full hookups, no tents, reservations (541)382-6206, showers, laundry, $20/night.
Take US 97 2.5 miles south of its junction with US 20.

SODA CREEK (Deschutes NF)   🔺 RV
7 units, trailers to 22', on Sparks Lake - no motors, fishing, hiking, elev. 5400', FREE.

Leave US 97 in town heading southwest on Century Drive Hwy. for 26.2 miles to campground.

SOUTH (Deschutes NF)
23 units, trailers to 22', picnic area, Hosmer Lake - speed limits, boat launch, fishing, canoeing, elev. 4900', $5/night.
Leave US 97 in town heading southwest on Century Drive Hwy. for 34 miles and FSR 4625 southwest 1 mile.

SWAMP WELLS (Deschutes NF)
6 units, no water, trailers to 22', horse trails, elev. 5400', FREE.
Take US 97 south 4 miles, FSR 18 east 5.4 miles, FSR 1810 south 5.8 miles, and FSR 1816 east 3 miles.

TODD LAKE (Deschutes NF)
11 hike-in sites, picnic area, lake - no motors, horse trails to Three Sisters Wilderness, hiking, fishing, elev. 6200', $3/night.
Leave US 97 in town heading southwest on Century Drive Hwy. for 24 miles, FSR 370 north .5 mile, and hike-in .5 mile to lake.

TUMALO (Oregon State Park)
21 sites w/full hookups, 67 tent sites, group area, reservations (800)452-5687, maximum site 44', showers, fishing, hiking trails, $13-19/night.
Follow US 20 northwest 5 miles.

LaPINE

BULL BEND (Deschutes NF)
12 units, on Deschutes River, boat ramp, fishing, swimming, canoeing, elev. 4300', $7/night.
Take US 97 northeast 2.4 miles, Pringle Falls Loop west 8 miles, and FSR 4370 southwest 1.5 miles.

CHIEF PAULINA HORSE CAMP (Deschutes NF)
14 horse camp units, reservations (800)280-CAMP, trailers to 32', near Paulina Lake, horse trails, elev. 6300', $11/night - can reserve entire camp.
US 97 north 5 miles, Paulina/East Lake Rd. 15 miles east.

CINDER HILL (Deschutes NF)
110 units, res. (800)280-CAMP, trailers to 32', flush toilets, on East Lake, boat launch, fishing, swimming, birdwatching, canoeing, hiking, elev. 6300', $12-14/night.
US 97 north 5 miles, Paulina/East Lake Rd. 18 miles east.

COW MEADOW (Deschutes NF)
21 units, trailers to 22', on north end of Crane Prairie Reservoir - speed limits, boat ramp, fishing, elev. 4400', $5/night.
US 97 north 5 miles, Paulina/East Lake Rd. 18 miles east.

CRANE PRAIRIE (Deschutes NF)
146 units, trailers to 22', on Crane Prairie Reservoir - speed limit, well, boat launch, $10-14/night.
US 97 north 2.4 miles, Pringle Falls Loop west 9 miles, Century Dr. west 8 miles, Odell/Lava Lake Rd. north 4.5 miles.

CRANE PRAIRIE RESORT (Private)
38 units w/hookups for water/elec./sewer, tents okay, reservations (541)383-3939, boat & motor rentals, boat ramp, store, boat gas, fishing, on Crane Prairie Reservoir, elev. 4400', open late April thru Oct., $20/night.
US 97 north 2.4 miles, Pringle Falls Loop west 9 miles, Century Dr. west 8 miles, Odell/Lava Lake Rd. north 4.5 miles.

CULTUS CORRAL HORSE CAMP (Deschutes NF)
12 units, trailers okay, reservations advised (541)388-5664, no tables, horse corral, river, boat ramp, swimming, fishing, water skiing, hiking, elev. 4400', $5/night.
US 97 north 2.4 miles, Pringle Falls Loop west 11 miles, FSR 42 west 9.5 miles, CR 46 north 8 miles, and FSR 620 west .5 mile.

CULTUS LAKE (Deschutes NF)
55 units, trailers to 22', picnic area, lake, boat launch, swimming, fishing, water skiing, windsurfing, elev. 4700', $10-20/night.
US 97 north 2.4 miles, Pringle Falls Loop west 9 miles, Century Dr. west 8 miles, Odell/Lava Lake Rd. north 6.4 miles, FSR 463 west 1 mile.

DESCHUTES BRIDGE (Deschutes NF)
12 units, trailers to 22', reservations (541)382-9443, picnic area, on Deschutes River, fishing, birdwatching, elev. 4600', $5/night - campground can be reserved for group @ $100/2 nights.
US 97 north 2.4 miles, Pringle Falls Loop west 9 miles, Century Dr. west 8 miles, Odell/Lava Lake Rd. north 10 miles.

EAST LAKE (Deschutes NF)
29 units, res. (800)280-CAMP, trailers to 32', flush toilets, lake - speed limit, boat launch, canoeing, fishing, swimming, birdwatching, hiking, elev. 6400', $12-14/night.
US 97 north 5 miles, Paulina/East Lake Rd. 17 miles east.

EAST LAKE RESORT & RV PARK (Private)
38 units w/ water & elec., tents okay, trailers to 36', reservations (541)536-2230, showers, laundry, store, cafe, cabins, trailer waste disposal, lake, boat launch/rental, swimming, fishing, hiking, elev. 6400', pets okay, open June thru Sept., $15/night.
US 97 north 5 miles, Paulina/East Lake Rd. 18 miles east.

FALL RIVER (Deschutes NF)
10 units, trailers to 22', hiking, stream, fly fishing, elev. 4300', $8/night.

Take US 97 northeast 2.4 miles, Pringle Falls Loop west 11 miles, and FSR 42 northeast .3 mile.

GULL POINT (Deschutes NF) 🏕️ RV
79 units, small group site, reservations (541)382-9443, trailers to 32', flush toilets, picnic area, trailer dump station, on Wickiup Reservoir, boat ramp, swimming, fishing, water skiing, elev. 4300', $10-24/night - groups $80/2 nights.
US 97 north 2.4 miles, Pringle Falls Loop west 9 miles, Century Dr. west 5.4 miles, FSR 4260 south 3.5 miles.

HIDDEN PINES RV PARK (Private) RV
18 units w/full hookups inc. cable, reservations (541)536-2265, tents okay, showers, laundry, trailer waste disposal, ice, propane, RV supplies, elev. 4200', $14-18/night.
US 97 north 2.4 miles, Pringle Falls Loop west 2.5 miles, Pine Forest Rd. south .7 mile, Wright Rd. 1 block to park.

HIGHLANDER MOTEL & RV PARK (Private) 🏕️ RV
28 pull thrus w/full hookups plus grassy tent area, reservations (541)536-2131, trailers to 35', showers, propane, gas, trailer waste disposal, $13/night..
Located in LaPine, at 51511 Hwy. US 97.

HOT SPRINGS (Deschutes NF) 🏕️ RV
52 units, reservations (800)280-CAMP, trailers to 32', on East Lake - speed limit, fishing, hiking, elev. 6400', $9/night - can reserve all or loop area for groups.
US 97 north 5 miles, Paulina/East Lake Rd. 17.6 miles east.

LAPINE (Oregon State Park) 🏕️ RV
145 units - 95 w/full hookups plus 50 w/elec. only, reservations (800)452-5687, maximum site 85', showers, wheelchair access, picnic area, trailer waste disp,, Deschutes River, boating, fishing, $10-15/night.
US 97 north 6 miles, LaPine Recreation Area Rd. west 3.2 miles.

LAVA LAKE (Deschutes NF) 🏕️ RV
43 units, trailers to 22', trailer waste disposal, lake - speed limits, boat ramp & rental, fishing, hiking, elev. 4800', $10-20/night.
US 97 north 2.4 miles, Pringle Falls Loop west 9 miles, Century Dr. west 8 miles, Odell/Lava Lake Rd. north 13.5 miles, FSR 500 northeast 1 mile.

LAVA LAKE LODGE & RV (Private) 🏕️ RV
24 units w/full hookups, tents okay, reservations (541)382-9443, showers, laundry, groceries, propane, gas, trailer waste disposal, lake - speed limits, boat launch & rental, swimming, fly fishing, hiking, elev. 4700', open mid-April thru Oct., $21/night.
US 97 north 2.4 miles, Pringle Falls Loop west 9 miles, Century Dr. west 8 miles, Odell/Lava Lake Rd. north 18 miles.

LITTLE CRATER (Deschutes NF) ▲ RV

50 units, reservations (800)280-CAMP, trailers to 32', on Paulina Lake, boat ramp, fishing, swimming, elev. 6300', $12-14/night. US 97 north 5 miles, Paulina/East Lake Rd. 15 miles east.

NEWBERRY GROUP CAMP (Deschutes NF) ▲ RV

3 group area, res. (800)280-CAMP, picnic area, on Paulina Lake - speed limit, fishing, swimming, hiking, elev. 6400', $55-85/night. US 97 north 5 miles, Paulina/East Lake Rd. 12.5 miles east.

NORTH COVE (Deschutes NF) ▲

6 tent units, hike-in/boat-in only, on Paulina Lake, water skiing, fishing, trails, elev. 6300', FREE. Us 97 north 5 miles, Paulina/East Lake Rd. east 13.1 miles, and boat north or follow Trail #57 to north shore of lake.

NORTH DAVIS CREEK (Deschutes NF) ▲ RV

17 units, trailers okay, well, on Wickiup Reservoir, boat launch, fishing, FREE. US 97 north 2.4 miles, Pringle Falls Loop west 11 miles, FSR 42 west 8.0 miles, FSR 46 Odell/Lava Lake Rd. north 4 miles.

OGDEN GROUP CAMP (Deschutes NF) ▲ RV

Groups only - 3 areas, reservations (800)280-CAMP, on Paulina Creek, hiking trails, elev. 4300', $50/area. US 97 north 5 miles, Paulina/East Lake Rd. 2.5 miles east.

PAULINA LAKE (Deschutes NF) ▲ RV

69 units, trailers to 32', reservations (800)280-CAMP, flush toilets, boat launch, fishing, swimming, hiking, elev. 6300', $12-14/night. US 97 north 5 miles, Paulina/East Lake Rd. 13.1 miles east.

PRAIRIE (Deschutes NF) ▲ RV

16 units, res. (800)280-CAMP, on Paulina Creek, fishing, hiking, elev. 4300', $9/night. US 97 north 5 miles, Paulina/East Lake Rd. 3 miles east.

PRINGLE FALLS (Deschutes NF) ▲ RV

6 units, trailers to 22', on Deschutes River, canoeing, rafting, fishing, hiking, elev. 4200', $7/night. US 97 north 5 miles, Paulina/East Lake Rd. Paulina/East Lake Rd. west 7.2 miles, FSR 4330-500 northeast .7 mile.

QUINN RIVER (Deschutes NF) ▲ RV

41 units, trailers to 32', picnic area, on Crane Prairie Reservoir - speed limits, boat ramp, Odell River, fishing, near Billy Quinn Historical Grave Site, elev. 4400', $9-18/night. US 97 north 2.4 miles, Pringle Falls Loop west 9 miles, Century Dr. west 8 miles, Odell/Lava Lake Rd. north 4 miles.

125

RESERVOIR (Deschutes NF) [A] [RV]
28 units, trailers to 22', on south shore of Wickiup Reservoir, boat launch, fishing, hiking, elev. 4400', $7/night.
US 97 north 2.4 miles, Pringle Falls Loop west 11 miles, FSR 42 west 8.0 miles, FSR 46 south 5 miles, and FSR 44 east 1.7 miles.

RIVERVIEW TRAILER PARK (Private) [A] [RV]
20 units w/full hookups plus grassy tent area, reservation (541)536-2382, trailers to 60', showers, laundry, Little Deschutes River, swimming, fishing, hiking, elev. 4300', small pets okay, 11-17/night..
US 97 north 2.4 miles, Pringle Falls Loop west 1 mile, Huntington Rd. north 1 mile to park.

ROCK CREEK (Deschutes NF) [A] [RV]
31 units, trailers to 22', on Crane Prairie Reservoir - speed limits, boat ramp, fishing, elev. 4400', $9-18/night.
US 97 north 2.4 miles, Pringle Falls Loop west 9 miles, Century Dr. west 8 miles, Odell/Lava Lake Rd. north 2.4 miles.

ROSLAND (Deschutes NF) [A] [RV]
11 units, trailers to 22', on Little Deschutes River, swimming, fishing, birdwatching, elev. 4200', $7/night.
US 97 north 2.4 miles, Pringle Falls Loop west 1.5 miles.

ROUNDUP TRAVEL TRAILER PARK (Private) [A] [RV]
27 units w/full hookups, reservations (541)536-2378, showers, laundry, $16/night.
Leave US 97 on Huntington Rd., go south 1 block, and take Finley Butte Rd. east 1 block to park.

SHEEP BRIDGE (Deschutes NF) [A] [RV]
18 units, trailers to 22', well, on Deschutes River at Wickiup Reservoir, boat launch, fishing, elev. 4400', $5/night.
US 97 northeast 2.4 miles, Pringle Falls Loop west 11 miles, FSR 42 west 4.6 miles, and FSR 4260 west .8 mile.

SOUTH TWIN LAKE (Deschutes NF) [A] [RV]
24 units, trailers to 22', flush toilets, lake - no motors, boat ramp, swimming, fishing, hiking, elev. 4300', $12-24/night.
US 97 north 2.4 miles, Pringle Falls Loop west 9 miles, Century Dr. west 5.4 miles, FSR 4260 south 1.6 miles.

TWIN LAKES RESORT (Private) [RV]
23 units w/hookups for water/elec./sewer, no tents, reservations (541)593-6526, flush toilets, showers, picnic tables, restaurant, groceries, tackle shop, on South Twin Lake - no gas motors allowed, row/paddle/kayak rentals, walk to Wickiup Reservoir, fishing, hiking, open April thru mid-Oct., elev. 4300', $24/night.
US 97 north 2.4 miles, Pringle Falls Loop west 9 miles, Century Dr. west 5.4 miles.

WEST CULTUS (Deschutes NF) [A]

12 tent sites, boat-in or hike-in only, on Cultus Lake, fishing, swimming, water skiing, elev. 4700', $5/night.
US 97 north 2.4 miles, Pringle Falls Loop west 9 miles, Century Dr. west 8 miles, Odell/Lava Lake Rd. north 6.4 miles, FSR 463 northwest 1.5 miles, boat across lake 2.7 miles or take Trail #16 for 3.2 miles to campground.

WEST SOUTH TWIN LAKE (Deschutes NF) [A] [RV]

24 units plus 2 group areas, trailers to 22', horse facilities, flush toilets, snack bar, on Deschutes River/Wickiup Reservoir - speed limits, boat launch & rental, water skiing, swimming, fishing, elev. 4300', $10-20/night.
US 97 north 2.4 miles, Pringle Falls Loop west 9 miles, Century Dr. west 5.4 miles, FSR 4260 south 1.7 miles.

WICKIUP BUTTE (Deschutes NF) [A] [RV]

8 units, trailers to 22', on east shore of Wickiup Reservoir, boating, water skiing, fishing, elev. 4400', $7/night.
Us 97 northeast 2.4 miles, Pringle Falls Loop west 10 miles, FSR 4380 southwest 3.6 miles, FSR 4260 west 3 miles.

WYETH (Deschutes NF) [A] [RV]

3 units, trailers to 22', horse facilities, no tables, on river, fishing, elev. 4300', $7/night.
US 97 northeast 2.4 miles, Pringle Falls Loop west 8 miles, FSR 4370 south .3 mile.

CRESCENT

CONTORTA POINT (Deschutes NF) [A] [RV]

15 units, trailers to 22', no drinking water, on south end of Crescent Lake, boating, sailing, fishing, swimming, water skiing, windsurfing, hiking, elev. 4800', FREE.
Take Crescent Cutoff Rd. west 12.2 miles, State 58 north 3.5 miles, and FSR 60 southwest 9.9 miles..

CRESCENT CREEK (Deschutes NF) [A] [RV]

10 units, trailers to 22', on creek, fishing, elev. 4500', $8/night.
Take Crescent Cutoff Rd. west 8.2 miles.

CRESCENT LAKE (Deschutes NF) [A] [RV]

47 units, trailers to 22', on lake, boat launch, swimming, fishing, wind surfing, water skiing, hiking, elev. 4800', $10-12/night.
Take Crescent Cutoff Rd. west 11.5 miles, State 58 northwest 3.5 miles, and FSR 60 southwest 2.7 miles to north end of lake.

CRESCENT RV PARK (Private) [A] [RV]

25 units w/full hookups plus grassy tent area, reservations (541)433-2950, trailers to 90', pull thrus, showers, wheelchair

accessible, laundry, store, trailer waste disposal, near river, fishing, hiking, pets okay, open year round, $11-16/night.
Located in Crescent, on US 97 at Potter St.

CY BINGHAM PARK (Klamath County) [A] [RV]
10 units, trailers okay, picnic tables, near river, pets okay, $8/night.
Located .3 mile west of US 97 on Crescent Cutoff Rd.

EAST DAVIS LAKE (Deschutes NF) [A] [RV]
33 units, trailers to 22', picnic area, lake - speed limit, boating, fishing, elev. 4000', $8/night.
Take Crescent Cutoff Rd. west 9 miles, FSR 46 north 6.5 miles, and FSR 855 west 1.5 miles to south end of Davis Lake.

LAVA FLOW (Deschutes NF) [A] [RV]
12 units, trailers to 22', east shore Davis Lake - speed limits, boat launch, fly fishing, lava formation, birdwatching, elev. 4400', FREE.
Take Crescent Cutoff Rd. west 8.2 miles.

ODELL CREEK (Deschutes NF) [A] [RV]
22 units, no drinking water, trailers to 22', res. (800)280-CAMP, on Odell Lake, boating, fly fishing, windsurfing, hiking trails, elev. 4800', $5/night.
Take Crescent Cutoff Rd. west 11.5 miles, and State 58 northwest 5 miles - on east end of lake, at the head of Odell Creek.

PEBBLE BAY (Deschutes NF) [A]
Boat-in camping along southwest shore of Odell Lake, swimming, fishing, water skiing, elev. 4800', $5/night.
Take Crescent Cutoff Rd. west 11.5 miles, State 58 northwest 5 miles to Odell Lake, and boat to Pebble Bay on southwest shore.

PRINCESS CREEK (Deschutes NF) [A] [RV]
46 units, trailers to 22', picnic area, on Odell Lake, boat launch, fishing, water skiing, wind surfing, elev. 4800', $10-12/night.
Take Crescent Cutoff Rd. west 11.5 miles, and State 58 northwest 9 miles.

SHELTER COVE RESORT (Private) [A] [RV]
58 sites w/hookups for elec. plus 11 w/out hookups, trailers to 40', tents okay, reservations (541)433-2548, showers, cabins, propane, gas, trailer waste disposal, on Odell Lake, boat launch & rental, moorage, fishing, hiking, downhill & cross country skiing - ski & snowshoe rentals, elev. 4800', $12-17/night.
Take Crescent Cutoff Rd. west 11.5 miles, State 58 northwest 6.9 miles, and FSR 5810 southwest 2.2 miles.

SIMAX GROUP CAMP (Deschutes NF) [A] [RV]
3 group sites - res. req. (800)280-CAMP, on Crescent Lake, boating, fishing, swimming, wind surfing, elev. 4850', $60-85.

Take Crescent Cutoff Rd. west 11.5 miles, State 58 northwest 3.5 miles, FSR 60 southwest 2 miles, and FSR 6015 south 1.6 miles.

SPRING (Deschutes NF)
68 units, trailers to 22', on Crescent Lake, boat launch, swimming, fishing, water skiing, wind surfing, hiking trails, elev. 4800', $10-12/night.
Take Crescent Cutoff Rd. west 11.5 miles, State 58 northwest 3.5 miles, FSR 60 southwest 9 miles.

SUMMIT LAKE (Deschutes NF)
3 units, no drinking water, trailers to 22', rough road, boating, sailing, swimming, fishing, mountain biking, hike to Pacific Crest Trail, Diamond Creek Wilderness, elev. 5600', FREE.
Take Crescent Cutoff Rd. west 12.2 miles, State 58 northwest 3.5 miles, FSR 60 southwest 7.2 miles, and FSR 6010 west 6.5 miles.

SUNSET COVE (Deschutes NF)
21 units, trailers to 22', picnic area, on Odell Lake, boat launch, fishing, wind surfing, elev. 4800', $10/night.
Take Crescent Cutoff Rd. west 11.5 miles, and State 58 northwest 6 miles.

TRAPPER CREEK (Deschutes NF)
32 units, trailers to 22', on Odell Lake, huckleberries, boat launch, sailing, fishing, hiking, near Diamond Peak Wilderness, elev. 4800', $10-12/night.
Take Crescent Cutoff Rd. west 11.5 miles, State 58 northwest 6.9 miles, and FSR 5810 southwest 1.8 miles.

WEST DAVIS LAKE (Deschutes NF)
25 units, trailers to 22', well, on Davis Lake - speed limit, fishing, birdwatching, elev. 4400', $8/night.
Take Crescent Cutoff Rd. west 9 miles, FSR 46 north 3.3 miles, FSR 4660 northwest 3.8 miles, and FSR 4669 east 2 miles to the south end of Davis Lake and campground.

WHITEFISH HORSE CAMP (Deschutes NF)
17 horse camp units - reservations req. (800)280-CAMP, trailers okay, stream, trails, horse stalls, at wet end of Crescent Lake, elev. 4800', $11-12/night.
Take Crescent Cutoff Rd. west 11.5 miles, State 58 northwest 3.5 miles, FSR 60 southwest 6.7 miles.

WINDY GROUP CAMP (Deschutes NF)
Group site, no drinking water, 1 picnic table & fire ring, trailers okay, fishing, hiking, elev. 4800', $40/night.
Take Crescent Cutoff Rd. west 11.5 miles, State 58 northwest 3.5 miles, and FSR 60 southwest 7.4 miles.

CHEMULT

CORRAL SPRINGS (Winema NF) [A] [RV]
6 units, trailers to 22', primitive, hiking into Sky Lakes or Pelican butte, mosquitoes, elev. 4900', FREE.
Take US 97 north 2.7 miles and FSR 9774 west 1.9 miles.

CRATER LAKE MOTEL & RV PARK (Private) [A] [RV]
10 units w/full hookups plus tent area, reservations (541)365-2241, showers, laundry, wheelchair accessible, space for horses, pets okay, open April thru Oct., $10-15/night..
Located right in the town of Chemult.

DIGIT POINT (Winema NF) [A] [RV]
64 units, trailers to 32', flush toilets, trailer waste disposal, on Miller Lake - speed limit, mosquitoes, boat ramp, swimming, fishing, trail to Mt. Thielsen Wilderness, elev. 5600', $5/night.
Take US 97 north 1 mile, and FSR 9772 west 12 miles.

JACKSON CREEK (Winema NF) [A] [RV]
12 units, trailers to 22', horse corral, hike into Yamsay Crater, fishing, elev. 4600', FREE.
US 97 south 24.5 miles, Military Crossing/Silver Lake Rd. northeast 22.1 miles, and FSR 49 southeast 5.3 miles.

SAND CREEK STATION (Private) [A] [RV]
10 units w/full hookups plus 4 w/water & elec., tents okay, information (541)365-4416, showers, wheelchair accessible, store, propane, gas, restaurant, horse corral, pets okay, open year round, $5-10/night.
Follow US 97 south 23 miles.

SILVER LAKE

ALDER SPRINGS (Fremont NF) [A] [RV]
3 sites, no potable water or tables, fire rings, historic site, FREE.
Take State 31 west 1 mile, Silver Creek Marsh Rd./FSR 27 southwest 13 miles, and FSR 021 1 mile.

BUNYARD CROSSING (Fremont NF) [A] [RV]
3 sites, no potable water, creek, fishing, birdwatching, hiking, FREE.
Take East Bay Rd./FSR 28 south 7 miles, FSR 2917 west 1 mile, and at the bridge take FSR 413 - campsites located back in canyon to the north.

CABIN LAKE (Fremont NF) [A] [RV]
14 units, trailers to 22', piped water, birdwatching, elev. 4500', FREE.
Take Picture Lane 17 miles north to Fort Rock and FSR 18 north 9.8 miles to campground.

CHINA HAT (Fremont NF)
14 units, trailers to 32', piped water, hiking, elev. 5100', FREE.
Take Picture Lane 17 miles north to Fort Rock and FSR 18 north
20.8 miles.

DUNCAN RESERVOIR (BLM)
5 units, picnic area, boat ramp, elev. 4800', $5/night.
Follow Duncan Reservoir Road southeast 8 miles.

EAST BAY (Fremont NF)
17 units, trailers to 32', on Thompson Res. - 10 mph speed limit,
boat ramp, swimming, fishing, elev. 5000', $6/night.
Take East Bay Rd./FSR 28 south 12.5 miles, and FSR 280014
west 1.5 miles.

LOWER BUCK CREEK (Fremont NF)
5 campsites - 2 w/tables, no potable water, fishing, FREE.
Take State 31 west 1 mile, Silver Creek Marsh Rd./FSR 27 southwest 10 miles, FSR 2804 south 2 miles and FSR 015 1 mile.

SILVER CREEK MARSH (Fremont NF)
8 units, trailers to 22', picnic area, well, horse corrals, stream,
fishing, bird watching, mountain biking, trailhead, FREE.
Take State 31 west 1 mile, Silver Creek Marsh Rd./ FSR 27 south
10 miles to campground.

THOMPSON RESERVOIR (Fremont NF)
19 units, trailers to 22', well, lake - 10 mph speed, boat ramp,
swimming, fishing, birdwatching, elev. 5000', FREE.
Take State 31 west 1 mile, Silver Creek Marsh Rd./FSR 27 south
13 miles and FSR 287 to campground.

UPPER BUCK (Fremont NF)
6 units - 3 tables, no potable water, fishing, birdwatching, FREE.
Take State 31 west 1 mile, Silver Creek Marsh Rd./FSR 27 southwest 10 miles, and FSR 2804 4 miles.

PAISLEY

CAMPBELL LAKE (Fremont NF)
15 units, trailers to 22', well, no firewood, picnic area, high mountain lake - electric motors only, birdwatching, hiking trails, boat
ramp, swimming, fishing, elev. 7200', FREE.
Take Twin Lakes Rd. west 1 mile, FSR 33 west 22.7 miles, FSR 28
south 3 miles, and FSR 033 west 2 miles.

DAIRY POINT (Fremont NF)
4 units, trailers to 30', well, picnic area, no firewood, stream, fishing, birdwatching, elev. 5200', FREE.
Take Twin Lakes Rd. west 1 mile, FSR 33 west 22.7 miles, FSR 28
south 2 miles, and FSR 3428 to campground.

DEADHORSE CREEK (Fremont NF)　　　　　　▲ RV

4 campsites, potable water @ nearby Clear Springs, fishing, bird-watching, elev. 5400', FREE.
Take State 31 north, turn left on Mill St./FSR 33, go 20 miles past the Y, turn left on FSR 28 for 2 miles, and FSR 047 for 3 miles.

DEADHORSE LAKE (Fremont NF)　　　　　　▲ RV

9 units plus 7 group sites, trailers to 22', well, no firewood, high mountain lake - electric motors only, boat ramp, fishing, hiking, elev. 7400', FREE.
Take Twin Lakes Rd. west 1 mile, FSR 33 west 22.7 miles, FSR 28 south 3 miles, and FSR 033 west 3 miles.

HAPPY CAMP (Fremont NF)　　　　　　　　▲ RV

9 units, trailers to 18', piped water, picnic shelters, on Dairy Creek, birdwatching, good fishing, elev. 5200', FREE.
Take Twin Lakes Rd. west 1 mile, FSR 33 west 22.7 miles, FSR 28 south 2.4 miles, and FSR 047 west 2 miles.

JONES CROSSING (Fremont NF)　　　　　　▲ RV

2 campsites along Chewaucan River, fishing, birdwatching, FREE.
Take State 31 north and turn left on Mill Rd./FSR 33; at the Y head to the left for an additional 9 miles.

LEE THOMAS (Fremont NF)　　　　　　　　▲ RV

8 units, trailers to 22', well, no firewood, river, birdwatching, hiking, remote, elev. 6200', mosquitoes early in season, FREE.
Take Twin Lakes Rd. west 1 mile, FSR 33 west 22.7 miles, FSR 28 1 mile, and FSR 3411 about 4 miles to campground.

MARSTER SPRING (Fremont NF)　　　　　　▲ RV

11 campsites, well, handicap accessible, fishing, birdwatching, hiking, elev. 4800', FREE.
Take State 31 north and turn left on Mill Rd./FSR 33; at the Y head to the left for an additional 7 miles.

PIKES CROSSING (Fremont NF)　　　　　　▲ RV

6 units, trailers to 32', river, fishing, elev. 5700', FREE.
Take State 31 west 10 miles, FSR 29 west 12 miles, FSR 28 west 3 miles, and campground road to Pikes Crossing.

ROCK CREEK (Fremont NF)　　　　　　　　▲ RV

5 sites, no potable water, fishing, birdwatching, nearby hiking, elev. 5800', FREE.
Take State 31 north 11 miles, FSR 29 west 12 miles, and FSR 28 south and watch for campground road. There are also several pull-off sites for the next 3 miles.

SANDHILL CROSSING (Fremont NF)　　　　▲ RV

5 units, trailers to 18', well, no firewood, near Gearhart Wilderness, birdwatching, fishing, hiking, mosquitoes early in season, elev. 6100', FREE.

Take Twin Lakes Rd. west 1 mile, FSR 33 west 18 miles, FSR 28 south 1 mile, and FSR 3411 west 8 miles.

SLIDE LAKE (Fremont NF)
2 tent sites - walk-in only, no potable water, fishing, birdwatching, trailhead, elev. 6000', FREE.
Take State 31 north and turn left on Mill Rd./FSR 33/3315, and at the Y head right for an additional 6 miles, take FSR 3360 north 9 miles and park at the Slide Lake Trailhead and walk in .3 mile.

SUMMER LAKE HOT SPRINGS (Private)
10 pull thrus w/hookups for water/elec./sewer plus tent area, reservations (541) 943-3931, trailers to 50', showers, laundry, hot spring swimming pool, nearby fishing, hiking, pets okay, $10-13/night inc. pool.
Located right in Paisley - on Hwy 31 at milepost 92.

UPPER JONES (Fremont NF)
2 units along Chewaucan River, fishing, birdwatching, elev. 4800', FREE.
Take State 31 north and turn left on Mill Rd./FSR 33, go 9 miles beyond the Y and look for unmarked sites in the trees along the river.

FORT KLAMATH

CRATER LAKE RESORT (Private)
25 units - 13 w/hookups for water/elec./sewer, 12 w/water & elec., plus large tent area, reservations (541)381-2349, showers, laundry, rec room, cabins, playfield, playground, trout pond, stream, fishing, elev. 4100', $12-17/night.
Take State 62 south 1.5 miles.

CRATER LAKE RV PARK (Private)
63 units - 7 w/hookups for water/elec./sewer, 41 w/water & elec., plus 15 tent sites, reservations (541)381-2275, showers, laundry, handicap access, playground, trout pond, stream, swimming, fishing, elev. 4300', $12-18/night.
Take State 62 northwest 5 miles.

FORT KLAMATH LODGE & RV PARK (Private)
16 units - 11 w/hookups for water/elec./sewer plus 5 tent sites, reservations (541)381-2234, showers, laundry, river, fishing, elev. 4100', $20/night.
Located on State 62, near city center.

JACKSON F. KIMBALL (Oregon State Park)
6 primitive campsites, maximum site 45', no drinking water, picnic tables, wildlife viewing, hiking, fishing, $7/night.
Take State 62 east to Ft. Klamath Junction, and Sun Mountain Rd. north 3 miles.

CHILOQUIN

AGENCY LAKE RESORT (Private) 　　　　　▲ RV

12 w/hookups for water/elec./sewer, 8 w/water & elec., plus grassy tent treed area, lake front, reservations (541)783-2489, showers, general store, cabins, boat launch & rental, marine gas, swimming, fishing, birdwatching, elev. 4200', pets okay, $8-16/night.
Just north of Chiloquin, leave US 97 on Chiloquin Hwy. and go west 6 miles to Lakeside Rd., then head south 3 miles.

COLLIER (Oregon State Park) 　　　　　▲ RV

68 campsites - 50 w/hookups for water/elec./sewer plus 18 tent sites, maximum site 60', showers, wheelchair access, picnic area, trailer waste disposal, horse facilities, hiking trails, fishing, historic logging museum & pioneer cabins, $10-17/night.
Take US 97 north about 5 miles to Collier State Park.

HEAD OF THE RIVER (Winema NF) 　　　　▲ RV

5 units, trailers to 32', no tables, primitive, fishing, elev. 4600', FREE.
Take Sprague River Rd. northeast 5 miles, Williamson River Rd. northeast 20 miles, and FSR 4648 north 1 mile.

SPORTSMAN'S RIVER RETREAT (Private) 　　▲ RV

27 units w/hookups for water/elec./sewer plus tent area, reservations (541)783-2675, trailers to 40', showers, laundry, picnic area, trailer waste disposal, on Williamson River, boat launch/dock & moorage, trout fishing, pets okay, elev. 4100', open May thru Oct., $15/night.
Take US 97 south 9 miles and Modoc Point Rd. northwest 6 miles.

SPRING CREEK (Winema NF) 　　　　　　▲ RV

5 units, flush toilets, picnic tables, fishing, not recommended for trailers, elev. 4200', FREE.
Take US 97 north 7 miles, FSR 9738 west .2 mile, and FSR 9732 northwest 3 miles.

WALT'S COZY CAMP (Private) 　　　　　▲ RV

34 units - 12 w/hookups for water/elec./sewer, 2 w/water & elec., plus 20 tent sites, reservations (541)783-2537, showers, elev. 4200', small pets okay, $12-14/night.
Located on US 97, south of Chiloquin at milepost #248.

WATER WHEEL CAMPGROUND (Private) 　　▲ RV

10 units w/hookups for water/elec./sewer, 18 w/water & elec., plus tent area, reservations (541)783-2738, showers, laundry, playground, trailer waste disposal, groceries, propane, Williamson River, boat launch, swimming, fishing, elev. 4200', pets okay, $15-19/night.
Located on US 97, near its junction with State 62.

WILLIAMSON RIVER (Winema NF)
10 units, trailers to 32', well, handicap access, picnic area, fishing, elev. 4200', $5/night.
Take US 97 north 5 miles, and FSR 9730 northeast 1 mile.

BLY

CORRAL CREEK (Fremont NF)
6 units, no potable water or firewood, handicap access, box horse stalls, birdwatching, hiking, fishing, elev. 5900', FREE.
Take State 140 east .5 mile, CR 1259 east .5 mile, FSR 34 northeast 15 miles, and FSR 012 to campground.

GERBER RESERVOIR (BLM)
50 units, trailers okay, handicap accessible, trailer dump station, boat launch, fishing platform, swimming, hiking, $6/night.
Leave State 140 at Bly and follow the signs southwest - it's about 19 miles to the campground on the west side of the reservoir.

LOFTON RESERVOIR (Fremont NF)
26 units, trailers to 30', well, grey water disposal, lake - electric motors only, boat ramp, accessible fishing pier, birdwatching, fishing, host in summer, elev. 6200', FREE.
Take State 140 southeast 12.9 miles, FSR 3715 south 7 miles, and FSR 013 northeast 1.3 miles.

LAKEVIEW

COTTONWOOD REC. AREA (Fremont NF) 🅰️ RV
21 units, trailers to 22', piped water, lake - electric motors only, boat ramps, 12 miles of trails, swimming, fishing, birdwatching, host in summer, elev. 6200', FREE.
Take State 140 west 24 miles, and FSR 3870 northeast 8 miles.

DEEP CREEK (Fremont NF) 🅰️ RV
6 units, trailers okay, fishing, birdwatching, elev. 5600', FREE.
Take State 140 east 6.5 miles, FSR 3915 south 15 miles, and FSR 4015 1 mile.

GOOSE LAKE (Oregon State Park) 🅰️ RV
48 units w/elec., trailers to 50', showers, picnic area, trailer waste disposal, boat launch, fishing, wildlife viewing, $10-12/night.
Take US 395 south 15 miles.

HUNTER'S RV (Private) 🅰️ RV
10 sites w/full hookups, 13 w/water & elec., plus tent area, reservations (541)947-4968, showers, laundry, groceries, trailer waste disposal, elev. 5000', $8-16/night.
Take US 395 north 2 miles.

JUNIPERS RESERVOIR RV RESORT (Private)
23 units w/full hookups, 17 w/water & elec., plus 6 tent sites, reservations (541)947-2050, showers, laundry, wheelchair access, trailer waste disposal, reservoir, stream, fishing, hiking, wildlife viewing, $18-20/night.
Follow State 140 west 10 miles - located in the middle of an 8,000 acre cattle ranch/wildlife viewing area.

MILE-HI TRAILER & RV PARK (Private) RV
20 units w/hookups for water/elec./sewer, no tents, reservations (541)947-2232, trailers to 40', showers, laundry, pets okay, open year round, $16/night.
Located in Lakeview, at 764 NE H St.

MUD CREEK (Fremont NF)
7 units, trailers to 18', piped water, fishing, birdwatching, FREE.
US 395 north 5.4 miles, State 140 east 8 miles, and FSR 3615 north 7 miles.

PARKWAY MOTEL & RV PARK (Private)
19 units - 18 w/hookups for water/elec./sewer plus 1 tent site, flush toilets, showers, reservations (541)947-2707, $8-15/night.
Located on State 140, 2 blocks west of US 395.

VALLEY FALLS STORE & CAMPGROUND (Private)
5 units w/hookups for water/elec./sewer, plus grassy tent area, reservations (541)947-2052, groceries, fuel, hiking, elev. 4200', $5-10/night.
Take US 395 north 23 miles.

WILLOW CREEK (Fremont NF)
8 units, no drinking water, trailers to 22', fishing, birdwatching, elev. 5800', FREE.
Take US 395 north 5.4 miles, State 140 east 6.5 miles, FSR 3915 south 9 miles, and FSR 4011 1 mile.

KLAMATH FALLS

ASPEN POINT (Winema NF)
61 units, trailers to 22', flush toilets, trailer waste disposal, at Lake of the Woods, boat launch, fishing, hiking, elev. 5000', $6/night.
Follow State 140 northwest 33 miles, FSR 3704 south .6 mile.

FOURMILE LAKE (Winema NF)
25 units, trailers to 20', horse facilities, trailhead access to Sky lakes Wilderness, fishing, boating, swimming, elev. 5800', $6/night.
Follow State 140 northwest 35 miles, FSR 3661 north 5.5 miles.

GREENSPRINGS RV PARK (Private)
18 units w/full hookups, no tents, information (541)882-0823, trailers to 50', small pets okay, open year round, $23/night. Located east of US 97 - at 2055 Greensprings Dr.

HAGELSTEIN PARK (Klamath County)
10 campsites, trailers okay, flush toilets, wheelchair accessible, on Klamath Lake, boat launch, fishing, pets okay, $8/night. Take US 97 north 10 miles.

KLAMATH FALLS KOA (Private)
73 units - 36 w/hookups for water/elec./sewer, 30 w/water & elec., plus 7 tent sites, reservations (541)884-4644, showers, laundry, pool, playground, trailer waste disposal, groceries, propane, stream, elev. 4100', $18-22/night. Take 5th St., go left on Washburn, and take Shasta Way to 3435.

LAKE OF THE WOODS RV RESORT (Private)
42 units - 27 w/hookups for water/elec./sewer, 5 w/elec. only, plus 10 tent sites, reservations (541)949-8300, trailers to 35', showers, laundry, trailer waste disposal, propane, restaurant, groceries, on lake, boat launch/gas & rental, swimming, fishing, hiking, pets okay, elev. 5000', $20/night. Follow State 140 northwest 33 miles, FSR 3704 south 1 mile, and resort road west .5 mile.

ODESSA (Winema NF)
5 units, trailers to 22', stream, boat ramp, fishing, primitive, elev. 4100', FREE. Take State 140 northwest 30 miles and FSR 3651 north 11 miles.

OREGON MOTEL & RV PARK (Private)
40 units - 22 w/hookups for water/elec./sewer, 3 w/water & elec., plus 15 tent sites, reservations (877)882-0482 or (541)882-0482, showers, laundry, swimming pool, game room, elev. 4100', pets okay, $13-18/night. Take US 97 north 3 miles.

ROCKY POINT RESORT & MARINA (Private)
18 units w/hookups for water/elec./sewer, 11 w/water & elec., plus 4 tent sites, reservations (541)356-2287, showers, laundry, store, trailer waste disposal, Upper Klamath Lake, paddleboat rental, boat launch, swimming, fishing, hiking, elev. 4200', pets okay, $14-18/night. Follow State 140 northwest 28 miles, and Rocky Point Rd. north 3 miles.

SUNSET (Winema NF)
67 units, trailers to 22', flush toilets, handicap access, at Lake of the Woods, boat ramp, swimming, fishing, hiking, elev. 5000', $5/night. Follow State 140 northwest 32.6 miles, FSR 3704 south 1 mile.

SURVEYOR (BLM) ▲ RV
8 campsites, water, elev. 5160', $3/night.
US 97 south 3 miles, State 66 southwest 13 miles, and Howard Prairie Lake Rd. 14 miles.

TINGLEY LAKE ESTATES (Private) ▲ RV
14 units - 4 w/hookups for water/elec./sewer, 6 w/water & elec., plus 4 tent units, reservations (541)882-8386, showers, pond, swimming, fishing, elev. 4100', $14-16/night.
Follow US 97 south 7 miles to the town of Midland, take Old Midland Rd. east 2 miles, and Tingley Ln. south .5 mile.

WISEMAN'S MOBILE COURT (Private)
26 units w/full hookups and 5 w/water & elec., no tents, reservations (541)884-4327, maximum site 40', showers, laundry, trailer waste disposal, small pets okay, elev. 4200', $14-16/night.
Located at 6800 S. 6th St.

KENO

KENO CAMP (Pacific Power) ▲ RV
26 campsites, information (503)813-6666, showers, handicap access, picnic area, trailer waste disposal, on Klamath River, boat launch, fishing, swimming, open May thru Oct., $15/night.
Take State 66 northwest 2 miles.

TOPSY (BLM) ▲
12 primitive tent sites, handicap accessible, picnic facilities, boat launch, swimming, elev. 3500', $3/night.
Follow State 66 northwest 6 mile, and Topsy County Rd. south 1 mile.

EASTERN OREGON
CAMPGROUNDS

See Page

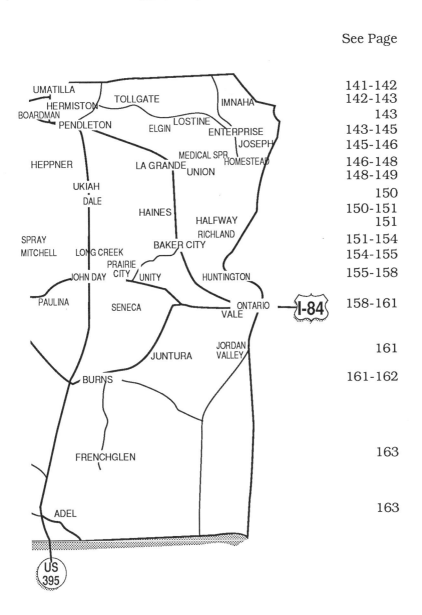

UMATILLA

UMATILLA MARINA & RV PARK (Port)
26 units - 9 w/hookups for water/elec./sewer, no tents, trailers to 65', pull thrus, showers, wheelchair access, trailer waste disposal, pets okay, open year round, $13/night.
From I-84/State 730 junction, go north .3 mile on Brownell Rd, then west .3 mile on 3rd St. - located at 1710 Quincy.

SAND STATION REC. AREA (Corp)
Camp area on Lake Wallula, tents okay, information (541)922-3211, picnic facilities, swimming, pets okay, $7-11/night.
Take State 730 east 10.5 miles.

SHADY REST RV PARK (Private)
24 units w/full hookups inc. cable, reservations (541)922-5041, showers, laundry, pool, $17/night.
Take US 730 west .4 mile.

WAREHOUSE BEACH REC. AREA (Corp)
10 units, on Columbia River, fire pits, sandy beach, swimming, $7-11/night.
Take State 730 east 9.5 miles and State 37 north .4 mile.

TOLLGATE

ALPINE SPRING (Umatilla NF)
3 tent units, no trailers, river, hiking, elev. 5000', FREE.
Take State 204 6 miles east to Balloon Tree Rd. and follow this 1 mile.

BEAR CANYON (Umatilla NF)
6 tent units, river, fishing, hiking, elev. 4900', FREE.
Take FSR 64 north 12 miles to Jubilee Lake and FSR 6413 east 14 miles.

DUSTY SPRING (Umatilla NF)
5 tent units, water, picnic area, hiking, berry picking, elev. 5100', FREE.
Take FSR 64 north 3 miles, FSR 6403 northeast 8.5 miles.

ELK FLATS (Umatilla NF)
3 tent sites, river, trailhead into Wenaha-Tucannon Wilderness, elev. 5000', $3/night.
Take FSR 64 north 12 miles to Jubilee Lake and FSR 6313 east 18 miles.

INDIAN (Umatilla NF)
2 tent sites, picnic area, river, hiking,. 5800', FREE.
Take FSR 64 north 3 miles, FSR 6403 northeast 14 miles, and FSR 64 north 20 miles.

JUBILEE LAKE (Umatilla NF)　　　　　　　 🔺 RV
51 sites trailers to 22', flush toilets, handicap access, lake - no motors, fishing, swimming, trail, elev. 4800', $14/night.
Take FSR 64 northeast 12 miles.

LUGER SPRINGS (Umatilla NF)　　　　　　　 🔺 RV
5 units - 2 trailers, water, picnic area, hiking, elev. 5000', FREE.
Take FSR 64 north 3 miles, FSR 6303 northeast 14 miles.

MOSIER SPRING (Umatilla NF)　　　　　　　 🔺 RV
4 sites - some trailers, water, picnic area, hiking, berry picking, elev. 4700', FREE.
Take FSR 64 north 12 miles to Jubilee Lake and FSR 6413 east 23 miles.

SQUAW SPRING (Umatilla NF)　　　　　　　　　　 🔺
5 tent units, water, picnic area, hiking, elev. 5100', FREE.
Take FSR 64 north 3 miles, FSR 6403 northeast 14 miles, and FSR 64 north 7 miles.

TARGET MEADOWS (Umatilla NF)　　　　　　 🔺 RV
20 units, trailers to 22', picnic area, hiking, elev. 4800', $10/night.
Take FSR 64 .1 mile and FSR 6401 north 2.2 miles.

TIMOTHY SPRINGS (Umatilla NF)　　　　　　 🔺 RV
3 sites - 1 trailer, water, picnic area, hiking, berry picking, elev. 4600', $3/night.
Take FSR 64 north 3 miles, FSR 6403 northeast 14 miles, and FSR 64 southeast 3.3 miles.

WOODWARD (Umatilla NF)　　　　　　　　　　 🔺 RV
18 units, trailers to 22', hike/bike trails, elev. 4950', $10/night.
Located at Tollgate.

HERMISTON

FORT HENRIETTA RV PARK (City)　　　　　　 🔺 RV
7 units w/hookups for water/elec./sewer plus grassy tent area, information (541)376-8411, showers, handicap access, fishing, trailer waste disposal, pets okay, $10-15/night.
Leave I-84 on exit #188 and go .5 mile south to Echo and park.

HAT ROCK CAMPGROUND (Private)　　　　　　 🔺 RV
27 units w/full hookups, 33 w/water & elec., plus 10 tent sites, reservations (541)567-4188, showers, pool, trailer waste disposal, river, boat launch, fishing, $14-15/night.
Take US 395 north 5 miles, US 730 east 8 miles, and Hat Rock State Park Rd. north 1 mile.

BOARDMAN

BOARDMAN MARINA PARK (City)   A RV
63 sites w/full hookups, tents okay, trailers to 40', pull thrus, reservations (541)481-7217, showers, laundry, wheelchair access, trailer waste disposal, on Columbia River, boat launch, fishing, hiking, pets okay, open mid March thru mid Dec., $15/night. Located just off I-84, at exit #164.

IMNAHA

HAT POINT (Wallowa-Whitman NF)   A RV
2 units, picnic area, no water, hiking, stock ramp, outstanding view, elev. 7000', FREE.
Take FSR 4240 southeast 23.4 miles and FSR 315 east .8 mile.

SADDLE CREEK (Wallowa-Whitman NF)   A RV
6 units, trailers to 18', no water, elev. 6600', FREE.
Take FSR 4240 southeast 19.7 miles.

SACAJAWEA (Wallowa-Whitman NF)   A
3 tent units, picnic area, no water, hiking, stock ramp, outstanding view, elev. 7000, FREE.
Take FSR 4240 southeast 25 miles and follow FSR 315 .7 mile.

PENDLETON

BROOKE RV PARK (Private)   RV
22 sites w/hookups for water/elec./sewer plus 6 w/water & elec., no tents, reservations (541)276-5353, showers, laundry, Umatilla River, walk to downtown, $16-18/night.
Leave I-84 on exit #210, take State 11 northeast .8 mile, SE Court Ave. west 2.5 miles, and SE 8th St. north 2 blocks.

EMIGRANT SPRINGS (Oregon State Park)   A RV
18 sites w/full hookups, 33 tent sites, group area, $13-17/night.
Take I-84 southeast 26 miles.

UMATILLA FORKS (Umatilla NF)   A RV
15 units, some trailers to 22', water, access to North Fork Umatilla Wilderness, fishing, hiking, horse trails, elev. 2400', $8/night.
Leave town heading east along the Umatilla River Rd. for 31 miles, and take FSR 32 southeast .6 mile.

ELGIN

MINAM (Oregon State Park)   A RV
12 sites, maximum site 71', picnic area, fishing, $10/night.
Take State 82 northeast 15 miles.

WOODLAND (Umatilla NF)　　　　　　　　　▲ RV
7 units, trailers to 22', no water, picnic facilities, on edge of North
Fork Umatilla Wilderness, elev. 5200', $3/night.
Take State 204 northwest 16 miles.

LOSTINE

BOUNDARY (Wallowa-Whitman NF)　　　　　▲ RV
8 units, trailers to 18', no water, creek, swimming, fishing, FREE.
Head northwest 11 miles to the town of Wallowa, and take Bear
Creek Rd./FSR 8250 south 6.9 miles.

SHADY (Wallowa-Whitman NF)　　　　　　　▲ RV
14 units, trailers to 18', no water, river, swimming, fishing, trailheads to wilderness, primitive, elev. 5400', $3/night.
Take Lostine River Rd./FSR 8210 south 15.5 miles.

TWO PAN (Wallowa-Whitman NF)　　　　　　▲ RV
6 units, trailers to 18', no water, river, swimming, fishing, trailheads to wilderness, primitive, elev. 5600', $3/night.
Take Lostine River Rd./FSR 8210 south 17.8 miles.

WILLIAMSON (Wallowa-Whitman NF)　　　　▲ RV
10 units, trailers to 18', no water, river, swimming, fishing, trailheads to wilderness, elev. 5000', $3/night.
Take Lostine River Rd./FSR 8210 south 10 miles.

ENTERPRISE

BUCKHORN SPRINGS (Wallowa-Whitman NF)　　▲ RV
6 units, trailers to 22', no water, picnic area, stock ramp, spring,
elev. 5200', FREE.
Take State 82 south 3 miles and Swamp Creek/FSR 46 about 36
miles to campground.

COYOTE (Wallowa-Whitman NF)　　　　　　▲ RV
6 units, trailers to 22', no water, primitive, elev. 4800', FREE.
Take State 3 north 15 miles and FSR 46 northeast 30 miles.

DOUGHERTY SPRINGS (Wallowa-Whitman NF)　▲ RV
10 units, trailers to 22', no water, elev. 4900', FREE.
Take State 3 north 15 miles and FSR 46 northeast 37 miles.

MUD CREEK (BLM)　　　　　　　　　　　　▲ RV
Scattered campsites, small boat ramp on Grande Ronde River,
information (541)523-4476, pets okay, FREE.
Take State 3 north 30 miles to Flora, Lost Prairie Rd. west 3 miles,
Troy Rd. northwest 3 miles to campground road and head south-
west 4 miles.

OUTPOST RV PARK (Private)   [A] [RV]
48 rv sites w/water/elec./sewer plus grassy tent area, reservations (541)426-4027, showers, elev. 3500', $10-17/night.
Take State 3 north .5 mile.

TROY WILDERNESS LODGE/RV PARK (Private)   [A] [RV]
20 units w/elec., plus grassy tent area w/firepits, reservations (541)426-4027, showers, gas, propane, elev. 3500', pets okay, $5-9/night.
Take State 3 north .5 mile.

VIGNE (Wallowa-Whitman NF)   [A] [RV]
7 units, trailers to 22', well, stream, fishing, primitive, elev. 3000', FREE.
Take State 3 north 15 miles and FSR 46 northeast 22 miles.

JOSEPH

BLACKHORSE (Hells Canyon NRA)   [A] [RV]
15 units, no water, trailers to 32', river, hiking, elev. 4000', FREE.
Take State 350 east 7.7 miles, and FSR 39 southeast 28.7 miles.

EVERGREEN GROUP CAMP (Wallowa-Whitman NF)   [A] [RV]
17 units, trailers to 32', no drinking water, river, swimming, fishing, hiking, in Hells Canyon Rec. Area, elev. 4500', FREE.
Take State 350 east 7.7 miles, FSR 39 south 28.8 miles, and FSR 3960 southwest 8 miles.

HIDDEN (Hells Canyon NRA)   [A] [RV]
10 units, trailers to 32', no water, fishing, hiking, elev. 4400', FREE.
Take State 350 east 7.7 miles, FSR 39 southeast 28.8 miles, and FSR 3960 southwest 7 miles.

HURRICANE CREEK (Wallowa-Whitman NF)   [A] [RV]
10 units, trailers to 18', no water, picnic area, fishing, trails into Eagle Cap Wilderness, primitive, elev. 4600', $3/night.
Head west of town 3.5 miles and take FSR 8205 south .5 mile.

INDIAN CROSSING (Hells Canyon NRA)   [A] [RV]
14 sites, no water, horse ramp, fishing, pets okay, elev. 4500', FREE.
Take State 350 east 7.7 miles, FSR 39 southeast 28.8 miles, and FSR 3960 southwest 8.8 miles.

OLLOKOT (Hells Canyon NRA)   [A] [RV]
12 units, trailers to 32', river, fishing, elev. 4000', FREE.
Take State 350 east 7.7 miles, and FSR 39 southeast 28.8 miles.

WALLOWA LAKE (Oregon State Park)   A RV

121 sites w/full hookups, 89 tent sites, plus 3 group tent areas, reservations (800)452-5687, maximum site 90', showers, wheelchair access, picnic area, trailer waste disposal, boating, fishing, swimming, edge of Eagle Cap Wilderness, $11-20/night.
Follow Wallowa Lake Rd. south 6 miles.

HEPPNER

ANSON WRIGHT PARK (Morrow County)   A RV

44 units - 16 w/full hookups, 2 w/elec., 4 w/water, 18 dry sites, and 2 group areas, tents okay, trailers to 30', showers, wheelchair access, picnic area, playground, stream, fishing - handicap accessible, hiking, stocked fish pond, rockhounding, open mid-May thru mid-Nov., elev. 2300', pets okay, $5-10/night.
Follow State 207 southwest 26 miles.

CUTSFORTH PARK (Morrow County)   A RV

42 units - 20 w/hookups for water/elec./sewer, 18 w/out hookups and 2 group areas, tents okay, trailers to 30', showers, wheelchair access, 2 disabled sites, picnic area, playground, stocked fish pond, fishing - handicap accessible, nature trails, open mid-May thru mid-Nov., elev. 3400', pets okay, $5-10/night.
Take State 207 southwest 2 miles, and Willow Creek Hwy. southeast 20 miles.

FAIRVIEW (Umatilla NF)   A

4 tent sites, some trailers, picnic area, no drinking water, elev. 4300', FREE.
Take State 207 south 34 miles.

PENLAND LAKE (Umatilla NF)   A RV

8 side-by-side sites, picnic area, no drinking water, boat ramp, lake - electric motors only, fishing, swimming, elev. 4950, FREE.
Take Willow Creek Rd. southeast 19 miles, FSR 53 south 2.5 miles, FSR 21 south 2.9 miles, FSR 2103 east 2.8 miles, and FSR 030 northeast .3 mile.

LA GRANDE

HILGARD JUNCTION (Oregon State Park)   A RV

18 campsites, maximum site 30', wheelchair access, trailer waste disposal, rafting, fishing, OR Trail display, $10/night.
Take I-84 northwest 8 miles.

HOT LAKE RV RESORT (Private)   A RV

100 pull thrus w/water/elec./sewer plus tent area, (541) 963-5253, trailers to 50', showers, laundry, wheelchair access, pool, trailer waste disposal, fishing, hiking, pets okay, $12-20/night.
I-84 to exit #265, State 203 southeast 5 miles, .3 mile to resort.

LA GRANDE RENDEZVOUS RESORT (Private) ⚠️ RV
66 RV units w/water/elec./sewer, tents okay - no fire rings,
(541)962-0909, max. 70', showers, wheelchair access, pets okay,
year round, $13-22/night.
Located at 2632 Bearco Loop.

MOSS SPRINGS (Wallowa-Whitman NF) ⚠️ RV
11 units, trailers to 22', picnic area, hiking/horse trails, horse
ramp & stall, elev. 5400', FREE.
Take State 237 east to Cove, follow Moss Springs Rd. southeast
1.5 miles, and FSR 6220 east 6.5 miles.

RIVER (Wallowa-Whitman NF) ⚠️ RV
6 units, trailers to 22', no drinking water, picnic area, river, fishing, primitive, elev. 3800', FREE.
Take I-84 west 9.1 miles, State 244 southwest 12.9 miles, and
FSR 51 south 9 miles.

SPOOL CART (Wallowa-Whitman NF) ⚠️ RV
16 units, trailers to 22', no drinking water, river, fishing, primitive,
elev. 3700', FREE.
Take I-84 west 9.1 miles, State 244 southwest 12.9 miles, and
FSR 51 south 4.5 miles.

SUNDOWNER MOBILE HOME PARK (Private) RV
24 trailer sites w/water/elec./sewer, no tents, reservations
(541)963-2648, showers, laundry, trailer waste disposal, elev.
2800', pets okay, $17/night.
Take State 82 east .3 mile, and Holmes St. south .2 mile.

TIME AND A HALF (Wallowa-Whitman NF) ⚠️ RV
5 units, trailers to 22', no drinking water, river, fishing, primitive,
elev. 3800', FREE.
Take I-84 west 9.1 miles, State 244 southwest 12.9 miles, and
FSR 51 south 6.5 miles.

WOODLEY (Wallowa-Whitman NF) ⚠️ RV
7 units, trailers to 22', piped water, picnic area, river, fishing, hiking trails, primitive, elev. 3800', FREE.
Take I-84 west 9.1 miles, State 244 southwest 12.9 miles, FSR 51
south 16 miles, and FSR 5125 southeast 5 miles.

UNION

CATHERINE CREEK (Oregon State Park) ⚠️ RV
18 units, maximum site 30', picnic area, fishing, $8/night.
Follow State 203 southeast 8 miles.

N. CATHERINE TRAILHEAD (Wallowa-Whitman NF) ⚠️ RV
3 units, trailers to 22', stream, fishing, hiking, wilderness, elev.
4400', $3/night.

Take State 203 southeast 10 miles and FSR 7785 northeast 6.5 miles.

THIEF VALLEY CAMPGROUND (Union County) 🔺 RV
Primitive camp area, pets & horses okay, FREE.
Take State 237 and Teloca Set Ln south/southeast to Thief Valley Reservoir - about 12 miles.

MEDICAL SPRINGS

TAMARACK (Wallowa-Whitman NF) 🔺 RV
20 units, trailers to 22', piped water, stream, fishing, elev. 4600', FREE.
Take FSR 67 southeast 15.7 miles and FSR 77 east .3 mile.

TWO COLOR (Wallowa-Whitman NF) 🔺 RV
14 units, trailers to 22', piped water, stream, fishing, elev., FREE.
Take FSR 67 southeast 15.5 miles and FSR 7755 northeast 1.5 miles.

HOMESTEAD

DOVE CREEK (Wallowa-Whitman NF) 🔺
4 tent units, hike in only, fishing, elev. 1700', FREE.
Take the road north for 6 miles and hike Trail #1890 north 6.5 miles.

KIRBY CREEK (Wallowa-Whitman NF) 🔺
4 tent units, hike in only, boating, swimming, fishing, elev. 1700', FREE.
Take the road north for 6 miles and hike Trail #1890 north 6.54miles.

LEEP CREEK (Wallowa-Whitman NF) 🔺
3 tent units, hike in only, picnic area, fishing, elev. 1700', FREE.
Take the road north for 6 miles and hike Trail #1890 north 4.7 miles.

LYNCH CREEK (Wallowa-Whitman NF) 🔺
3 tent units, hike in only, fishing, elev. 1700', FREE.
Take the road north for 6 miles and hike Trail #1890 north 7.3 miles.

VERMILLION BAR (Wallowa-Whitman NF) 🔺
2 tent units, hike in only, fishing, elev. 1700', FREE.
Drive north 6 miles and hike Trail #1890 north 6.9 miles.

UKIAH

BEAR WALLOW (Umatilla NF) ▲ RV
6 units, trailers to 18', picnic area, no water, handicap access - inc. short trail along stream, fishing, elev. 3900', FREE.
Take State 244 northeast 11 miles.

BIG CREEK MEADOWS (Umatilla NF) ▲ RV
8 sites, no water, hiking, fishing, elev. 5100', FREE.
Take Ukiah-Granite Rd./FSR 52 southeast 23 miles.

DRIFT FENCE (Umatilla NF) ▲
5 tent sites, no water, elev. 4250', FREE.
Take FSR 52 southeast 8 miles.

FOUR CORNERS SNO-PARK (Umatilla NF) ▲ RV
2 campsites, no water, winter recreation, FREE.
Take State 244 east 20 miles.

FRAZIER (Umatilla NF) ▲ RV
18 units, some trailers to 32', no water, group picnic area, stream, fishing, elev. 4300', FREE.
Take State 244 east 18.1 miles, FSR 5226 south .5 mile, and FSR 20 east .2 mile.

LANE CREEK (Umatilla NF) ▲ RV
8 units, some trailers to 32', no water, picnic area, fishing, elev. 3850', FREE.
Take State 244 northeast 10.5 miles.

NORTH FORK JOHN DAY (Umatilla NF) ▲ RV
12 sites, trailers to 22', no potable water, river, fishing, access to N. Fork John Day Wilderness, nearby horse facilities, elev. 5200', FREE.
Take FSR 52 southeast 38.5 miles - scenic drive.

PEARSON WOODS (Umatilla NF) ▲ RV
4 sites, no water, hiking trails, FREE.
Take FSR 52 southeast 13.5 miles.

UKIAH-DALE FOREST (Oregon State Park) ▲ RV
25 units, trailers to 25', on N. Fork John Day River, fishing, $10/night.
Take US 395 southwest 3 miles.

WINOM CREEK (Umatilla NF) ▲ RV
7 units, no water, trails, wilderness access, elev. 5000', FREE.
Take FSR 52 southeast 20 miles and FSR 52440 for .2 mile.

DALE

GOLD DREDGE (Umatilla NF)
8 tent sites, no drinking water, picnic facilities, on North Fork John Day Wild & Scenic River, fishing, hiking, trail bikes, elev. 4300', FREE.
Take US 395 northeast 1 mile, FSR 55 northwest 5 miles, and FSR 5506 southeast 1.9 miles.

MEADOWBROOK LODGE (Private)
22 sites w/water & elec., tents okay, reservations (541)421-3104, showers, laundry, game room, miniature golf, trailer waste disposal, groceries, propane, pets okay, $13/night.
Follow US 395 south to milepost #71 and campground.

OLIVE LAKE (Umatilla NF)
24 units, trailers to 32', no drinking water, picnic area, lake - speed limits, elev. 6000', FREE.
Take US 395 northeast 1 mile, FSR 55 southeast .6 mile, FSR 10 southeast 26.3 miles, and FSR 420 southwest .3 mile.

ORIENTAL CREEK (Umatilla NF)
7 tent sites, no drinking water, on North Fork John Day Wild & Scenic Rive, fishing, hiking, elev. 3500', FREE.
Take US 395 northeast 1 mile, FSR 55 northwest 5 miles, and FSR 5506 southeast 8 miles.

TOLLBRIDGE (Umatilla NF)
7 units, trailers to 32', piped water, stream, fishing, at mouth of Desolation Creek, elev. 3800', FREE.
Take US 395 northeast 1 mile, FSR 55 southeast .6 mile, and FSR 10 southeast .1 mile.

WELCH CREEK (Umatilla NF)
5 units, trailer to 22', no water, picnic area, fishing, elev. 4500', FREE.
Take US 395 northeast 1 mile, FSR 55 southeast .6 mile, and FSR 10 southeast 13.9 miles.

HAINES

ANTHONY LAKES (Wallowa-Whitman NF)
37 units, trailers to 22', ice, snack bar, small lake - no motors, boat launch & rental, swimming, fishing, hiking, wheelchair access includes trails & fishing, elev. 7100', $5/night.
Follow the Elkhorn Scenic Byway northwest 17 miles, and FSR 73 west 7 miles.

GRANDE RONDE (Wallowa-Whitman NF)
8 units plus group area, trailers to 18', small lake - no motors, boat launch, swimming, fishing, elev. 7200', $3/night.

Follow the Elkhorn Scenic Byway northwest 17 miles, FSR 73 west 8.5 miles, and FSR 43 northwest .5 mile.

MUD LAKE (Wallowa-Whitman NF) ⚠️ 🅡🅥
7 units, trailers to 18', small lake, boating, swimming, fishing, periodic mosquito problems, elev. 7100', $3/night.
Follow the Elkhorn Scenic Byway northwest 17 miles, and FSR 73 west 7.3 miles.

N. FORK ANTHONY CREEK (Wallowa-Whitman NF) ⚠️
4 tent sites, fishing, hiking, primitive, elev. 5300', FREE.
Take State 30 north 4 miles and Pilcher Creek Rd. southwest 11 miles.

PILCHER CREEK CAMPGROUND (Union County) ⚠️ 🅡🅥
12 units, primitive, information (541)963-1001, boat ramp, pets & horses okay, open April thru Sept., FREE.
Take north 4 miles and head west on the Pilcher Creek Rd./FSR 4330 about 9.3 miles to the west side of the reservoir.

HALFWAY

DUCK LAKE (Wallowa-Whitman NF) ⚠️ 🅡🅥
2 units, no potable water, boating, swimming, fishing, hiking, rough roads, elev. 5700', FREE.
Take State 86 east 9.2 miles, FSR 39 north 13 miles, FSR 66 west 5.8 miles, and FSR 3980 north .7 mile.

FISH LAKE (Wallowa-Whitman NF) ⚠️ 🅡🅥
15 units, trailers to 22', piped water, stream, boating, swimming, fishing, elev. 6600', FREE.
Take Pine Creek Rd. north 5 miles, and FSR 66 north 18.6 miles.

LAKE FORK (Hells Canyon NRA) ⚠️ 🅡🅥
8 sites, trailers to 22', stream, fishing, hiking, elev. 3200', FREE.
State Highway 86 east 9.2 miles, FSR 39 north 8.3 miles.

McBRIDE (Wallowa-Whitman NF) ⚠️ 🅡🅥
2 campsites, trailers to 18', creek, elev. 4800', FREE.
Take State 413 northwest 5 miles, FSR 7710 west 2.5 miles, and FSR 77 west 2.1 miles.

TWIN LAKES (Wallowa-Whitman NF) ⚠️ 🅡🅥
6 units, trailers to 22', no potable water, boating, swimming, fishing, hiking, elev. 6500', FREE.
Take State 86 east 9.2 miles, FSR 39 north 13 miles, and FSR 66 west 10.9 miles.

RICHLAND

EAGLE FORKS (Wallowa-Whitman NF) [A] [RV]
7 units, trailers to 18', piped water, picnic area, stream, fishing, elev. 4000', FREE.
Take Eagle Creek Rd. northwest 8.1 miles and FSR 7735 north 2.7 miles.

EAGLE VALLEY RV/MH PARK (Private) [A] [RV]
24 units w/full hookups, 16 w/water/elec./cable tv, plus grassy tent area, reservations (541)893-6161, showers, laundry, wheelchair access, trailer waste disposal, propane, $10-17/night.
Take State 86 east .2 mile - located near milepost #42.

HEWITT PARK (Baker County) [A] [RV]
38 units - 17 w/hookups for water & elec., 16 w/out hookups, plus 5 tent sites, trailers to 32', flush toilets, wheelchair access - includes fishing dock, river, boat launch, fishing, hiking, open mid March thru mid Nov., pets okay, $10-13/night.
Follow signs at east end of town for 2.5 miles to park.

SWEDES LANDING (BLM) [A] [RV]
Camping area, restrooms, boat ramp, on Snake River, FREE.
Take the Brownlee Reservoir/Snake River Rd. southeast 14 miles.

TUNNEL LAUNCH (BLM) [A] [RV]
Camping area, boat ramp, on Snake River, FREE.
Take the Brownlee Reservoir/Snake River Rd. southeast 34 miles.

BAKER CITY

BAKER CITY MOTEL/RV CENTER (Private) [A] [RV]
20 units w/full hookups inc. cable, tent area, reservations (800)931-9229, showers, laundry, pets okay, $8-14/night.
Located at 880 Elm St.

BASSER DIGGINS (BLM) [A] [RV]
Open camp area, water, picnic facilities, hiking, pets okay, elev. 6800', FREE.
Leave I-84 at the Lookout Mountain exit and follow Lookout Mountain Rd. 15 miles to campground.

DEER CREEK (Wallowa-Whitman NF) [A]
8 tent sites, no water, picnic area, fishing, primitive, elev. 4600', FREE.
Take State 7 southwest 2 miles, and FSR 6550 north 3 miles.

FOURTH CREEK (Wallowa-Whitman NF) [A] [RV]
2 campsites, primitive, creek, trails, FREE.
Take State 7 southwest 33 miles and N. Fork Burnt River Rd. south 4 miles.

McCULLEY FORK (Wallowa-Whitman NF)
6 units plus 2 group sites, no water, stream, fishing, elev. 4600', FREE.
Take State 7 southwest 27 miles, and State 410 7 miles northwest.

MILLERS LANE (Wallowa-Whitman NF)
6 units, trailers to 18', no water, lake, boating, swimming, fishing, water skiing, elev. 4100', FREE.
Take State 7 southwest 33 miles, Phillips Lake South shore Rd. south 2 miles, and FSR 2220 southeast 2 miles.

MOUNTAIN VIEW TRAV-L-PARK (Private)
68 units w/full hookups plus 14 tent sites, reservations (541)523-4824, showers, laundry, trailer waste disposal, swimming pool, playground, groceries, propane, meeting room, $15-19/night.
Leave I-84 at exit #304, travel west .5 mile on Campbell, north 1 mile on Cedar, and west 1 mile on Hughes Ln.

OREGON TRAILS WEST RV (Private)
49 units w/hookups for water/elec./sewer, plus grassy tent area, trailers to 40', pull thrus, reservations (541)523-3236, showers, laundry, groceries, propane, gas, pets okay, $12-18/night.
Campground is located just off I-84, at exit #302.

SOUTHWEST SHORE (Wallowa-Whitman NF)
18 units, no water, trailers to 18', on Phillips Lake, swimming, fishing, water skiing, boat ramp, elev. 4100', FREE.
Take State 7 southwest 33 miles, Phillips Lake South shore Rd. south 1.5 miles.

SUMPTER PINE RV PARK (Private)
14 units w/full hookups, tents okay, reservations (541)894-2328, trailers to 60', fishing, pets okay, $10-16/night.
State 7 southwest 25 miles, Sumpter Rd. north 2 miles.

UNION CREEK (Wallowa-Whitman NF)
24 sites w/full hookups, 34 standard units, 12 tent sites, plus group area, trailers to 22', reservations (541)894-2260, flush toilets, wheelchair access, trailer waste disposal, on Phillips Reservoir, ice, bait, boat launch/rentals & gasoline, swimming, fishing, water skiing, hiking, bicycling, elev. 4100', $10-16/night.
Take State 7 southwest 20 miles.

SPRAY

ASHER'S RV PARK (Private)
20 campsites w/elec., tents okay, restroom, no drinking water, reservations (541)934-2712, play area, hiking, fishing, fossil area, $8-10/night.
State 19 southeast to Kimberly - near the John Day Fossil Beds.

BIG BEND (BLM) ▲ RV
4 campsites, no drinking water, elev. 1500', FREE.
Take State 19 southwest 15 miles to Kimberly and head northeast on the County Road 3 miles.

BULL PRAIRIE (Umatilla NF) ▲ RV
28 units, trailers to 32', picnic area, on 24 acre Bull Prairie Lake - no motors, fishing, trail, elev. 4000', $10/night.
State 207 northeast 14.5 miles, FSR 2039 northeast 3 miles.

FAIRVIEW (Umatilla NF) ▲ RV
5 units, trailers to 18', no water, elev. 4100', FREE.
Take State 19 east 2.5 miles, State 207 north 11.5 miles, and FSR 400 west .5 mile.

MULESHOE (BLM) ▲ RV
11 units, picnic area, on John Day River, boat ramp, fishing, swimming area, elev. 600', FREE.
Take State 207 west; campground is located about 13 miles west.

MITCHELL

ALLEN CREEK (Ochoco NF) ▲ RV
5 units, no drinking water, 5 horse corrals, nearby Allen Creek Reservoir, elev. 4200', FREE.
Take Johnson Creek Rd./FSR 22 south 20 miles to the northeast edge of Big Summit Prairie.

BARNHOUSE (Ochoco NF) ▲ RV
6 units, trailers to 22', no drinking water, FREE.
Take US 26 east 13 miles and FSR 12 south 5 miles to the summit of Ochoco Pass.

COTTONWOOD (Ochoco NF) ▲ RV
6 units, no water, elev. 5700', FREE.
Take US 26 southwest 13 miles and FSR 12 south 15 miles to FSR 200 and campground.

SCOTTS CAMP (Ochoco NF) ▲ RV
3 units, spring, elev. 4100', FREE.
Take Johnson Creek Rd./FSR 22 south 17.5 miles.

LONG CREEK

BEECH CREEK (Malheur NF) ▲ RV
5 units, trailers to 18', fishing, primitive, elev. 4500', FREE.
Take US 395 south 16 miles.

HITCHING POST TRAILER COURT (Private) 🔺 RV
19 units w/full hookups plus grassy tent area, reservations (541)421-3043, trailers to 40', showers, laundry, propane, pets okay, open April thru Nov., $15/night.
Located right in town - 2 blocks from the store.

JOHN DAY

BILLY FIELDS (Malheur NF) 🔺 RV
6 units, trailers to 22', stream, fishing, picnic area, near Cedar Grove Botanical Area, elev. 4000', FREE.
Take US 26 10 miles beyond Mt. Vernon and follow FSR 21 south 7 miles to campground.

CANYON MEADOWS (Malheur NF) 🔺 RV
18 units, trailers to 18', piped water, picnic area, reservoir - no motors, boating,hiking,fishing, wilderness access, elev. 5100', FREE.
Take US 395 south 10 miles, FSR 15 southeast 9 miles, and FSR 1520 northeast 5 miles.

CLYDE HOLLIDAY (Oregon State Park) 🔺 RV
30 campsites w/elec., maximum site 60', showers, wheelchair access, picnic area, trailer waste disposal, fishing, $10-15/night.
Take US 26 west 7 miles.

CRESCENT (Malheur NF) 🔺 RV
4 sites, trailers to 18', stream, fishing, elev. 520', FREE.
Take US 26 east 13 miles to Prairie City, South River Rd. southeast 8.3 miles, and FSR 14 south 8.5 miles.

DEPOT PARK (Prairie City) 🔺 RV
20 units w/full hookups plus grassy tent area, information (541)820-3605, cable & telephone hookups avail., showers, wheelchair access, trailer waste disposal, hiking, open May thru Oct., pets okay, $9-13/night.
Take US 26 east 13 miles to Prairie City and follow signs.

DIXIE (Malheur NF) 🔺 RV
11 sites, trailers to 22', well, picnic area, berry picking, elev. 5000', FREE.
Take US 26 northeast 21 miles and FSR 848 north .5 mile.

ELK CREEK (Malheur NF) 🔺 RV
5 units, trailers to 22', no water, stream, fishing, adjacent to N. Fork Malheur River, hiking, elev. 5000', FREE.
Take US 26 east 13 miles to Prairie City, South Shore River Rd. south 8.3 miles, FSR 13 southeast 16 miles, and FSR 16 south 1.3 miles.

INDIAN SPRINGS (Malheur NF) 🔺

10 tent sites, primitive, hiking trails, stream, wilderness access, 6000', FREE.
Take US 26 east 13 miles to Prairie City, South Shore River Rd. south 11 miles, FSR 14 southeast 11 miles, FSR 16 west 11.3 miles, and FSR 1640 north 6.5 miles.

JOHN DAY TRAILER PARK (Private) RV

5 units w/hookups for water/elec./sewer, no tents, reservations (541)575-1557, trailers to 50', laundry, near John Day River, small pets okay, restrooms closed in winter, $15/night.
Located in John Day, at 660 W. Main.

LITTLE CRANE (Malheur NF) 🔺 RV

5 units, trailers to 32', stream, fishing, hiking tail, elev. 5500', FREE.
Take US 26 east 13 miles to Prairie City, South Shore River Rd. south 8.3 miles, FSR 13 south 16 miles, and FSR 16 south 5.7 miles.

MAGONE LAKE (Malheur NF) 🔺 RV

25 units, some trailers to 18', picnic area, piped water, lake - speed limits, boat launch, boating, fishing, swimming, hiking trails, elev. 5000', FREE.
Take US 26 west to Mt. Vernon and head north on US 395 for 9 miles, FSR 36 northeast 8 miles, FSR 3620 north 1.5 miles, and FSR 3618 west 1 mile.

McNAUGHTON SPRING (Malheur NF) 🔺 RV

4 units, trailers to 22', stream, fishing, wilderness access, elev. 4800', FREE.
Take US 26 east 13 miles to Prairie City, Strawberry Rd. south 8.7 miles, and FSR 6001 south .3 mile.

NORTH FORK MALHEUR (Malheur NF) 🔺 RV

5 units, trailers okay, on N. Fork Malheur River, fishing, hiking, elev. 4700', FREE.
Take US 26 east 13 miles to Prairie City, South Shore River Rd. southeast 8.3 miles, FSR 13 southeast 16 miles, FSR 16 south 2 miles, and FSR 1675 south 2.7 miles.

OREGON MINE CAMPGROUND (Malheur NF) 🔺 RV

6 units, trailers to 22', stream, fishing, elev. 4300', FREE.
Take US 26 west of Mt. Vernon 10 miles, FSR 21 south 14 miles, and FSR 2170 northwest 1 mile.

RAY COLE (Malheur NF) 🔺 RV

1 units, trailer to 22', no drinking water, stream, fishing, wilderness access, elev. 4300', FREE.
Take US 395 south 10 miles, FSR 15 southeast 3 miles, and FSR 1510 north 1 mile.

SLIDE CREEK (Malheur NF) 🏕️ RV

1 group site, trailers to 22', stream, fishing, hiking, wilderness access, horse corral, elev. 4900', FREE.
Take US 26 east 13 miles to Prairie City, Strawberry Rd. south 8.7 miles, and FSR 6001 south .6 mile.

STRAWBERRY (Malheur NF) 🏕️ RV

11 units, trailers to 22', piped water, stream, boating, fishing, trailhead to Strawberry Mountain Wilderness, horse corrals, elev. 5700', $3/night.
Take US 26 east 13 miles to Prairie City, Strawberry Rd. south 8.7 miles, and FSR 6001 south 2.3 miles.

TROUT FARM (Malheur NF) 🏕️ RV

9 units, trailers to 22', picnic shelter, piped water, small fishing pond, hiking, elev. 4900', FREE.
Take US 26 east 13 miles to Prairie City, South Shore River Rd. southeast 8.3 miles, and FSR 14 south 6.9 miles. Rough road.

WICKIUP (Malheur NF) 🏕️ RV

9 units, trailers to 18', picnic area, piped water, stream, fishing, elev. 4300', FREE.
Take US 395 south 10 miles and FSR 15 southeast 8 miles.

UNITY

ELDORADO (Wallowa-Whitman NF) 🏕️ RV

Campsites, trailers to 18', no water, picnic area, stream, fishing, elev. 4000', FREE.
Take US 26 southeast 10 miles and FSR 16 southwest 2 miles.

ELK CREEK (Wallowa-Whitman NF) 🏕️ RV

Campsites, no water, fishing, elev. 4500', FREE.
Take Burnt River Rd. west/southwest 6 miles and FSR 6005 southwest 2 miles.

LONG CREEK (Wallowa-Whitman NF) 🏕️ RV

Camp area, trailers to 18', no water, FREE.
Take FSR 1680 south 9 miles.

MAMMOTH SPRINGS (Wallowa-Whitman NF) 🏕️ RV

Camp area, trailers to 18', no drinking water, creek, fishing, elev. 4400', FREE.
Take Burnt River Rd. west/southwest 6 miles and FSR 6005 southwest 2.5 miles.

OREGON (Wallowa-Whitman NF) 🏕️ RV

11 units, trailers to 18', no drinking water, picnic area, hiking, elev. 5000', FREE.
Take US 26 northwest 10.5 miles.

SOUTH FORK (Wallowa-Whitman NF) △ RV
14 units, trailers to 18', piped water, fishing, elev. 4400', FREE.
Take Burnt River Rd. west/southwest 6 miles, and FSR 6005 southwest 1 mile.

STEVENS CREEK (Wallowa-Whitman NF) △ RV
Campsites, no drinking water, fishing, trail, elev. 4500', FREE.
Take Burnt River Rd. west/southwest 6 miles and FSR 6005 southwest 1.5 miles.

UNITY LAKE (Oregon State Park) △ RV
21 sites w/elec., trailers to 50", wheelchair access, trailer waste disposal, boat ramp, fishing, elev. 4000', $10-15/night.
Take US 26 northwest 2.5 miles.

UNITY MOTEL & RV PARK (Private) △ RV
10 sites w/full hookups plus grassy tent area, reservations (541)446-3431, showers/$3, laundry, trailer waste disposal, $5-15/night.
Follow US 26 to the east end of town and park.

WETMORE (Wallowa-Whitman NF) △ RV
16 units, trailers to 18', piped water, picnic area, wheelchair access inc. trail, hiking, elev. 4400', FREE.
Take US 26 northwest 8.2 miles.

YELLOW PINE (Wallowa-Whitman NF) △ RV
21 units, trailers to 18', piped water, picnic area, wheelchair access inc. trails, trailer waste disposal, hiking, elev. 4500', FREE.
Take US 26 northwest 9.2 miles.

HUNTINGTON

FAREWELL BEND (Oregon State Park) △ RV
53 units w/elec., 43 primitive sites, plus group sites, reservations (800)452-5687, maximum site 56', showers, wheelchair accessible, picnic area, trailer waste disposal, river, boat launch, fishing, swimming, Oregon Trail display, open year round, $12-16/night.
Take I-84 southeast 5 miles.

SPRING (BLM) △ RV
14 sites, river, boat ramp, rough road, elev. 2500', $4/night..
Take Snake River Rd. northeast 4 miles.

PAULINA

BIG SPRINGS (Ochoco NF) △ RV
6 units, no water, primitive, elev. 5000', FREE.
Take Paulina-Suplee Rd. east 3.5 miles, Beaver Creek Rd. north 6.6 miles, FSR 42 northwest 14 miles, and FSR 4270 for 2 miles.

FRAZIER (Ochoco NF) 🔺 RV
5 units, trailers to 22', no drinking water, fishing, bicycle path, primitive, elev. 5000', FREE.
Take Paulina-Suplee Rd. east 3.5 miles, Beaver Creek Rd. north 2.2 miles, Puitt Rd east 10 miles, FSR 58 east 6.3 miles, and FSR 1548 northeast 1.1 miles.

MUD SPRINGS (Ochoco NF) 🔺 RV
4 units, trailers to 22', no drinking water, elev. 5000', FREE.
Take Paulina-Suplee Rd. east 3.5 miles, Beaver Creek Rd. north 2.2 miles, Puitt Rd. east 10 miles, FSR 58 east 4.2 miles, and FSR 5840 north 6 miles.

SUGAR CREEK (Ochoco NF) 🔺 RV
20 units, fishing, swimming, handicap access - inc. 3/4 mile trail, hiking, wildlife, elev. 4000', $8/night.
Take Paulina-Suplee Rd. east 3.5 miles, Beaver Creek Rd. north 6.5 miles, and FSR 58 east 1.8 miles.

WOLF CREEK (Ochoco NF) 🔺 RV
12 units, trailers to 22', no drinking water, elev. 4100', $6/night.
Take Paulina-Suplee Rd. east 3.5 miles, Beaver Creek Rd. north 6.6 miles, and FSR 42 north 1.6 miles to campground road.

SENECA

BIG CREEK (Malheur NF) 🔺 RV
14 units, trailers to 22', well, stream, fishing, elev. 5100', FREE.
Take FSR 16 east 20.5 miles and FSR 815 north .5 mile; campground is on edge of Logan Valley.

MURRAY (Malheur NF) 🔺 RV
5 units, trailers to 22', stream, fishing, hiking, elev. 5200', FREE.
Take FSR 16 east 19 miles and FSR 934 north 2 miles.

PARISH CABIN (Malheur NF) 🔺 RV
17 units plus 3 group areas, trailers to 22', picnic area, piped water, stream, fishing, elev. 4900', FREE.
Take FSR 16 east 12 miles.

STARR (Malheur NF) 🔺 RV
8 units, trailers, no water, picnic area, elev. 5100', $5/night.
Take US 395 north 9.1 miles.

ONTARIO

COUNTRY CAMPGROUNDS (Private) 🔺 RV
15 sites w/full hookups, tents okay, reservations (541)889-6042, showers, laundry, waste disposal, hiking, fishing, $7-10/night.
Located 2 miles west of the Ontario airport, at 660 Sugar Ave.

IDLE WHEELS VILLAGE (Private) `RV`
6 units w/full hookups, no tents, reservations (541)889-8433, showers, laundry, trailer waste disposal, $15/night.
Located in town, at 198 SE 5th St.

COUNTY FAIRGROUNDS (Malheur County) `A` `RV`
Open camping area - 20 sites w/elec., tents okay, information (541)889-3431, restrooms, trailer waste disposal, $5/night.
Located at 795 NW 9th St.

VALE

BULLY CREEK RESERVOIR (Malheur County) `A` `RV`
66 units - 64 w/elec., information (541)473-2969, showers, trailer waste disposal, lake, swimming, boat launch, fishing, swimming, $6-8/night.
Follow Graham Blvd. west 9 miles to reservoir and park.

LAKE OWYHEE (Oregon State Park) `A` `RV`
40 units - 10 w/elec, reservations (800)452-5687, max. site 55', picnic area, showers, trailer waste disposal, boat launch, fishing, open March-Nov., $13-15/night.
Follow Lake Owyhee State Park Rd south 41 miles.

LAKE OWYHEE RESORT (Private) `A` `RV`
61 units w/hookups for water & elec., tents okay, trailers to 35', reservations (541)339-2444, groceries, lake, boat launch & rental, tackle shop, swimming, fishing, open April thru Nov., $10/night.
Follow Lake Owyhee State Park Rd. south 38 miles.

PROSPECTOR RV PARK (Private) `A` `RV`
34 sites w/full hookups plus tent area, reservations (541) 473-3879, showers, laundry, ice, trailer waste disposal, $5-18/night.
Take US Hwy. 26 north .1 mile to Hope St. - park is 1 block east.

SIMPSON'S RV PARK (Private) `A` `RV`
30 pull thru campsites - 20 w/full hookups plus 10 w/water & elec., tents okay, trailer waste disposal, $10-12/night.
Drive southeast to Nyssa - located at 489 Columbia Ave.

SNIVELY HOT SPRINGS (BLM) `A` `RV`
Primitive campsite clearing, no water, hot spring, FREE.
Take Lake Owyhee State Park Rd. south about 29 miles. Located 1 mile south of the Lower Owyhee Watchable Wildlife Site.

SUCCOR CREEK (Oregon State Park) `A` `RV`
19 units, no drinking water, picnic area, hiking, rockhounding, wildlife viewing area, colorful rock formations, $9/night.
Take Lake Owyhee State Park Rd. south 15 miles, go east 2 miles to State 201 and head south 13 miles south to Succor Creek State Recreation Area Rd. - park is southwest 16.5 miles.

TWIN SPRINGS (BLM)

5 units, no drinking water, picnic sites, open May thru Oct., rough road, elev. 3200', FREE.
Take US 20 west 3.5 miles and Dry Creek Rd. south 34 miles.

WESTERNER RV PARK (Private)

15 units w/full hookups - some w/cable, tents okay, reservations (541)473-3947, showers, laundry, trailer waste disposal, on river, fishing, pets okay, $10/night.
Located at the junction of US Hwy. 20 and US Hwy. 26.

JUNTURA

CHUKAR PARK (BLM)

18 units,trailers okay, on Beulah Reservoir, swimming, hiking, elev. 3100', $4/night.
Take US 20 west 4 miles, and Beulah Res. Rd. north 6 miles.

OASIS CAFE/MOTEL/RV PARK (Private)
22 trailer sites w/hookups for water/elec./sewer plus grassy tent area, reservation information (541)277-3605, showers, North Fork Malheur River, fishing, elev. 2900', pets okay, $12/night.
Located right on US 20, in Juntura.

JORDAN VALLEY

LESLIE GULCH (BLM)
8 units, no drinking water, picnic sites, on Owyhee River, boat ramp, swimming, elev. 2800', FREE.
Take US 95 north 18 miles and Leslie Gulch Rd. west 25 miles.

ROME CAMPGROUND (BLM)
5 units, drinking water, picnic facilities, Owyhee River, boat ramp, open March thru Nov., pets okay, elev. 3400', FREE.
Take US 95 west toward Rome; located adjacent to the boat ramp.

BURNS

CHICKAHOMINY REC. SITE (BLM)
Open camp area, drinking water, handicap access, firepits, picnic tables, lake - water level varies by season, boat ramp, fishing, wildlife viewing, open April thru Sept., $4/night.
Take US 20 west 34 miles.

CRYSTAL CRANE HOT SPRINGS CAMP (Private)
6 units w/hookups for elec. plus large tent area, reservations (541)493-2312, showers, horse corrals, cabins, pond, hiking, pets okay, $8-12/night.
Take State 78 east 25 miles.

DELINTMENT LAKE (Ochoco NF) ⚠ RV
29 units, trailers to 32', well water, pit toilets, wheelchair access inc. fishing dock, boat launch, pets okay, elev. 5600', $8/night.
Go northwest on FSR 47 for 15 miles, and FSR 41 for approximately 30 miles to lake and campground.

EMIGRANT (Ochoco NF) ⚠ RV
7 units, no potable water, fly fishing, hiking, pets okay, elev. 5100', $5/night.
Go northwest on FSR 47 for 15 miles, and FSR 41 for 20 miles.

FALLS (Ochoco NF) ⚠ RV
6 units, well water, pit toilets - handicap access, stream, fishing, pets okay, elev. 5000', $6/night.
Go northwest on FSR 47 for 15 miles, and FSR 41 for 18 miles.

HINES MOBILE HOME PARK (Private) ⚠ RV
9units w/full hookups plus grassy tent area, trailers to 70', reservations (541)573-3955, pull thrus, showers, laundry, trailer waste disposal, pets okay, $8-15/night.
Take US 395/20 south 2 miles to Hines - at 12671 Hwy. 20.

IDLEWILD (Malheur NF) ⚠ RV
24 sites, trailers to 32', piped water, picnic area, elev. 5300', FREE.
TAke US 395 north 17 miles.

ROCK SPRINGS (Malheur NF) ⚠ RV
8 units, trailers to 22', water, elev. 5000', FREE.
Take US 395 north 33.8 miles, FSR 17 east 4.5 miles, and FSR 054 southeast 1 mile.

SANDS OVERNIGHT TRAILER PARK (Private) ⚠ RV
26 units - 10 pull-thrus w/hookups for water/elec./sewer plus 6 tent sites, information (541)573-7010, showers, nearby golf & fishing, $10/night.
Take US 395/20 south 1 mile to park.

VILLAGE RV PARK (Private) RV
41 units w/hookups for water/elec./sewer, no tents, reservations (541)573-7640, showers, laundry, playground, propane, nearby fishing, small pets okay - limit two @ 20 lbs. or less, $20/night.
Take US 395/20 northeast to Seneca Dr. - at 1273 Seneca Dr.

YELLOW JACKET (Malheur NF) ⚠ RV
20 units, trailers to 22', piped water, lake - speed limits, boat launch, swimming, fishing, elev. 4800', FREE.
Take US 20 south 1 mile, FSR 47 northwest 32 miles, FSR 37 east 4 miles, and FSR 3745 south .5 mile.

FRENCHGLEN

FISH LAKE (BLM)
23 sites - trailers to 22', pit toilets - accessible, lake - no motors, fishing, hiking, corral, grey water station, elev. 7500', camp host July thru Oct., $4/night.
Follow Steens Mountain Loop east 17 miles.

JACKMAN PARK (BLM)
6 units, handicap access, hiking, grey water station, elev. 8100', camp host July thru Aug., $4/night.
Follow Steens Mountain Loop east 20 miles.

PAGE SPRINGS (BLM)
36 sites, trailers to 24', pit toilets - accessible, drinking water, fire pits, borders wildlife refuge, fishing, hiking, water & camp host May thru Oct., grey water station, elev. 4339', summer camp host, $4/night.
Located 4 miles southeast of Frenchglen, via Steens Mtn. Loop Road, on the Blitzen River.

SOUTH STEENS (BLM) 🄰 RV
21 sites - 15 w/horse hitches, drinking water, pit toilet - accessible, picnic tables, grey water station, wildlife viewing, hiking & horse trails, horse ramp, nearby fishing, elev. 5300', open May thru October, camp host in summer, $4/night.
Follow Steens Mountain Loop east 28 miles - near Donner und Blitzen River.

STEENS MT. RESORT/CAMPER CORRAL (Private) 🄰 RV
90 sites - 45 w/full hookups, 45 w/water & elec., plus large group tent area, some pull thrus, reservations (541)493-2415, showers, laundry, fire pits, trailer waste disposal, groceries, hiking, fishing, pets okay, elev. 4100', $10-15/night.
Located just south of the Frenchglen Hotel.

ADEL

ADEL STORE & RV PARK (Private) RV
7 trailer sites w/hookups for water/elec./sewer, reservations (541)947-3850, groceries & hot food, nearby fishing, located 25 miles south of Hart National Antelope Refuge, $15/night.
This park is located in right Adel, next to grocery store.

WASHINGTON'S CAMPGROUNDS

Tenters will enjoy Washington's wealth of natural campsites; those traveling by RV will be thrilled with its luxurious resorts. Everyone will find plenty of places to choose from, no matter where their travels take them.

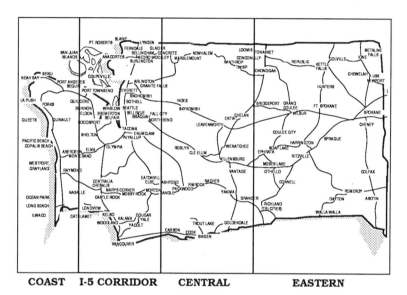

COAST   I-5 CORRIDOR   CENTRAL   EASTERN

THE WASHINGTON COAST

The northern portion of Washington's Pacific Ocean coastline harbors America's last unspoiled wilderness beach. Together, the Olympic National Park and Olympic National Forest protect most of the north coast's best features. This area has lush rain forests, old growth forests, wildlife refuges, great whale watching, hiking trails, and high-mountain lakes.

Along the southern Washington coast you'll encounter the world's longest driveable beach, a couple of wonderful old forts, aging lighthouses, colorful cranberry bogs, charter fishing boats, and lots of great beachcombing areas.

WASHINGTON'S I-5 CORRIDOR

A journey along I-5 provides access to several of the state's best-known attractions. These include Mt. St. Helens, where you can see an active volcano up close; Mt. Rainier

National Park, which protects the 14,410' Mt. Rainier; Puget Sound; and the spectacular San Juan Islands.

History buffs will enjoy Port Townsend, Coupeville, Snohomish, Fort Lewis and Olympia. At 55-65 mph it all goes by in a quick blur, but anyone taking the time to leave the freeway will find plenty of great camping spots.

CENTRAL WASHINGTON

Heading east over the Cascade Mountains, toward Central Washington, you'll find a slightly drier climate. These mountains do not run due north and south, so you'll find some of the cities in this section are actually on upper the western slopes.

The full glory of the Cascade Loop unfolds here. Most of the land it passes is protected by National Forests and Parks. Along the way, you'll have the chance to visit pristine wilderness areas, hike a multitude of trails, cruise a 55-mile long lake, and watch bald eagles. The town of Winthrop looks like a town out of the old west, and Leavenworth resembles a Bavarian village.

EASTERN WASHINGTON

In eastern Washington you'll find a dry, desert climate. That's probably why some of this region's most popular campgrounds are those along the Snake, Columbia and Pend Oreille Rivers. Lake Conconully, Roosevelt Lake and Potholes Reservoir are also good places to cool off.

This region is where you'll find the state's largest limestone cave, the reconstructed 1880 Fort Spokane, tragic Whitman Mission, remnants of the Ice Age Missoula Flood, and the Ginkgo Petrified Forest.

WASHINGTON COAST
CAMPGROUNDS

See Page

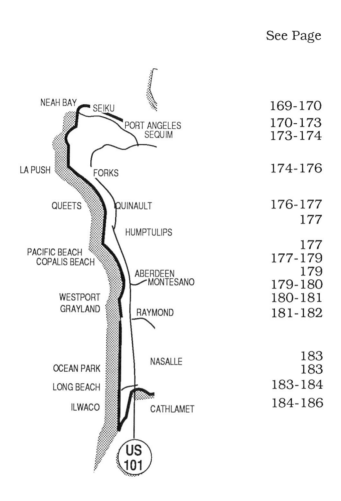

NEAH BAY

CAPE MOTEL & RV PARK (Private)
54 units w/full hookups, information (360)645-2250, tent area, trailers to 70', showers, laundry, trailer waste disposal, fishing, hiking, pets okay, $12-16/night..
Located in Neah Bay, just past the museum on Bayview Ave.

HOBUCK BEACH PARK (Private)
28 units, tents okay, reservations (360)645-2422, trailers to 30', on bay, fishing, hiking, pets okay, $10/night.
Located 3 miles southwest of town, on bay.

TYEE MOTEL & RV PARK (Private)
20 pull thrus w/full hookups, tents okay, reservations (360)645-2223, trailers to 30', showers, trailer waste disposal, fishing, pets okay, open mid-April thru mid-Sept., $15/night.
Located right in Neah Bay.

SEIKU

BAYVIEW RV PARK (Private)
39 units w/full hookups plus tent area, reservations (360)963-2750, trailers to 40', showers, laundry, wheelchair access, fishing, pets okay, $8-13/night.
Located right in Seiku, on Airport Rd.

COHO RESORT (Private)
150 units - 44 w/full hookups, 50 w/water & elec., plus 56 tent sites, information (360)963-2333, trailers to 50', showers, laundry, ice, trailer waste disposal, fishing, boat launch/rental & gas, pets okay, open March thru Oct., $18/night.
Located at Seiku's east end.

CURLEY'S RESORT (Private)
10 sites w/full hookups plus dry camp, tents only w/rv, reservations (800)542-9680, on Strait of Juan de Fuca, trailers to 22', scuba shop & tours, $10 pet fee, open April thru Oct., $15/night.
Located right in Seiku.

MURALT'S MH/RV/CABINS (Private)
8 units w/full hookups plus 3 tent sites, reservations (360)963-2394, trailers to 40', showers, laundry, fishing, hiking, pets okay, $4-16/night.
Located 4 miles east of Seiku, in Clallam Bay.

OLSON'S RESORT (Private)
50 w/full hookups, 10 w/elec., 90 dry sites, tents okay, reservations (360)963-2311, trailers to 40', showers, laundry, wheelchair access, groceries, fishing, boat launch/gas & rental, $12/night.
Located right in Seiku.

OZETTE (Olympic NP) [A]
15 tent sites - walk-in, hiking, beach access, elev. 80', $10/night. Located at Ozette Lake; take State 112 west 2.8 miles and Hoko/Ozette Rd. southwest.

PILLAR POINT (Clallam County) [A] [RV]
37 primitive sites, flush toilets, picnic shelter, small-boat launch & dock, fishing, open May thru Sept., $10/night. Take State 112 west of Seiku 7 miles.

SAM'S TRAILER & RV PARK (Private) [A] [RV]
26 units - 20 w/hookups for water/elec./sewer plus 6 tent sites, reservation (360)963-2402, maximum site 40', 8 pull thrus, showers, laundry, ocean access, boat launch & moorage, fishing, pets okay, $10-14/night.
Located 4 miles east of Seiku, at the east end of Clallam Bay.

SURFSIDE CAMPLAND (Private) [A] [RV]
20 units - 10 w/full hookups plus 10 tent sites, reservations (360)963-2723, trailers to 40', showers, laundry, trailer waste disposal, fishing, pets okay, open May thru Sept., $10-14/night. Located right in Seiku.

TRETTEVIKS TRAILER PARK (Private) [A] [RV]
29 w/hookups for water/elec./sewer plus 20 tent sites, information (360)963-2688, trailers to 70', on Strait of Juan de Fuca, fishing, sandy beach, pets okay, $14-18/night. Take State 112 west of Seiku 3 miles.

VAN RIPER'S RESORT & RV PARK (Private) [A] [RV]
52 units - 42 w/hookups for water & elec. plus 10 tent sites, information (360)963-2334, showers, wheelchair access, snacks, ice, trailer waste disposal, fishing, boat launch & rental, salmon charters, pets okay, open March thru Sept., $11-16/night. Located right in Seiku.

PORT ANGELES

AL'S RV PARK (Private) [A] [RV]
31 units w/full hookups plus tent area, reservations (360)457-9844, trailers to 40', pull thrus, showers, laundry, wheelchair access, game room, playground, trailer waste disposal, nearby fishing & hiking, pets okay, $12-19/night.
US 101 east 1.5 miles, Lee's Creek Rd. north .3 mile.

ALTAIRE (Olympic NP) [A] [RV]
30 campsites, trailers to 21', handicap accessible restrooms, on Elwha River, elev. 450', open June thru Sept., $10/night. US 101 west 7 miles, Olympic Hot Springs Rd. south 5 miles.

ARNEY'S DAM RV PARK (Private) 🏕️ [RV]
37 units w/hookups for water/elec./sewer plus grassy tent area, reservations (425)452-7054, trailers to 40', showers, wheelchair access, propane, pets okay, $12-17/night.
Take US 101 west 5 mile, and State 112 west to Lower Dam Rd.

CAROL'S CRESCENT BEACH RV PARK (Private) 🏕️ [RV]
60 units w/hookups for water/elec./sewer, tents okay, reservations (360)928-3344, trailers to 35', showers, groceries, laundry, ocean beach, swimming, fishing, pets okay, $25/night.
US 101 west 5 miles, State 112 west 6.5 miles to Joyce, Crescent Beach Rd. north 3 miles.

CONESTOGA QUARTERS RV PARK (Private) 🏕️ [RV]
34 units w/hookups for water/elec./sewer, plus 11 w/out hookups, tents okay, reservations (800)808-4637, trailers to 40', showers, wheelchair access, playground, trailer waste disposal, charter fishing, pets okay, $16-20/night.
Take US 101 east 7 miles, and Seibertt Creek Rd. 1 mile to park.

DEER PARK (Olympic NP) 🏕️
18 tent sites, water, elev. 5400', $6/night.
Take US 101 east 6 miles and follow Blue Mountain Rd. south 18 miles to its end.

ELMER'S TRAILER PARK (Private) [RV]
12 units w/hookups for water/elec./sewer, no tents, reservations needed - (360)457-4392, trailers to 70', pets okay, $16/night.
Follow US 101 east 1.5 miles.

ELWHA (Olympic NP) 🏕️ [RV]
41 campsites, trailers to 21', handicap accessible restrooms, on Elwha River, hiking, elev. 390', $10/night.
US 101 west 7 miles, Olympic Hot Springs Rd. south 3 miles.

FAIRHOLM CAMPGROUND (Olympic NP) 🏕️ [RV]
87 units, trailers to 21', handicap access, trailer waste disposal, on Crescent Lake, swimming, fishing, boat launch & rental, hiking, elev. 580', $10/night.
Take US 101 west 26 miles.

HARRISON BEACH (Private) 🏕️ [RV]
12 units, information (360)928-3006, trailers to 32', on water, surf fishing, hiking, pets okay - $2 fee, rock hunting, seal & whale watching, $12-16/night..
Take US 101 west 5 miles, State 112 west 15 miles, West Lyre River Rd. to Harrison Beach Rd. and camp.

HEART O' THE HILLS (Olympic NP) 🏕️ [RV]
105 units, trailers to 21', wheelchair access, hiking, elev. 1807', $10/night.
Leave US 101 on Race St., and follow south 6 miles.

INDIAN VALLEY MOTEL/RV/CAMP (Private)   ⚠️ RV
8 units w/full hookups plus tent area, (360)928-3266, trailers to 30', shower, restaurant, pets okay, $8-12/night.
Take US 101 west 13 miles.

KLAHOWYA (Olympic NF)   ⚠️ RV
55 units, trailers to 30', reservations (800)280-2267, flush toilets, handicap access, river, ramp, fishing, hiking, elev. 800', $12/night.
Take US 101 west 40 miles to milepost #212 and campground.

LINCOLN PARK (City)   ⚠️ RV
35 units, trailers to 25', information (425)452-2928, flush toilets, showers, wheelchair access, pets okay, open summer only, $10/night.
Take US 101 west 5 miles, and State 112 just west of junction.

LYRE RIVER (DNR)   ⚠️ RV
11 sites, drinking water, covered picnic shelter, fishing, FREE.
Take US 101 west 5 miles and follow State 112 west 17 miles to the Lyre River and campground.

LYRE RIVER PARK (Private)   ⚠️ RV
44 w/hookups for water/elec./sewer, 32 w/water & elec., plus tent sites, reservations (360)928-3436, showers, laundry, wheelchair access, groceries, trailer waste disposal, on Lyre River - inner tubing, fishing, hiking, pets okay, $14-25/night.
Take US 101 west 5 miles, State 112 west 15 miles, and West Lyre River Rd. north .5 mile.

PEABODY CREEK RV PARK (Private)   ⚠️ RV
36 units w/hookups for water/elec./sewer plus tent area, reservations (800)392-2361, trailers to 35', showers, laundry, propane, creek, pets okay, $12-20/night.
Located in Port Angeles - at 127 South Lincoln.

PORT ANGELES KOA (Private)   ⚠️ RV
100 units - 20 w/full hookups, 50 w/water/elec./tv, plus 30 tent sites, (360)457-5916, trailers to 50', showers, laundry, wheelchair access, pool, playground, groceries, propane, trailer waste disposal, pets okay, open April thru Oct., $21-27/night.
Take US 101 east 5 miles - located at O'Brien.

SALT CREEK REC. AREA (Clallam County)   ⚠️ RV
90 units, information (360)928-3441, trailers to 70', flush toilets, showers, wheelchair access, trailer waste disposal, boat ramp, swimming, fishing, hiking, pets okay, $8-10/night.
Take US 101 west 5 miles, State 112 west 9 miles, and Camp Hayden Rd. north 3.5 miles.

SHADOW MOUNTAIN (Private)
60 units - 40 w/hookups for water/elec./sewer plus 20 tent sites, reservations (360)928-3043, trailers to 70', showers, laundry, wheelchair access, playground, store, propane, gas, trailer waste disposal, at Crescent Lake, boat launch, swimming, fishing, hiking, pets okay, $13-19/night.
Take US 101 west 15 miles.

SOL DUC HOT SPRINGS RESORT (Private)
20 units w/hookups for water & elec., no tents, reservations (425)327-3583, no restrooms, trailers to 28', hot springs extra, restaurant, groceries, open daily mid May thru Sept. - weekends only April & Oct., $17/night.
US 101 west 28 miles, Soleduck River Rd. southeast 12 miles.

SOLEDUCK (Olympic NP)
80 units, group area, trailers to 21', handicap access, trailer waste disp., on river, swimming, fishing, hiking, elev. 1680', $12/night.
US 101 west 28 miles, Soleduck River Rd. southeast 12 miles.

WELCOME INN TRAILER & RV PARK (Private)
75 trailer sites w/full hookup, no tents, reservations (360)457-1553, trailers to 70', pull thrus, showers, laundry, wheelchair access, trailer waste disposal, pets okay, $20/night.
Located near the west end of Port Angeles, on US 101.

WHISKEY CREEK BEACH (Private)
15 sites w/hookups for water & sewer plus 38 w/out hookups, tents okay, reservations (360)928-3489, trailers to 26', fishing, hiking, pets okay, open May thru Oct., $10-12/night.
Take US 101 west 5 miles, State 112 west 9.5 miles, and Whiskey Creek Beach Rd. north to campground.

SEQUIM

DUNGENESS FORKS (Olympic NF)
9 tent sites, stream, fishing, hiking elev. 1000', $8/night.
US 101 east 4 miles, FSR 28 to FSR 2880, and south 7.5 miles.

DUNGENESS REC. AREA (Clallam County)
65 units, information (360)683-5847, trailers to 40', showers, wheelchair access, playground, trailer waste disposal, pond, boat launch, swimming, fishing, hiking, open Feb. thru Oct., $10 and up/night.
Take US 101 west 7 miles, and Kitchen Rd. north 4 miles.

EAST CROSSING (Olympic NF)
9 tent sites, stream, fishing, hiking, elev. 1200', $8/night.
US 101 east 4 miles, FSR 28 to FSR 2860, and south 9 miles.

RAINBOW'S END RV PARK (Private)   🏕 RV
38 units w/full hookups inc. cable, a few pull-thrus plus tent area, (360)683-3863, trailers to 40', showers, laundry, wheelchair access, propane, trailer waste disposal, pets okay, $14-21/night. West of Sequim. US 101 west 1.5 miles.

SEQUIM BAY (WA State Park)   🏕 RV
86 units - 26 w/hookups for water/elec./sewer plus 60 standard sites, trailers to 60', accessible showers, trailer waste disposal, boat launch, moorage buoys, fishing, scuba diving, $10-16/night. Take US 101 east 4 miles.

SEQUIM BAY RESORT (Private)   RV
43 units w/full hookups, no tents, (425)681-3853, trailers to 40', accessible showers, laundry, fishing, pets okay, $16/night. Take West Sequim Bay Rd. northwest 2.5 miles.

SEQUIM WEST RV PARK & INN (Private)   RV
29 units w/full hookups, no tents, reservations (360)683-4144, trailers to 65', showers, ice, motel, pets okay, $19/night. Located at 740 West Washington (US 101).

SOUTH SEQUIM BAY RV PARK (Private)   🏕 RV
30 units - 24 w/hookups for water/elec./sewer plus 6 w/water, tents okay, reservations (360)683-7194, trailers to 40', showers, trailer waste disposal, pets okay, $11-18/night. US 101 east 5 miles, and Old Blyn Highway northeast .3 mile.

SUNSHINE RV PARK (Private)   🏕 RV
57 units w/hookups for water/elec./sewer plus tent area, reservations (360)683-4769, trailers to 40', pull thrus, showers, laundry, stream, pets okay, $15-20/night. West of Sequim. US 101 west 4 miles.

LA PUSH

LAPUSH OCEAN PARK RESORT (Private)   RV
55 units w/hookups for water & elec., no tents, reservations (800)487-1267, trailers to 50', showers, laundry, wheelchair access, propane, trailer waste disposal, ocean access, fishing, hiking, pets okay, $15/night. Located right in La Push.

MORA CAMPGROUND (Olympic NP)   🏕 RV
94 campsites plus walk-in group site, group res. (360)374-5460, trailers to 21', handicap access, trailer waste disposal, ocean access, on Quinault River, swimming, fishing, hiking,$10/night - group site $20 plus $1/person. Located right in La Push.

174

OCEAN PARK/SHORELINE RESORT (Private) `RV`
55 units w/hookups for water & elec., no tents, reservations (800)487-1267, trailers to 50', showers, laundry, wheelchair access, surf fishing, hiking, pets okay, $15/night. Located right in La Push.

THREE RIVERS RESORT (Private) `A` `RV`
5 sites w/full hookups, 9 w/water & elec. plus 10 tent sites, reservations (360)374-5300, showers, laundry, cabins, playground, groceries, propane, restaurant, pets okay, $8-12/night. Take La Push Rd. east 6 miles.

FORKS

BEAR CREEK (DNR)
10 campsites, no drinking water, hiking, fishing, FREE. Take US 101 northeast 15 miles to milepost #206; campground is 2 miles east of Sappho on Hoh River Rd.

BOGACHIEL (WA State Park) `A` `RV`
42 units - 6 w/hookups for water & elec. plus 36 standard sites, trailers to 35', flush toilets, showers, comm. kitchen, trailer waste disposal, on river, fishing, $7-16/night. Take US 101 south 6 miles.

COTTONWOOD (DNR)
9 sites, no drinking water, river, boat ramp, hiking, fishing, FREE. Take US 101 south 13 miles, Oil City Rd. for 4 miles, and Road H-4060 .9 mile.

FORKS MOBILE HOME & RV PARK (Private) `RV`
7 trailer sites w/full hookups, reservations (360)374-5510, trailers to 32', laundry, no dogs, $12/night. Leave US 101 on Calawah Way and go east 3 blocks to park.

FORKS 101 RV PARK (Private) `A` `RV`
40 w/full hookups plus tent area, reservations (360)374-5073, sites to 70', pull thrus, showers, laundry, some pets, $16-24/night. Located right in Forks, on US 101.

HARD RAIN CAFE & RV PARK (Private) `A` `RV`
7 units w/hookups for water/elec./sewer plus 6 w/water & elec., tents okay, reservations (360)374-9288, trailers to 35', cafe, showers, wheelchair access, pets okay, $13-15/night. Take US 101 south 13 miles, and Lower Hoh Rd. west 6 miles.

HOH RIVER (Olympic NP) `A` `RV`
89 units, trailers to 21', handicap access, trailer waste disposal, river, fishing, hiking, elev. 578', $10/night. Take US 101 south 14 miles, and Hoh River Rd. east 19 miles.

HOH RIVER RESORT & RV PARK (Private)

20 w/full hookups, 4 w/water & elec., grassy tent area, reservations (360)374-5566, showers, laundry, groceries, propane, river trail, fishing, hiking, pets okay, $15/night.
Follow US 101 south 15 miles.

HOH OXBOW (DNR)

8 campsites, picnic area, river, boat ramp, fishing, FREE.
Take US 101 south 14 miles; located on north side of Hoh bridge, at milepost #176.

MINNIE PETERSON (DNR)

8 campsites, no drinking water, river, FREE.
Take US 101 south 12 miles and Upper Hoh Rd. east 4.5 miles.

SOUTH FORK HOH (DNR)

3 campsites, river, FREE.
Take US 101 south 14 miles, Hoh-Clearwater Mainline Rd. east 6.6 miles, and Road H-1000 north 7.4 miles.

WILLOUGHBY CREEK (DNR)

3 campsites, river, fishing, FREE.
Take US 101 south 2 miles and Upper Hoh Rd. east 3.5 miles.

YAHOO LAKE (DNR)

4 walk-in campsites, trails, fishing, FREE.
Take US 101 south 14 miles, Hoh-Clearwater Mainline Rd. east 12.5 miles, Road C-3000 north 4.8 miles, Road C-3100 east 5.5 miles, and keep left .6 mile to trailhead.

QUEETS

COPPERMINE BOTTOM (DNR)

9 campsites, picnic shelter, boat ramp, fishing, hiking, FREE.
Take US 101 southeast 5.4 miles, Clearwater Rd. north 12.6 miles, and Road C-1010 for 1.5 miles.

KALALOCH (Olympic NP)

175 units plus small group site, group reservations (360)962-2283, handicap access, trailer waste disp., fishing, hiking, elev. 50', $12/night - groups $20 +$1/person.
Take US 101 north of Queets 6 miles.

UPPER CLEARWATER (DNR)

9 campsites, no drinking water, picnic shelter, boat ramp, fishing, FREE.
Take US 101 southeast 5.4 miles, Clearwater Rd. north 12.9 miles, and Road C-3000 for 3.2 miles.

QUINAULT

FALLS CREEK (Olympic NF)
31 units, trailers to 16', flush toilets, wheelchair access, on Lake Quinault, boat ramp, swimming, fishing, hiking, $7-13/night. Take South Shore Rd. northeast .2 mile.

GATTON CREEK (Olympic NF)
5 tent sites, on Lake Quinault, swimming, fishing, $7-10/night. Take South Shore Rd. northeast .5 mile.

RAIN FOREST RESORT VILLAGE & RV PARK (Private)
31 units w/hookups for water & elec., no tents, information (253)288-2535, trailers to 38', showers, laundry, groceries, restaurant, on Lake Quinault, swimming, fishing, hiking, canoe rental, pets okay, $16/night. Take South Shore Rd. northeast 1.5 miles.

WILLABY (Olympic NF)
22 units, trailers to 16', flush toilets, on Lake Quinault, boat ramp, swimming, fishing, hiking, $13/night. Take South Shore Rd. northeast .5 mile.

HUMPTULIPS

CAMPBELL TREE GROVE (Olympic NF)
11 units, trailers to 16, pit toilets, well, stream, fishing, hiking, primitive, elev. 1100', FREE. Take US 101 northeast 4 miles and follow FSR 2204 northeast 21.5 miles to campground.

PACIFIC BEACH

PACIFIC BEACH (WA State Park)
138 units - 20 w/hookups for water & elec. plus 188 standard sites, reservations (800)452-5687, trailers to 45', flush toilets, showers, trailer waste disposal, fishing, beachcombing, clamming, $10-16/night. Located at Pacific Beach, just off State 109.

COPALIS BEACH

BLUE PACIFIC MOTEL & RV PARK (Private)
19 units - 13 w/hookups for water/elec./sewer plus 6 w/water & elec., tents okay, reservations (360)289-2262, trailers to 38', showers, laundry, pets okay, $14-17/night. Take State 109 south of town 2.5 miles.

COPALIS BEACH SURF/SAND RV PARK (Private) 🔺 RV
43 units w/full hookups, 5 w/water & elec., plus tent area, reservations (800)867-2707, trailers to 40', showers, wheelchair access, playground, restaurant/lounge, trailer waste disposal, fishing, hiking, pets okay, $15-22/night.
Located in Copalis Beach, on beach access road.

DUNES RV RESORT (Private) 🔺 RV
29 units w/full hookups, 9 w/water & elec., plus 6 tent sites, (360)289-3873, trailers to 50', accessible showers, trailer waste disposal, fishing, hiking, pets okay, $9-19/night.
Located on State 109, near milepost #20.5.

ECHOES BY THE SEA (Private) 🔺 RV
28 units w/water/elec./tv, plus 7 w/out hookups, tents okay, (360)289-3358, showers, trailer waste disposal, $12-16/night.
Located on State 109, just north of the Copalis Beach bridge.

OCEAN CITY (WA State Park) 🔺 RV
29 units w/hookups for water/elec./sewer plus 149 campsites, group reservations (800)452-5687, trailers to 55', flush toilets, showers, disabled access, trailer waste disp., fishing, $10-16/night.
Take State 109 south 5.5 miles.

SILVER MAPLE RV PARK (Private) RV
30 units w/full hookups, reservations (360)289-0166, trailers to 40', showers, pets okay, $15/night.
Take State 109 south 3.5 miles.

RIVERSIDE RV RESORT (Private) 🔺 RV
67 units w/hookups for water/elec./sewer plus tent area, reservations (360)289-2111, showers, hot tub, trailer waste disposal, river, boat ramp, fishing, pets okay, $17/night.
Located on State 109, just north of the Copalis Beach bridge.

ROD'S BEACH RESORT & RV PARK (Private) RV
80 units w/full hookups, no tents, reservations (360)289-2222, trailers to 40', showers, rec room, pool, playground, store, motel, trailer waste disposal, fishing, pets okay, open March thru Oct., $17/night.
On State 109, just south of Copalis Beach.

TIDELANDS ON THE BEACH RV PARK (Private) 🔺 RV
16 units w/hookups for water/elec./sewer, 39 w/water & elec., plus 50 tent sites, (360)289-8963, trailers to 40', showers, trailer waste disposal, pets okay, $12-16/night.
Take State 109 south .6 mile.

STURGEON TRAILER HARBOR (Private)   A RV

54 units w/hookups for water/elec./sewer plus 16 w/water & elec., no tents, reservations (360)289-2101, trailers to 35', showers, propane, horses & pets okay, $12/night.
Take State 109 south 3 miles to Ocean City and park.

ABERDEEN

ARCTIC RV PARK (Private)   A RV

10 units w/full hookups plus 15 w/water/elec./tv, roomy tent area, reservations (360)533-4470, trailers to 50', showers, laundry, wheelchair access, trailer waste disposal, fishing, hiking trail, pets w/approval, $10-14/night.
Take US 101 south to milepost #75 and park.

MONTESANO

CHETWOOT (Olympic NF)   A

8 tent sites, hike-in or boat-in only, lake, primitive, swimming, fishing, waterskiing, hiking trails, elev. 800', FREE.
Take Wynoochee Lake Rd./FSR 22 north 33 miles, FSR 23 north 2.5 miles, and Trail #878 east .5 mile.

COHO (Olympic NF)   A RV

58 campsites, trailers to 36', flush toilets, wheelchair access, on Wynoochee Lake, paved nature trail, elev. 900', $8-12/night.
Wynoochee Lake Rd./FSR 22 north 32 miles, and FSR 23 north 1.5 miles.

LAKE SYLVIA (WA State Park)   A RV

35 campsites plus group area, group reservations (425)249-3621, maximum site 30', flush toilets, showers, disabled access, community kitchen, snack bar, groceries, trailer waste disposal, on lake, boat launch & rental, fishing, swimming, $10/night - groups $20 +$1/person.
Leave State 12 on the Lake Sylvia park road at Montesano.

SCHAFER (WA State Park)   A RV

55 units - 6 w/hookups for water & elec. plus 47 standard sites, trailers to 40', flush toilets, showers, community kitchen, trailer waste disposal, on river, fishing, $10-15/night.
Take State 12 east 5 miles, and Satsop River Rd. north 5 miles.

TENAS (Olympic NF)   A

9 tent sites, hike-in or boat-in only, lake, no picnic tables, swimming, fishing, hiking trails, elev. 800', FREE.
Take Wynoochee Lake Rd./FSR 22 north 32 miles, FSR 2202 north 2 miles, and Trail #878 about .5 mile west.

WYNOOCHEE FALLS (Olympic NF)

12 tent sites, river, fishing, elev. 1000', FREE.
Take Wynoochee Lake Rd./FSR 22 north 44.2 miles, and FSR 2312 northeast 10 miles.

WESTPORT

COHO RV PARK (Private)

76 units w/full hookups, no tents, reservations (800)572-0177, trailers to 60', pull thrus, showers, laundry, wheelchair access, ice, large meeting room w/kitchen, fishing & charter, crab pot & fish cleaning room, pets okay, $20/night.
Located in Westport, in the dock area.

GRIZZLY JOE'S RV PARK (Private)

36 units w/hookups for water/elec./sewer, no tents, reservations (360)268-5555, trailers to 40', showers, laundry, wheelchair access, boat dock, fishing, hiking, pets okay, $18/night.
Located at end of town, at 743 Neddie Rose Dr.

HAMMOND RV PARK (Private)

35 units w/hookups for water/elec./sewer, no tents, reservations (360)268-9645, trailers to 40', showers, laundry, nearby stores/restaurants/fishing, pets okay, $12/night.
From city center take Montesano St. south 1 mile - park is at 1845 Roberts Rd.

HOLAND CENTER RV PARK (Private)

80 rv sites w/full hookups, reservations (360)268-9582, trailers to 38', showers, laundry, pets okay, $17/night.
Located on State 105, 2 blocks off docks.

ISLANDER RV PARK (Private)

55 units w/hookups for water/elec./sewer, no tents, reservations (360)268-9166, trailers to 40', pull thrus, showers, laundry, wheelchair access, ice, swimming pool, coffee shop, lounge, meeting room, waterfront sites, ocean access, fishing & charter, fish cleaning area, pets okay, $18/night.
On Revetment Dr., at northwest end of the boat basin.

JOLLY ROGERS (Private)

30 units w/full hookups, tents okay, reservations (360)268-0265, trailers to 40', showers, on jetty, harbor & surf fishing, salmon fishing off private dock, moorage, pets okay, $16-18/night.
Located in the dock area, on the north side of the boat basin.

KILA HANA CAMPERLAND (Private)

70 units w/full hookups, 40 w/elec., plus 50 tent sites, reservations (360)268-9528, trailers to 60', pull thrus, showers, wheelchair access, rec hall, propane, trailer waste disposal, fishing, hiking, pets okay, $9-17/night.

Located 1 mile north of the State 105/105 spur intersection, at 931 S. Forrest Ave.

PACIFIC AIRE RV PARK (Private)
120 units w/full hookups plus large tent area, reservations (800)569-2267 or (360) 268-0207, trailers to 40', showers, laundry, wheelchair access, pool, propane, pets okay, $14-18/night. Located in dock area, at 1209 N. Montesano St.

PACIFIC MOTEL & RV PARK (Private)
80 units w/full hookups inc. cable, plus 10 tent sites, reservations (360)268-9325, trailers to 40', pull thrus, showers, heated pool, laundry, rec room, $13-18/night.
On State 105, just south of town.

TOTEM RV PARK (Private) 🅰️ RV
46 units w/full hookups, 70 w/water & elec., 6 w/water, grassy tent area, reservations (360)268-0025, trailers to 40', showers, laundry, groceries, drive-in restaurant, trailer waste disposal, fishing, pets okay, $15-17/night.
Located in the dock area.

TWIN HARBORS (WA State Park) 🅰️ RV
49 units w/hookups for water/elec./sewer plus 272 standard sites, reservations (800)452-5687, group reservations (360)268-9717, trailers to 35', flush toilets, showers, disabled access, trailer waste disposal, fishing, hiking, $10-16/night.
Located on State 105, 3 miles south of town.

GRAYLAND

BAYSHORE RV PARK (Private) 🅰️ RV
44 units w/full hookups plus 6 w/water & elec., tents okay, reservations (800)638-7555 or (425)267-2625, trailers to 40', showers, trailer waste disposal, ocean, fishing, pets okay, $15-24/night.
Take State 105 south 8 miles, and Tokeland Rd. southeast 2 miles to Tokeland - located at 2941 Kindred.

GRAYLAND BEACH (WA State Park) 🅰️ RV
60 units w/hookups for water/elec./sewer, reservations (800)452-5687, trailers to 40', flush toilets, showers, disabled access, self-guided trail, beachcombing, fishing, $15/night.
Located in Grayland, on State 105.

KENANNA RV PARK (Private) 🅰️ RV
90 pull thrus w/full hookups plus 20 tent sites, reservations (800)867-3515, showers, wheelchair access, laundry, rec room, playfield, playground, ball courts, mini golf, groceries, camping cabins, ice, propane, trailer waste disposal, ocean access, sandy beach, fishing, pets okay, $14-18/night.
Located on State 105, 2 miles south of town.

OCEAN GATE RESORT (Private)   🏕️ RV
48 units - 24 w/full hookups plus 24 tent sites, reservations (425)267-1956, trailers to 40', showers, playground, ocean access, surf fishing, pets okay, $13-19/night.
Located in Grayland, on State 105.

ROAMER'S ROOST RV PARK (Private)   🏕️ RV
41 units w/full hookups inc, cable plus 8 w/water & elec., tents okay, adult park, reservations (800)438-1474, trailers to 50', showers, laundry, pets okay, open mid-May thru mid-Sept., $17-20/night.
Leave State 105 on Schmid Rd., park is east .1 mile.

WESTERN SHORES MOTEL /RV PARK (Private)   🏕️ RV
21 units w/full hookups, tents okay, reservations (425)267-6115, trailers to 40', showers, laundry, pets okay, $13/night.
Located in Grayland, on State 105.

WILLAPA RV PARK (Private)   🏕️ RV
48 units w/full hookups plus 13 tent sites, reservations (425)267-7710, trailers to 35', showers, laundry, wheelchair access, small store w/sandwiches, on bay, fishing, pets okay, $12-17/night.
Take State 105 south 8 miles, and Tokeland Rd. south 2 miles.

RAYMOND

BAY CENTER KOA (Private)   🏕️ RV
10 units w/full hookups, 34 w/water & elec., 16 tent sites plus bicycle camp w/shelter, reservations (253)875-6344, trailers to 40', showers, laundry, game room, small store, propane, playground, playfield, trailer waste disposal, sandy beach, fishing, hiking, pets & horses okay, open March thru Oct., $18-24/night.
Take US 101 southwest 15.5 miles, Bay Center Rd. west 3 miles.

SOUTH BEND MOBILE & RV PARK (Private)   🏕️ RV
10 units w/full hookups plus tent area, reservations (253)875-5165, trailers to 50', pull thrus, showers, laundry, trailer waste disposal, pets okay, $5-15/night.
Take US 101 south 5 miles to South Bend - park is located 4 blocks from downtown, at 524 Central.

TIMBERLAND RV PARK (Private)   🏕️ RV
24 pull thrus w/hookups for water/elec./sewer plus tent area, reservations (253)942-3325, showers, pets okay, $9-15/night.
State 105 west .2 mile to Crescent St., park is 2 blocks south.

WILLAPA HARBOR GOLF & RV (Private)   RV
20 units w/hookups for water/elec./cable, no tents, reservations (253)942-2392, trailers to 50', showers, wheelchair access, golf, trailer waste disposal, pets okay, $17/night.
Take Fowler St. off US 101 and follow 2 miles to golf course.

NASALLE

CHINOOK RV PARK/CAMPGROUND (Private)
64 sites w/full hookups, 16 w/out hookups, 20 tent sites, reservations (360)777-8475, showers, laundry, picnic facilities, groceries & tackle, trailer waste disposal, across street from Columbia River, fishing, pets okay, $10-25/night.
Take State 401 south 9 miles.

NASALLE TRAILER COURT (Private)
24 trailer sites w/hookups for water/elec./sewer, no tents, reservations (360)484-3351, showers, laundry, $10-15/night.
Located on State 4 just east of town.

OCEAN PARK

CLAM TIDE RV PARK (Private)
16 units w/hookups for water/elec./sewer plus 4 tent sites, reservations (425)665-3545, trailers to 36', showers, laundry, wheelchair access, near ocean, no dogs, $10/night.
Located at 25210 Vernon Ave.

EVERGREEN COURT (Private)
34 units w/full hookups plus dry camp, tents okay, reservations (425)665-6351, showers, trailer waste disposal, $10-13/night.
Take State 103 south 1 mile.

OCEAN AIRE TRAILER PARK (Private)
46 units w/full hookups, no tents, trailers to 35', reservations (425)665-4027, showers, laundry, well mannered pets okay, $15/night.
Leave State 103 on 260th St., and go east .1 mile.

OCEAN PARK RESORT (Private)
80 units w/full hookups plus tent area, reservations (425)665-4585, showers, laundry, rec room, pool in summer, spa, playground, ice, propane, pets okay, $15/night.
Leave State 103 on 259th St., and go east .1 mile.

WESTGATE RV PARK & MOTEL (Private)
39 units w/full hookups (11 pull-thrus), no tents, reservations (425)665-4211, showers, ocean fishing, pets okay, $17-18/night.
Take State 103 south 2 miles to Klipsan Beach.

LONG BEACH

ANDERSEN'S ON THE OCEAN (Private)
59 units w/full hookups plus 15 tent sites, reservations (800) 645-6795, trailers to 70', showers, laundry, playground, rec. hall,

cable tv, group facilities, propane, trailer waste disposal, nearby surf fishing, hiking, pets okay, $14-18/night.
Take State 103 north 3.5 miles.

ANTHONY'S HOME COURT (Private)   RV

25 units w/hookups for water/elec./sewer, reservations (360)642-2802, showers, laundry, pets okay, $15-18/night.
Located at 1310 Pacific Highway North.

CRANBERRY RV & TRAILER PARK (Private)   RV

24 units w/full hookups, no tents, adults only, reservations (360)642-2027, trailers to 40', pull thrus, showers, rec room w/tv, ice, walk to beach, fishing, hiking, pets okay, open March thru Oct., $12/night.
Take State 103 north 3 miles, and Cranberry Rd. east .3 mile.

DRIFTWOOD RV PARK & MOTEL (Private)   RV

56 units w/full hookups, some pull-thrus, group facilities, reservations (360)642-2711, showers, cable tv, laundry, picnic area, near Columbia River & fishing, pets okay, $18/night.
In Long Beach, on State 103.

MA & PA'S PACIFIC RV PARK (Private)   [A] RV

44 sites w/full hookups, 6 w/water & elec, plus grassy tent area, (360)642-3253, showers, laundry, near ocean, pets okay - $2 fee, $19/night.
Take State 103 north 2 miles.

OCEAN BAY MOBILE/RV PARK (Private)   [A] RV

15 units w/full hookups plus 10 tents sites, reservations (425)665-6933, showers, nearby grocery store, pets okay, $10-15/night.
Located north of Long Beach at 2515 Bay Ave.

OCEANIC RV PARK (Private)   RV

20 sites w/full hookups, no tents, reservations (360)642-3836, showers, wheelchair access, pets okay, $15/night.
Located at the corner of Pacific and Fifth Sts.

PEGG'S OCEANSIDE RV PARK (Private)   RV

30 units w/full hookups, no tents, reservations (360)642-2451, showers, laundry, rec room, ocean access, pets okay, $14-18/night.
Take State 103 north 4.5 miles.

PIONEER RV PARK (Private)   [A] RV

34 units w/full hookups, grassy tent area, reservations (360)642-3990, trailers to 35', showers, walk to ocean, hiking, near stores & restaurant, pets okay, $15-17/night.
On State 103, at north end of town.

SAND CASTLE RV PARK (Private)
38 units w/hookups for water/elec./sewer, no tents, reservations (360)642-2174, showers, laundry, ocean access, $18-23/night. On State 103, at north end of town.

SAND-LO MOTEL & TRAILER PARK (Private)
15 units w/hookups for water/elec./sewer plus 4 tent sites - no fire pits, reservations (800)676-2601, showers, laundry, nearby groceries & restaurant, 4 blocks to beach, fish cleaning area, pets okay, $12-16/night.
North of Long Beach. State 103 north 1 mile.

SOU'WESTER LODGE & TRAILER PARK (Private)
50 units w/hookups for water/elec./sewer/cable tv, tenters welcome, reservations (360)642-2542, showers, laundry, o/n trailer rental, ocean access, fishing, $16-26/night.
Located south of Long Beach, in Seaview, on Seaview Beach Rd.

WILDWOOD RV PARK (Private)
50 units - 30 w/hookups for water/elec./sewer plus 20 tent sites, reservations (360)642-2131, showers, picnic area, trailer waste disposal, private lake, game area, fishing, $15-17/night.
Take State 103 south to junction with US 101, US 101 east .5 mile, and Sandridge Rd. north .8 mile to park.

ILWACO

BEACON RV PARK (Private)
60 units - 40 w/full hookups plus 20 w/elec. only, no tents, reservations (360)642-2138, trailers to 40', showers, ice, on Columbia River, fishing & charters, hiking, nearby shops, pets okay, $18-20/night.
Located in Ilwaco, at the east end of docks.

CHINOOK BAIT/TACKLE & RV (Private)
100 units - 75 w/water & elec. plus grassy tent area, reservations (360) 777-8475, showers, laundry, trailer waste disposal, picnic area, near river, small pets okay, $12-16/night.
Take State Hwy. 401 3 miles north of junction with US Hwy. 101.

COVE RV PARK (Private)
43 units w/full hookups (6 pull-thrus), some tent sites, reservations (360)642-3689, showers, laundry, trailer waste disposal, ocean access - by Baker Bay, fishing, pets okay, $15/night.
Located in Ilwaco, at the west end of port area.

FORT CANBY (WA State Park)
60 sites w/hookups for water/elec./sewer plus 190 standard units, reservations (800)452-5687, trailers to 45', flush toilets, showers, disabled access, trailer waste disposal, Lewis & Clark

Trail Interpretive Center, boat launch, ocean fishing, hiking, $10-16/night.
Follow signs southwest 2.5 miles.

ILWACO KOA (Private) 🔺 RV

200 campsites - 36 w/hookups for water/elec./sewer, 90 w/elec. only, plus 74 tent units, reservations (360)642-3292, showers, laundry, playground, rec room, groceries, propane, trailer waste disposal, creek, ocean access, pets okay, $20-26/night.
Located on US 101, about halfway between Ilwaco and Chinook.

MAUCH'S SUNDOWN RV PARK (Private) 🔺 RV

40 units w/hookups for water/elec./sewer plus 10 w/water & elec., tents okay, reservations (360)777-8713, showers, laundry, trailer waste disposal, on river, fishing, pets okay, $8-15/night.
Take US 101 southeast 8.5 miles - located just west of the Astoria Bridge.

RIVER'S END RV (Private) 🔺 RV

100 units - 20 w/hookups for water/elec./sewer, 40 w/water & elec., plus grassy tent area, reservations (360)777-8317, showers, laundry, rec room, playground, trailer waste disposal, river, fishing, $14-18/night.
Take US 101 east 4.3 miles.

SNAG LAKE (DNR) 🔺 RV

4 campsites, picnic area, lake, hiking, FREE.
Take US 101 northeast 16 miles, State 4 east 4.3 miles, C-Line up the hill .9 mile north, Road C-4000 east 1.4 miles, and Road C-2600 north .8 mile to campground road.

TUNERVILLE (DNR) 🔺 RV

3 campsites, horse corral, stream, hiking & horse trails, FREE.
Take State 401 to State 4 and go east 3.5 miles, and Salmon Creek Rd. northeast 8.5 miles. Stay left at the fork for 1 mile.

WESTERN LAKES (DNR) 🔺 RV

3 campsites, picnic area, fishing, hiking tails, FREE.
Take US 101 northeast 16 miles, State 4 east 4.3 miles, C-Line up the hill .9 mile north, Road C-4000 east 1.4 miles, and Road C-2600 north .9 mile to campground road.

CATHLAMET

SKAMOKAWA VISTA PARK (Private) 🔺 RV

23 rv sites w/hookups for elec. & cable, plus space for 15 w/out hookups, tents okay, reservations (360)795-8605, group area available, trailers to 40', wheelchair accessible restrooms, showers, play area, ball courts & field, on Columbia River, fishing, swimming, pets okay - no leash law, $10-17/night.
Take State 4 west 7 miles to Skamokawa and park.

WASHINGTON I-5 CORRIDOR CAMPGROUNDS

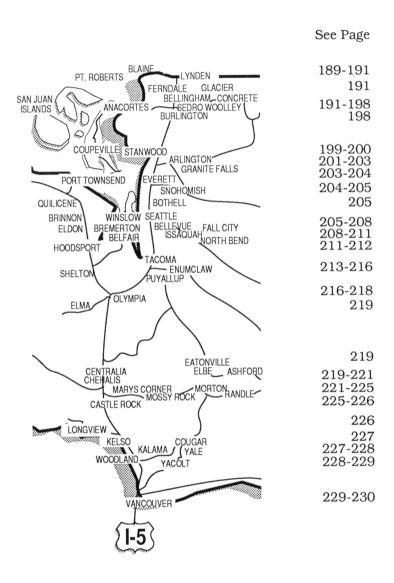

BLAINE

BALL BAY VIEW RV PARK (Private)
42 units w/hookups for water/elec./sewer, 7 w/water & elec., plus tent area, reservations (253)371-0334, trailers to 38', showers, laundry, small pets okay, $12-19/night.
Take I-5 to exit #270, go west 4 miles, and take Birch Bay Dr. south 2 miles to Jackson Rd. - located at 7387 Jackson Rd.

BEACHSIDE RV PARK (Private)
26 units w/hookups for water/elec./sewer plus 15 tent sites, reservations (253)371-5962, trailers to 40', showers, laundry, trailer waste disposal, pets okay, $13-20/night.
Take I-5 to exit #270, go west 4 miles, and take Birch Bay Dr. south to 7630 Birch Bay Dr.

BELAIR TRAILER COURT (Private)
4 units w/hookups for water/elec./sewer, no tents, reservations (425)332-8633, trailers to 50', showers, laundry, trailer waste disposal, pets okay, $12/night.
Take the first Blaine exit off I-5 and head toward town.

BIRCH BAY (WA State Park)
167 units - 20 w/hookups for water & elec., 147 standard sites plus group area, reservations (800)452-5687, sites to 70', flush toilets, showers, disabled access, trailer waste disposal, scuba diving area, fishing, hiking, $10-15/night.
Take I-5 to exit #270, go west 4 miles, and take Birch Bay Dr. south 3 miles to park.

BIRCH BAY RESORT PARK (Private)
442 trailer sites - 337 w/full hookups plus 40 w/out hookups,no tents, reservations (253)371-7922, cable, showers, laundry, rec room, activities, propane, trailer waste disposal, swimming, fishing, $17-25/night.
Take I-5 to exit #270, go west about 4 miles, and then south to 8080 Harborview Rd.

EVERGREEN MANOR & RV PARK (Private)
16 units w/hookups for water/elec./sewer, no tents, reservations (360)384-1241, trailers to 35', showers, laundry, wheelchair access, pets okay, weekly only - $70.
Take I-5 to exit #266, Grandview Rd. east .5 mile, and Enterprise Rd. .01 mile to park.

PLAZA RV & MOBILE HOME PARK (Private)
20 units w/full hookups, 20 w/water & elec. plus 22 tent sites, reservations (253) 371-7822, trailers to 50', showers, laundry, small pets okay, close to bay - crabbing & fishing, nearby waterslides, $14-16/night.
Take I-5 to exit #270 and Birch Bay-Lynden Rd. east 2 miles.

POINT ROBERTS

LIGHTHOUSE MARINE PARK (Whatcom County) [A] [RV]
30 tent/trailer sites, information (360)945-4911, beach, lookout tower, on Strait, boat ramps, fishing, clamming, $10/night. Located at 811 Marine Dr.

WHALEN'S RV PARK (Private) [A] [RV]
50 RV sites w/hookups for water & elec., plus large tent/dry camp, reservations (253)945-2874, trailers to 70', accessible showers, trailer waste disposal, ocean access, fishing, pets okay, open May thru Sept., $13-18/night.
Take Roosevelt Rd. east 1 mile to park.

LYNDEN

BERTHUSEN PARK (City) [A] [RV]
25 units w/hookups for water & elec. plus dry sites, tents okay, information (360)354-2424, trailers to 50', trailer waste disposal, old growth, stream, fishing, hiking, pets okay, open April thru Oct., $10-15/night.
Follow signs from downtown - located on Berthusen Rd.

HIDDEN VILLAGE RV PARK (Private) [A] [RV]
25 pull thrus w/hookups for water/elec./sewer, 38 w/water & elec., plus tent area, reservations (360)398-1041, showers, laundry, trailer waste disposal, pets okay, $10-20/night.
Take State 539 south 3 miles.

LYNDEN KOA (Private) [A] [RV]
45 sites w/full hookups, 25 w/water & elec., plus 30 tent sites, reservations (425)354-4772, pull thrus, showers, laundry, playground, swimming pool, groceries, restaurant, propane, trailer waste disposal, pond fishing, boat rental, miniature golf, pets okay, $23-28/night.
Take State 546 east 3 miles and Line Rd. south 1.5 miles.

SILVER LAKE PARK (Whatcom County) [A] [RV]
50 units w/hookups for water & elec. plus 30 w/out hookups, tents okay, information (360)599-2776, trailers to 36', showers, wheelchair access, trailer waste disposal, on lake, swimming beach, boat launch/moorage & dock, fishing, canoe & paddleboat rentals, horse stalls, pets okay, $10-15/night.
Take State 546 east 5 miles, State 9 south 3 miles, South Pass Rd. east 17 miles and Silver Lake Rd. south 3 miles..

SUMAS RV PARK (Private) [A] [RV]
19 units w/full hookups, 10 w/water & elec., 10 w/out hookups, plus tent area, reservations (360)988-8875, trailers to 35', accessible showers, laundry, trailer waste disposal, pets okay, $8-17/night.

Take State 546 east 5 miles, State 9 north to Sumas, and Cherry St. .01 mile to campground.

WINDMILL INN MOTEL & RV PARK (Private)　　　RV
8 units w/full hookups inc. cable, no tents, reservations (425)354-3424, trailers to 35', showers, telephone hookups, pets okay, $18/night.
Located on Front St.

FERNDALE

THE CEDARS RV RESORT (Private)　　　A　RV
72 units w/full hookups, 33 w/water & elec., 8 w/elec., plus lots of dry & tent sites, reservations advised (360)384-2622, pull thrus, cable tv & telephone hookups, showers, laundry, pool, game room, playfield, playground, groceries, trailer waste disposal, pond, pets okay, $17-26/night.
Leave I-5 on exit #263 and take Portal Way north 1 mile.

GLACIER

DOUGLAS FIR (Mt. Baker-Snoqualmie NF)　　　A　RV
30 campsites, reservations (800)280-CAMP, trailers to 26', picnic area, community. kitchen, Nooksack River, fishing, hiking, elev. 1000', pets okay, $12/night.
Take State 542 east 2 miles.

EXCELSIOR CAMP (Mt. Baker-Snoqualmie NF)　　　A　RV
1 group site, reservations (800)280-2267, not recommended for trailers, no water, on N. Fork Nooksack River, fishing, pets okay.
Take State 542 east 7 mile.

SILVER FIR (Mt. Baker-Snoqualmie NF)　　　A　RV
21 campsites, trailers to 32', res. (800)280-CAMP, picnic area, community kitchen, Nooksack River, fishing, elev. 2000', pets okay, $12/night.
Take State 542 east 12.5 miles.

SAN JUAN ISLANDS

BLIND ISLAND (WA State Park)　　　A
4 tent sites, boat-in only, buoys, primitive, no drinking water, beach access, $6/night.
Blind Island is located north of Shaw Island.

CLARK ISLAND (WA State Park)　　　A
8 boat-in campsites, no water, mooring buoys, tide pools, hiking, fishing, scuba diving, $6/night.
Clark Island is 1.8 miles off the northeast tip of Orcas Island.

191

CYPRESS ISL.~CYPRESS HEAD (DNR)
5 boat-in sites, picnic area, rest rooms, mooring buoys, FREE.
On Cypress Island.

CYPRESS ISL.~PELICAN BEACH (DNR)
4 sites - boat-in or hike-in only, picnic area & shelter, restrooms, buoys, hiking trails, open Feb. thru mid July, FREE.
On Cypress Island, 4 miles north of Cypress Head, on northeast side. To hike in, take trail out of Cypress Head Campground for 1.2 miles.

DOE ISLAND (WA State Park)
5 boat-in campsites, no water, small secluded island, floats, fishing, scuba diving, hiking, $6/night.
Doe Island is just a short distance from Orcas Island's Doe Bay.

HOPE ISLAND (WA State Park)
5 tent sites, boat-in only, no drinking water, primitive, $6/night.
Hope Island is located in Skagit Bay, 2 miles north of the entrance to Swinomish Bay, near Whidbey Island.

JAMES ISLAND (WA State Park)
13 campsites, boat-in only, buoys, no drinking water, picnic facilities, hiking trails, scuba diving, $6/night.
Located on James Island.

JONES ISLAND (WA State Park)
21 boat-in campsites, mooring buoys, picnic facilities, fishing, scuba diving, hiking, $6/night.
Jones Island is 1 mile west of Orcas Island's southwest tip.

LOPEZ ISL.~ODLIN PARK (WA State Park)
30 units, boat launch, fishing, hiking, $13-15/night.
Lopez Island is accessible via the Anacortes ferry - park is 1.3 miles south of the ferry landing.

LOPEZ ISL.~SPENCER SPIT (WA State Park)
34 units, group area - reservations & rates (800)452-5687, trailers to 20', disabled access, trailer waste disposal, fishing, $11/night.
Park is located on the northeast side of Lopez Island.

LUMMI ISLAND CAMPGROUND (DNR)
5 campsites, boat-in only, buoys, restroom, FREE.
Located on southeast tip of Lummi Island, 1 miles south of Reil Harbor.

MATIA ISLAND (WA State Park)
6 boat-in campsites, no water, mooring buoys, fishing, scuba diving, tide pools, short trail, $6/night.
Matia Island is 2.5 miles north of Orcas Island.

ORCAS ISL.~DOE BAY VILLAGE RESORT (Private)
3 reservable sites w/elec., 22 w/out hookups plus 13 walk-in tent sites, reservations (360)376-2291 - fee, trailers to 32', showers, wheelchair access, hot tub, mineral baths, sauna, natural foods cafe/store, fishing, hiking, pets off-season only, $12 and up.
Orcas Island is accessible via the Anacortes ferry - follow the main road and signs toward Olga.

ORCAS ISL.~MORAN (WA State Park)
151 campsites, reservations (800) 452-5687, trailers to 45', flush toilets, showers, disabled access, trailer waste disposal, boat launch & rental, fishing, located on Mt. Constitution, $11/night.
On northeast side of Orcas Island, past Eastsound.

ORCAS ISL.~OBSTRUCTION PASS (DNR)
9 campsites, boat-in or hike-in only, 2 buoys, hiking trails, FREE.
Campground is on Orcas Island, 5 miles southwest of Rosario. To hike in: leave Olga on Doe Bay Rd., head east .6 mile, turn right on Obstruction Pass Rd. for .7 mile keeping right at the Y and go an additional .8 mile to parking lot. Follow trail .5 mile.

ORCAS ISL.~OBSTRUCTION PASS (DNR)
2 campsites, boat-in only, rest rooms, view of Canadian Gulf Islands, FREE.
Campground is on north end of Orcas Island, 3 miles northwest of Eastsound. Check navigational map for objects and currents.

ORCAS ISL.~WEST BEACH RESORT (Private)
35 units w/hookups for water & elec. plus 35 tent sites, reservations (877)937-8224 or (360)376-2240, trailers to 50', showers, laundry, wheelchair access, hot tub, meeting room, playground, groceries, marina, scuba air, trailer waste disposal, swimming, fishing, boat launch & rental, hiking, pets w/fee, $18-30/night.
On Orcas Island, 3.5 miles west of Eastsound.

PATOS ISLAND (WA State Park)
4 boat-in campsites, no water, mooring buoys, fishing, scuba diving, tide pools, $6/night.
Patos Island is 5.5 miles north of Orcas Island.

POSEY ISLAND (WA State Park)
Primitive boat-in camping, no water, fishing, scuba diving, tide pools, $5/night.
Posey Island is just north of San Juan Island's Roche Harbor.

SADDLEBAG ISLAND (WA State Park)
5 tent sites, boat-in only, primitive, no drinking water, fishing, beachcombing, crabbing, $6/night.
Saddlebag Island is 2 miles northeast of Anacortes, at the north end of Padilla Bay.

SAN JUAN ISL.~LAKEDALE CAMPGROUND (Private) 🔺 RV

125 units - 18 w/hookups for water & elec., 82 dry/tent sites, 15 site bicycle camp, group sites, reservations (800)617-CAMP, trailers to 50', showers, wheelchair access, cabins, store, 3 lakes, swimming, fishing, boat & bicycle rental, pets okay - fee, open mid March thru mid Oct., $24-28/night - bicycle camp $6-8/person. San Juan Island is accessible via Anacortes ferry, then follow Roche Harbor Rd. 4 miles north of Friday Harbor.

SAN JUAN ISL.~PEDAL INN BICYCLE CAMP (Private) 🔺

25 walk-in tent sites, no parking - bicycle/hikers only, information (360)378-3049, showers, laundry, small store, no ground fires, pond, fishing, hiking, no pets, open April thru Oct., $5/night.
On San Juan Island - take Cattle Point Rd. 4 miles, turn right on False Bay Dr. and follow signs.

SAN JUAN COUNTY PARK (County) 🔺 RV

20 sites, picnic area, reservations (360)378-2992, trailers to 25', flush toilets, handicap access, boat ramp, pets okay, $16/night.
On San Juan Island - take 2nd St. to West Valley Rd., go 6 miles to Mitchell Bay Rd. and follow 4 miles to park.

SAN JUAN ISL.~SNUG HARBOR (Private) 🔺 RV

4 waterfront rv sites - 2 w/water & elec., plus dry/tent area, reservations only - (360)378-4762, trailers to 25', showers, groceries, propane, marina, boat & kayak rental, boat launch & dock, fishing, whale watching tours, events, swimming, hiking, pets - $5/fee, $20-40/night - $10-25 off-season.
On San Juan Island - take Beaverton Valley Rd. 8 miles west of Friday Harbor to Mitchell Bay and marina.

SHAW ISL.~SOUTH BEACH (Island County) 🔺 RV

11 units plus overflow area - 2 sites will take small trailers, small boat launch, beach, good biking, $10-12/night.
Shaw Island is accessible via Anacortes ferry. Take road to first left and turn onto paved road - park is .5 mile.

SKAGIT ISLAND (DNR) 🔺

Boat-in camping, no facilities on shore, mooring buoys, $4/night.
Island is located in Skagit Bay.

STRAWBERRY ISLAND (DNR) 🔺

3 campsites, boat-in only, restrooms, FREE.
Island is located .5 mile west of Cypress Island. Strong currents & submerged rocks make this spot accessible only to low draft skiffs and kayaks - check navigational charts.

STUART ISLAND (WA State Park) 🔺

19 primitive boat-in sites, mooring buoys & floats, no drinking water, fishing, $5/night.
Stuart Island is northwest of San Juan Island.

SUCIA ISLAND (WA State Park)

51 primitive boat-in sites, mooring buoys & floats, no drinking water, picnic shelter, scuba diving area, fishing, $5/night.
Sucia Island is about 2.5 miles north of Orcas Island.

TURN ISLAND (WA State Park)

10 primitive boat-in sites, mooring buoys, no drinking water, fishing, trails, $5/night.
Turn Island is east of San Juan Island's Friday Harbor.

ANACORTES

ANACORTES RV PARK (Private)

50 units w/hookups inc. cable & telephone, tent area, reservations (360)293-3700, trailers to 35', showers, laundry, pets extra, $12-17/night.
Located at 1225 State Highway 20.

LIGHTHOUSE RV PARK (Private)

31 rv sites w/full hookups, no tents, reservations (360) 293-7523, trailers to 31', showers, laundry, pets okay, $20/night.
Follow signs toward ferry - located at 5809 Sands Way.

WASHINGTON PARK (City)

46 units w/hookups for water & elec. plus 24 tent sites, information (360)293-1927, trailers to 70', accessible showers, laundry, trailer waste disposal, swimming, fishing, boat launch, hiking, pets okay, $12-15/night.
Take State 20 to 12th St., go west 2 miles and veer left to park.

BELLINGHAM

EAGLE'S HAVEN RV PARK (Private)
35 sites w/full hookups, tents okay, reservations (360)758-2420, handicap access, showers, conv. store - sandwiches/videos, cable & telephone avail., quiet, city bus, pets okay, $10-18/night.
Leave I-5 at exit 260 and follow signs for 9 miles to 2924 Haxton Way.

LARRABEE (WA State Park)
26 units w/hookups for water/elec./sewer plus 61 standard sites, group area, reservations (800)452-5687 & (360)676-2093, trailers to 60', flush toilets, showers, trailer waste disposal, on Puget Sound, tidal pools, boat launch, fishing, trails, $10-15/night.
Follow State 11 south 7 miles.

WILDWOOD RESORT (Private)
35 sites - 3 w/full hookups, 3 w/water & elec., plus 30 w/out hookups, tents okay, reservations (360)595-2311, flush toilets, trailer waste disposal - fee, rec hall, cabins, groceries, on lake,

boat launch/rental & moorage, fishing, swimming, water skiing, no dogs, $14-20/night.
Take I-5 south to exit #240, Cain Lake Rd. east .5 mile, and head north at the Y for .2 mile to resort.

CONCRETE

BOULDER CREEK (Mt. Baker-Snoqualmie NF) [A] [RV]
8 units plus group area, group reservations (800)280-CAMP, no water, trailers to 16', elev. 1100', pets okay, $7/night - groups $55.
Take State 20 west of town, Burpee Hill/Baker Lake Rd. north 9.6 miles, and FSR 11 north 5.4 miles.

CLARK'S SKAGIT RIVER RV PARK (Private) [A] [RV]
72 units - 38 w/full hookups, 20 w/water & elec., 6 dry sites, plus tent sites, reservations (425)873-2250, showers, laundry, restaurant, river, fishing, hiking, pets okay, $12-25/night.
Take State 20 east 14.5 miles - located 6 miles past Rockport.

CREEKSIDE CAMPING (Private) [A] [RV]
22 units w/full hookups, 2 w/water & elec., plus grassy tent area w/fire pits & tables, reservations (360)826-3566, showers, laundry, groceries, playground, trailer waste disposal, fishing, pets okay, $22/night.
Take State 20 west 7 miles and Baker Lake Rd. north .2 mile.

GRANDY LAKE (Skagit County) [A] [RV]
20 sites, pit toilets, primitive, fishing, hiking, $6/night.
Take State 20 to west 7 miles, Baker Lake Rd. north 4-5 miles and follow signs to Grandy Lake Park.

HORSESHOE COVE (Mt. Baker-Snoqualmie NF) [A] [RV]
34 units plus group area, group reservations (800)280-CAMP, trailers to 22', flush toilets, handicap access, on Baker Lake, boat launch, swimming, fishing, pets okay, $12/night - groups $50.
Take State 20 west of town, Burpee Hill/Baker Lake Rd. north 9.6 miles, FSR 11 north 2.4 miles, and FSR 1118 east 2 miles.

HOWARD MILLER STEELHEAD PARK (County) [A] [RV]
70 units - 60 w/hookups for water & elec. plus 10 tent sites, reservations (253)853-8808, showers, wheelchair access, playground, picnic shelter, trailer waste disposal, river, boat launch, swimming, fishing, hiking, pets okay, $12-18/night.
Take State 20 east 10 miles and follow signs to park.

MAPLE GROVE (Mt. Baker-Snoqualmie NF) [A]
5 tent sites, boat-in or hike-in only, lake, swimming, fishing, water skiing, trails, pets okay, elev. 700', FREE.
Head north off State 20 at milepost #82, heading north 9.6 miles to FSR 11, go north 2.4 miles, east 2 miles on FSR 1106, cross

dam and follow FSR 1107 to trailhead. Hike 3 miles north along
east shore of Baker Lake.

PANORAMA POINT (Mt. Baker-Snoqualmie NF)
15 campsites, trailers to 24', reservations (800)280-CAMP, on
Baker Lake, boat launch, swimming, fishing, water skiing, elev.
700', $7/night.
Take State 20 west of town, Burpee Hill/Baker Lake Rd. north 9.6
miles, and FSR 11 north 6.4 miles.

PARK CREEK (Mt. Baker-Snoqualmie NF)
12 units plus 2 group sites, group reservations (800)280-CAMP,
no water, trailers to 22', elev. 800', pets okay, $7/night.
Take State 20 west of town, Burpee Hill/Baker Lake Rd. north 9.6
miles, FSR 11 north 7.4 miles, and FSR 1144 west .1 mile.

ROCKPORT (WA State Park)
59 units - 50 w/hookups for water/elec./sewer plus 8 standard
sites, group area - reservations (253)853-4705, trailers to 45',
flush toilets, showers, disabled access - inc. old growth trail, picnic shelter, trailer waste disposal, old growth forest, fishing, hiking, pets okay, open April thru mid Nov., $10-16/night.
Take State 20 east 8 miles.

SAUK PARK (Skagit County) RV
20 sites for self-contained units, very primitive, picnic area, fishing, hiking, $6/night.
Take State 20 to west 7 miles, Baker Lake Rd. north 4-5 miles and
follow signs to Grandy Lake Park.

SHANNON CREEK (Mt. Baker-Snoqualmie NF)
19 units, reservations (800)280-CAMP, trailers to 26', on Baker
Lake, boat ramp, water skiing, swimming, fishing, elev. 800',
$12/night.
Take State 20 west of town, Burpee Hill/Baker Lake Rd. north 9.6
miles, FSR 11 north 12.2 miles, and FSR 3830 east .5 mile.

TIMBERLINE RV PARK (Private)
39 units in treed park w/full hookups inc. cable, tents okay,
reservations (360)826-3131, showers, laundry, wheelchair access,
groceries, propane, rec room, playfield, playground, pets okay,
$12-20/night.
Take State 20 west 5 miles, Russell Rd. north to Challenger Rd.,
and go east .3 mile to park - at 736 Wilde Rd.

WILDERNESS VILLAGE (Private)
38 units w/full hookups plus 6 tent sites, reservations (425)873-
2571, showers, laundry, river, fishing, pets okay.
Take State 20 east 14 miles.

SEDRO WOOLLEY

HUTCHINSON CREEK (DNR) 🅰 RV
11 units, picnic area, on creek, FREE.
Take State 9 north 16 miles to Acme, Mosquito Lake Rd. east 2.4 miles, and campground road .4 mile to campground.

RIVERVIEW PARK (Private) RV
6 units w/hookups for water & elec. plus 24 w/out hookups, no tents, reservations (360)595-2672, trailers to 70', wheelchair access, trailer waste disposal - fee, firewood, S. Fork Nooksack River - no motors, fly fishing, swimming, innertube rental, no pets, open April thru Sept., $14-17/night.
Take State 9 north 16 miles to Acme and park.

BURLINGTON

BAY VIEW (WA State Park) 🅰 RV
9 sites w/full hookups plus 67 dry/tent sites, reservations (800)452-5687, trailers to 40', community kitchen, showers, on Padilla Bay, $10-16/night.
Take State 20 west 6 miles; and follow signs 1.3 miles north.

BLAKE'S RV PARK & MARINA (Private) 🅰 RV
29 sites w/full hookups plus 32 dry sites, tents okay, reservations (253)445-6533, trailers to 50', showers, laundry, wheelchair access, propane, on N. Fork Skagit River, boat launch/moorage & dock, fishing, hiking, pets okay, $12-20/night.
Leave I-5 on exit #221 and follow signs 6 miles to park.

BURLINGTON KOA (Private) 🅰 RV
52 units w/full hookups, 10 w/water & elec., 18 w/elec., plus 40 tent sites, reservations (360)724-5511, showers, wheelchair access, laundry, propane, rec. room, cable tv, indoor pool, sauna, hot tub, playground, trailer waste disposal, $17-25/night.
Take I-5 exit #232, Cook Rd. east .2 mile, and Old Highway 99 north 3.5 miles.

LILY~LIZARD LAKES (DNR) 🅰
6 tent sites @ Lily Lake plus 3 hike/horse-in sites @ Lizard Lake, trails, FREE.
Take I-5 north to exit #240, follow Samish Lake Rd. north .5 mile, turn left on Barrel Springs Rd. for 1 mile, take Road SW-C-1000 for 1.5 miles to Lily Lake. Hike or ride 1.7 miles to Lizard Lake.

RIVERBEND PARK (Private) 🅰 RV
75 units w/hookups for water/elec./sewer plus 30 tent sites, reservations (360)428-4044, showers, wheelchair access, laundry, trailer waste disposal, fishing, pets okay, $6-19/night.
Take I-5 exit #227, College Way west to Freeway Dr., and go north .5 mile.

COUPEVILLE

DECEPTION PASS (WA State Park)
246 campsites, trailers to 30', group area - information (360)675-2417, flush toilets, wheelchair access, community kitchen, trailer waste disposal, boat launch/buoys/floats, hiking, swimming, fishing, scuba diving, pets okay, $11/night.
Located 16 miles north of Coupeville, at bridge, on State 20.

FORT CASEY (WA State Park)
38 sites, trailers to 40', flush toilets, wheelchair access, explore old fort, boat launch, fishing, hiking, scuba diving, $11/night.
Take Engle Rd. 3 miles south to west side of island.

FORT EBEY (WA State Park)
50 units, reservations (800)452-5687, trailers to 70', flush toilets, showers, disabled access, historic defense bunker, fishing, hiking, scuba diving, $11/night.
Located on the west side of island, 6 miles from Coupeville.

ISLAND COUNTRY FAIRGROUND (Private)
50 units w/hookups for water & elec. plus large tent area, reservations (360)221-4677, trailers to 70', showers, wheelchair access, near town, box stalls for horses, pets okay, $10-15/night.
Take State 20 south 5 miles, State 525 south 18 miles, and head north 4 miles to Langley - located at 819 Camano Ave.

JAMES ISLAND (WA State Park) 🔺
13 boat-in campsites, no water, mooring buoys, fishing, scuba diving, short trail, $6/night.
From Deception Pass State Park, boat north - James Island is near northeast tip of Decatur Island.

MUTINY BAY RESORT (Private) RV
25 units w/hookups for water/elec./sewer, no tents, reservations (360)331-4500, trailers to 30', showers, ice, ocean access, swimming, fishing, pets okay, $20/night.
Located south of Coupeville, in Freeland - take Fish Rd. south 1 mile, and follow Mutiny Bay Rd. to resort.

NORTH WHIDBEY RV PARK (Private) 🔺 RV
100 units w/full hookups plus 10 tent sites, reservations (360)675-9597, trailers to 70', showers, near laundry, wheelchair access, play area, pets okay, no dogs in tent area, $20-22/night.
Located 16 miles north of Coupeville, on the north end of island.

OAK HARBOR CITY BEACH (City) 🔺 RV
56 units w/hookups for water & elec. plus overflow & tent area, information (360)679-5551, showers, tennis, playground, trailer waste disposal, reservable kitchen area, ocean access, swimming - lifeguard area in summer, fishing, boat launch, pets okay, $8-15/night.

Take State 20 north toward Oak Harbor - campground is just south of Oak Harbor, at Pioneer Rd.

RHODODENDRON (DNR) 🅰 [RV]
6 sites, water, picnic area, handicap access, hiking trails, FREE. Take State 525 southeast 2 miles.

SOUTH WHIDBEY (WA State Park) 🅰 [RV]
56 campsites, trailers to 45', showers, disabled access, group sites, reservations (800)452-5687, picnic area, trailer waste disposal, scuba diving, fishing, hiking, $11/night.
Take State 20 south 5 miles, State 525 south 6 miles, and take the road leading southwest toward the water and campground.

STANWOOD

CAMANO ISLAND (WA State Park) 🅰 [RV]
87 units, group area - reservations (360)387-3031, trailers to 45', flush toilets, showers, trailer waste disposal, boat launch, fishing, scuba diving area, nature trail, $11/night.
Take State 532 west 5 miles to Camano Island, and head south 7 miles to this state park campground.

CEDAR GROVE SHORES RV PARK (Private) [RV]
48 units w/full hookups plus 20 w/water & elec., no tents, reservations (360)652-7083, showers, laundry, rec room, lake, swimming, fishing, boat launch, pets okay, $21-28/night.
Take I-5 south to exit #206, Lakewood Rd. west 5 miles, and 52nd Ave. NW south .5 mile.

KAYAK POINT PARK (Island County) 🅰 [RV]
32 sites w/hookups for elec. & gray water, 2 w/handicap access - reservations (360)652-7992, flush toilets, yurts, boat launch, fishing, pets okay, no hookups Nov. to Feb., $15/night.
Take Marine Dr. south 9 miles.

LAKE GOODWIN RESORT (Private) 🅰 [RV]
68 units w/hookups for water/elec./sewer, 17 w/water & elec., plus 18 tent sites, reservations (360)652-8169, propane, playground, groceries, trailer waste disposal, swimming, fishing, water skiing, boat launch & rental, small pets okay.
Take I-5 south to exit #206, Lakewood Rd. west 5 miles, and follow signs.

WENBERG (WA State Park) 🅰 [RV]
10 units w/hookups for water & elec. plus 65 standard sites, reservations (800)452-5687, trailers to 50', flush toilets, showers, groceries, trailer waste disposal, on east shore of Lake Goodwin, boat launch, fishing, swimming, $10-15/night.
Take I-5 south to exit #206, Lakewood Rd. west 5 miles, and follow signs south 2 miles to campground.

ARLINGTON

RIVER MEADOWS PARK (Snohomish County)
80 tent/trailer sites, no hookups, information (360)435-3441, trailers to 70', wheelchair accessible restrooms, on river, fishing, swimming, canoeing, nature & mountain bike trails, pets okay, $10/night.
Take Arlington Heights Rd. east 2 miles, bear right onto Jordan Rd., and follow 3 miles to park.

SMOKEY POINT RV PARK (Private)
97 units w/hookups for water/elec./sewer, tents okay, reservations (360)652-7300, showers, laundry, rec room, trailer waste disposal, nearby store & restaurant, pets okay, $14-24/night.
Located in Arlington, at 17019 28th Dr. NE.

SQUIRE CREEK PARK (Snohomish County)
34 campsites, 2 picnic shelters, no alcohol, information (360)436-1283, trailers to 70', wheelchair access, old growth trees, trailer waste disposal, pets okay, $10/night.
Take State 530 northeast 26 miles - located just off highway.

GRANITE FALLS

BEAVER CREEK (Mt. Baker-Snoqualmie NF)
4 group sites - 25 people, no water, reservations (800)280-CAMP, fishing, elev. 1600', pets okay, $40/night.
Take Mountain Loop Hwy. east 24.4 miles.

BEAVER PLANT LAKE (DNR)
6 hike-in campsites, small lake, hiking, fishing, FREE.
Leave State 92 on Mountain Loop Hwy. heading north 15.2 miles, take FSR 4020 for 2.6 miles to Ashland Lakes Trailhead and hike in 2.1 miles.

BEDAL (Mt. Baker-Snoqualmie NF)
18 campsites, trailers to 22', handicap access, picnic area, river, fishing, pets okay, elev. 1300', $7/night.
Take Mountain Loop Hwy. east 30.1 miles and FSR 20 northeast 6.5 miles.

BOARDMAN CREEK (Mt. Baker-Snoqualmie NF)
8 tent & 2 trailer sites plus group area, fishing, pets okay, elev. 1200', $7/night.
Take Mountain Loop Hwy. east 16.6 miles.

BOARDMAN LAKE (Mt. Baker-Snoqualmie NF)
8 hike-in tent sites, lake - no motors, fishing, swimming, hiking, elev. 3100', FREE.
Take Mountain Loop Hwy. east 15.5 miles, FSR 4020 south 6.9 miles, and Trail #704 south 1 mile.

COAL CREEK BAR (Mt. Baker-Snoqualmie NF) 🔺 RV
5 group sites - 25 people, no water, reservations (800)280-CAMP, trailers to 18', fishing, elev. 1600', pets okay, groups $40/night.
Take Mountain Loop Hwy. east 23.5 miles.

ESSWINE CAMP (Mt. Baker-Snoqualmie NF) 🔺 RV
Group site - 25 people, no water, reservations (360)436-1155, fishing, pets okay, groups $40/night.
Take Mountain Loop Hwy. east 16 miles.

GOLD BASIN (Mt. Baker-Snoqualmie NF) 🔺 RV
92 units, 3 group sites - 40 people - reservations (800)280-2267, trailers to 32', wheelchair access, interpretive trail, river, fishing, elev. 1100', $12/night - groups $50.
Take Mountain Loop Hwy. east 13.4 miles.

LOWER ASHLAND LAKE (DNR) 🔺
6 campsites, hike-in only, small lake, fishing, FREE.
Take Mountain Loop Hwy. north 15.2 miles, follow FSR 4020 2.6 miles to Ashland Lakes Trailhead and hike 3 miles.

MARTEN CREEK (Mt. Baker-Snoqualmie NF) 🔺 RV
4 group sites - 25 people, no water, reservations (800)280-CAMP, trailers to 18', fishing, elev. 1400', groups $40/night.
Take Mountain Loop Hwy. east 20.6 miles.

MT. PILCHUCK (Mt. Baker-Snoqualmie NF) 🔺 RV
5 campsites, trailers to 32', group sites, picnic area, water, hiking, elev. 3000', FREE.
Take Mountain Loop Hwy. east 12 miles, and FSR 42 southwest 6.9 miles.

RED BRIDGE (Mt. Baker-Snoqualmie NF) 🔺 RV
16 units, trailers to 32', river, fishing, pets okay, elev. 1300', $7/night.
Take Mountain Loop Hwy. east 18.1 miles.

TULALIP MILLSITE (Mt. Baker-Snoqualmie NF) 🔺 RV
12 group sites - 60 people, no water, reservations (800)280-CAMP, trailers to 32', elev. 1400', fishing, pets okay, groups $65/night.
Take Mountain Loop Hwy. east 18.6 miles.

TURLO (Mt. Baker-Snoqualmie NF) 🔺 RV
19 units, reservations (800)280-2267, trailers to 32', handicap access, river, swimming, fishing, elev. 900', pets okay, $12/night.
Take Mountain Loop Hwy. east 10.8 miles.

TWIN FALLS LAKE (DNR) 🔺
5 hike-in sites, small waterfall, fishing, hiking, FREE.
Leave State 92 on Mountain Loop Hwy. heading north 15.2 miles, take FSR 4020 for 2.6 miles to Ashland Lakes Trailhead and hike in 4.5 miles.

UPPER ASHLAND LAKE (DNR)
6 hike-in sites, fishing, FREE.
Take Mountain Loop Hwy. north 15.2 miles, follow FSR 4020 2.6 miles to Ashland Lakes Trailhead and hike 2.5 miles.

VERLOT (Mt. Baker-Snoqualmie NF)
26 units, trailers to 32', reservations (800)280-CAMP, flush toilets, handicap access, river, fishing, swimming, elev. 900', pets okay, $12/night.
Take Mountain Loop Hwy. east 11 miles.

WILEY CREEK (Mt. Baker-Snoqualmie NF)
3 group tent sites - 100 people, no water, reservations (800)280-CAMP, shelters, fishing, hiking, elev. 1200', groups $60/night.
Take Mountain Loop Hwy. east 15 miles.

PORT TOWNSEND

CHIMACUM PARK (Jefferson County)
18 tent/trailer sites, picnic facilities, $10/night.
Take US 20 southwest 6 miles, Four Corners Rd. east 1 mile, and Chimacum-Beaver Valley Rd. south 3 miles.

FAIRGROUNDS (Jefferson County)
70 sites - some w/water & elec., information (360)385-1013, trailers to 70', showers, horse track, $10-14/night.
Located in Port Townsend, at the north end of town.

FORT FLAGLER (WA State Park)
14 units w/water & elec., 102 standard sites plus group area, trailers to 50', flush toilets, showers, disabled access, trailer waste disposal, boat launch, fishing, scuba diving area, $10-16/night.
Take State 20 southwest about 5 miles to the road marked Hadlock/Fort Flagler State Park and follow signs.

FORT WORDEN (WA State Park)
80 units w/full hookups plus 30 w/water & elec., information (360)385-4730, trailers to 50', flush toilets, showers, wheelchair access, community kitchen, snack bar, groceries, trailers waste disposal, boat launch, scuba diving area, fishing, $10-16/night.
Located in Port Townsend, at the north end of town.

OAK BAY PARK (Jefferson County)
68 tent/trailer units - some w/elec., swimming beach, boat launch, fishing, hiking, $10-14/night.
Take US 20 southwest 6 miles, Four Corners Rd. east 1 mile, Chimacum-Beaver Valley Rd. south 2 miles, Hadlock Rd. east 2 miles, and Oak Bay Rd. south 2 miles.

OLD FORT TOWNSEND (WA State Park)
40 units, trailers to 40', flush toilets, showers, community

kitchen, playfield, historic fort, trailer waste disposal, beach access, fishing, clamming, open May thru mid Sept., $11/night. Take State 20 southwest 4 miles and follow signs east.

POINT HUDSON RESORT (Private) `RV`
18 units w/hookups for water/elec./sewer, no tents, reservations (800)452-5687, showers, laundry, wheelchair access, motel, fishing, boat launch, marina, restaurant, pets okay, $20/night. Located at the docks - follow Water St. to the end.

PORT LUDLOW RV PARK (Private) `A` `RV`
37 units w/hookups for water/elec./sewer, tents okay, reservations (360)437-0513, trailers to 40', pull thrus, showers, trailer waste disposal, groceries, pets okay, $10-16/night. Take US 20 southwest 6 miles, Four Corners Rd. east 1 mile, Chimacum-Beaver Valley Rd. south 10 miles, Port Ludlow Rd. east 1.5 miles, and Ludlow-Paradise Rd. east 2 miles to park.

SMITTY'S RV PARK RETREAT (Private) `RV`
40 units w/hookups for water/elec./sewer, no tents, reservations (360)385-2165, propane, quiet, fishing, pets okay, $10-16/night. Take State 20 southwest about 5 miles to the road marked Hadlock/Fort Flagler State Park and follow signs - Smitty's is 1 mile south of park.

EVERETT

LAKESIDE RV PARK (Private) `A` `RV`
155 units w/full hookups plus 9 tent sites, reservations (800)468-7275, trailers to 60', pull thrus, showers, laundry, wheelchair access, propane, gas, trailer waste disposal, private lake, fishing, hiking, pets okay, $15-28/night. Leave I-5 at exit #186, go west 1.3 miles, and turn left onto State 99S - located at 12321 Highway 99S.

SILVER SHORES RV PARK (Private) `A` `RV`
87 units w/hookups for water/elec./sewer, 8 w/water & elec., plus 15 tent sites, reservations (425)337-8741, showers, laundry, rec room, tennis, trailer waste disposal, on Silver Lake, swimming, fishing, small pets okay, $17-27/night. Leave I-5 at exit #186, go west to 4th Ave., north to 112th St., over the freeway, and follow 14th Ave./Silver Lake Rd. south to 11621 W. Silver Lake Rd.

SNOHOMISH

FERGUSON PARK (City) `A` `RV`
11 units w/hookups for water & elec. plus tent area, information (360)568-3115, trailers to 34', showers, wheelchair access, playground, trailer waste disposal, lake - no motors, swimming, fish-

ing, boat launch, no pets, open year round - no water in winter, $10-14/night.
Located in Snohomish, near junction of US 2 and State 9.

FLOWING LAKE PARK (Snohomish County)　△ RV
28 units w/water & elec., 10 tent sites, 3 reservable sites for disabled - (360)568-2274, picnic area, boat launch, swimming, fishing, pets okay, $10-14/night.
Head east on Three Lakes Rd. - park is about 4 miles.

LAKE ROESIGER PARK (Snohomish County)　△
10 walk-in sites, wheelchair access, lake - no motors, swimming, fishing, trail, pets okay, open mid May thru Sept., $10/night.
Head east on Three Lakes Rd., after about 8 miles you'll see signs pointing north to lake and park.

QUILCENE

DOSEWALLIPS (Olympic NP)　△ RV
32 units, handicap access, summer nature program, elev. 1540', $6/night.
Take US 101 south 13 miles and D River Rd. west 15 miles.

FALLS VIEW CAMPGROUND (Olympic NF)　△ RV
35 campsites, reservations (800)280-2267, trailers to 21', flush toilets, picnic area, fishing, hiking trails, elev. 500', $10/night.
Take US 101 southwest 3.5 miles.

LAKE LELAND PARK (Jefferson County)　△ RV
22 tent/trailer sites, boat launch, fishing, swimming, $10/night.
Take US 101 north 6 miles and follow signs to east side of lake.

QUILCENE PARK (Jefferson County)　△ RV
8 tent/trailer sites, picnic facilities, play area, $10/night.
Located just south of town on US 101.

BOTHELL

LAKE PLEASANT RV PARK (Private)　RV
167 units w/full hookups plus 12 w/water & elec., reservations (800)742-0386, pull thrus, showers, laundry, fishing, hiking, $20-25/night.
Leave I-405 at exit #26 and take Bothell Highway 1 mile south.

SEATTLE

AQUA BARN RANCH (Private)　△ RV
105 units w/hookups for water/elec./sewer, 65 w/water & elec., plus 25 tent sites, reservations (425)255-4618, trailers to 35',

showers, pool, hot tub, restaurant, trailer waste disposal, horse rentals, hiking, pets okay, $17-25/night.
Leave I-405 on State 169 and go east 3.5 miles.

BLAKE ISLAND (WA State Park) 🛖
54 boat-in units, group area - reservations advised (360)731-0770, floats & buoys, marine pump out station, scuba diving area, fishing, nature trail, hiking, $5-11/night.
Located on Blake Island, in Puget Sound, 3 miles west of Seattle.

SEATTLE/TACOMA KOA (Private) 🛖 RV
133 units w/hookups for water/elec./sewer plus 18 w/water & elec., tents okay, reservations (253)872-8652, trailers to 50', showers, laundry, wheelchair access, playground, pool, rec room, groceries, propane, pets okay, $23-29/night.
Leave I-5 south at exit #152 and go east on Orillia Rd.

TWIN CEDARS RV PARK (Private) RV
70 trailer sites w/hookups for water/elec./sewer, no tents, reservations (425)742-5540, trailers to 40', showers, laundry, wheelchair access, club house w/pool table, trailer waste disposal, pets okay, $24/night.
Take I-5 north to Lynnwood exit #183, 164th St. west 1.3 miles to State 99, and go south to 17826 Highway 99N.

BELLEVUE

TRAILER INNS RV PARK (Private) RV
100 blacktop trailer sites w/full hookups, reservations (800)659-4684, trailers to 40', showers, laundry, pool, sauna, rec room, playground, pets okay, $17-29/night.
Located at 15531 SE 37th.

VASA PARK RESORT (Private) 🛖 RV
6 units w/full hookups plus 16 w/water, tents okay, reservations (425)746-3260, trailers to 50',showers, playground, trailer waste disposal, on Sammamish Lake, fishing, swimming, pets okay, open mid May thru early Oct., $15-20/night.
Leave I-90 on Lake Rd. and follow signs north to resort.

WINSLOW

CAPTAINS LANDING (Private) 🛖 RV
22 units w/hookups for water/elec./sewer, tents okay, reservations (253)638-2257, trailers to 70', showers, gas, groceries, restaurant, fishing, pets okay, $18-22/night.
Take State 305 northwest 7 miles, cross bridge, and follow Millers Bay/Hansville Rd. north 15 miles.

FAY BAINBRIDGE (WA State Park)
26 units w/hookups for water only, trailers to 30', flush toilets, showers, disabled access, trailer waste disposal, on Puget Sound, boat launch, scuba diving area, fishing, $15/night.
Take Madison Ave. north 5 miles and follow signs.

KITSAP MEMORIAL (WA State Park)
43 units, group area - reservations (253)779-3205, trailers to 30', flush toilets, showers, disabled access, playfield, trailer waste disposal, on Hood Canal, fishing, $10/night.
Take State 305 northwest 13 miles, and State 3 north 4 miles.

BRINNON

COLLINS (Olympic NF)
16 units, trailers to 21', river, fishing, elev. 200', $8/night.
Take US 101 south 2 miles, and FSR 2510 west 4.8 miles.

COVE RV PARK (Private)
25 rv sites w/water/elec./sewer, reservations (253) 796-4723, showers, laundry, propane, trailer waste disposal, fishing. no dogs, $15 and up.
Take US 101 north 3 miles.

DOSEWALLIPS (WA State Park)
40 units w/full hookups plus 87 standard sites, group area, reservations (800)452-5687, trailers to 60', flush toilets, showers, disabled access, trailer waste disposal, on Dosewallips River & Hood Canal, fishing, clamming, $10-15/night.
Take US 101 south 1 mile.

ELKHORN (Olympic NF)
18 units, trailers to 21', river, fishing, hiking, elev. 600', $8/night.
Take US 101 north 1 mile, and FSR 2610 west 10 miles.

SEAL ROCK (Olympic NF)
35 units, trailers to 21', res. (800)280-2267, flush toilets, dis. access, on Hood Canal, swimming, fishing, trail, $10-12/night.
Take US 101 north 2 miles.

ELDON

LENA CREEK (Olympic NF)
14 units, trailers to 21', well, swimming, fishing, Lena Lakes Trailhead, elev. 700', $8/night.
Take US 101 north 1.7 miles and FSR 25 west 9 miles.

LENA CREEK (Olympic NF)
29 tent sites, hike-in only, no tables, fishing, swimming, geology, mountain climbing, elev. 1800', FREE-$3/night.

Take US 101 north 1.7 miles, FSR 25 west 9 miles, and Trail #810
4 miles to campground.

HAMMA HAMMA (Olympic NF) 🔺 RV
15 units, trailers to 21', river, swimming, fishing, hiking, bicycling, elev. 600', $8/night.
Take US 101 north 1.7 miles, FSR 25 west 6.5 miles.

BREMERTON

ILLAHEE (WA State Park) 🔺 RV
33 units, group site - reservations (360)478-6460, trailers to 30',
flush toilets, showers, wheelchair access, community kitchen,
trailer waste disposal, bay, boat launch, pier fishing, $10/night.
Take State 306 east 3 miles to park.

MANCHESTER (WA State Park) 🔺 RV
50 units, trailers to 42', reservations (800)452-5687, flush toilets,
showers, disabled access, picnic shelter, trailer waste disposal,
historic site, scuba diving area, fishing, open year round - weekends only in winter, $10/night.
Leave State 3 south of town on State 160, follow to Port Orchard,
and take the road around the point 6 miles to park.

SCENIC BEACH (WA State Park) 🔺 RV
50 units, group area, reservations (800)452-5687, trailers to 40',
flush toilets, showers, wheelchair access, community kitchen,
trailer waste disposal, on Hood Canal, fishing, open year round -
weekends only Oct. thru March, $10/night.
Take Seabeck Hwy. northwest 12 miles.

BELFAIR

ALDRICH LAKE (DNR) 🔺 RV
4 sites, picnic area, lake, boat ramp, fishing, trail, elev. 50', FREE.
Take State 300 southwest 13 miles, Maggie Lake Rd. to Dewatto
Rd., 2.1 miles to Robbins Lake Rd., and after .6 mile turn right on
campground road and go .7 mile.

BELFAIR (WA State Park) 🔺 RV
47 units w/full hookups plus 134 standard sites, reservations
(800)452-5687, trailers to 60', showers, wheelchair access, picnic
shelter, trailer waste disposal, fishing, $10-15/night.
Take State 300 southwest 3 miles.

CAMP SPILLMAN (DNR) 🔺 RV
6 sites, picnic area, hiker/horse/motorbike trail, elev. 60', FREE.
Take State 300 1 mile and turn right on Sandhill Rd., at the Y
take Goat Ranch Rd. to the left. The third road on the right leads
to the campground.

GREEN MOUNTAIN HORSE CAMP (DNR)
12 sites, horse facilities, water, horse/hike/bicycle trail, elev. 100', FREE.
Take State 300 for 1 mile, turn right on Sandhill Rd., stay right at the Y for an additional 8 miles to Green Mountain Rd. This will lead you to the campground.

HOWELL LAKE (DNR)
5 sites, water, picnic area, hiking/horse/mountain bike trail, fishing, elev. 50', FREE.
Take State 300 southwest 4 miles, turn on Haven Lake Rd., stay left at Y and follow to Howell Lake.

JARRELL COVE (WA State Park)
20 units, group area - reservations (360)426-9226, trailers to 30', flush toilets, showers, wheelchair access, fishing, $10/night.
Take State 3 southwest 17 miles and follow park road east 7 miles to campground.

KAMMENGA CANYON (DNR)
2 sites, no drinking water, hike/horse/atv/mountain bike trails, stream, FREE.
Take State 300 for 3.5 miles, turn right on Belfair/Tahuya Rd. for 1.9 miles, Elfendahl Rd. for 2.9 miles, and turn left.

PENROSE POINT (WA State Park)
83 units, group area, reservations (800)452-5687, trailers to 35', flush toilets, showers, wheelchair access, community kitchen, trailer waste disposal, on Carr Inlet, fishing, clamming, open year round - weekends only in winter, $10/night.
Take State 3 south 4 miles, State 302 southeast 12 miles, and Longbranch Rd. south 7 miles to park.

ROBIN HOOD VILLAGE (Private)
14 trailer sites w/hookups for water & elec. plus tent area, reservations (360)898-2163, showers, laundry, sauna, beauty shop, fishing, $12-18/night.
Take State 3 south 1 mile, and State 106 southwest 13.5 miles.

SNOOZ JUNCTION RV PARK (Private)
12 units w/hookups for water/elec./sewer plus 30 w/water & elec., no tents, reservations (360)275-2381, trailers to 70', showers, wheelchair access, trailer waste disposal, propane, on Hood Canal, fishing, pets okay, $20/night.
Take State 300 southwest 2.5 miles.

TAHUYA RIVER HORSE CAMP (DNR)
8 sites, horse facilities, water, hiker/horse trails, elev. 60', FREE.
Take State 300 southwest 1 mile, turn right on Sandhill Rd., at Y take Goat Ranch Rd. to the left. The second road on left leads to campground.

TOONERVILLE (DNR)
4 sites, picnic area, hiker/horse/mountain bike trails, elev. 60', FREE.
Take State 300 southwest 1 mile, turn right on Sandhill Rd., at Y take Goat Ranch Rd. to the left. The first road on the right leads you to the campground; it's about 4 miles.

TWANOH (WA State Park)
9 units w/hookups for water/elec./sewer plus 38 standard sites, group area - reservations (360)275-2222, trailers to 35', flush toilets, showers, community kitchen, wheelchair access, on Hood Canal, boat launch, fishing, swimming, water skiing, tennis court, open mid April thru Sept., $10-15/night.
Take State 3 south 1 mile, and State 106 southwest 8 miles.

TWIN LAKES (DNR)
6 sites, picnic area, boat ramp, fishing, elev. 60', FREE.
Take State 300 southwest 1 mile, turn right on Sandhill Rd., at Y take Goat Ranch Rd. to the left, and follow the fourth road on the right to the campground.

FALL CITY

SNOQUALMIE RIVER CAMPGROUND (Private)
80 units w/hookups for water & elec. plus 100 w/out hookups, tents okay, reservations (425)222-5545, some group sites, showers, pavilion, playground, on the Snoqualmie River, fishing, swimming, boating, pets okay, open April thru Oct., $16-19/night.
Located in Fall City, on SE 44th St.

TOLT MACDONALD PARK (King County)
17 units plus 12 walk-in tent sites, information (206)296-2966, trailers okay, showers, wheelchair access, on river, swimming, fishing, pets okay, $10/night.
Take State 203 north 6 miles, head west on NE 32nd St., and follow signs.

ISSAQUAH

BLUE SKY RV PARK (Private)
51 units w/full hookups, no tents, reservations (425)222-7910, trailers to 40', showers, laundry, wheelchair access, covered pavilion, pets okay, $25/night.
Leave I-90 at exit #22 - located at 9002 302nd Ave. SE.

ISSAQUAH HIGHLANDS CAMPING CLUB (Private)
100 non-member units w/water & elec., tents okay, reservations (425)392-2351, trailers to 70', showers, laundry, pool, trailer waste disposal, pets okay.
Take the Renton-Issaquah Rd. south of town 3.5 miles.

ISSAQUAH VILLAGE RV PARK (Private) `RV`
128 rv sites w/full hookups, no tents, reservations (800)258-9223, trailers to 40', showers, laundry, wheelchair access, playground, trailer waste disposal, pets okay, $30/night.
Leave I-90 at exit #17, go north 1 block, and take 2 quick right turns - located at 650 First Ave. N.E.

NORTH BEND

COMMONWEALTH (Mt. Baker-Snoqualmie NF) `A`
6 tent sites, picnic area, stream, near Pacific Crest National Scenic Trail, hiking, horse trails, mountain climbing, elev. 3000', FREE-$3/night.
Take I-90 southeast 22 miles and FSR 58 north .2 mile. Located at Snoqualmie Pass.

DENNY CREEK (Mt. Baker-Snoqualmie NF) `A` `RV`
33 units, 3 group areas - 35 people - reservations (800)280-CAMP, trailers to 22', handicap access, fishing, hiking, elev. 2200', $12/night - groups $75.
Take I-90 southeast 17 miles, and FSR 58 northeast 2.2 miles.

TINKHAM (Mt. Baker-Snoqualmie NF) `A` `RV`
48 units, reservations (800)280-2267, trailers to 22', handicap access, river, waterfall, fishing, nature trail, elev. 1520', $12/night.
Take I-90 southeast 10 miles, and FSR 55 southeast 1.5 miles.

HOODSPORT

BIG CREEK (Olympic NF) `A` `RV`
23 units, trailers to 30', swimming, fishing, hiking, elev 700', $8/night.
Take Lake Cushman Rd. northwest 8 miles, and FSR 24 south .1 mile.

GLEN AYR RV PARK & MOTEL (Private) `RV`
49 units w/hookups for water/elec./sewer, adults only, no tents, reservations (360)877-9522, trailers to 42', showers, laundry, propane, therapy pool, rec room, lounge, on Hood Canal, swimming, fishing, hiking, pets okay, $22/night.
Take US 101 north 1 mile.

LAKE CUSHMAN RESORT (Private) `A` `RV`
25 units w/water & elec. plus 25 tent sites, reservations (800)588-9630, trailers to 40', showers, wheelchair access, meeting hall, groceries, cabins, on lake, swimming, fishing, boat launch, canoe & paddleboat rental, hiking, pets okay, $13-23/night.
Take Lake Cushman Rd. northwest 5 miles.

LAKE CUSHMAN (WA State Park)
30 units w/hookups for water/elec./sewer plus 51 standard sites, group area, reservations (800)452-5687, trailers to 60', flush toilets, showers, community kitchen, disabled access, trailer waste disposal, on lake, boat launch, fishing, hiking trails, $10-16/night.
Take Lake Cushman Rd. northwest 7 miles.

LILLIWAUP (DNR)
6 sites, drinking water, creek, FREE.
Take Cushman-Jorstad Rd. 4 miles northeast of Lake Cushman to Lilliwaup Creek and campground.

MELBOURNE (DNR)
6 units, lake, FREE.
Take US 101 north to Jorstad Creek Rd. and go northwest 5.5 miles and west 2.5 miles keeping left at Y.

MIKE'S BEACH RESORT (Private)
25 sites, tents okay, information (360)877-5324, trailers to 30', showers, laundry, store, cabins, beach, boat ramp & gas, moorage, kayak rentals, surf fishing, hiking, pets okay, open Feb. thru Nov., $12-18/night.
Take US 101 north about 8 miles to Lilliwaup and resort.

MINERVA BEACH (Private)
40 units w/full hookups plus 20 tent sites, reservations (360)877-5145, showers, laundry, wheelchair access, trailer waste disposal, store, propane, on Hood Canal, scuba diving area, diving center, fishing, clamming, pets okay, open $15-20/night.
Take US 101 south 3.2 miles.

POTLATCH (WA State Park)
18 units w/hookups for water/elec./sewer plus 17 standard sites, trailers to 60', flush toilets, showers, trailer waste disposal, on Hood Canal, scuba diving area, fishing, clamming, $10-16/night.
Take US 101 south 3 miles.

REST A WHILE RV PARK (Private)
80 units w/full hookups plus some tent sites, reservations (360)877-9474, trailers to 45', showers, laundry, wheelchair access, propane, groceries, drive-in restaurant, swimming, fishing, boat launch & rental, pets okay, $19-20/night.
Take US 101 north 2.5 miles.

STAIRCASE CAMPGROUND (Olympic NP)
59 units, trailers to 21', handicap access, on Elk Creek, swimming, fishing, hiking, open year round, elev. 765', $12/night.
Take Lake Cushman Rd. northwest 16 miles.

SHELTON

BROWN CREEK (Olympic NF) [A] [RV]
19 units, trailers to 21', swimming, fishing, hiking, elev. 600', $8/night.
Take US 101 north 7.5 miles, Skykomish Valley Rd. northwest 5.3 miles, FSR 23 north 8.7 miles, and FSR 2353 east .5 mile.

LAKE NAHWATZEL RESORT (Private) [RV]
17 units w/hookups for water/elec./sewer plus 5 w/water & elec., no tents, reservations (360)426-8323, trailers to 35', showers, wheelchair access, restaurant, trailer waste disposal, on lake, fishing, pets extra, $18-20/night.
Follow Shelton Matlock Rd. west 10.5 miles.

JARRELL'S COVE MARINA (Private) [A] [RV]
4 units w/water & elec., reservations (360) 426-8823, trailers to 27', showers, laundry, groceries, bait, gas, play area, trailer waste disposal, swimming, fishing, hiking, pets okay, $20/night.
Take State 3 northeast 8 miles, Spencer Lake Rd. east 4 miles, North Island Dr. north 3 miles, and Haskell Hill Rd. west 1 mile.

SPENCER LAKE RESORT & RV (Private) [RV]
25 rv sites w/full hookups, no tents, no restrooms, reservations (360) 426-3178, trailers to 40', trailer waste disposal, on lake, fishing, pets okay, $17/night.
Take State 3 northeast 8 miles and Spencer Lake Rd. east 1 mile.

WE & YOU MOBILE HOME & RV PARK (Private)
16 units w/full hookups plus grassy tent area, reservations (360) 426-3169, trailers to 40', showers, laundry, small pets okay, $8-14/night.
Take the first Shelton exit off US 101 and head north - located at 261 SE Craig Rd.

TACOMA

DASH POINT (WA State Park) [A] [RV]
136 units - 28 w/hookups for water & elec., trailers to 35', group area, reservations (800)452-5687, flush toilets, showers, trailer waste disposal, on sound, fishing, $10-15/night.
Leave State 99 just north of Federal Way on State 509 and drive west 5 miles to park.

GIG HARBOR RV RESORT (Private) [RV]
65 units w/full hookups, reservations (253)858-8138, trailers to 40', showers, laundry, pool in summer, playground, groceries, propane, trailer waste disposal, pets okay, $25/night.
Take State 16 over the Narrows Bridge plus 6 miles, and head north on Burnham Dr. 1 mile to resort.

KARWAN VILLAGE MH/RV PARK (Private) `RV`

7 trailer sites w/hookups for water/elec./sewer, adults only, reservations (253)588-2501, trailers to 40', showers, laundry, no pets, $15/night.
Leave I-5 south at exit #129 (north #128) and go west on 84th St.

KOPACHUCK (WA State Park) `A` `RV`

41 standard units, trailers to 35', flush toilets, showers, disabled access, picnic shelter, trailer waste disposal, on Henderson Bay, scuba diving area, clamming, $11/night.
Take State 16 north of the bridge 6 miles and follow signs.

OAKNOLL RV PARK (Private) `RV`

36 rv units w/full hookups plus 2 w/water & elec., no tents, reservations (253)588-8867, trailers to 40', showers, laundry, trailer waste disposal, pets okay - $10 fee, $15/night.
Leave I-5 at exit #125 - located at 110404 S. Tacoma Way.

SALTWATER (WA State Park) `A` `RV`

52 units, group area - reservations (206)764-4128, trailers to 60', flush toilets, showers, disabled access, trailer waste disposal, on sound, scuba diving area, hiking, $11/night.
Follow State 509 north of Federal Way following State 509 when they split - park is northwest 3 miles.

PUYALLUP

BENBOWS CAMPGROUND (Private) `A` `RV`

38 units w/water/elec./sewer plus 23 w/water & elec., plus 12 tent spaces, reserva-tions (360)879-5426, trailers to 40', showers, laundry, wheel-chair access, cabins, on Lake Tanwax, fishing, pets okay, $10-18/night.
Take State 161 south 20 miles and watch for signs.

HENLEY'S SILVER LAKE RESORT (Private) `A` `RV`

20 units w/hookups for water & elec., 12 w/elec. only, plus tent area, reservations (360)832-3580, trailers to 50', cabins, fishing dock, boat launch & rental, pets okay, open April thru Oct., $8-12/night.
Take State 161 south 26 miles, 352nd Ave. west 4 miles, State 7 south 3 miles, and follow signs.

MAJESTIC MOBILE MANOR/RV PARK (Private) `A` `RV`

118 units w/full hookups plus 12 tent sites, reservations (253) 845-3144, trailers to 40', showers, wheelchair access, pool, trailer waste disposal, pets okay, $18-24/night.
Follow State 167/River Rd. west 3 miles.

RAINBOW RESORT (Private) `RV`

52 units w/hookups for water/elec./sewer, no tents, reservations (360)879-5115, trailers to 40', showers, laundry, wheelchair

access, rec room, groceries, propane, on Lake Tanwax, swimming, fishing, boat rental, pets okay, $14/night.
Take State 161 south 15 miles and Tanwax Dr. east .5 mile.

RAINIER VIEW RV PARK (Private)
55 rv sites w/full hookups, adults only, no tents, reservations (253)847-7153, trailers to 60', showers, laundry, clubhouse, exercise & game room, pets okay, $20/night.
Follow State 161 south 3 miles.

SIERRA-RAINIER RV PARK (Private)
8 rv sites w/hookups for water/elec./sewer, no tents, restrooms only in summer, reservations (360)893-6422, trailers to 38', playground, stream, fishing, hiking, mini-railroad, small pets okay, $12/night.
Take State 161 south 12 miles, 264th St. east 5 miles, and Orville Rd. north to 25916 Orville Rd. E.

ENUMCLAW

CORRAL PASS (Mt. Baker-Snoqualmie NF)
20 tent sites, stream, berry picking, horse ramp, near Mountain Goat Reserve & Norse Peak Wilderness, elev. 5600', FREE.
Take State 410 southeast 31 miles and FSR 7174 east 6.1 miles.

ECHO LAKE (Mt. Baker-Snoqualmie NF)
13 hike-in tent sites, shelter, swimming, fishing, elev. 3800', FREE.
Take State 410 southeast 32.1 miles, FSR 185 east 6.7 miles, and Trail #1176 northeast 5.2 miles.

EVANS CREEK (Mt. Baker-Snoqualmie NF)
34 units, picnic shelter, trailbike & atv trails, elev. 3200', FREE.
Take State 165 south of Buckley 12 miles, continue 7 miles onto gravel road and follow FSR 7920 about 2 miles to campground.

IPSUT CREEK (Mt. Rainier NP)
32 units, res. (800)280-CAMP, hiking, elev. 4400', $10/night.
Take State 165 south 12 miles to Carbonado - located 5 miles east of Mt. Rainier Nat'l Park's Carbon River Entrance.

KANASKAT-PALMER (WA State Park)
19 units w/hookups for elec. plus 31 standard sites, trailers to 30', group area, reservations (800)452-5687, flush toilets, showers, disabled access, community kitchen, trailer waste disposal, on Green River, boating, fishing, $10-15/night.
Take State 410 east 1 mile and Palmer Rd. northeast 9 miles.

SILVER SPRINGS (Mt. Baker-Snoqualmie NF)
56 units, trailers to 22', reservations (800)280-CAMP, picnic area, wheelchair access, fishing, elev. 2600', $10-12/night.

Follow State 410 southeast 31.3 miles - located 1 mile north of Mt. Rainier Nat'l Park boundary.

SOUTH PRAIRIE CREEK RV PARK (Private) `RV`

105 units w/full hookups plus 70 w/out hookups, no tents, no restrooms, reservations (360)897-8465, trailers to 40', trailer waste disposal, creek, small pets okay, $10-15/night.
Take State 410 west 3 miles, State 165 south 2 miles, and State 162 west to South Prairie and park.

THE DALLES (Mt. Baker-Snoqualmie NF) `A` `RV`

44 units, trailers to 22', group area - reservations (800)280-CAMP, fishing, hiking, elev. 2200', $12/night - groups $50 and up.
Follow State 410 southeast 25.4 miles - located 7 miles north of Mt. Rainier Nat'l Park boundary.

WHITE RIVER (Mt. Rainier NP) `A` `RV`

112 sites, group area - reservations (800)280-CAMP, hiking, $12/night.
Follow State 410 southeast 36 miles - located 5 miles west of White River Entrance for Mt. Rainier Nat'l Park.

OLYMPIA

ALDERBROOK MOTOR HOME PARK (Private) `A` `RV`

21 units w/full hookups plus small tent area, reservations (360)357-9448, pull thrus, showers, laundry, wheelchair access, club house, pets okay, $15/night.
Leave I-5 south at exit #102 and go 7 blocks to 2110 54th Ave.

AMERICAN HERITAGE CAMPGROUND (Private) `A` `RV`

24 units w/full hookups, 52 w/water & elec., plus 19 tent sites, reservations (360)943-8778, trailers to 35', showers, laundry, groceries, pool, playground, propane, trailer waste disposal for overnighters, pets okay, open summer only, $18-26/night.
Take exit #99 off I-5, go east .3 mile, and turn south to 9610 Kimmie St. SW.

COACH POST (Private) `RV`

25 sites w/full hookups inc. cable plus 1 w/water & elec., no tents, reservations (360)754-7580, trailers to 70', showers, laundry, wheelchair access, telephone hookups avail., pets okay, $25/night.
Leave US 101 north on the Evergreen College exit, turn right at the fire station, go up the hill, turn onto Kaiser for a few blocks and take 7th Ave. to 3633 7th Ave.

COLUMBUS PARK (Private) `A` `RV`

48 units w/full hookups, 31 w/water & elec., plus 2 tent sites, reservations (360)786-9460, trailers to 35', showers, laundry, wheelchair access, playground, trailer waste disposal, on Black

Lake, swimming, fishing, boat launch & docks, paddle boat rental, pets okay, $15-17/night.
Leave I-5 on US 101, go west 2 miles, and take Black Lake Blvd. south 3.5 miles.

FALL CREEK (DNR) A RV
8 sites, drinking water, horse/hiking/mountain bike trails, horse facilities, FREE.
Campground is located 5 miles west of the Delphi entrance to Capitol Forest Multiple Use Area, on Fall Creek.

LAKESIDE RV PARK & CAMPGROUND (Private) A RV
3 units w/hookups for water/elec./sewer plus 40 w/water & elec., tents okay, reservations (360)491-3660, showers, laundry, wheelchair access, groceries, boat launch/dock & rental, pets okay, $15/night.
Take I-5 north 6 miles - located at 7225 14th Ave. SE.

MARGARET MCKENNY (DNR) A RV
25 campsites, drinking water, horse/hiking/mountain bike trails, horse facilities, FREE.
Campground is 3 miles northwest of Littlerock, along Waddell Creek Rd., in Capitol Forest Multiple Use Area.

MARTIN WAY MH/RV PARK (Private) RV
10 units w/hookups for water/elec./sewer plus 4 w/water & elec., no tents, reservations (360)491-6840, trailers to 40', showers, laundry, no pets, open year round, $13-21/night.
Take I-5 north to exit #111, State 510 east .8 mile, and Martin Way south .1 mile.

MIDDLE WADDELL (DNR) A RV
24 campsites, drinking water, hiking/trailbike trails, FREE.
Campground is 4.2 miles northwest of Littlerock, on Waddell Creek Rd., in Capitol Forest Multiple Use Area.

MILLERSYLVANIA (WA State Park) A RV
52 units w/hookups for water & elec. plus 135 standard sites, group sites, reservations (800)452-5687, trailers to 45', flush toilets, showers, wheelchair access, community kitchen, trailer waste disposal, boat launch, fishing, swimming, $10-15/night.
Take I-5 south of Olympia about 10 miles.

MIMA FALLS TRAILHEAD (DNR) A RV
5 campsites, hiking/horse/mountain bike trails, picnic area, horse facilities, FREE.
Campground is 4 miles west of Littlerock, at trailhead, in Capitol Forest Multiple Use Area.

NISQUALLY PLAZA RV PARK (Private) RV
49 rv units w/full hookups, no tents, reservations (360)491-3831, showers, laundry, wheelchair access, groceries, pool, playground,

trailer waste disposal, gas, propane, river, fishing, boat launch, pets okay, $20/night.
Take I-5 north to exit #114 and campground.

NORTH CREEK (DNR)
5 campsites, drinking water, hiking/mountain bike trails, FREE.
Campground is 6 miles northeast of Oakville, on Cedar Creek Rd., in Capitol forest Multiple Use Area.

OLYMPIA CAMPGROUND (Private)
28 units w/full hookups, 45 w/water & elec., plus 22 tent sites, reservations (360)352-2551, trailers to 40', 28 pull thrus, showers, laundry, pool, playground, groceries, propane, gas, trailer waste disposal, pets okay, $17-24/night.
Take exit #99 off I-5, go east .3 mile to Kimmie Rd., and north 1 mile to 83rd Ave. - located at 1441 83rd Ave. SW.

PORTER CREEK (DNR)
16 campsites, drinking water, hiking/horse/mountain bike trails, horse facilities, FREE.
Campground is 5 miles northeast of Porter, on Porter Creek Rd., in Capitol Forest Multiple Use Area.

RIVERBEND CAMPGROUND (Private)
30 units w/hookups for water/elec./sewer, 20 w/water & elec., 10 w/water, plus tent sites, reservations (360)491-2534, trailers to 40', trailer waste disposal, on Nisqually River, boat launch, fishing, swimming, hiking, pets okay, $10-18/night.
Take I-5 north to exit #116 and follow signs - it's 4 miles.

SALMON SHORE RESORT (Private)
30 units w/hookups for water/elec./sewer, 15 w/water & elec., 10 w/elec., plus tent area, reservations (360)357-8618, trailers to 40', showers, laundry, picnic shelter, playfield, playground, groceries, trailer waste disposal, on Black Lake, swimming, fishing, boat launch & rental, pets okay, $13-16/night.
Leave I-5 to on US 101, go west 2 miles, and take Black Lake Blvd. south 3.3 miles.

SHERMAN VALLEY "Y" (DNR)
7 campsites, drinking water, hiking/mountain bike trails, FREE.
Campground is 9 miles west of Littlerock, along Cedar Creek, in Capitol forest Multiple Use Area.

THURSTON COUNTY ORV PARK (County)
Lots of tent/trailer & group sites, no hookups, information (360) 495-3243, trailer waste disposal, ORV trails/all levels, children's motocross-style riding area, access to Capitol Forest Multi-use Rec. Area, meeting hall, pets okay, open April thru Sept., $8/night.
US 101 to State 8, then west 11 miles to county line and park.

ELMA

ELMA RV PARK (Private)　　　　　　　　[A] [RV]
60 units w/full hookups plus 2 grassy tent areas, reservations
(425)482-4053, trailers to 40', showers, laundry, propane, trailer
waste disposal, river, fishing, pets okay, $9-18/night.
Located in Elma, at 4730 Highway 12.

TRAVEL INN RESORT (Private)　　　　　　[A] [RV]
180 units w/full hookups plus grassy tent area, reservations
(425)482-3877, trailers to 40', showers, laundry, wheelchair
access, swimming pool, trailer waste disposal, pets okay, mem-
bership resort - non-members when space available @ $25/night.
Located in Elma, at 801 E. Main St.

EATONVILLE

ALDER LAKE PARK (Private)　　　　　　　[A] [RV]
37 units w/full hookups, 45 w/water & elec., plus 16 tent sites,
reservations (253)569-2778, trailers to 40', showers, wheelchair
access, trailer waste disposal, fishing, boat launch & moorage,
pets okay, open Jan. thru mid Dec., $10-15/night.
Located in Eatonville, at 50324 School Rd.

ELBE

ALDER LAKE (DNR)　　　　　　　　　　　[A] [RV]
25 campsites, drinking water, picnic area, group shelter, boat
ramp, fishing, FREE.
Take State 7 south to Pleasant Valley Rd., follow this 3.5 miles,
keeping left at the Y.

BEAVER CREEK (DNR)　　　　　　　　　　[A] [RV]
6 sites, picnic facilities, hiking/horse/mountain bike trail, FREE.
Take State 706 east 6.3 miles, Stone Rd. north 2.3 miles, take left
fork at second intersection and go 1.9 miles to trailhead.

COUGAR ROCK (Mt. Rainier NP)　　　　　　[A] [RV]
200 campsites, trailers to 30', group area - reservations (800)280-
CAMP, trailer waste disposal, hiking, closes in mid Oct., elev.
3100', $10/night.
Take State 706 east 22.2 miles - located .8 mile east of Nisqually
Entrance to Mt. Rainier Nat'l Park.

EAGLE'S NEST MOTEL & RV PARK (Private)　　[A] [RV]
9 rv sites w/hookups for water/elec./sewer, grassy tent area,
reservations (253)569-2533, trailers to 35', handicap access,
laundry, on Alder Lake, fishing, hiking, small pets okay, $10-
15/night.
Take State 7 northwest 3 miles.

ELBE HILLS ORV TRAILHEAD (DNR) 🅰 RV
6 sites, no water, picnic area, group shelter, jeep trails, FREE.
Take State 706 east 6.1 miles, turn left just before National and follow this road 3.7 miles to campground.

MEMORIAL TRAILHEAD (DNR) 🅰 RV
6 sites, hiking/horse/mountain bike trail, FREE.
Take State 706 east 6.3 miles, Stone Rd. north 2.3 miles, take left fork at second intersection and go 4.2 miles to gated road and turn left for approximately 1.6 miles.

SAHARA CREEK HORSE CAMP (DNR) 🅰 RV
18 units, picnic area & shelter, horse/mountain bike trail, FREE.
Take State 706 east 5.3 miles.

SUNSHINE POINT (Mt. Rainier NP) 🅰 RV
20 campsites, trailers to 25', reservations (800)280-CAMP, on Nisqually River, fishing, elev. 2000', $10/night.
Take State 706 east 22.6 miles - located .5 mile east of Nisqually Entrance to Mt. Rainier Nat'l Park.

ASHFORD

ASHFORD VALLEY GROCERY & RV PARK (Private) RV
23 pull thrus w/hookups for water/elec./sewer, no tents, reservations (253)569-2560, trailers to 70', restrooms in store, trailer waste disposal, propane, gas, no pets, $14/night.
Located in Ashford, right on State 706.

CENTRALIA

HARRISON RV PARK (Private) 🅰 RV
35 units w/water/elec./sewer, 9 w/water & elec., plus grassy tent area, reservations (425)330-2167, trailers to 70', showers, laundry, wheelchair access, pets okay, $14-17/night.
Leave I-5 at exit #82 and take Harrison Ave. west 2 miles.

MID-WAY RV PARK (Private) RV
20 pull thrus w/full hookups inc. cable, no tents, reservations (360)736-3200, showers, laundry, handicap access, group room, restaurant, pets okay, $21/night.
Leave I-5 at exit #82 and take Harrison Ave. west 1 mile to Galvin, turn left and go .2 mile to 3200 Galvin Rd.

OFFUT LAKE RESORT & RV PARK (Private) 🅰 RV
35 units w/full hookups, 16 w/elec., plus 12 tent sites, reservations (360)264-2438, showers, laundry, playground, cabins, trailer waste disposal, swimming, fishing, boat rental, $17-20/night.
Take State 507 north 12 miles to Tenino, Pacific Hwy. north 4 miles, and Offut Lake Rd. east 1 mile to lake and resort.

PEPPERTREE WEST INN/RV PARK (Private)
28 units w/hookups for water/elec./sewer, 14 w/water & elec.,
plus grassy tent area, reservations (360)736-1124, trailers to 50',
showers, laundry, wheelchair access, trailer waste disposal,
restaurant/lounge, pets okay, $10-20/night.
Leave I-5 at exit #81 - located on east side of freeway.

ROTARY RIVERSIDE PARK (City)
16 units w/hookups for water & elec. plus 15 tent sites, information (360)330-7688, trailers to 36', showers, wheelchair access,
trailer waste disposal, pets okay, $8-12/night.
Leave I-5 at exit #82 - park is 2 blocks east.

CHEHALIS

CHEHALIS KOA (Private)
30 units w/water/elec./sewer plus 20 dry sites, reservations
(360)262-9220, trailers to 37', wheelchair access, showers, hot
tub, groceries, propane, fishing, pets okay, $17-20/night.
Take I-5 south to exit #68; campground is on US 12.

RAINBOW FALLS (WA State Park)
47 units, trailers to 32', group area - reservations (253)291-3767,
flush toilets, showers, wheelchair access, community. kitchen,
trailer waste disposal, on Chehalis River, old growth trail,
$10/night.
Take State 6 west approximately 17 miles - located near Doty.

STAN HEDWALL PARK (City)
29 units w/water & elec., tents okay, reservations (360)748-0271,
trailers to 40', wheelchair access, showers, playground, trailer
waste disposal, swimming, fishing, hiking, pets okay, $10/night.
Leave I-5 at Chehalis exit #76 and take Rice Rd. west .5 mile.

MARYS CORNER

LEWIS & CLARK (WA State Park)
25 units, trailers to 60', flush toilets, showers, nature trail,
$10/night.
Leave US 12 at Marys Corner and follow signs south to park.

MOSSYROCK

BARRIER DAM CAMPGROUND (Private)
26 units w/hookups for water & elec. plus 14 tent sites, 2 group
areas w/shelters, reservations (360)985-2495, trailers to 44',
showers, playground, groceries, bait/tackle, trailer waste disposal, walk to Cowlitz River, $12-18/night.
Take US 12 west 6 miles and Fuller Rd. south 1 mile.

HARMONY LAKESIDE RV PARK (Private)
48 units w/water/elec./sewer plus 32 w/water & elec., tents okay, reservations (253)983-3804, trailers to 40', showers, wheelchair access, playfield, trailer waste disposal, on Mayfield Lake, fishing, boat launch, pets okay, $20-22/night.
Take Harmony Rd. northwest 2.5 miles at flashing light.

IKE KINSWA (WA State Park)
41 units w/water/elec./sewer plus 60 w/out, trailers to 60', reservations (800)452-5687, flush toilets, showers, disabled access, trailer waste disposal, boat launch, fishing, swimming, horse trails, $10-15/night.
Take US 12 west 6 miles and follow signs north to park.

LAKE MAYFIELD RESORT/RV/MARINA (Private)
60 units w/water & elec. plus tent sites, reservations (360)985-2357, trailers to 38', showers, swimming, fishing, boat launch & rental, pets okay.
Take US 12 west 5 miles and follow signs.

MAYFIELD LAKE PARK (Lewis County)
64 units, group area, reservations (360)985-2364, showers, wheelchair access, playground, trailer waste disposal, swimming, fishing, boat launch, hiking, open May thru Sept., $12-15/night.
Take US 12 west 3 miles, turn at the dam and drive .3 mile.

MOSSYROCK PARK (Private)
105 units w/water & elec., tents okay, trailers to 36', (253)983-3900, showers, wheelchair access, trailer waste disposal, on lake, fishing, pets okay, open Jan. 2 thru Dec. 19.
Take US 12 east 2 miles and follow signs.

MOUNTAIN ROAD MOBILE & RV PARK (Private)
7 units w/water/elec./sewer, 3 w/water & elec., plus dry/tent camp, information (253)983-3094, trailers to 40', showers, disabled access, trailer waste disposal, pets okay, $8-12/night.
Located west of town, at 262 Mossyrock.

WINSTON CREEK (DNR)
11 campsites, FREE.
Take US 12 east about 5 miles to Mayfield Lake, and Longbell County Rd. southeast 5 miles.

MORTON

BACKSTROM PARK (City)
10 units w/full hookups, 17 w/water & elec., plus tent area, information (360)496-6844, trailers to 36', showers, pets okay.
Located in Morton, at 715 Main Ave.

CARTER'S COUNTRY ROADHOUSE (Private) ⚠️ RV
10 sites w/elec. plus dry/tent area, information (360)496-5029, trailers to 36', restaurant & pub, pets okay, $15-20/night. Located 1 mile west of Morton, on US 12.

ROY'S MOTEL & RV PARK (Private) RV
7 units w/hookups for water/elec./sewer, no tents, reservations (360)496-5000, no restrooms, no pets, walk to restaurants, $20/night. Located in Morton, at 161 N. Second St.

TAIDNAPAM PARK (Private) ⚠️ RV
19 units w/water/elec./sewer, 33 w/water & elec., plus 16 tent sites, information (425)497-7707, trailers to 70', showers, wheelchair access, trailer waste disposal, on Riffe Lake, fishing, open Jan. 2 thru Dec. 20. Take US 12 east of town and follow signs to east end of lake.

RANDLE

ADAMS FORK (Gifford Pinchot NF) ⚠️ RV
24 units, reservations (800)280-CAMP, nearby orv trails, swimming, fishing, elev. 2600', $11-27/night. Take Woods Creek Rd. south 3 miles, FSR 23 southeast 15.7 miles, FSR 21 southeast 4.7 miles, and FSR 56 east .2 mile.

BLUE LAKE CREEK (Gifford Pinchot NF) ⚠️ RV
11 units, reservations (800)280-CAMP, fishing, hiking, elev. 1900', $10/night. Take Woods Creek Rd. south 3 miles and FSR 23 southeast 13.2 miles.

CAT CREEK (Gifford Pinchot NF) ⚠️ RV
5 sites, trailers to 16', Cispus River, fishing, elev. 3000, $9/night. Take Woods Creek Rd. south 3 miles, FSR 23 southeast 15.7 miles, and FSR 21 east 6.1 miles.

CHAIN-OF-LAKES (Gifford Pinchot NF) ⚠️ RV
3 campsites, trailers to 16', lake - speed limits, swimming, fishing, hiking trails, near Mt. Adams Wilderness, trailhead to horse camp, elev. 4400', $9/night. Take Woods Creek Rd. south 3 miles, FSR 23 southeast 28.9 miles, FSR 2329 north 1.2 miles, and FSR 22 north 1 mile. Last 5 miles are gravel roads.

COUNCIL LAKE (Gifford Pinchot NF) ⚠️ RV
9 units, trailers to 16', lake - speed limit, boating, swimming, fishing, hiking trails, near Mt. Adams Wilderness, elev. 4300', $9/night. Take Woods Creek Rd. south 3 miles, FSR 23 southeast 30.2 miles, and FSR 2334 west 1.2 miles. Last 3 miles are gravel roads.

COWLITZ FALLS PARK (Lewis County) [A] [RV]
12 units w/water & elec., 73 w/out hookups, group area, tents okay, reservations (425)497-7175, trailers to 36', showers, wheelchair access, trailer waste disposal, on Lake Scanwa, boat ramp & dock, fishing, pets okay, open May thru Oct., $9-13/night.
Take US 12 west 2 miles and follow Peters Rd. south to park.

HORSESHOE LAKE (Gifford Pinchot NF) [A] [RV]
10 sites, trailers to 16', lake - speed limits, primitive boat ramp, swimming, fishing, trails, near Mt. Adams Wilderness, elev. 4200', FREE.
Take Woods Creek Rd. south 3 miles, FSR 23 southeast 28.9 miles, FSR 2329 northeast 6.8 miles, and FSR 78 west 1.3 miles. Last 12 miles are gravel roads.

IRON CREEK (Gifford Pinchot NF) [A] [RV]
98 units, trailers to 42', res. (800)280-CAMP, on river, fishing, hiking, old-growth, open thru mid Oct., elev. 1200', $12-24/night.
Take Woods Creek Rd. south 2 miles and FSR 25 southwest 9 miles.

KEENES HORSE CAMP (Gifford Pinchot NF) [A] [RV]
14 units, trailers to 22', stream, horse trails/ramp/corrals, water trough, trails, near Mt. Adams wilderness, elev. 4300', FREE.
Take Woods Creek Rd. south 3 miles, FSR 23 southeast 28.9 miles, FSR 2329 southeast 7.2 miles, and FSR 82 west .1 mile.

KILLEN CREEK (Gifford Pinchot NF) [A] [RV]
8 sites, trailers to 22', wilderness trailhead to north face of Mt. Adams, berry picking, elev. 4400', FREE-$3/night.
Take Woods Creek Rd. south 3 miles, FSR 23 southeast 28.9 miles, FSR 2329 southeast 6.2 miles, and FSR 72 west .1 mile.

NORTH FORK (Gifford Pinchot NF) [A] [RV]
33 units, group sites - 40 people, reservations (800)280-CAMP, trailers to 32', fishing, hiking, on N. Fork Cispus River, bicycling, open mid May thru mid Oct., elev. 1500', $11-13/night - groups $43-59.
Take Woods Creek Rd. south 3 miles and FSR 23 southeast 8.7 miles.

OLALLIE LAKE (Gifford Pinchot NF) [A] [RV]
5 sites, trailers to 22', lake - speed limit, boating, swimming, fishing, view of Mt. Adams, elev. 4200', $9/night.
Take Woods Creek Rd. south 3 miles, FSR 23 southeast 28.9 miles, FSR 2329 north .8 mile, and FSR 5601 north .6 mile.

POLE PATCH (Gifford Pinchot NF) [A] [RV]
12 units, stream, berry picking, rough road, elev. 4400', FREE.
Take Woods Creek Rd. south 2 miles, FSR 25 south 20.3 miles, FSR 28 east 2.8 miles, and FSR 77 north 6.1 miles.

SHADY FIRS CAMPGROUND/RV PARK (Private)   🏕️ RV
17 units w/water & elec. plus tent area, reservations (425)497-6108, trailers to 70', showers, laundry, playground, horses & pets okay, fishing, trailer waste disposal, $8-14/night.
Take US 12 east 3 miles - located at 107 Young Rd.

SPRING CREEK (Gifford Pinchot NF)   🏕️ RV
3 sites, trailers to 16', hiking, near Mt. Adams Wilderness, berry picking, elev. 4300', FREE.
Take Woods Creek Rd. south 3 miles, FSR 23 southeast 28.9 miles, FSR 2329 northeast 7.5 miles, and FSR 85 west 1.3 miles.

TAKHLAKH LAKE (Gifford-Pinchot NF)   🏕️ RV
54 units, trailers to 22', res. (800)280-CAMP, lake - speed limits, boating, fishing, swimming, nearby lava flow, elev. 4500', $11-22/night.
Take Woods Creek Rd. south 3 miles, FSR 23 southeast 28.9 miles, and FSR 2329 north 1.6 miles.

TOWER ROCK (Gifford Pinchot NF)   🏕️ RV
22 units, reservations (800)280-CAMP, trailers to 22', on river, fishing, open mid May thru early Oct., elev. 1100', $11-13/night.
Take Woods Creek Rd. south 3 miles, FSR 23 southeast 6.8 miles, and FSR 2306 west 1.8 miles.

TOWER ROCK U-FISH RV PARK (Private)   🏕️ RV
29 units w/water/elec./sewer plus tent area, reservations (425)497-7680, restaurant, trailer waste disposal, trout ponds, horses & pets okay, $12-14/night.
Take Woods Creek Rd. south 3 miles, FSR 23 southeast 6.8 miles, and follow signs - located 2 miles past Cispus Learning Center.

CASTLE ROCK

CEDARS RV PARK (Private)   🏕️ RV
26 sites w/full hookups plus tent area, showers, laundry, pets okay, hiking trails, $11-15/night.
Leave I-5 at exit #46 and go to 115 Beauvais Rd.

DREWS TRAILER PARK (Private)   RV
14 rv units w/water/elec./sewer, no tents, no restrooms, reservations (360)274-8920, trailers to 40', groceries/sandwiches/videos, gas & diesel, no pets, $12/night.
Take State 504 east 10 miles to Toutle and park.

FOX PARK RV (Private)   🏕️ RV
44 sites w/full hookups, 8 w/water & elec., plus grassy tent area, reservations (360)274-6785, trailers to 50', some pull thrus, showers, laundry, near Toutle & Cowlitz Rivers, small pets okay, $12-15/night.
Leave I-5 at exit #52 (Toutle Park Rd.) and go to 112 Burma Rd.

FROST ROAD TRAILER PARK (Private) [A] [RV]

21 units w/full hookups, tents okay, reservations (425)785-3616, showers, laundry, trailer waste disposal, $16/night.
I-5 to exit #63, go east .8 mile, north 1.5 mile, and west .5 mile.

MT. ST. HELENS RV PARK (Private) [A] [RV]

49 sites w/full hookups, 30 w/water & elec. plus tent sites, (360)274-8522, trailers to 70', showers, handicap access, trailer waste disposal, pets okay, $15-20/night.
Take State 504 east 2 miles - located on hill behind grocery store.

PARADISE COVE RESORT & RV PARK (Private) [A] [RV]

40 sites w/full hookups plus 6 w/water & elec., tents okay, reservations (253)274-6785, showers, handicap facilities, laundry, groceries, $12-18/night.
Leave I-5 just north of Castle Rock on exit #52 - park is .6 mile.

SEAQUEST (WA State Park) [A] [RV]

16 units w/water/elec./sewer plus 76 standard sites, group reservations (800)452-5687, trailers to 50', flush toilets, showers, wheelchair access, trailer waste disposal, fishing, $10-16/night.
Take State 504 east 5 miles.

SILVER LAKE MOTEL & RESORT (Private) [A] [RV]

7 units w/water/elec./sewer, 14 w/water & elec., plus tent sites, (360)274-6141, trailers to 35', showers, groceries, playground, rec room, swimming, fishing, boat launch/rental, pets okay, $12-20/night.
Take State 504 east 6 miles.

KELSO

BROOKHOLLOW RV PARK (Private) [RV]

132 units w/full hookups, no tents, trailers to 70', reservations (360) 577-6474, showers, laundry, group clubhouse, exercise room, modem-friendly hookups, pets - fee, $20/night.
Leave I-5 at exit #39 and head east .8 mile on Allen.

LONGVIEW

MARV'S RV PARK (Private) [A] [RV]

20 units w/full hookups plus tent area, (360)795-3453, trailers to 40', showers, wheelchair access, rec room, propane, trailer waste disposal, fishing, pets okay, $15/night.
Take State 4 west 20 miles.

OAKS TRAILER & RV PARK (Private) [RV]

94 units w/full hookups, reservations (360)425-2708, trailers to 40', pull thrus, showers, wheelchair access, play area, pets okay.
Located at 636 California Way in Longview.

COUGAR

BEAVER BAY CAMP (Pacific Power)
78 campsites, large group area, res. (503)464-5035, flush toilets, showers, handicap access, trailer waste disposal, playground, on Yale Reservoir, boat launch, fishing, swimming, water skiing, open April thru Sept., $15/night - call for rates on group area.
Follow State 503 east 2 miles.

COUGAR CAMP (Pacific Power)
60 tent sites, large group area, res. (503)464-5035, flush toilets, showers, handicap access, playground, on Yale Reservoir, boat launch, fishing, swimming, water skiing, open summer only, $15/night - call for rates on group area.
Follow State 503 east 1 mile.

COUGAR RV PARK (Private)
14 units w/full hookups plus 7 tent sites, reservations (425)238-5224, trailers to 70', showers, pets okay, $10-14/night.
Located at 16730 Lewis River Rd.

LAKE MERRILL (DNR)
11 sites, picnic area, drinking water, boat ramp, fishing, FREE.
Located on the east shore of Lake Merrill, 6 miles north of Cougar via FSR 81.

LONE FIR RESORT (Private) 🅰 RV
32 units w/hookups for water/elec./sewer, grassy tent area, reservations (425)238-5210, trailers to 40', showers, laundry, ice, swimming pool, pets okay, $13-18/night.
Located on Lewis River Rd. - follow signs.

LOWER FALLS REC. AREA (Nat'l Volcanic Mon.) 🅰 RV
43 campsites, group site, trailers to 32', reservations (800)280-CAMP, on Lewis River, waterfalls, pets okay, open thru Labor Day, elev. 1300', $9-27/night.
Take State 503 east 18 miles, and FSR 90 north 12 miles - located at monument headquarters.

SWIFT CAMP (Pacific Power) 🅰 RV
93 campsites, trailers okay, flush toilets, handicap access, trailer waste disposal, on Swift Reservoir, boat launch, fishing, swimming, water skiing, open May thru Oct., $12/night.
Take State 503 east 18 miles and FSR 90 a short distance to campground.

YALE

CRESAP BAY CAMP (Pacific Power) 🅰 RV
73 campsites plus large group area, reservations (503)464-5035, flush toilets, showers, handicap access, trailer waste disposal, on

Lake Merwin, boat ramp & moorage, swimming, fishing, water skiing, interpretive trail, open summer only, $15/night - call for group rates.
Take State 503 east 2 miles, and Lewis River Highway south 4 miles to camp.

SADDLE DAM (Pacific Power)
14 tent/trailer units, flush toilets, showers, handicap access, trailer waste disposal, on Lake Merwin, boat ramp, swimming, fishing, water skiing, open late April thru early Nov., $15/night.
Take State 503 east 2 miles, and Lewis River Highway south 4 miles to campground.

KALAMA

CAMP KALAMA RV PARK (Private)
65 units w/full hookups inc. cable, 31 w/water & elec., plus grassy tent area, reservations (360)673-2456, pull thrus, showers, laundry, wheelchair access, groceries & rv supplies, bait & tackle, gift shop, game room, playground, trailer waste disposal, on Kalama River, swimming, fishing, boat launch, pets okay, $12-21/night.
Leave I-5 at exit #32 and follow Kalama River Rd. east .1 mile.

RASMUSSEN RV PARK (Private)
22 units w/hookups for water/elec/sewer, 5 dry sites, plus tent area, reservations (360)673-2626, trailers to 40', showers, wheelchair access, trailer waste disposal, on Columbia River, fishing, nature trail, pets okay, $9-14/night.
Leave I-5 northbound at exit #27 (southbound exit #30) - located at 268 Hendrickson Dr.

WOODLAND

COLUMBIA RIVERFRONT RV PARK (Private)
76 units w/full hookups, tents okay, reservations (800)845-9842, trailers to 40', showers, laundry, wheelchair access, seasonal heated pool, volleyball & basketball courts, propane, on Columbia River, fishing, hiking, pets okay, $20-22/night.
Leave I-5 at exit #22 and follow the dike access road for 2 miles.

WOODLAND CAMP (DNR)
10 campsites, picnic area, drinking water, FREE.
Take State 503 to East CC St. and turn right, turn right again on CR 1 south of bridge for .3 mile, and left on CR 38 for 2.5 miles.

YACOLT

COLD CREEK (DNR)
6 campsites, picnic area w/shelter, drinking water, hiking & mountain bike trails, FREE.
Take County Rd. 16 south 3 miles, County Rd. 12 southeast 2.5 miles, and Dole Valley Rd. south 5.5 miles.

ROCK CREEK (DNR)
19 campsites, drinking water, picnic area & shelter, handicap access, trails for hikers/horses/mountain bikes, horse facilities, FREE.
Take County Rd. 16 south 3 miles, County Rd. 12 southeast 2.5 miles, and Dole Valley Rd. south 3.5 miles.

SUNSET FALLS (Gifford Pinchot NF)
16 units, reservations (800)280-CAMP, trailers to 22', wheelchair access - inc. trail, East Fork Lewis River, fishing, hiking, pets okay, elev. 1000', $11/night.
Take County Rd. 16 south 3 miles, County Rd. 12 east 8 miles, and FSR 42 to campground.

VANCOUVER

BATTLE GROUND LAKE (WA State Park)
35 units plus 15 primitive horse campsites, group area, reservations (800)452-5687, trailers to 50', flush toilets, showers, disabled access, community kitchen, snack bar, trailer waste disposal, on lake, boat launch, scuba diving area, fishing, swimming, horse trails, $7-10/night.
Take I-5 north 9 miles, State 502 east 10 miles, and follow signs northeast 4 miles to park.

BEACON ROCK RESORT (Private)
50 units w/full hookups plus tent area, (360)427-8473, trailers to 60', showers, laundry, wheelchair access, on Columbia River, propane, boat launch/dock & moorage, fishing, hiking, pets okay.
Take State 14 east about 32 miles to the town of Skamania - located at 62 Moorage Rd.

BEACON ROCK (WA State Park)
33 units, group area - reservations (360)427-8265, trailers to 50', flush toilets, showers, disabled access, community kitchen, trailer waste disposal, on Columbia River, boat launch, fishing, trail to top of monolith, pets okay, $11/night.
Take State 14 east 35 miles to Beacon Rock and campground.

BIG FIR CAMPGROUND (Private)
37 units w/water/elec./sewer plus 38 tent sites, (253)887-8970, trailers to 70', 3 pull thrus, showers, pets okay, $15-18/night.
Take I-5 north to exit #14 and go east 4 miles to campground.

DOUGLAN CREEK (DNR)
7 campsites, picnic area, drinking water, river, FREE.
Take State 14 east 16 miles to Washougal and follow Washougal River Rd. for 16.4 miles. Located in Yacolt Multiple Use Area.

LEWIS RIVER RV PARK (Private)
25 units w/water/elec./sewer, 45 w/water & elec., 15 tent sites, (253)225-9556, trailers to 60', showers, laundry, wheelchair access, pool, trailer waste disposal, groceries, fishing, pets okay, $16-20/night.
Take I-5 north 20 miles to exit #21 and State 503 east 5 miles.

99 MOBILE LODGE & RV PARK (Private)
60 units w/hookups for water/elec./sewer, no tents, reservations (253)573-0351, showers, laundry, pets extra, $20/night.
Take I-5 north to 134th St. exit - located on State 99 at 129th St.

NORTHWEST GUIDE RV PARK (Private)
4 units w/water/elec./sewer, 5 w/water & elec., plus 3 dry sites, tents okay, reservations (360)427-4625, trailers to 40', showers, trailer waste disposal, pets okay, open March thru Dec., $7-15/night.
Take State 14 east to milepost #33 and turn onto Woodard Creek Rd. - located at 202 Woodard Creek Rd.

PARADISE POINT (WA State Park)
70 units, reservations (800)452-5687, trailers to 45', flush toilets, showers, trailer waste disposal, on E. Fork Lewis River, boat launch, fishing, hiking trail, open year round - weekends only Oct. thru March, $10/night.
Take I-5 north 15 miles.

REED ISLAND (WA State Park)
5 primitive boat-in sites, no water, on Columbia River, picnic facilities, fishing, $6/night.
Take State 14 east 16 miles to the Camas/Washougal Marina and boat to campground - located 1 mile east of Washougal.

CENTRAL WASHINGTON CAMPGROUNDS

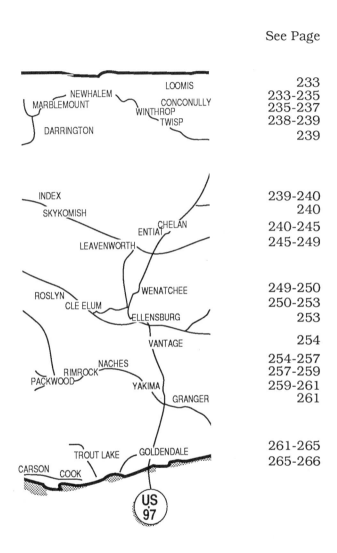

LOOMIS
NEWHALEM
MARBLEMOUNT
CONCONULLY
WINTHROP
TWISP
DARRINGTON

INDEX
SKYKOMISH
CHELAN
ENTIAT
LEAVENWORTH

ROSLYN
CLE ELUM
WENATCHEE
ELLENSBURG

VANTAGE

NACHES
RIMROCK
PACKWOOD
YAKIMA
GRANGER

TROUT LAKE
GOLDENDALE
CARSON
COOK

US 97

LOOMIS

CHOPAKA LAKE (DNR)
15 sites, drinking water, boat ramp, fishing, birdwatching, FREE.
Take Palmer Lake Rd. north 2.1 miles, Toats Coulee Rd. west 1.4
miles, Chopaka Creek Rd. northwest 5.1 miles, turn right on and
go another 2 miles to campground.

COLD SPRINGS (DNR)
9 sites in mountainous area, spring water, picnic area, stream,
trails for hikers & horses, horse facilities, FREE.
Take Palmer Lake Rd. north 2.1 miles, Toats Coulee Rd. west 5.6
miles, OM-T-1000 for 2.1 miles, Cold Creek Rd. .4 mile, then keep
to the right for 1.8 miles, veer left and go another 2.7 miles to
campground.

LONG SWAMP (Okanogan NF)
3 sites, trailers to 18', stream, hiking, elev. 5000', $5/night.
Take Palmer Lake Rd. north 2.1 miles, Toats Coulee Rd. north 1
mile, and FSR 39 west 20.5 miles.

NORTH FORK NINE MILE (DNR)
11 units, drinking water, picnic area, stream, fishing, FREE.
Take Palmer Lake Rd. north 2.1 miles, Toats Coulee Rd. west 5.6
miles, and OM-T-1000 for 2.5 miles.

PALMER LAKE (DNR)
6 campsites, FREE.
Take Palmer Lake Rd. north 8.5 miles.

TOATS COULEE (DNR)
9 sites, picnic area, stream, FREE.
Take Palmer Lake Rd. north 2.1 miles, and Toats Coulee Rd. west
5.5 miles.

NEWHALEM

DEVIL'S PARK (Okanogan NF)
Dispersed hike-in tent camping in the Pasayten Wilderness,
creek, horse trails - meager grazing & scarce water in late sum-
mer, $5/night.
Take State 20 approximately 15 miles east of Newhalem to Devil's
Park Trailhead #738, and follow trail 3.5 miles to campground.

McMILLAN PARK (Okanogan NF)
Dispersed hike-in tent camping in the Pasayten Wilderness,
creek, horse trails - meager grazing & scarce water in late sum-
mer, $5/night.
Take State 20 approximately 15 miles east of Newhalem to Devil's
Park Trailhead #738, and follow trail 2 miles to campground.

MARBLEMOUNT

COLONIAL CREEK (N. Cascades NP)　　　🔺 RV
164 units, trailers to 22', flush toilets, well water, wheelchair access, picnic area, summer program, trailer waste disposal, at Diablo Lake, boat launch, fishing, hiking, pets okay, $10/night.
Take State 20 east of Marblemount 24 miles.

GOODELL CREEK (N. Cascades NP)　　　🔺 RV
22 units, small trailers okay, on Skagit River, raft/canoe launch, fishing, hiking, $10/night.
Take State 20 east 13 miles.

MARBLE CREEK (Mt. Baker-Snoqualmie NF)　　🔺 RV
24 units, trailers to 26', picnic area, pit toilets, fishing, pest okay, elev. 900', $7/night.
Take Cascade River Rd. to FSR 15; campground is 8 miles east.

MINERAL PARK (Mt. Baker-Snoqualmie NF)　　🔺 RV
8 campsites, picnic area, pit toilets, river, fishing, elev. 1400', pets okay, FREE.
Take Cascade River Rd. to FSR 15; campground is 16 miles.

NEWHALEM CREEK (N. Cascades NP)　　🔺 RV
129 units, trailers to 22', flush toilets, wheelchair access, trailer waste disposal, on Skagit River, fishing, hiking, $10/night.
Take State 20 east 14 miles.

CONCONULLY

CONCONULLY (WA State Park)　　　🔺 RV
75 units, trailers to 60', flush toilets, showers, community kitchen, trailer waste disposal, boat launch, fishing, swimming, trail, open year round - weekends only Oct. thru March, $10/night.
Follow signs - at south end of town.

JACK'S RV PARK & MOTEL (Private)　　🔺 RV
66 units w/hookups for water/elec./sewer, tents okay, reservations (509)826-0132, trailers to 40', showers, laundry, pool, trailer waste disposal, propane, on Conconully Reservoir, fishing, hiking, mountain biking, pets okay.
Located in town, 1 block east of Main St.

KERR (Okanogan NF)　　　🔺 RV
13 units, trailers to 22', stream, fishing, elev. 3100', $5/night.
Take Salmon Creek N. Fork Rd. northwest 1.8 miles and FSR 38 northwest 2 miles.

KOZY CABINS & RV PARK (Private)   🅰 RV
14 units w/full hookups, tents okay, reservations (509)826-6780, showers, creek, fishing, $8-12/night.
Located in town, at 111 Broadway.

LAZE DAZE RV PARK (Private)   RV
43 rv sites w/hookups for water/elec./sewer, no tents, reservations (509) 826-0326, trailers to 38', showers, laundry, wheelchair access, on reservoir, pets okay, open April thru Sept/Oct., $16/night.
Located in town, 1 block east of Main St.

LIARS COVE RESORT (Private)   🅰 RV
30 units w/hookups for water/elec./sewer, tents okay, reservations (509)826-1288, showers, lake, swimming, fishing, boat launch & rental.
Located at the east end of town.

MAPLE FLATS RV PARK (Private)   🅰 RV
25 units w/full hookups, grassy tent area, reservations (509)826-4231, wheelchair access, showers, laundry, walk to restaurants/lake & fishing, $10-15/night.
Located just east of Main, on A St.

ORIOLE (Okanogan NF)   🅰 RV
10 units, stream, fishing, elev. 2900', $5/night.
Take Salmon Creek N. Fork Rd. northwest 1.8 miles and FSR 38 northwest an additional .8 mile.

SALMON MEADOWS (Okanogan NF)   🅰 RV
7 units, picnic area, stream, hiking trails, horse corral, elev. 4500', $5/night.
Take Salmon Creek N. Fork Rd. northwest 1.8 miles and FSR 38 northwest an additional 6.9 miles.

SHADY PINES RESORT (Private)   🅰 RV
23 units w/water/elec./sewer, tents okay, reservations (509)826-2287, showers, swimming, fishing, boat rental.
Located 1 mile out of town, on west shore of Conconully Res.

SUGAR LOAF (Okanogan NF)   🅰 RV
5 units, trailers to 22', lake - speed limit, boat ramp, swimming, fishing, elev. 2400', $5/night.
Take Sinlahekin Rd northeast 4.5 miles.

WINTHROP

BALLARD (Okanogan NF)   🅰 RV
6 sites, trailers to 22', river, fishing, elev. 2500', $5/night.
Take State 20 northwest 13.2 miles, Mazama Rd. northwest 6.9 miles, and FSR 5400 northwest 2.1 miles.

BIG TWIN LAKE CAMPGROUND (Private) [A] [RV]
20 units w/hookups for water/elec./sewer, 26 w/water & elec., 40 w/out hookups, plus tent area, reservations (509)996-2650, pull-thrus, showers, laundry, playground, trailer waste disposal, on lake, swimming, fishing, boat rentals, $11-14/night.
Take State 20 south 3 miles and Twin Lake Rd. west 2.3 miles.

CAMP FOUR (Okanogan NF) [A] [RV]
5 units, trailers to 18', stream, fishing, elev. 2400', $5/night.
Take West Chewack Rd. north 6.6 miles and FSR 5160 northeast 11.3 miles.

CHEWUCH (Okanogan NF) [A] [RV]
4 units, trailers to 16', stream, fishing, elev. 2200', $5/night.
Take West Chewack Rd. north 6.6 miles and FSR 5160 northeast 8.6 miles.

DERRY'S RESORT ON PEARRYGIN LAKE (Private) [A] [RV]
64 units w/full hookups plus 90 tent sites, reservations (509)996-2322, showers, laundry, groceries, trailer waste disposal, swimming, fishing, boat launch, pets okay, $15-18/night.
Take Riverside north .5 mile, Bluff St. east 2 miles, and Pearrygin Lake Rd. east 1 mile.

EARLY WINTERS (Okanogan NF) [A] [RV]
13 units, a few trailers to 24', wheelchair access, river, fishing, elev. 2160', $5/night.
Follow State 20 northwest 16 miles.

FALLS CREEK (Okanogan NF) [A] [RV]
7 units, trailers to 18', fishing, swimming, short hike to waterfall, elev. 2100', $5/night.
Take W. Chewack Rd. north 6.6 miles and FSR 51 north 5.3 miles.

FLAT (Okanogan NF) [A] [RV]
12 units, trailers to 18', pit toilets, wheelchair access, stream, fishing, pets okay, $5/night.
Take W. Chewack Rd. north 6.6 miles, FSR 51 north 2.8 miles, and FSR 5130 northwest 2 miles.

HARTS PASS (Okanogan NF) [A]
5 tent sites, near entrance to Pacific Crest National Scenic Trail & Pasayten Wilderness, elev. 6200', $5/night.
Take State 20 northwest 13.2 miles, Mazama Rd. northwest 6.9 miles, and FSR 5400 northwest 12.5 miles.

HONEYMOON (Okanogan NF) [A] [RV]
6 units, trailers to 18', stream, fishing, elev. 3300', $5/night.
Take West Chewack Rd. north 6.6 miles, FSR 5160 north 2.8 miles, and FSR 5130 northwest 8.9 miles.

KLIPCHUCK (Okanogan NF)
46 units, a few trailers to 34', flush toilets, wheelchair access, stream, fishing, hiking, rattlesnake area, elev. 2920', $5/night.
Take State 20 northwest 17.2 miles and FSR 300 north 1 mile.

LONE FIR (Okanogan NF)
27 units, trailers to 22', wheelchair access, piped & well water, creek, fishing, hiking, views of Silver Star Glacier, elev. 3640', $5/night.
Follow State 20 northwest 26.8 miles.

MEADOWS (Okanogan NF)
14 tent units, stream, access to Pacific Crest National Scenic Trail & Alpine Meadows, elev. 6200', $5/night.
Take State 20 northwest 13.2 miles, Mazama Rd. northwest 6.9 miles, FSR 5400 northwest 12.5 miles, and FSR 5400-500 south 1 mile.

NICE (Okanogan NF)
3 tent sites, stream, fishing, elev. 2700', $5/night.
Take West Chewack Rd. north 6.6 miles, FSR 5160 north 2.8 miles, and FSR 5130 northwest 3.8 miles.

PEARRYGIN LAKE (WA State Park)
30 units w/full hookups, 27 w/water, and dry sites, trailers to 60', group area, reservations (800)452-5687, flush toilets, showers, wheelchair access, trailer waste disposal, boat launch, fishing, open April thru mid Nov., $11-16/night.
Take Riverside north .5 mile, Bluff St. east 2 miles, and follow Pearrygin Lake Rd. to campground.

PINE-NEAR RV PARK (Private)
28 units w/hookups for water/elec./sewer plus 25 tent sites, reservations (509)996-2391, showers, laundry, trailer waste disposal, pets okay, $9-14/night.
Take Riverside north .5 mile and Bluff St. east .1 mile.

RUFFED GROUSE (Okanogan NF)
4 units - 2 will accommodate trailers to 14', stream, fishing, elev. 3200', $5/night.
Take West Chewack Rd. north 6.6 miles, FSR 5160 north 2.8 miles, and FSR 5130 northwest 7.8 miles.

WINTHROP/CASCADE NP KOA (Private)
16 units w/hookups for water/elec./sewer, 52 w/water & elec., plus 52 tent sites, reservations (509)996-2258, trailers to 70', showers, laundry, playground, pool, groceries, trailer waste disposal, on river, boat launch, fishing, hiking, bicycle rental, horse tie up area, pets okay, open mid April thru Oct., $20-25/night.
Follow State 20 south 1 mile.

TWISP

BLACK PINE LAKE (Okanogan NF)   [A] [RV]
23 units, trailers to 22', picnic area, piped water, lake - no motors, wheelchair access - includes trail, boat launch & docks, fishing, hiking, pets okay, elev. 4200', $5/night.
Take Poorman Creek Rd. west 11 miles, FSR 43 south 8 miles.

FOGGY DEW (Okanogan NF)   [A] [RV]
13 units, trailers to 18', stream, hiking trails, elev. 2400', $5/night.
Take State 153 south 12.2 miles, Gold Creek Rd. southwest 1.1 miles, and FSR 4340 west 4.1 miles.

J R (Okanogan NF)   [A] [RV]
6 units, trailers to 25', wheelchair access, stream, bicycling, elev. 3900', $5/night.
Follow State 20 east 12.1 miles.

LOUP LOUP (Okanogan NF)   [A] [RV]
25 units, trailers to 22', stream, access to mountain bike trails, elev. 4200', $5/night.
Follow State 20 east 13 miles and FSR 42 north .6 mile.

MYSTERY (Okanogan NF)   [A] [RV]
4 units, river, fishing, hiking trails, elev. 2800', $5/night.
Take Poorman Creek Rd. west 10.8 miles and FSR 44 northwest 7.3 miles.

POPLAR FLAT (Okanogan NF)   [A] [RV]
16 units, trailers to 22', wheelchair access, pit toilets, picnic area, piped water, river, fishing, hiking trails, pets okay, elev. 2900', $5/night.
Take Poorman Creek Rd. west 10.8 miles, FSR 44 northwest 9.4 miles.

RIVER BEND RV PARK (Private)   [A] [RV]
69 units w/hookups for water/elec./sewer plus 35 tent sites, reservations (509)997-3500, showers, laundry, playground, trailer waste disposal, fishing, pets okay, $14-18/night.
Follow State 20 southeast 6 miles.

ROADS END (Okanogan NF)   [A]
4 tent sites, river, fishing, hiking trails, elev. 3600', $5/night.
Take Poorman Creek Rd. west 10.8 miles and FSR 44 northwest 14.4 miles.

SOUTH CREEK (Okanogan NF)   [A] [RV]
4 units, trailers to 15', fishing, hiking trails, elev. 3100', $5/night.
Take Poorman Creek Rd. west 10.8 miles and FSR 44 northwest 11.3 miles.

WAR CREEK (Okanogan NF) △ RV
10 units, trailers to 25', fishing, hiking, elev. 2400', $5/night.
Take Poorman Creek Rd. west 10.8 miles, FSR 44 west 3.3 miles.

DARRINGTON

BUCK CREEK (Mt. Baker-Snoqualmie NF) △ RV
26 units, trailers to 22', shelter, picnic area, interpretive trail, fishing, hiking, pets okay, elev. 1200', $7/night.
Take State 530 north 7.7 miles and FSR 26 east 15.2 miles.

CLEAR CREEK (Mt. Baker-Snoqualmie NF) △ RV
18 units, trailers to 22', handicap access, picnic area, fishing, Frog Lake Trailhead, pets okay, elev. 600', $7/night.
Take Mountain Loop Hwy. southeast 4 miles.

SULPHUR CREEK (Mt. Baker-Snoqualmie NF) △ RV
20 units, trailers to 18', fishing, Sulphur Creek Trailhead, pets okay, elev. 1500', $7/night.
Take State 530 north 7.7 miles and FSR 26 east 22.5 miles.

WHITECHUCK (Mt. Baker-Snoqualmie NF) △ RV
5 units, trailers okay, river, fishing, hiking, elev. 900', FREE.
Take Mountain Loop Hwy. southeast 10.2 miles.

WILLIAM C. DEARINGER (DNR) △ RV
12 campsites, picnic area, river, FREE.
Take Mountain Loop Hwy. 9.9 miles, East Sauk Prairie Rd. for .8 mile, stay right on SW-D-5000 for 2.7 miles, stay left at Y for .8 mile, and go left on SW-D-5400 for 2 miles.

INDEX

BIG GREIDER LAKE (DNR) △
5 hike-in sites, sub-alpine lake, fishing, hiking, FREE.
Take US 2 west to Sultan, Sultan Basin Rd. northeast 13.8 miles, at fork go straight on SLS-4000 8.7 miles to Greider Lake Trailhead and hike 3 miles.

BOULDER LAKE (DNR) △
9 hike-in sites, sub-alpine lake, fishing, hiking, FREE.
Take US 2 west to Sultan, Sultan Basin Rd. northeast 13.8 miles, at fork go straight on SLS-4000 8.7 miles to Greider Lake Trailhead, stay right on SLS-7000 for 1.1 mile to Boulder Lake Trailhead, and hike 3.8 miles.

CUTTHROAT LAKE (DNR) △
10 hike-in campsites, fishing, hiking, FREE.
Take US 2 west to Sultan, Sultan Basin Rd. northeast 22 miles to East Bald Mountain Trailhead #37, and hike 4.5 miles.

LITTLE GREIDER LAKE (DNR)
9 hike-in campsites, sub-alpine lake, fishing, hiking, FREE.
Take US 2 west to Sultan, Sultan Basin Rd. northeast 13.8 miles,
at fork go straight on SLS-4000 8.7 miles to Greider Lake
Trailhead and hike 2.2 miles.

SAN JUAN (Mt. Baker-Snoqualmie NF)
8 campsites, river, fishing, primitive, elev. 1500', $7/night.
Take Index-Galena Rd. northeast 14 miles.

TROUBLESOME CREEK (Mt. Baker-Snoqualmie NF)
30 units, trailers to 22', group area, reservations (800)280-CAMP,
handicap access, picnic area, fishing, interpretive trail, elev.
1300', $12/night.
Take Index-Galena Rd. northeast 12 miles.

WALLACE FALLS (WA State Park)
6 tent units, picnic shelter, disabled access, on Wallace River,
waterfalls, $10/night.
Take US 2 west 6 miles - located 2 miles northeast of Gold Bar.

SKYKOMISH

BECKLER RIVER (Mt. Baker-Snoqualmie NF)
27 units, trailers to 22', reservations (800)280-CAMP, well water,
fishing, swimming, on site caretaker, elev. 900', $12/night.
Take US 2 east 1 mile and FSR 65 north 2 miles.

MILLER RIVER (Mt. Baker-Snoqualmie NF)
Group sites - 100 people - reservations required (800)280-CAMP,
trailers to 22', swimming, fishing, elev. 1000', $50 and up.
Take US 2 west 2.5 miles, FSR 64 southeast 1 mile, and FSR 6410
south 1 mile.

MONEY CREEK (Mt. Baker-Snoqualmie NF)
24 units plus group sites, reservations (800)280-CAMP, trailers to
22', wheelchair access, pit toilets, well water, swimming, fishing,
on site caretaker, pets okay, elev. 900', $12/night.
Take US 2 west 2.5 miles and FSR 64 southeast .1 mile.

CHELAN

ALTA LAKE (WA State Park)
16 units w/hookups for water & elec. plus 149 standard sites,
trailers to 40', reservable group area (509)923-2473, flush toilets,
showers, wheelchair access, community kitchen, trailer waste disposal, boat launch, fishing, swimming, trail, $10-15/night.
Take US 97 northeast 17 miles, State 153 west 2 miles, and follow campground road south 2 miles.

BIG CREEK (Wenatchee NF)
4 tent sites, boat-in only, 4-boat dock, on Lake Chelan, shelter, swimming, fishing, water skiing, nearby waterfall, elev. 1100', $5/night.
Boat northwest 27 miles; on west shore.

BOILING LAKE (Wenatchee NF)
3 tent sites, hike-in only, FREE.
Boat northwest on Lake Chelan for 35.2 miles; on west shore.

CORRAL CREEK (Wenatchee NF)
2 tent sites, boat-in only, 6-boat dock, on Lake Chelan, swimming, fishing, water skiing, $5/night.
Boat northwest on Lake Chelan for 27.6 miles to Prince Creek Trail on east shore, and hike Trail #1255 10 miles.

CUB LAKE (Wenatchee NF)
3 tent sites, hike-in only, elev. 5200', FREE.
Boat northwest on Lake Chelan for 27.6 miles to Prince Creek Trail on east shore, and hike Trail #1255 6.5 miles.

DAROGA (WA State Park)
25 units w/hookups for water & elec. plus 17 walk-in/boat-in tent sites, group area - reservations (509)884-8702, showers, wheelchair access, playfield & ball courts, trailer waste disposal, swimming beach, boat launch & moorage, fishing, windsurfing, hiking, open April thru Oct., $5-15/night.
Take State 150 southeast 2 miles to where it meets US 97, cross the Columbia River and continue south 15 miles.

DEER POINT (Wenatchee NF)
4 tent sites, boat-in only, 8-boat dock, on Lake Chelan, swimming, fishing, water skiing, elev. 1100', $5/night.
Boat northwest on Lake Chelan for 21.7 miles; on east shore.

DOMKE FALLS (Wenatchee NF)
3 tent sites, boat-in only, 6-boat dock, on Lake Chelan, fishing, swimming, water skiing, elev. 1100', $5/night.
Boat northwest on Lake Chelan for 37.5 miles; on west shore.

DOMKE LAKE (Wenatchee NF)
6 tent sites, boat-in/hike-in only, on Lake Chelan, shelter, fishing, swimming, water skiing, elev. 1100', $5/night.
Boat northwest on Lake Chelan for 40 miles; on west shore.

GRAHAM HARBOR CREEK (Wenatchee NF)
9 tent sites, boat-in only, on Lake Chelan, fixed docks/6-10 boats, shelter, fishing, swimming, water skiing, elev. 1100', $5/night.
Boat northwest on Lake Chelan for 31 miles; on west shore.

GROUSE MOUNTAIN SPRING (Wenatchee NF) [A]

4 tent sites, trailers to 18', piped water, adjacent to Devil's Backbone ORV trails, elev. 4500', FREE.
Take US 97 west 3.1 miles, South Shore Rd. northwest 16 miles, and FSR 5900 west 8.1 miles.

HANDY SPRING (Wenatchee NF) [A]

1 tent site, adjacent to Devil's Backbone ORV trails, elev. 6300', FREE.
Take US 97 west 3.1 miles, South Shore Rd. northwest 16 miles, FSR 5900 west 14.5 miles, and FSR 114 south .7 mile.

JUNIOR POINT (Wenatchee NF) [A] [RV]

5 units, no water, adjacent to Devil's Backbone ORV trails, elev. 6600', FREE.
Take US 97 west 3.1 miles, South Shore Rd. northwest 16 miles, and FSR 5900 west 14.3 miles.

KAMEI RESORT (Private) [A] [RV]

10 units w/hookups for water/elec./sewer plus 45 w/water & elec., tents okay, reservations (509)687-3690, trailers to 34', showers, snack bar, on Wapato Lake, fishing, boat launch/rental & dock, pets okay, open May thru Labor Day.
Take State 150 along the north shore of Lake Chelan 5 miles and follow Swartout/Wapato Lake Rd. an additional 5 miles to resort.

LAKE CHELAN (WA State Park) [A] [RV]

17 units w/full hookups, 127 standard sites, group area, reservations (800)452-5687, trailers to 30', showers, disabled access, picnic shelter, snack bar, trailer waste disposal, boat launch, scuba diving, fishing, swimming, water skiing, $10-16/night.
Follow the road leading around south side of Lake Chelan - campground is 9 miles west of city.

LAKESHORE WATERFRONT RV PARK (City) [A] [RV]

151 units w/full hookups plus 9 w/water & elec., tents okay - no fire rings, information (509)682-8023, trailers to 70', showers, playground, trailer waste disposal, on Lake Chelan, swimming, fishing, bumper & paddleboat rentals, go carts, mini golf, no dogs or fires, $11-26/night.
Located right in Chelan, on State 150.

LUCERNE (Wenatchee NF) [A]

2 tent sites, boat-in only, on Lake Chelan, dock & boat basin - 11 boats, well, fishing, swimming, water skiing, Domke Lake Trailhead, adjacent to ranger station, elev. 1100', $5/night.
Boat northwest on Lake Chelan for 41.2 miles; on west shore.

MITCHELL CREEK (Wenatchee NF) [A]

6 tent sites, boat-in only, on Lake Chelan, 17-boat dock, picnic shelter, fishing, swimming, water skiing, elev. 1100', $5/night.
Boat northwest on Lake Chelan for 14.9 miles; on east shore.

MOORE POINT (Wenatchee NF) 🏕

4 tent sites, boat-in or hike-in only, on Lake Chelan, 3-boat dock, shelter, swimming, fishing, water skiing, hiking, elev. 1100', $5/night.
Boat northwest on Lake Chelan for 43 miles; on east shore.

PRINCE CREEK (Wenatchee NF) 🏕

6 tent sites, boat-in only, on Lake Chelan, 3-boat dock, picnic area, fishing, swimming, water skiing, hiking, elev. 1100', $5/night.
Boat northwest on Lake Chelan for 35.2 miles; on east shore.

RAMONA TRAILHEAD (Wenatchee NF) 🏕

7 tent sites, trailers to 22', stream, fishing, water skiing, hiking, elev. 2000', $5/night.
Take US 97 west 3.1 miles, South Shore Rd. northwest 20 miles, FSR 5900 west 3.1 miles, and FSR 8410 to campground.

REFRIGERATOR HARBOR (Wenatchee NF) 🏕

4 tent sites, boat-in only, on Lake Chelan, 4-boat dock, Domke Lake Trailhead, elev. 1100', $5/night.
Boat northwest on Lake Chelan for 41 miles; on west shore.

SAFETY HARBOR (Wenatchee NF) 🏕

2 tent sites, boat-in only, on Lake Chelan, 6-boat dock, stream, no picnic tables, fishing, swimming, water skiing, elev. 1100', $5/night.
Boat northwest on Lake Chelan for 25 miles; on east shore.

SOUTH NAVARRE (Wenatchee NF) 🏕

4 tent sites, horse camping - stock water, summit trail, elev. 6500', FREE.
Take State 150 northwest 5.8 miles, CR 10 north 16 miles, and FSR 8200 northwest .5 mile.

TWENTYFIVE MILE CREEK (WA State Park) 🏕

23 units w/hookups for water/elec./sewer plus 63 standard sites, trailers to 30', group area - reservations (509)687-3710, flush toilets, showers, trailer waste disposal, lake, boat launch & dock, swimming, $10-16/night.
Follow the road leading around south side of Lake Chelan - campground is 20 miles west of city.

WINDY CAMP (Wenatchee NF) 🏕

2 tent sites, elev. 6000', FREE.
Take US 97 west 3.1 miles, South Shore Rd. northwest 20 miles, FSR 5900 west 3.1 miles, and FSR 8410 15 miles southwest of Ramona Park.

ENTIAT

BIG HILL (Wenatchee NF)

1 tent site, shelter, no water, elev. 6800', FREE.
Take US 97 southwest 1.4 miles and Entiat Valley Rd. northwest 25.2 miles, FSR 317 northwest 3.5 miles, FSR 298 north 7.9 miles, and FSR 298A north 1.5 miles.

COTTONWOOD (Wenatchee NF)

25 campsites plus group area, trailers to 22', river, fishing, hiking, elev. 3100', $10/night.
US 97 southwest 1.4 miles, Entiat Valley Rd. northwest 39 miles.

ENTIAT CITY PARK (City)

31 rv units w/hookups for elec. plus 50 tent sites, reservations (509)784-1500, showers, wheelchair access, playground, trailer waste disposal, lake, swimming, fishing, boat launch & moorage, no pets, open year round - no water Nov. to March, $13-16/night.
Leave US 97 in Entiat on Lakeshore Dr., and follow to park.

FOX CREEK (Wenatchee NF)

16 campsites, some trailers, fishing, elev. 2100', $10/night.
US 97 southwest 1.4 miles, Entiat Valley Rd. northwest 27 miles.

HALFWAY SPRING (Wenatchee NF)

5 tent sites, piped water, hiking, elev. 5000', $4/night.
Take US 97 southwest 1.4 miles and Entiat Valley Rd. northwest 25.2 miles, FSR 317 northwest 3.5 miles, and FSR 298 north 2 miles.

LAKE CREEK (Wenatchee NF)

18 campsites, trailers to 18', fishing, hiking, elev. 2200', $10/night.
US 97 southwest 1.4 miles, Entiat Valley Rd. northwest 28.2 miles.

NORTH FORK (Wenatchee NF)

8 tent sites plus 1 trailer to 22', river, fishing, trail, elev. 2700', $10/night.
Take US 97 southwest 1.4 miles, Entiat Valley Rd. northwest 33.5 miles.

PINE FLAT (Wenatchee NF)

7 units, no water, river, fishing, hiking, elev. 1900', $10/night.
Take US 97 southwest 1.4 miles, Entiat Valley Rd. northwest 9 miles, and FSR 5700 northwest 3 miles.

SHADY PASS (Wenatchee NF)

1 tent site, picnic table, elev. 5400', FREE.
Take US 97 southwest 1.4 miles and Entiat Valley Rd. northwest 25.2 miles, FSR 317 northwest 3.5 miles, and FSR 298 north 5.1 miles.

SILVER FALLS (Wenatchee NF)
31 tent sites plus 4 trailers to 22', small group area - reservations (509)784-1511, limited handicap access, well, picnic area, stream, fishing, hiking, waterfall, pets okay, elev. 2400', open mid May thru mid Oct., $10/night - groups $60 and up.
Take US 97 southwest 1.4 miles and Entiat Valley Rd. northwest 30.4 miles.

SPRUCE GROVE (Wenatchee NF)
2 tent sites, river, fishing, elev. 2900', $4/night.
Take US 97 southwest 1.4 miles, Entiat Valley Rd. northwest 25.2 miles, and FSR 5100 northwest 9.8 miles.

THREE CREEK (Wenatchee NF)
3 tent sites, fishing, nearby hiking trail, elev. 2900', $4/night.
Take US 97 southwest 1.4 miles and Entiat Valley Rd. northwest 25.2 miles, and FSR 5100 northwest 10.5 miles.

LEAVENWORTH

ALDER CREEK HORSE CAMP (Wenatchee NF)
Group horse camp - up to 24 horses, elev. 2400', FREE.
Take US 2 northwest 15.9 miles, State 207 north 4 miles, Chiwawa Loop Rd. east 1 miles, and FSR 6200 northwest 4.5 miles.

ALPINE MEADOW (Wenatchee NF)
4 tent sites, river, fishing, elev. 2700', $4/night.
Take US 2 northwest 15.9 miles, State 207 north 4 miles, Chiwawa Loop Rd. east 1 mile, and FSR 6200 northwest 19.5 miles.

ATKINSON FLAT (Wenatchee NF)
8 units, trailers to 22', river, fishing, elev. 2500', $4/night.
Take US 2 northwest 15.9 miles, State 207 north 4 miles, Chiwawa Loop Rd. east 1 mile, and FSR 6200 northwest 15 miles.

BLACKPINE CREEK HORSECAMP (Wenatchee NF)
10 units, trailers to 22', horse ramp, elev. 3000', $9/night.
Take US 2 west .5 mile and Icicle Rd. southwest 19.2 miles.

BLUE SHASTIN TRAILER & RV PARK (Private)
86 units w/hookups for water/elec./sewer, tenters welcome, reservations (888)548-4184, showers, laundry, rec room, pool, trailer waste disposal, river, fishing, hiking, pets okay, $17-21/night.
Take US 2 southeast 4 miles and US 97 south 7 miles.

BRIDGE CREEK (Wenatchee NF)
6 units, trailers to 18', fishing, hiking, elev. 1900', $9/night.
Take US 2 west .5 mile and Icicle Rd. southwest 9.4 miles.

CHALET RV PARK (Private) △ RV
18 units w/full hookups, 14 w/water & elec., plus 12 tent sites, reservations (800)477-2697, showers, laundry, nearby fishing & stores, pets okay, $16-22/night.
At east end of Leavenworth, on US 2.

CHATTER CREEK (Wenatchee NF) △ RV
12 units, trailers to 22', group area - reservations (800)274-6104, fishing, hiking, elev. 2800', $9/night.
Take US 2 west .5 mile and Icicle Rd. southwest 16.1 miles.

CHIWAWA HORSE CAMP (Wenatchee NF) △ RV
21 sites, barrier free, elev. 2500', $4/night.
Take US 2 northwest 15.9 miles, State 207 north 4 miles, Chiwawa Loop Rd. east 1 mile, and FSR 6200 northwest 15 miles.

COUGAR INN RV (Private) △ RV
50 units, tents okay, trailers to 70', reservations (509)763-3354, showers, disabled access, restaurant, on lake, pedal/row boat rentals, boat launch, fishing, hiking, pets okay, $10/night.
Take US 2 northwest 16 miles and follow State 207 north to the head of Lake Wenatchee.

COVE RESORT (Private) △ RV
10 units w/water/elec./sewer, 25 w/water & elec., plus 65 tent sites, (509)763-3130, trailers to 34', showers, on Fish Lake, boat rentals/launch, fishing, hiking, pets okay.
Take US 2 northwest 16 miles, State 207 north 5 miles, and Chiwawa Loop Rd east 1 mile.

DEEP CREEK (Wenatchee NF) △ RV
3 campsites, fishing, elev. 2000', FREE.
Take US 2 northwest 15.9 miles, State 207 north 4 miles, Chiwawa Loop Rd. east 3 miles, and FSR 6100 north 2.2 miles.

DEER CAMP (Wenatchee NF) △
3 tent sites, stream, elev. 4000', FREE.
Take US 2 northwest 15.9 miles, State 207 north 4 miles, Chiwawa Loop Rd. east 3 miles, FSR 6100 north 1.5 miles, and FSR 6101 northeast 2 miles.

EIGHTMILE (Wenatchee NF) △ RV
45 units, trailers to 20', group area - reservations (800)274-6104, handicap access, stream, fishing, hiking, elev. 1800', open mid May thru mid Oct., $9/night.
Take US 2 west .5 mile and Icicle Rd. southwest 8 miles.

FINNER (Wenatchee NF) △
3 tent sites, trailers to 32', piped water, stream, fishing, trails, elev. 2500', $4/night.
Take US 2 northwest 15.9 miles, State 207 north 4 miles, Chiwawa Loop Rd. east 1 mile, and FSR 6200 northwest 11 miles.

GLACIER VIEW (Wenatchee NF)

23 tent units plus 16 walk-in sites on Lake Wenatchee shore, boat launch, swimming, fishing, water skiing, elev. 1900', $9/night.
Take US 2 northwest 15.9 miles, State 207 northeast 3.4 miles, South Shore Rd. west 3.9 miles, and FSR 290 west 1.5 miles.

GOOSE CREEK (Wenatchee NF)

29 campsites - some okay for trailers, fishing, elev. 2200', $7/night.
Take US 2 east of town .3 mile, State 209 north 17.5 miles, and FSR 6100 north 3.2 miles.

GRASSHOPPER MEADOWS (Wenatchee NF)

5 tent sites, river, fishing, elev. 2000', FREE.
Take US 2 northwest 15.9 miles, State 207 north 4 miles, Chiwawa Loop Rd. east .9 mile, and FSR 6400 northwest 7.9 miles.

ICICLE RIVER RANCH (Private)

52 units w/full hookups plus 12 tent sites, (509)548-5420, showers, spa, putting green, river, swimming, fishing, pets okay, $16-25/night.
Take US 2 west .5 mile and Icicle Rd. southwest to #7305.

IDA CREEK (Wenatchee NF)

10 units, trailers to 20', handicap access, fishing, hiking, $8-9/night.
Take US 2 west .5 mile and Icicle Rd. southwest 14.2 miles.

JOHNNY CREEK (Wenatchee NF)

65 units, trailers to 20', handicap access, hand pump well, pit toilets, fishing, hiking, elev. 2300', open mid May thru mid Oct., $8-9/night.
Take US 2 west .5 mile and Icicle Rd. southwest 12.4 miles.

LAKE CREEK (Wenatchee NF)

8 tent sites, fishing, elev. 2300', FREE.
Take US 2 northwest 15.9 miles, State 207 north 9 miles, and FSR 6500 northwest 9.8 miles.

LAKE WENATCHEE (WA State Park)

197 sites, group area, reservations (800)452-5687, trailers to 60', picnic shelter, showers, disabled access, trailer waste disposal, boat launch, swimming, horse trails & rental, pets okay, $10-11/night.
Take US 2 northwest 16 miles and State 207 north 6 miles.

LEAVENWORTH/WENATCHEE KOA (Private)

46 units w/full hookups inc. cable tv, 60 w/water & elec., plus 29 tent sites, pull-thrus, (509)548-7709, kitchen area, showers, laundry, groceries, picnic shelter, playground, trailer waste dis-

posal, swimming pool, hot tub for adults, river, swimming, fishing, hiking, pets okay, $23-30/night.
Take US 2 east .3 mile and River Bend Dr. north to #11401.

LITTLE WENATCHEE FORD (Wenatchee NF)

3 tent sites, stream, fishing, hiking trails, primitive, elev. 2900', FREE.
Take US 2 northwest 15.9 miles, State 207 north 9 miles, and FSR 6500 northwest 14.7 miles.

MEADOW CREEK (Wenatchee NF)

4 units, fishing, elev. 2300', FREE.
Take US 2 northwest 15.9 miles, State 207 north 4 miles, Chiwawa Loop Rd. east 1 mile, and FSR 6200 northeast 2.4 miles.

MIDWAY VILLAGE RV & GROCERY (Private)

14 rv sites w/full hookups, tents okay, reservations (509)763-3344, trailers to 40', shower, laundry, gas, pizza, pets okay, $9-15/night.
Take US 2 northwest 16 miles, State 207 north 5 miles, and Chiwawa Loop Rd east .5 mile.

NAPEEQUA (Wenatchee NF)

5 units - some trailers to 32', river, fishing, entrance to Glacier Peak Wilderness, elev. 2000', FREE.
Take US 2 northwest 15.9 miles, State 207 north 4 miles, Chiwawa Loop Rd. east .9 mile, and FSR 6400 northwest 5.9 miles.

NASON CREEK (Wenatchee NF)

73 units plus group site, trailers to 32', flush toilets, river, fishing, Nason Ridge Trailhead, pets okay, elev. 1800', $10/night.
Take US 2 northwest 16 miles, State 207 north 3.4 miles, and South Shore Rd. west .1 mile.

NINETEEN MILE (Wenatchee NF)

4 units, trailers to 22', river, fishing, elev. 2600', $4/night.
Take US 2 northwest 15.9 miles, State 207 north 4 miles, Chiwawa Loop Rd. east 1 mile, and FSR 6200 northwest 18 miles.

PHELPS CREEK (Wenatchee NF)

7 tent sites, fishing, horse trails to Glacier Peak Wilderness, horse ramp, elev. 2800', $4/night.
Take US 2 northwest 15.9 miles, State 207 north 4 miles, Chiwawa Loop Rd. east 1 mile, and FSR 6200 northwest 21 miles.

ROCK CREEK (Wenatchee NF)

4 sites, fishing, trails, elev. 2500', $4/night.
Take US 2 northwest 15.9 miles, State 207 north 4 miles, Chiwawa Loop Rd. east 1 mile, and FSR 6200 northwest 15 miles.

ROCK ISLAND (Wenatchee NF)
22 units, trailers to 22', handicap access, stream, fishing, hiking, elev. 2900', $8-9/night.
Take US 2 west .5 mile and Icicle Rd. southwest 17.7 miles.

SCHAEFER CREEK (Wenatchee NF)
6 units, fishing, elev. 2600', $4/night.
Take US 2 northwest 15.9 miles, State 207 north 4 miles, Chiwawa Loop Rd. east 1 mile, and FSR 6200 northwest 15.8 miles.

SODA SPRINGS (Wenatchee NF)
5 tent sites, stream, fishing, trails, elev. 2000', FREE.
Take US 2 northwest 15.9 miles, State 207 north 9 miles, and FSR 6500 west 7.2 miles.

THESEUS CREEK (Wenatchee NF)
2 units, trailers to 18', fishing, primitive, elev. 2300', FREE.
Take US 2 northwest 15.9 miles, State 207 northwest 9 miles, FSR 6500 west 6 miles, and FSR 6701 west 4.5 miles.

TUMWATER (Wenatchee NF)
84 units, trailers to 20', large group site w/shelter - reservations (800)274-8104, flush toilets, handicap access, stream, fishing, hiking, elev. 2050', open mid May thru mid Oct., $11/night.
Follow US 2 northwest 9.9 miles to campground.

VALLEY COTTAGE MOTEL RV (Private)
5 units w/hookups for water/elec./sewer, no tents, no restrooms, reservations (509)548-5731, trailers to 40', on river, fishing, hiking, no pets, $10/night.
Follow US 2 east 7 miles to Dryden - located at 8912 Motel Rd.

WHITE RIVER FALLS (Wenatchee NF)
5 tent sites, fishing, entrance to Glacier Peak Wilderness, elev. 2100', FREE.
Take US 2 northwest 15.9 miles, State 207 north 4 miles, Chiwawa Loop Rd. east .9 mile, and FSR 6400 northwest 9 miles.

WHITEPINE (Wenatchee NF)
4 units, trailers to 22', stream, fishing, elev. 1900', FREE.
Take US 2 northwest 24.9 miles, and FSR 6950 west .5 mile.

WENATCHEE

BEEBE BRIDGE PARK (PUD)
27 units w/water & elec., tents okay, trailers to 30', showers, wheelchair access, trailer waste disposal, river, boat launch, fishing, hiking, no pets, open May thru Oct.
Take State 28 north 5 miles and US 2/97 north 34 miles.

LINCOLN ROCK (WA State Park) 🔺 RV

32 units w/water/sewer/elec., 35 w/water & elec., plus 27 tent sites, reservations (800)452-5687, trailers to 65', flush toilets, showers, disabled access, trailer waste disposal, boat launch, fishing, water skiing, $10-15/night.
Take State 28 north 4 miles and US 2 north 2 miles.

SQUILCHUCK (WA State Park) 🔺 RV

Group campsites - reservations required (509)664-6373.
Follow Squilchuck Rd southwest 9 miles.

WENATCHEE CONFLUENCE (WA State Park) 🔺 RV

51 units w/full hookups plus 8 tent sites, reservations (800)452-5687, trailers to 65', showers, wheelchair access inc. trail, playground, trailer waste disposal, Columbia & Wenatchee Rivers, boat launch, fishing, swimming, water skiing, $10-15/night.
North of town take Euclid Ave. south .8 mile and follow signs.

ROSLYN

CLE ELUM RIVER (Wenatchee NF) 🔺 RV

35 units, trailers to 22', fishing, hiking, elev. 2200', $10/night.
Take State 903 northwest 8 miles and Salmon La Sac Rd. northwest 7 miles.

FISH LAKE (Wenatchee NF) 🔺

15 tent sites, pit toilets, stream, fishing, hiking, primitive, elev. 3400', FREE.
Take State 903 northwest 8 miles, Salmon La Sac Rd. northwest 10.7 miles, and FSR 4330 northeast 11 miles.

OWHI (Wenatchee NF) 🔺

23 tent sites, picnic area, Cooper Lake - no motors, boat ramp, swimming, fishing, trailhead to Pacific Crest Trail & Alpine Lakes Wilderness, elev. 2800', FREE.
Take State 903 northwest 8 miles, Salmon La Sac Rd. northwest 9.7 miles, FSR 46 northwest 4.9 miles, and FSR 4616 north .2 mile.

RED MOUNTAIN (Wenatchee NF) 🔺

9 tent sites, pit toilets, river, hiking, fishing, elev. 2200', FREE.
Take State 903 northwest 8 miles, and Salmon La Sac Rd. northwest 8.3 miles.

SALMON LA SAC (Wenatchee NF) 🔺 RV

127 units, reservations (800)879-4496, trailers to 22', flush toilets, handicap access, picnic shelter, fishing, hiking, horse ramp/corrals, trailhead to Cascade Crest Trail & Alpine Lakes Wilderness, elev. 2400', $10/night.
Take State 903 northwest 8 miles, Salmon La Sac Rd. northwest 10.7 miles.

SCATTER CREEK (Wenatchee NF) [A] [RV]
12 units, trailers to 32', fishing, elev. 3300', FREE.
Take State 903 northwest 8 miles, Salmon La Sac Rd. northwest
10.7 miles, FSR 4330 northeast 10.9 miles.

TUCQUALA MEADOWS (Wenatchee NF) [A] [RV]
9 units, trailers to 18', stream, trailhead to Alpine Lakes
Wilderness, elev. 3400', FREE.
Take State 903 northwest 8 miles, Salmon La Sac Rd. northwest
10.7 miles, and FSR 4330 northeast 12.9 miles.

WISH POOSH (Wenatchee NF) [A] [RV]
39 units, trailers to 22', flush toilets, picnic area, on Cle Elum
Lake, boat launch, swimming, fishing, water skiing, occasionally
closes late in season due to low water, elev. 2400', $10/night.
Take State 903 northwest 7 miles and FSR 112 west .1 mile.

CLE ELUM

BEVERLY (Wenatchee NF) [A] [RV]
16 units, trailers to 22', no drinking water, river, fishing, near
horse & motorcycle trails, elev. 3100', FREE.
Take State 970 east 8 miles, Teanaway Rd. north 13 miles, and
FSR 9737 north 4 miles.

BUCK MEADOWS (Wenatchee NF) [A] [RV]
5 units, trailers to 18', no water, pit toilets, horse & motorcycle
trails, stream, fishing, elev. 4300', FREE.
Take I-90 southeast 12 miles, Taneum Rd. southwest 3 miles,
FSR 33 northwest 8 miles, FSR 3300 south 8 miles, and FSR 31
south 5 miles.

CRYSTAL SPRINGS (Wenatchee NF) [A] [RV]
25 units, trailers to 22', picnic area & shelter, fishing, berry &
mushroom picking, elev. 2400', $10/night.
Take I-90 west 20.7 miles and FSR 212 northwest .4 mile.

DE ROUX (Wenatchee NF) [A]
4 tent sites, stream, fishing, hiking trail, elev. 3800', FREE.
Take State 970 east 8 miles, Teanaway Rd. north 13 miles, and
FSR 9737 north 8 miles.

HANEY MEADOWS (Wenatchee NF) [A] [RV]
19 units, horse loading/tethering, trails, elev. 5500', FREE.
Take State 970 east 12 miles, US 97 north 8.1 miles, and FSR
9722 east 10 miles.

ICEWATER CREEK (Wenatchee NF) [A] [RV]
17 units, picnic area, drinking water, trail, fishing, $6/night.
Take I-90 southeast 12 miles, Taneum Rd. southwest 3 miles,
FSR 33 northwest 5 miles.

INDIAN CAMP (Wenatchee NF) ▲

9 tent sites, river, fishing, FREE.
Take State 970 east 8 miles, Teanaway Rd. west .6 mile, West Fork Teanaway Rd. .6 mile south, and Middle Fork Teanaway Rd. west 3.9 miles.

KACHESS (Wenatchee NF) ▲ RV

180 units, trailers to 32', group area - 50 people - reservations (800)879-4496, flush toilets, on Lake Kachess, boat launch, swimming, fishing, water skiing, hiking, interpretive trail, occasionally closes late in season due to low water, elev. 2300', $10/night.
Take I-90 west 20.7 miles and FSR 49 northeast 5.4 miles.

LAKE EASTON (WA State Park) ▲ RV

45 units w/hookups for water/elec./sewer plus 92 standard sites, trailers to 60', group area, reservations (800)452-5687, flush toilets, showers, disabled access, trailer waste disposal, boat launch, fishing, swimming, $10-15/night.
Take I-90 west to exit# 70 - located 1 mile west of Easton.

LIBERTY REC. AREA (BLM) ▲ RV

Dispersed camping, no restrooms, creek, hiking, wildlife, FREE.
Take State 970 east 12 miles, US 97 north 4 miles, and Liberty Rd. west 1 mile. Camp area on right.

MINERAL SPRINGS (Wenatchee NF) ▲ RV

12 units, fishing, elev. 2700', $10/night.
Take State 970 east 12 miles and US 97 north 9 miles.

MINERAL SPRINGS RESORT & RV (Private) ▲ RV

20 units w/elec. plus grassy tent area, reservations (509)857-2361, restaurant, hiking, gold panning, agate beds, pets okay, $6-12/night.
Take State 970 east 12 miles and US 97 north 9 miles.

QUARTZ MOUNTAIN (Wenatchee NF) ▲ RV

3 units, trailers to 18', no drinking water, horse & ORV trails, elev. 6200', FREE.
Take I-90 east 12 miles, Taneum Rd. west 3 miles, and FSR 33 northwest 8 miles, FSR 3330 south 8 miles, FSR 1904 west 4 miles, and FSR 3100 northwest 7 miles.

RED TOP (Wenatchee NF) ▲

3 tent sites, pit toilet, fire lookout, horse trails, agate beds, rough road - no trailers, elev. 5100', FREE.
Take State 970 east 12 miles, US 97 north 6.1 miles, and FSR 9702 for about 10 miles. Located near Red Top Lookout.

RV TOWN INC. (Private) ▲ RV

20 units w/hookups for water/elec./sewer plus 52 w/water & elec., tents okay, reservations (509)656-2360, trailers to 40',

showers, laundry, playground, pool, restaurant, trailer waste disposal, stream, fishing, hiking, pets & horses okay, $8-19/night.
Take I-90 west to exit #70 - located in Easton.

SOUTH FORK MEADOW (Wenatchee NF) 🅰 RV
4 units, trailers to 18', stream, fishing, hiking/motorcycle trails, elev. 3500', FREE.
Take I-90 southeast 12 miles, Taneum Rd. west 3 miles, and FSR 33 northwest 13 miles.

TAMARACK SPRING (Wenatchee NF) 🅰
3 tent sites, no drinking water, pit toilet, horse/motorcycle trails, elev. 4500', FREE.
Take I-90 east 12 miles, Taneum Rd. west 3 miles, and FSR 33 northwest 8 miles, FSR 3330 south 8 miles, and FSR 3120 east 2 miles.

TANEUM (Wenatchee NF) 🅰 RV
13 units, picnic area, hiking, horse & motorcycle trails, stream, fishing, elev. 2400', $10/night.
Take I-90 east 12 miles, Taneum Rd. west 3 miles, and FSR 33 northwest 4.2 miles.

TRAILER CORRAL RV PARK (Private) 🅰 RV
15 units w/hookups for water/elec./sewer, 7 w/water & elec., plus 2 w/out hookups, tents okay, reservations (509)674-2433, showers, cabins, trailer waste disposal, $13-18/night.
Take I-90 east to exit #85 and follow State 970 east 1 mile.

ELLENSBURG

ELLENSBURG KOA (Private) 🅰 RV
12 units w/hookups for water/elec./sewer, 88 w/water & elec., plus 40 tent sites, reservations (509)925-9319, showers, wheelchair access, laundry, groceries, rec room, playground, swimming pool, trailer waste disposal, on river, boat launch, rafting, fishing, nearby restaurant & horse facilities, $18-25/night.
Leave I-90 at exit #106 and follow signs to campground.

LION ROCK SPRING (Wenatchee NF) 🅰
3 tent sites, picnic area, pit toilets, hiking/horse/motorcycle trails nearby, elev. 6300', FREE.
Take Green Canyon Rd. north 12.4 miles, FSR 35 north 9.7 miles, and FSR 124 west .8 mile.

RIVERVIEW CAMPGROUND (Private) 🅰 RV
34 units w/water & elec. plus 76 tent sites, reservations (509) 952-6043, trailers to 35', coin showers, Yakima River, boat rental, fishing, hiking, pets okay, open March thru mid Nov., $5/person plus $3/elec.
Located on State 821, between mileposts 14 & 15.

VANTAGE

GINKGO/WANAPUM (WA State Park) [A] [RV]
50 units w/hookups for water/elec./sewer, reservations (800)452-5687, trailers to 60', flush toilets, showers, on reservoir, boat launch, fishing, swimming, trail, in Ginkgo Petrified Forest, open year round, pets okay, $15/night.
Take Huntzinger Rd south 3 miles.

VANTAGE KOA (Private) [A] [RV]
114 units w/hookups for water/elec./sewer plus 36 tent sites, reservations (509)856-2230, showers, laundry, groceries, rec room, playground, pool, hot tub, trailer waste disposal, on Columbia River, swimming, fishing, pets okay, $17-22/night.
Leave I-90 on exit #136 - located 2 blocks north.

NACHES

BUMPING CROSSING (Wenatchee NF) [A] [RV]
12 units, trailers to 18', river, fishing, hiking, reduced service, elev. 3200', FREE.
Take US 12 west 4.3 miles, State 410 northwest 27.8 miles, and FSR 1800 northwest 9.9 miles.

BUMPING DAM (Wenatchee NF) [A] [RV]
28 units, trailers to 18', river, fishing, reduced service, elev. 3400', $4/night.
Take US 12 west 4.3 miles, State 410 northwest 27.8 miles, FSR 174 southwest 10.8 miles, and FSR 1602 north .6 mile.

BUMPING LAKE (Wenatchee NF) [A] [RV]
45 units, trailers to 30', reservations (800)280-CAMP, boat launch, swimming, fishing, water skiing, elev. 3400', open mid May thru mid Oct., $10/night.
Take US 12 west 4.3 miles, State 410 northwest 27.8 miles, and FSR 1800 southwest 11.4 miles.

CEDAR SPRINGS (Wenatchee NF) [A] [RV]
15 units, trailers to 22', reservations (800)280-CAMP, on Bumping River, fishing, elev. 2800', open mid May thru mid Oct., $10/night.
Take US 12 west 4.3 miles, State 410 northwest 27.8 miles, and FSR 1800 southwest .5 mile.

CLEAR LAKE (Wenatchee NF) [A] [RV]
26 units, picnic area, stream, lake - 5 mph speed limit, fishing, hiking, reduced service, elev. 3100', open mid May thru mid Oct., $6/night.
Take US 12 west 35.6 miles, FSR 143 south .9 mile, and FSR 1312 south 1 mile.

COTTON WOOD (Wenatchee NF)
16 units, trailers to 22', reservations (800)280-CAMP, on Naches River, fishing, elev. 2300', $10/night.
Take US 12 west 4.3 miles and State 410 northwest 17.7 miles.

COUGAR FLAT (Wenatchee NF)
12 units, trailers to 20', reservations (800)280-CAMP, on Bumping River, fishing, elev. 3100', open mid May thru mid Oct., $10/night.
Take US 12 west 4.3 miles, State 410 northwest 27.8 miles, and FSR 1800 southwest 6 miles.

CROW CREEK (Wenatchee NF)
15 units, trailers to 18', fishing, ORV, reduced service, elev. 2900', $4/night.
Take US 12 west 4.3 miles, State 410 northwest 24.8 miles, and FSR 1900 northwest 3.1 miles.

DEEP CREEK (Wenatchee NF)
6 units, trailers to 18', trailhead into Cougar Lakes Area, elev. 4300', FREE.
Take US 12 west 4.3 miles, State 410 northwest 27.8 miles, FSR 174 southwest 13.3 miles, and FSR 162 southwest 7 miles.

EAGLE ROCK RESORT (Private)
10 units w/water/elec./sewer, trailers to 35', (509) 658-2905, disabled access, propane, groceries, restaurant, on Naches River, fishing, hiking, pets okay, $15/night.
Take US 12 west 4.3 miles and State 410 northwest 7.7 miles.

GRANITE LAKE (Wenatchee NF)
8 units, trailers to 18', boating, swimming, fishing, elev. 5000, FREE.
Take US 12 west 4.3 miles, State 410 northwest 27.8 miles, FSR 174 southwest 13.9 miles, and FSR 163 southwest 3.7 miles.

HALFWAY FLAT (Wenatchee NF)
8 units, trailers to 18', river, fishing, reduced service, elev. 2100', $6/night.
Take US 12 west 4.3 miles, State 410 northwest 21.2 miles, and FSR 1704 northwest 2.9 miles.

HELLS CROSSING (Wenatchee NF)
18 units, trailers to 20', reservations (800)280-CAMP, picnic area, on American River, fishing, elev. 3200', open mid May thru mid Oct., $10/night.
Take US 12 west 4.3 miles and State 410 northwest 33.7 miles.

HUCKLEBERRY (Wenatchee NF)
8 tent sites, river, fishing, berry picking, elev. 5300', FREE.
Take US 12 west 4.3 miles, State 410 northwest 24.3 miles, FSR 197 northwest 3 miles, and FSR 182 for 7 miles.

INDIAN FLAT (Wenatchee NF) ⛺ RV
11 units, trailers to 20', on Bumping River, fishing, elev. 2600', $8/night.
Take US 12 west 4.3 miles and State 410 northwest 26.6 miles.

KANER FLAT (Wenatchee NF) ⛺ RV
41 units, trailers to 30', near Little Naches River, fishing, historic wagon train camp on Old Naches Trail, elev. 2700', $8/night.
Take US 12 west 4.3 miles, State 410 northwest 24.9 miles, and FSR 1900 northwest 2.5 miles.

LITTLE NACHES (Wenatchee NF) ⛺ RV
21 units plus 3 group areas, reservations (800)280-CAMP, trailers to 20', on Little Naches River, fishing, elev. 2600', open mid May thru mid Oct., $10/night.
Take US 12 west 4.3 miles, State 410 northwest 24.9 miles, and FSR 1900 northwest .1 mile.

LODGEPOLE (Wenatchee NF) ⛺ RV
33 units, trailers to 20', reservations (800)280-CAMP, picnic area, river, fishing, elev. 3500', open mid May thru mid Oct., $10/night.
Take US 12 west 4.3 miles and State 410 northwest 40.6 miles.

LONGMIRE MEADOW (Wenatchee NF) ⛺ RV
13 units, trailers to 18', river, fishing, elev. 2800', $6/night.
Take US 12 west 4.3 miles, State 410 northwest 24.3 miles, and FSR 197 northwest 4.1 miles.

LOST LAKE (Wenatchee NF) ⛺
3 tent sites, boating, swimming, fishing, elev. 3500', FREE.
Take US 12 west 22.6 miles, FSR 143 south .2 mile, and FSR 1402 southeast 4.6 miles.

MILK POND (Wenatchee NF) ⛺ RV
5 units, lake, fishing, hiking, FREE.
Take US 12 west 4.3 miles, State 410 northwest 25 miles, and FSR 1708 northeast 1.7 miles.

PENINSULA (Wenatchee NF) ⛺ RV
15 units, trailers to 18', lake, boating, swimming, fishing, boat landing, water skiing, reduced service, elev. 3000', $6/night.
Take US 12 west 22.6 miles, FSR 143 south 2.9 miles, and FSR 1200 west 1 mile.

PINE NEEDLE (Wenatchee NF) ⛺
6 tent sites, river, fishing, reduced service, elev. 3000', FREE.
Take US 12 west 4.3 miles, State 410 northwest 30.8 miles.

PLEASANT VALLEY (Wenatchee NF) ⛺ RV
16 units, trailers to 22', reservations (800)280-CAMP, river, fishing, hiking, elev. 3300', $10/night.
Take US 12 west 4.3 miles and State 410 northwest 37 miles.

RIMROCK BOAT LANDING (Wenatchee NF)　　　🅰 RV
5 units, lake, fishing, swimming, boating, water skiing, $6/night.
Take US 12 west 29.6 miles.

SAWMILL FLAT (Wenatchee NF)　　　🅰 RV
25 units, 1 barrier-free site, trailers to 24', wheelchair access, on
Naches River, fishing, elev. 2500', $8/night.
Take US 12 west 4.3 miles and State 410 northwest 23.7 miles.

SODA SPRINGS (Wenatchee NF)　　　🅰 RV
26 units, trailers to 30', on Bumping River, shelters, fishing, natural mineral springs, elev. 3100', $8/night.
Take US 12 west 4.3 miles, State 410 northwest 27.8 miles, and
FSR 1800 southwest 4.8 miles.

SOUTH FORK (Wenatchee NF)　　　🅰 RV
9 units, trailers to 18', river, fishing, reduced service, elev. 3000',
open mid May thru mid Oct., $6/night.
Take US 12 west 22.6 miles, FSR 143 south 4.1 miles, and FSR
1326 south .5 mile.

SQUAW ROCK RESORT (Private)　　　🅰 RV
28 units w/full hookups plus 38 w/water & elec., tents okay,
reservations (509)658-2926, trailers to 35', showers, playground,
pool, hot tub, groceries, restaurant, trailer waste disposal, on
Naches River, fishing, hiking, most dogs okay, $20/night.
Take US 12 west 4.3 miles and State 410 northwest 15 miles.

WILD ROSE (Wenatchee NF)　　　🅰 RV
8 units, trailers to 32', no water, river, fishing, reduced service,
elev. 2400', $6/night.
Take US 12 west 20.4 miles.

WINDY POINT (Wenatchee NF)　　　🅰 RV
15 units, trailers to 22', reservations (800)280-CAMP, on Tieton
River, fishing, elev. 2000', $10/night.
Take US 12 west 12.7 miles.

RIMROCK

COVE RESORT (Private)　　　RV
58 sites w/full hookups, no restrooms, reservations (509)672-
2470, trailers to 35', Rimrock Lake, boat ramp/moorage, fishing,
hiking, swimming, pets okay, open April thru Oct., $18/night.
Located west of Rimrock, near milepost #164 on US 12.

HAUSE CREEK (Wenatchee NF)　　　🅰 RV
42 units, 1 barrier-free site, reservations (800)280-CAMP, trailers
to 30', flush toilets, wheelchair access, on Tieton River, fishing,
elev. 2500', $10/night.
Take US 12 east of Rimrock 6.9 miles.

INDIAN CREEK (Wenatchee NF)

39 units, trailers to 30', reservations (800)280-CAMP, near 2 lakes, elev. 3000', open mid May thru mid Oct., $10/night.
Take US 12 west of Rimrock 6.8 miles.

RIVER BEND (Wenatchee NF)
6 units, trailers to 20', on Tieton River, fishing, elev. 2500', $6/night.
Take US 12 east of Rimrock 3.2 miles.

US 12 WEST RESORT (Private)
30 rv sites w/water & elec., no tents, reservations (509)672-2460, showers, propane, restaurant, on Rimrock Lake, boat launch, fishing, hiking, pets okay, $15/night.
Located west of Rimrock, past Cove Resort, at 37590 US 12.

WILLOWS (Wenatchee NF)
16 units, trailers to 20', reservations (800)280-CAMP, on Tieton River, fishing, elev. 2400', open mid May thru mid Oct., $10/night.
Take US 12 east of Rimrock 5 miles.

PACKWOOD

BYPASS (Gifford Pinchot NF)

5 hike-in sites, creek, wilderness area, elev. 5500', $4/night.
Take US 12 southwest 2 miles, FSR 21 south 11 miles, FSR 2150 northwest 3 miles to Chambers Lake Campground and follow Trail #96 about 4 miles.

DOG LAKE (Gifford Pinchot NF)
11 units, trailers to 18', boat ramp, fishing, hiking trails, elev. 3400', $10/night.
Take US 12 northeast 22.2 miles.

LA WIS WIS (Gifford Pinchot NF)
105 units - some trailers to 24', walk-in sites, flush toilets, some wheelchair access, fishing, hiking, elev. 1400', $12-24/night.
Take US 12 east 7 miles and follow campground road.

LOST LAKE (Gifford Pinchot NF)
2 wilderness camp areas - 8 tent sites, hike-in only, elev. 5200', $4/night.
Take Packwood Lake Rd. 4 miles and hike Trail #78 4 miles to Packwood Lake then an additional 3.6 miles to Lost Lake.

OHANAPECOSH (Mt. Rainier NP)
232 units, trailers to 30', trailer waste disposal, hiking, old growth trees, on Ohanapecosh River, fishing, closes in late Oct., elev. 2000', $12/night.

Take US 12 east 8 miles and State 123 north 4 miles - located 1.5 miles south of Mt. Rainier NP entrance.

PACKWOOD RV PARK (Private)
69 w/full hookups, grassy tent area, (360)494-5145, trailers to 70', pull thrus, showers, laundry, trailer waste disposal. Located in Packwood, at city center.

SODA SPRINGS (Gifford Pinchot NF)
8 tent sites, no drinking water, trailhead to William O. Douglas Wilderness, fishing, elev. 3200', $6/night.
Take US 12 northeast 8.9 miles, FSR 45 west 1 mile, and FSR 4510 northwest 5 miles.

SUMMIT CREEK (Gifford Pinchot NF)
6 units, no drinking water, fishing, rough road, elev. 2400', $6/night.
Take US 12 northeast 8.9 miles, FSR 45 west 1 mile, and FSR 4510 northwest 2.1 miles.

WALUPT LAKE (Gifford Pinchot NF)
43 units, trailers to 22', reservations (800)280-CAMP, wheelchair access, lake - speed limits, fishing, horse facilities, trail into Goat Rocks Wilderness, elev. 3900', $11-22/night.
Take US 12 west 2.7 miles, FSR 21 southeast 16.4 miles, and FSR 2160 east 4.5 miles.

WHITE PASS HORSE CAMP (Gifford Pinchot NF)
6 sites, shelter, horse watering area & hitch rails, river, boating swimming, fishing, trails, elev. 4500', $6/night.
Take US 12 northeast 20.9 miles and FSR 1310 north .3 mile.

WHITE PASS LAKE (Gifford Pinchot NF)
16 units, trailers to 18', lake - no motors, boat ramp, Pacific Crest Trailhead, swimming, fly fishing, reduced service, elev. 4500', $6/night.
Take US 12 northeast 20.9 miles and FSR 1310 north .3 mile.

YAKIMA

AHTANUM MEADOWS (DNR)
18 campsites, drinking water, creek, fishing, hiking, FREE.
Take Ahtanum Rd. west 18 miles to Tampico and Middle Fork Ahtanum Creek Rd. 9.5 miles; campground is on left.

CIRCLE H RV RANCH (Private)
57 units w/full hookups, tents okay, reservations (509)457-3683, trailers to 60', showers, laundry, wheelchair access, playground, pool, spa, lounge, pets okay, $17-20/night.
Leave I-82 at exit #34 and take 18th St. north .3 mile.

CLOVER FLATS (DNR)
9 campsites, drinking water, rough roads, FREE.
Take Ahtanum Rd. west 18 miles to Tampico and Middle Fork
Ahtanum Creek Rd. 18.7 miles.

GREEN LAKE (DNR)
6 units, fishing, FREE.
Take Ahtanum Rd. west 18 miles to Tampico and Middle Fork
Ahtanum Creek Rd. 9.5 miles, North Fork Ahtanum Rd. for 4.5
miles, and keep left for an additional 3.6 miles to campground
road.

SNOW CABIN (DNR)
8 campsites, creek, horse facilities, fishing, FREE.
Take Ahtanum Rd. west 18 miles to Tampico and Middle Fork
Ahtanum Creek Rd. for 14 miles. Keep left at Y - campground is
2.6 miles further.

TRAILER INNS RV PARK (Private)
101 units w/full hookups plus 7 tent sites, reservations (509)452-
9561, trailers to 60', showers, laundry, wheelchair access, playground, fireside lounge, arcade room, indoor pool, sauna, therapy
pools, trailer waste disposal, pets okay, $15-21/night.
Leave I-82 at exit #31 - located at 1610 N. First St.

TREE PHONES (DNR)
14 campsites, picnic area, group shelter, horse facilities, creek,
trail, FREE.
Take Ahtanum Rd. west 18 miles to Tampico and Middle Fork
Ahtanum Creek Rd. 15.2 miles. Turn left on campground road.

WOODLAND PARK (Private)
30 units w/full hookups, no tents, reservations (509)453-9353,
trailers to 60', no restrooms, playground, on Berglund Lake - no
motors, boat launch/moorage & dock, paddle boat rental, fishing,
hiking, bicycle path, pets okay, $12-15/night.
Leave I-82 at exit #31 - located at 2008 N. First St.

YAKIMA KOA (Private)
50 units w/full hookups, 30 w/water & elec., plus 120 tent sites,
reservations (509)248-5882, trailers to 40', showers, laundry,
wheelchair access, playground, game room, groceries, propane,
trailer waste disposal, 2 ponds, fishing, canoe rentals, pets okay,
$20-26/night.
Take State 24 east 1 mile and Keyes Rd. north .3 mile.

YAKIMA RIVER CANYON (BLM)
3 campsites at Squaw Creek, 5700 public acres, picnic area &
boat ramp at Roza, Yakima River, rafting, fishing, water sports,
wildlife viewing, FREE.
Take State 821 along the Yakima River; campground is about 23
miles.

YAKIMA SPORTSMAN (WA State Park)

36 units w/hookups for water/elec./sewer plus 28 standard sites, reservations (800)452-5687, trailers to 60', flush toilets, showers, community kitchen, trailer waste disposal, on Yakima River, fishing, children's fishing pond, $10-15/night.
Take State 24 east 1 mile and Keyes Rd. north to park.

GRANGER

GRANGER RV PARK (Private)

45 units w/hookups for water/elec./sewer, tents okay, reservations (509) 854-1300, trailers to 36', pull thrus, showers, laundry, propane, trailer waste disposal, pets okay, $15/night.
Leave I-82 on State 223 and go south .3 mile.

SMITTY'S RV OVERNIGHTER (Private)

14 units w/full hookups, no tents, reservations (509)882-5858, trailers to 70', pull thrus, no restrooms, trailer waste disposal, pets okay, $14/night.
Leave I-82 on exit #82 - located at 608 W. Wine Country Rd.

YAKIMA NATION RV PARK (Private)

95 units w/full hookups, tent area, reservations (800)874-3087, trailers to 60', showers, laundry, wheelchair access, swimming pool, hot tub, game room, playground, basketball court, restaurant, propane, trailer waste disposal, pets okay, $12-20/night.
Take State 223 west 3 miles, State 22 northwest 6 miles to Toppenish, and follow signs.

GOLDENDALE

BROOKS MEMORIAL (WA State Park)

23 units w/full hookups, 22 standard sites, trailers to 30', group area - reservations (509)773-5382, flush toilets, showers, community kitchen, trailer waste disposal, fishing, hiking trails, $10-15/night.
Take State 97 north 15 miles.

COLUMBIA HILLS RV PARK (Private)

35 sites w/full hookups, tents okay, reservations (509)767-2277, showers, laundry, store, propane, pets okay, $5-18/night.
Take US 97 south 10 miles and State 14 west 21 miles to US 197 and head south; located 1.5 miles north of The Dalles Bridge.

CROW BUTTE (WA State Park)

50 campsites w/hookups for water/elec./sewer, trailers to 60', group area, reservations (800)452-5687, pull thrus, flush toilets, showers, disabled access, picnic shelter, trailer waste disposal, boat launch, fishing, water skiing, $15/night.
Take US 97 south 10 miles and State 14 east 49 miles.

HORSETHIEF LAKE (WA State Park)　　　　　[A] [RV]
12 sites, trailers to 30', flush toilets, trailer waste disposal, boat launch, on Columbia River & Horsethief Lake, scuba diving area, fishing, swimming, windsurfing, hiking, pets okay, $10/night.
Take US 97 south 10 miles and State 14 west 18 miles.

PEACH BEACH RV PARK (Private)　　　　　[A] [RV]
6 units w/hookups for water/elec./sewer, 46 w/water & elec., plus 30 tent sites, reservations (509)773-4698, showers, trailer waste disposal, river, fishing, swimming, hiking, pets okay.
Take US 97 north to Park exit, and drive 1 mile to Peach Beach.

MARYHILL (WA State Park)　　　　　　　[A] [RV]
50 units w/full hookups, reservations (800)452-5687, trailers to 50', flush toilets, showers, disabled access, community kitchen, trailer waste disposal, on Columbia River, boat launch, scuba diving area, fishing, swimming, windsurfing, water skiing, hiking, pets okay - not on beach, $10-16/night.
Take US 97 south 10 miles and State 14 east 2 miles.

PINE SPRINGS RESORT (Private)　　　　　[A] [RV]
12 units w/full hookups, 10 w/water & elec., plus 12 tent sites, reservations (509)773-4434, play area, trailer waste disposal, restaurant, store, propane, fishing, hiking, pets okay, $5-12/night.
Take US 97 north 12 miles.

SUNSET RV PARK (Private)　　　　　　　[A] [RV]
33 units w/hookups for water/elec./sewer, tents okay, reservations (509)773-3111, showers, wheelchair access, heated pool, play area, trailer waste disposal, near observatory, pets okay, open April thru Nov., $16/night.
Located right in Goldendale, at the corner of US 97 & Simcoe Dr.

TROUT LAKE

ATKISSON GROUP CAMP (Gifford Pinchot NF)　[A] [RV]
Group area - 50 people, (800)280-CAMP, trailers, no water, elev. 2700', $60.
Take State 141 north out of Trout Lake and follow it southwest 4 miles to this Sno-Park campground.

BIRD CREEK (DNR)　　　　　　　　　　[A] [RV]
8 campsites, picnic area, FREE.
Take the road east to Glenwood; campground is 6 miles northwest of Glenwood along Bird Creek Rd.

COLD SPRINGS (Gifford Pinchot NF)　　　　　[A]
3 tent sites, primitive, Mt. Adams Trailhead, elev. 5700', FREE.
Take State 141 southeast .2 mile, CR 17 north 1.9 miles, FSR 80 north 3.5 miles, and FSR 8040 north 8 miles.

CULTUS CREEK (Gifford Pinchot NF)
51 units, trailers to 32', reservations (800)280-CAMP, wheelchair access, stream, trail to Indian Heaven, elev. 4000', $11-22/night.
Take State 141 north out of Trout Lake, follow this southwest 5.5 miles to FSR 24, and go northwest 12.6 miles.

ELK MEADOWS RV PARK (Private)
24 units w/hookups for water/elec./sewer, 24 w/water & elec., 10 tent sites, plus group area, reservations (509)395-2400, trailers to 40', showers, laundry, wheelchair access, club house, trailer waste disposal, fishing, hiking, pets okay, $10-16/night.
Take State 141 north of town to milepost #25 and follow the signs to Elk Meadows - it's about 1 mile.

FORLORN LAKES (Gifford Pinchot NF)
8 units, trailers to 18', no drinking water, 5 lakes - no motors, swimming, fishing, primitive & isolated, elev. 3600', FREE.
Take State 141 west 5.5 miles, FSR 24 west 2.5 miles, FSR 60 west 5 miles, and FSR 6040 north 2.5 miles.

GOOSE LAKE (Gifford Pinchot NF)
37 units, trailers to 18', reservations (800)280-CAMP, no drinking water, lake - speed limit, boat launch, swimming, fishing, trail, $11-13/night.
Take State 141 southwest 5.5 miles, FSR 24 west 2.5 miles, and FSR 60 southwest 5.2 miles.

GULER-MT. ADAMS PARK (Klickitat County) 🅰 RV
10 units w/hookups for water & elec., plus 40 w/water, trailers to 40', tents okay, group area - reservations (509)395-2237, showers, trailer waste disposal, pets okay, open March thru mid Nov., $8/night.
Follow the signs - located just south of Trout Lake.

ICE CAVE (Gifford Pinchot NF) 🅰 RV
7 units, trailers to 18', picnic facilities, no water, lava tube cave, primitive, elev. 2800', $6/night.
Take State 141 southwest 5.5 miles, FSR 24 west .9 mile, and FSR 31 south .2 mile.

ISLAND CAMP (DNR) 🅰 RV
6 campsites, covered picnic shelter, winter sports, FREE.
Take road east to Glenwood; campground is 8 miles northwest of town along Bird Creek Rd.

LEWIS RIVER (Gifford Pinchot NF) 🅰
4 tent sites, on Upper Lewis River, swimming, fishing, hiking, primitive, elev. 1500', FREE.
Take State 141 west 1.4 miles, FSR 88 northwest 12.3 miles, FSR 8851 north 7.2 miles, FSR 100 west 5.1 miles, and FSR 3241 to campground. Gravel roads last 15 miles

LITTLE GOOSE (Gifford Pinchot NF) 　　　　 [A] [RV]
28 units, trailers to 18', piped water, berry picking, stream, hiking trails, primitive, elev. 4000', FREE.
Take State 141 southwest 5.5 miles, and FSR 24 northwest 10.1 miles. Gravel road last 6 miles.

MORRISON CREEK (Gifford Pinchot NF) 　　　 [A] [RV]
12 units, no drinking water, Mt. Adams Wilderness Trailhead, horse corral & loading ramp, elev. 4600', FREE.
Take State 141 southeast .2 mile, CR 17 north 1.9 miles, FSR 80 north 3.5 miles, and FSR 8040 north 6.1 miles.

PETERSON PRAIRIE (Gifford Pinchot NF) 　　 [A] [RV]
30 units, trailers to 32', reservations (800)280-CAMP, wheelchair access, hiking, berry picking, elev. 2800', $11-22/night.
Take State 141 north out of Trout Lake, follow this southwest 5.5 miles to FSR 24, and go west 2.5 miles.

PETERSON PRAIRIE GROUP (Gifford Pinchot NF) 　 [A] [RV]
2 group sites, trailers to 22', reservations (800)280-CAMP, wheelchair access, hiking, elev. 2800', $27-60.
Take State 141 north out of Trout Lake, follow this southwest 5.5 miles to FSR 24, and go west 2.5 miles.

SADDLE (Gifford Pinchot NF) 　　　　　　 [A] [RV]
12 units huckleberry area, no water, primitive, elev. 4200', FREE.
Take State 141 southeast 5.5 miles, FSR 24 northwest 18.3 miles, and FSR 2480 north 1.3 miles.

SMOKEY CREEK (Gifford Pinchot NF) 　　　 [A] [RV]
3 units, trailers to 22', no drinking water, berry picking, elev. 3700', FREE.
Take State 141 southwest 5.5 miles and FSR 24 northwest 7.3 miles.

SOUTH (Gifford Pinchot NF) 　　　　　　 [A] [RV]
8 units, trailers to 18', well, huckleberry area, elev. 4000', FREE.
Take State 141 southwest 5.5 miles, FSR 24 northwest 18.3 miles, and FSR 2480 east .3 mile.

TILLICUM (Gifford Pinchot NF) 　　　　　 [A] [RV]
32 units, trailers to 18', piped water, stream, berry picking, hiking, elev. 4300', FREE.
Take State 141 southwest 5.5 miles and FSR 24 northwest 19.1 miles.

TWIN FALLS (Gifford Pinchot NF) 　　　　 [A] [RV]
8 units, on east bank of Upper Lewis River, fishing, primitive, elev. 2700', $9/night.
Take State 141 west 1.4 miles, FSR 88 northwest 16.3 miles, and FSR 150 north 5.2 miles.

WICKY SHELTER (Gifford Pinchot NF) △ RV
1 unit, log shelter, hiking, primitive, elev. 4000', FREE.
Take State 141 southeast .2 mile, CR 17 north 1.9 miles, FSR 80
for 3.5 miles, and FSR 8040 north 1.5 miles.

CARSON

BEAVER (Gifford Pinchot NF) △ RV
24 campsites, 2 group areas - 40 people each, trailers to 25', some
res. (800)280-CAMP, flush toilets, wheelchair access, hiking, fishing, near Trapper Creek Wilderness, pets okay, elev. 1100', $11-22/night - groups $65.
Take Wind River Rd. northwest 12.2 miles.

BIG FOOT TRAILER PARK (Private) △ RV
19 units w/full hookups, tents okay, res. (509)427-4441, trailers
to 70', showers, laundry, wheelchair access, near Columbia River,
fishing, hiking, trailer waste disposal, pets okay, $5-10/night.
Located in Carson, on Metzger Rd.

CARSON HOT SPRINGS (Private) RV
12 units w/full hookups plus tent sites, res. (509) 427-8292,
showers, handicap access, picnic area, hot springs, therapy
baths, golf, trailer waste disposal, fishing, hiking, pets okay, $13-15/night.
Go up the hill, past the golf course, take a left and go down the
hill to resort.

CREST (Gifford Pinchot NF) △ RV
3 sites, trailers to 18', no drinking water, horse facilities, trails to
Pacific Crest Trail & Indian Heaven Wilderness, elev. 3500',
FREE-$3/night.
Take Wind River Rd. northwest 9 miles, FSR 6517 east 1.5 miles,
FSR 65 northwest 8 miles, and FSR 60 east 1.8 miles.

FALLS CREEK HORSE CAMP (Gifford Pinchot NF) RV
10 units, trailers to 18', horse trails/loading ramp/corrals, trailhead to Indian Heaven Wilderness & historic Indian race track,
elev. 3500', FREE-$3/night.
Take Wind River Rd. northwest 9 miles, FSR 6517/Warren Gap
Rd. east 1.5 miles, and FSR 65 north 12.5 miles.

HOME VALLEY GROCERY/RV PARK (Private) △ RV
5 units w/water & elec. plus grassy tent area, reservations
(509)427-5300, pit toilets, $3-8/night.
Located in Carson.

LEWIS & CLARK CAMP/RV PARK (Private) △ RV
20 units w/hookups for water/elec./sewer, 40 w/water & elec.,
plus 10 tent sites, reservations (509)427-5559, showers, laundry,
rec room, trailer waste disposal, river, fishing, hiking, nearby golf.

Take State 14 west to milepost #37 - park is about 1 mile west of North Bonneville, on Evergreen Dr.

PANTHER CREEK (Gifford Pinchot NF)   [A] [RV]
33 units, trailers to 25', some reservations (800)280-CAMP, near Pacific Crest Trail, well, stream, fishing, hiking, horse trails & loading ramp, pets okay, elev. 1000', $11-22/night.
Take Wind River Rd. northwest 9 miles, FSR 6517 east 1.5 miles, and FSR 65 south .1 mile.

PARADISE CREEK (Gifford Pinchot NF)   [A] [RV]
42 units, trailers to 25', some res. (800)280-CAMP, dis. access, fishing, Lava Butte Trailhead, pets okay, elev. 1500', $11-22/night.
Take Wind River Rd. northwest 13.8 miles and Meadow Creek Rd. north 6.3 miles.

COOK

HOME VALLEY PARK (Skamania County)   [A] [RV]
23 units, information (509)427-9478, showers, picnic area, wheelchair access, on Columbia River, swimming, fishing, wind surfing, pets okay, $7-12/night.
Take State 14 west of Cook to milepost #50 and park.

OKLAHOMA (Gifford Pinchot NF)   [A] [RV]
23 units, trailers to 22', some reservations (800)280-CAMP, on river, wheelchair access, well, fishing, pets okay, elev. 1700', $6-11/night.
Just east of town, take the road to Willard 7 miles north, and follow Oklahoma/FSR 18 north another 8 miles to campground.

MOSS CREEK (Gifford Pinchot NF)   [A] [RV]
17 units, trailers to 32', some reservations (800)280-CAMP, on Little White Salmon River, wheelchair access, piped water, fishing, pets okay, elev. 1400', $9-11/night.
Just east of town, take the road to Willard north 7 miles, and follow Oklahoma/FSR 18 north 1 mile to the campground.

EASTERN WASHINGTON CAMPGROUNDS

See Page

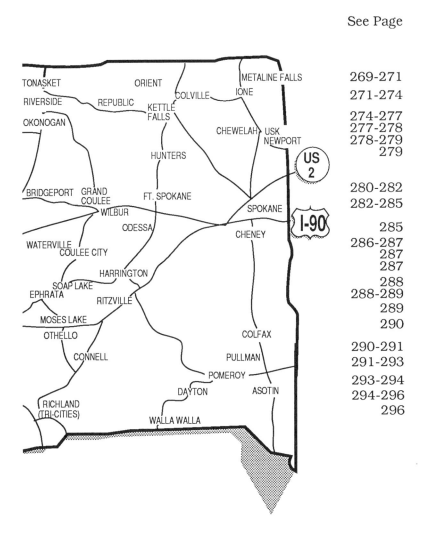

269-271
271-274

274-277
277-278
278-279
279

280-282
282-285

285
286-287
287
287
288
288-289
289
290

290-291
291-293

293-294
294-296
296

TONASKET

BETH LAKE (Okanogan NF)   🔺 RV
15 units, boating, swimming, fishing, hiking, elev. 2900', FREE.
Take State 20 east 20 miles, Bonaparte Lake Rd. north 6 miles,
FSR 32 northeast 6 miles, and head northwest 1 mile.

BONAPARTE LAKE (Okanogan NF)   🔺 RV
26 units, group area, trailers to 32', flush toilets, wheelchair
access, boat launch, swimming, fishing, hiking, elev. 3600'.
Take State 20 east 20 miles, Bonaparte Lake Rd. north 3 miles,
and FSR 32 north .7 mile - located south of the resort.

BONAPARTE LAKE RESORT (Private)   🔺 RV
32 units w/water/elec./sewer, tents okay, reservations (509)486-
2828, trailers to 35', showers, laundry, cafe, cabins, groceries,
propane, trailer waste disposal, fishing dock, swimming, boat
launch & rental, pets extra, open mid April thru Oct., elev. 3500',
$10-12/night.
Take State 20 east 20 miles, Bonaparte Lake Rd. north 6 miles.

LOST LAKE (Okanogan NF)   🔺 RV
18 units, trailers to 32', group area - reservations (509)486-2186,
flush toilets, wheelchair access, boat launch, swimming, fishing,
hiking, elev. 3800'.
Take State 20 east 20 miles, Bonaparte Lake Rd. north 6 miles,
FSR 32 northeast 3 miles, FSR 33 northwest 3.5 miles, and FSR
50 south .5 mile to campground.

LYMAN LAKE (Okanogan NF)   🔺 RV
4 sites, trailers to 32', fishing, elev. 2900', FREE.
Take State 20 east 12.6 miles, Aeneas Valley Rd. southeast 13
miles, FSR 3785 south 2.4 miles, and FSR 358 northwest .2 mile.

ORCHARD RV PARK (Private)   🔺 RV
41 units w/hookups for water/elec./sewer plus grassy tent area,
reservations (509)476-2669, trailers to 60', pull thrus, showers,
wheelchair access, on Lake Osoyoos, boat ramp, fishing, swimming beach, hiking, pets okay, $12-16/night.
Take State 97 north 18.5 miles, Eastside Osoyoos Lake Rd.
around the lake, and Thorndyke Loop Rd. to the park.

OSOYOOS LAKE (WA State Park)   🔺 RV
80 units, trailers to 45', reservations (800)452-5687, flush toilets,
showers, snackbar, trailer waste disposal, boat launch, fishing,
swimming, water skiing, open year round - weekends only Nov.
thru March, $10/night.
Take State 97 north 18.5 miles - located just north of Oroville.

RAINBOW RESORT (Private)   🔺 RV
37 units w/hookups for water/elec./sewer, 15 w/water & elec.,
plus tent area, reservations (509)223-3700, trailers to 35', wheel-

chair access, showers, on Spectacle Lake, swimming, fishing, boat launch & rental, pets okay, open April thru Oct., $16/night.
Take US 97 north approximately 7 miles and Loomis Rd. west 6 miles to resort.

RIVERVIEW TRAILER COURT (Private)   [RV]
4 trailer sites w/hookups for water/elec./sewer, no tents, reservations (509)486-2491, no restrooms, trailers to 40', on Okanogan River, fishing, hiking, pets okay, $10/night.
Located just off US 97, in Tonasket, at 1305 W. Fourth.

SPECTACLE FALLS RESORT (Private)
20 units w/hookups for water/elec./sewer, 10 w/water & elec., plus small tent area, reservations (509)223-4141, showers, ice, trailer waste disposal, on Spectacle Lake, swimming, fishing, boat launch/rental & gas, pets okay, $15/night.
Take US 97 north approximately 7 miles and Loomis Rd. west 8 miles to resort.

SPECTACLE LAKE RESORT (Private)
34 units w/hookups for water/elec./sewer plus 6 tent sites, reservations (509)223-3433, trailers to 40', showers, laundry, ice, swimming pool, playfield, playground, on lake, swimming, fishing, boat launch & rental, pets okay, $14/night.
Take US 97 north approximately 7 miles and Loomis Rd. west 5 miles to resort.

SUN COVE RESORT (Private)   [A] [RV]
20 units w/full hookups, 7 w/water & elec., 15 dry sites, tents okay, reservations (509)476-2223, trailers to 35', showers, laundry, cafe, rec room, heated pool, trailer waste disposal, groceries, tavern, Wannacut Lake, boat ramp, canoeing, fishing, hiking, pets okay, open April thru Oct., $18/night.
Take US 97 north 16 miles to Oroville, Wannacut Lake Rd. west 10 miles, and resort road north 1 mile.

ORIENT

DAVIS LAKE (Colville NF)   [A] [RV]
4 units, trailers to 18', no drinking water, boat ramp, fishing, elev. 4600', FREE.
Take US 395 south 16 miles, just before the town of Boyds take FSR 480 northwest 8 miles to lake.

PIERRE LAKE (Colville NF)   [A] [RV]
15 units, trailers to 32', well, boat launch, swimming, fishing, water skiing, elev. 2000', FREE.
Take Orient Rd. east 3.8 miles and Pierre Lake Rd. north 3.2 miles.

SUMMIT LAKE (Colville NF) ▲

4 units, no trailers, well, boat launch, fishing, elev. 3600', FREE.
Take Orient Rd. east 3.8 miles and Pierre Lake Rd. north 5 miles.

METALINE FALLS

BOUNDARY DAM CAMP (BLM) ▲ RV

4 primitive sites, picnic facilities, fire rings, on Pend Oreille River,
fishing, swimming, rafting, hiking, FREE.
Leave State 31 on Boundary Rd. and head north 6 miles, about
1.5 miles north of Ledbetter Lake turn east on the primitive road
and follow for 2.5 miles.

MILLPOND (Colville NF) ▲ RV

10 units, trailers to 28', stream, fishing, elev. 2600', $8/night.
Take State 31 northeast 1.5 miles and Sullivan Lake Rd. east 3.5
miles.

MT. LINTON RV PARK (Private) ▲ RV

42 units w/full hookups plus grassy tent area, reservations
(509)446-4553, trailers to 50', pull thrus, showers, laundry, nearby river & fishing, pets okay, $13-18/night.
Take State 31 south 2 miles to the town of Metaline and park.

SULLIVAN LAKE (Colville NF) ▲ RV

34 units, trailers to 28', group area, reservations (800)280-CAMP,
on lake, fishing, swimming, water skiing, hiking, elev. 2600', $8-
16/night.
Take State 31 northeast 1.5 miles and Sullivan Lake Rd. east 5
miles.

IONE

EDGEWATER (Colville NF) ▲ RV

23 units, trailers to 20', no water, river, boat ramp, fishing, water
skiing, elev. 2100', $6/night.
Take State 31 south 1 mile, Sullivan Lake Rd. east .3 mile,
Canyon-LeClerc Rd. north 2 miles and FSR 33101 for 1.8 miles.

IONE MOTEL & RV PARK (Private) ▲ RV

16 units w/hookups for water/elec./sewer plus 2 w/water & elec,
tents okay, reservations (509)442-3213, showers, laundry, on
Pend Oreille River, boat launch, paddle boat rentals, fishing,
swimming, water skiing, pets okay, $5-18/night.
Located at the south end of town.

NOISY CREEK (Colville NF) ▲ RV

19 sites, trailers to 28', reservations (800)280-CAMP, boat ramp,
swimming, fishing, water skiing, hiking, elev. 3200', $8-10/night.
State 31 south 1 mile, Sullivan Lake Rd. northeast 9 miles.

COLVILLE

BEAVER LODGE RV PARK (Private) ▲ RV
8 units w/full hookups, 7 w/water & elec., 27 w/out hookups, tents okay, reservations (509)684-5657, showers, laundry, groceries, cabins, propane, on lake, boat launch, fishing, swimming, canoe/motor/paddle boat rental, elev. 3300', $8-14/night. Take State 20 east 25 miles.

DEER CREEK SUMMIT (Colville NF) ▲ RV
7 sites, trailers to 18', no drinking water, hiking trails, elev. 4600', FREE.
Take State 21 north approximately 26 miles to Curlew and head east on Deer Creek Rd. for 11.5 miles.

DOUGLAS FALLS (DNR) ▲ RV
8 campsites, drinking water, wheelchair access, waterfalls, hiking trails, FREE.
Take State 20 east .5 mile, Aladdin Rd. 2 miles, and Douglas Falls Rd. 3 miles north.

FAIRGROUNDS PARK (Stevens County) ▲ RV
40 units w/hookups for water & elec., 40 w/elec., plus 20 tent sites, information (509)684-2585, trailers to 70', showers, wheelchair access, trailer waste disposal, playfield, pets okay, open April thru Nov.
Take US 395 to Colville's Fairgrounds exit and follow signs.

FLODELLE CREEK (DNR) ▲ RV
8 sites, water, fishing, hiking/mountain bike trails, FREE.
Take State 20 east 21 miles and Flodelle Creek Rd. .2 mile.

LAKE GILLETTE (Colville NF) ▲ RV
43 units, trailers to 32', some multi-family sites, flush toilets, wheelchair access, trailer waste disposal, on lake, hiking, nearby motorcycle trails, bicycling, elev. 3200', $6-10/night.
Take State 20 east 25 miles.

LAKE LEO (Colville NF) ▲ RV
8 units, trailers to 18', on lake, boat launch, swimming, fishing, elev. 3200', $5/night.
Take State 20 east 29 miles.

LAKE THOMAS (Colville NF) ▲
15 tent sites, no drinking water, boating, swimming, fishing, water skiing, nearby motorcycle trails, bicycling, elev. 3200', $5/night.
Take State 20 east 25.5 miles and campground road east 1 mile.

ROCKY LAKE (DNR) ▲ RV
8 campsites, drinking water, fishing, FREE.
Campground is located 3 miles southeast of Colville, off US 395, on Rocky Lake.

SHERRY CREEK (DNR) [A] [RV]
2 campsites, fishing, FREE.
Take State 20 east 23.8 miles and head south on gravel road .4 mile to campground.

STARVATION LAKE (DNR) [A] [RV]
6 units, handicap fishing facilities, FREE.
Take State 20 east 11 miles.

WILLIAMS LAKE (DNR) [A] [RV]
10 campsites, drinking water, interpretive site, hiking/mountain bike trails, FREE.
Campground is 16 miles north of Colville, along Echo Rd., on Williams Lake.

RIVERSIDE

CRAWFISH LAKE (Okanogan NF) [A] [RV]
18 units, trailers to 32', boat launch, fishing, elev. 4500', FREE.
Take Tunk Creek Rd. east 17.7 miles, FSR 3612 south 1.7 miles, and FSR 3525 southeast .4 mile.

REPUBLIC

BLACK BEACH RESORT (Private) [A] [RV]
60 units w/full hookups plus grassy tent area, reservations (509) 775-3989, showers, laundry, wheelchair access, playground, trailer waste disposal, groceries, on Lake Curlew, swimming, fishing, boat launch & rental, $12-19/night.
Take State 21 east and north 6 miles, West Curlew Lake Rd. north 8 miles, and Black Beach Rd. east 1 mile.

CURLEW LAKE (WA State Park) [A] [RV]
18 units w/hookups for water/elec./sewer, 7 w/water & elec., plus 57 standard sites, trailers to 30', flush toilets, showers, wheelchair access, trailer waste disposal, boat launch, fishing, hiking, open April thru Oct., $10-15/night.
Take State 21 east and north 10 miles.

FERRY LAKE (Colville NF) [A] [RV]
8 units, trailers to 22', boat ramp, fishing, elev. 3300', FREE.
Take State 21 south 7 miles, FSR 53 southwest 6 miles, FSR 5330 north 1 mile, and lake road north .5 mile.

LONG LAKE (Colville NF) [A] [RV]
6 units, trailers to 22', no drinking water, lake - no motors, fly fishing, swimming, elev. 3300', FREE.
Take State 21 south 7 miles, FSR 53 southwest 8 miles, and FSR 400 south 1.5 miles.

PINE POINT RESORT (Private) ⚠️ RV
32 units w/full hookups, tents okay, reservations (509)775-3643, showers, laundry, cabins, playground, groceries, trailer waste disposal, on Curlew Lake, swimming, fishing, boat launch & rental, pets okay, open late April thru Oct., $17/night.
Take State 21 east and north 10 miles.

SWAN LAKE (Colville NF) ⚠️ RV
19 units, trailers to 32' in 25 sites, community kitchen, boat ramp, swimming, fishing, hiking trails, elev. 3700', FREE.
Take State 21 south 7 miles and FSR 53 southwest 8 miles.

TIFFANY'S RESORT (Private) ⚠️ RV
14 units w/full hookups, 2 w/water & elec., 3 tent sites, reservations advised (509)775-3152, trailers to 50', showers, laundry, playground, groceries, propane, gas, on Curlew Lake, swimming, fishing, boat launch & rental, pets okay, open mid April thru Oct., $17/night.
Take State 21 east and north 6 miles, West Curlew Lake Rd. north 10 miles.

KETTLE FALLS

BRADBURY BEACH (Lake Roosevelt NRA) ⚠️ RV
5 units, trailers okay, drinking water, picnic area, picnic area, elev. 1285', $10/night.
Take State 25 south 8 miles.

CANYON CREEK (Colville NF) ⚠️ RV
12 units, trailers to 32', no drinking water, fishing, primitive, elev. 2200', FREE.
Take State 20 northwest 14.5 miles and FSR 136 south .2 mile.

CIRCLE-UP RV PARK (Private) ⚠️ RV
7 units w/full hookups, 10 tent sites, reservations (509)738-6617, trailers to 40', pull thrus, showers, store, trailer waste disposal, nearby fishing, hiking, bicycling, pets okay, open April thru Oct., $15/night.
Take US 395 south 2 miles.

EVANS (Lake Roosevelt NRA) ⚠️ RV
34 units, trailers okay, trailer waste disposal, summer programs, boat ramp & dock, swimming, elev. 1285', $10/night.
Follow State 25 north approximately 9 miles to campground.

GRANDVIEW INN MOTEL & RV PARK (Private) ⚠️ RV
28 units w/full plus grassy tent area, reservations (509)738-6733, trailers to 50', showers, laundry, wheelchair access, pool, hot tub, groceries, propane, lake view, fishing, hiking, horses & pets okay, open April thru Nov., $16/night.
Located at the intersection of US 395 & State 25, in Kettle Falls.

HAGG COVE (Lake Roosevelt NRA) [A] [RV]
8 units, trailers okay, drinking water, picnic area, boat dock, $10/night.
Take US 395 northwest 3.5 miles, State 20 south 4 miles, Kettle Falls Rd. southwest along the river for 2 miles.

KAMLOOPS ISLAND (Lake Roosevelt NRA) [A] [RV]
17 campsites, trailers okay, water, boat dock, $10/night.
Take State 20 across the river and follow US 395 north 4 miles.

KETTLE FALLS (Lake Roosevelt NRA) [A] [RV]
89 units plus group sites, trailers okay, wheelchair access, boat & trailer waste disposal, boat ramp & dock, swimming, summer programs, elev. 1234', $10/night.
Take Kettle Park Rd. towards the river and campground.

KETTLE RIVER (Lake Roosevelt NRA) [A] [RV]
12 units, trailers okay, water, boat dock, elev. 1237', $10/night.
Take State 20 across the river and follow US 395 up the Kettle River. The campground is just before Boyd.

LOCUST GROVE (Lake Roosevelt NRA) [A] [RV]
2 group sites, reservations (509)738-6266, tents okay, trailers to 70', wheelchair access, picnic shelter w/elec., on Lake Roosevelt, fishing, trail, pets okay.
Take Kettle Park Rd. towards the river and campground.

MARCUS ISLAND (Lake Roosevelt NRA) [A] [RV]
27 units, trailers okay, boat dock & ramp, elev. 1281', $10/night.
Follow State 25 north approximately 5 miles to campground.

NE LAKE ELLEN (Colville NF) [A] [RV]
11 units, trailers to 22', well, boat launch, swimming, fishing, elev. 2400', FREE.
Take US 395 northwest 3.5 miles, State 20 south 4 miles, Kettle Falls Rd. southwest 4.5 miles, and FSR 2014 southwest 5.5 miles.

NORTH GORGE (Lake Roosevelt NRA) [A] [RV]
12 units, trailers okay, water, boat ramp & dock, on Columbia River, elev. 1282', $10/night.
Take State 25 northeast 18 miles.

SHEEP CREEK (DNR) [A] [RV]
20 campsites, picnic area, drinking water, FREE.
Take State 25 northeast 33 miles to Northport; then Sheep Creek Rd northwest 4 miles.

SHERMAN PASS (Colville NF) [A] [RV]
9 campsites, trailers okay, picnic area, piped water, hiking & horse trails, elev. 5300', FREE.
Take State 20 west 22 miles to Sherman Pass.

SNAG COVE (Lake Roosevelt NRA) 🔼 RV
4 units, trailers okay, on Columbia River, boat dock, $10/night.
Take US 395 northwest 3.5 miles, State 20 north 4 miles, turn
right and travel 8 miles.

SUMMER ISLAND (Lake Roosevelt NRA) 🔼
Tent area, hike-in or boat-in only, boat dock, FREE.
Located on Upper Lake Roosevelt.

TROUT LAKE (Colville NF) 🔼 RV
4 sites, trailers to 18', boat ramp, fishing, elev. 3000', FREE.
Take US 395 northwest 3.5 miles, State 20 west 5.5 miles, and
FSR 20 northwest 5 miles.

UPPER SHEEP CREEK (DNR) 🔼 RV
2 campsites, FREE.
Take State 25 northeast 33 miles to Northport; then Sheep Creek
Rd northwest 5.2 miles.

WHISPERING PINES RESORT (Private) 🔼 RV
44 units w/full hookups plus tent area, reservations (509)738-
2593, pull thrus, showers, laundry, game room, playground, basketball court, store, ice, walk to river, lake, swimming, fishing,
hiking, pets okay, $9-15/night.
Take US 395 north 6.5 miles and follow signs.

OKANOGAN

COUNTY FAIRGROUNDS (Okanogan County) RV
52 units w/full hookups plus 36 w/water & elec., no tents, reservations (509)422-1621, trailers to 30', showers, wheelchair
access, on Okanogan River, fishing, horse corral & stalls, pets
okay, open March thru Sept., $12/night.
Located on east shore of Okanogan River, 1 mile north of town.

CARL PRECHT MEM. RV PARK (City of Omak) 🔼 RV
65 sites w/full hookups, 5 tent sites, trailers to 36', showers,
wheelchair access, tennis, city pool, trailer waste disp., Okanogan
River, boat launch, fishing, pets okay, open March to Oct.
Take State 20 north 5 miles to Omak - located on the east side of
town, near the fairgrounds.

LEADER LAKE (DNR) 🔼 RV
16 sites, picnic area, boat launch, fishing, FREE.
Take State 20 west 8.4 miles and Leader Lake Rd. .4 mile.

LEGION PARK (City of Okanogan) 🔼 RV
49 units, information (509)422-3600, trailers to 40', flush toilets,
showers, wheelchair access, on Okanogan River, nearby boat
launch, fishing, pets okay, open mid April thru Oct., $5/night.
Located in Okanogan, on State 215, at the north end of town.

PONDEROSA MOTOR LODGE & RV PARK (Private)
10 units w/full hookups, reservations (509)422-0400, trailers to 30', showers, laundry, wheelchair access, swimming pool, deli, nearby river & fishing, small pets okay, $12/night.
Located in Okanogan, at 1034 Second St.

ROCK CREEK (DNR)
6 sites, picnic area, drinking water, FREE.
Take State 20 west 9.8 miles and Loup Loup Creek Rd. north 3.9 miles.

ROCK LAKES (DNR)
8 sites, hiking trails, fishing, FREE.
Take State 20 wet 9.8 miles, Loup Loup Creek Rd. north 4.8 miles, and Rock Lakes Rd. northwest 5.8 miles.

CHEWELAH

CHEWELAH PARK (City)
Campsites, water, creek.
Follow signs to city park.

FORTYNINER CAMPGROUND & MOTEL (Private)
24 units w/full hookups, reservations (509)935-8613, showers, ice, indoor pool, jacuzzi, trailer waste disposal, $17/night.
Located on US 395 at the south edge of town.

GRANITE POINT PARK (Private)
80 units w/full hookups plus 5 w/water & elec., no tents, trailers to 35', reservations (509)233-2100, showers, laundry, groceries, rec room, playground, lake, swimming, fishing, boat launch & rental, no pets, $16-18/night.
Take US 395 southeast 17.5 miles - located about 1.5 miles south of Loon Lake.

SHORE ACRES RESORT (Private)
34 units w/full hookups, tents okay, reservations (509)233-2474, trailers to 40', showers, general store, cabins, playground, volley ball court, Loon Lake, swimming, fishing, boat launch, row/fishing/paddle boat rental, open April thru Sept., $17-19/night.
Take US 395 southeast 16 miles, State 292 west 1.8 miles, and Shore Acres Rd. south 1.8 miles.

SILVER BEACH RESORT (Private)
33 units w/full hookups, 14 w/water & elec., plus 6 w/elec. only, no tents, reservations (509)937-2811, trailers to 35', showers, laundry, dis. access, playground, restaurant, groceries, propane, trailer waste disposal, lake, boat launch/rental & moorage, swimming, fishing, pets okay, open April thru Sept., $20/night.
Take US 395 south 4 miles, State 231 south 2 miles, and Waitts Lake Rd. west 3 miles.

USK

BLUESLIDE RESORT (Private) [A] [RV]
31 sites w/full hookups, 29 w/elec., plus grassy tent area, reservations (509)445-1327, trailers to 60', group facilities, showers, laundry, wheelchair access, playground, heated pool, ball courts, play area, cabins & rooms, trailer waste disposal, on on Pend Oreille River, boat launch, boat gas, fishing, propane, groceries, hiking, pets okay, open Mem. Day thru Sept., $12-16/night.
Take State 20 north 21 miles.

SKOOKUM CHINOOK CAMPGROUND (Private) [A] [RV]
30 units, tents okay, reservations (509)447-4158, trailers to 26', showers, wheelchair access, on N. Skookum Lake, boat launch/moorage & dock, canoe & boat rentals, fishing, hiking, horses & pets okay, open mid April thru Oct., $10/night.
Take Kings Lake Rd. northeast 8.5 miles.

SKOOKUM CREEK (DNR) [A] [RV]
10 campsites, drinking water, FREE.
Campground is 4 miles east of Usk on Skookum Creek.

SOUTH SKOOKUM LAKE (Colville NF) [A] [RV]
14 units, trailers to 22', lake - speed limits, boat launch, fishing, hiking, elev. 3600', $8/night.
Take Kings Lake Rd. northeast 7.5 miles.

NEWPORT

JERRY'S LANDING RV PARK (Private) [A] [RV]
24 units w/full hookups plus 10 w/water & elec., tents okay, reservations (509)292-2337, trailers to 40', showers, wheelchair access, groceries, trailer waste disposal, on Lake Eloika, swimming, fishing, boat launch & rental, small pets okay, open April thru Sept., $15/night.
Take US 2 southwest approximately 19 miles and Oregon Rd. west 1 mile to Eloika Lake and RV park.

MARSHALL LAKE RESORT (Private) [A] [RV]
15 units w/full hookups, 20 w/water & elec., 7 w/water, plus tent area, reservations (509)447-4158, trailers to 36', showers, small store, motor boat/canoe/paddleboat rentals, boat launch & dock, horse corral, hiking, swimming, fishing, pets okay, $12-14/night.
Cross the Pend Oreille River bridge on US 2, turn left and travel along the river for 2.5 miles, turn right onto Bead Lake Rd. for 2.5 miles, turn right onto Marshall Lake Rd. and follow 1.5 miles.

OLD AMERICAN KAMPGROUND (Private) [A] [RV]
64 units w/full hookups plus tent area, reservations (509)447-3663, trailers to 40', wheelchair accessible restroom, showers,

laundry, trailer waste disposal, on Pend Oreille River, boat launch/dock, fishing, pets okay, $10-25/night.
Located in Newport, at 701 N. Newport Ave.

PEND OREILLE PARK (Pend Oreille County)
40 units, trailers to 20', information (509)447-4821, flush toilets, showers, wheelchair access, old growth trees, hiking & horse trails, horses & pets okay, open Mem. Day thru Labor Day.
Take US 2 southwest 16 miles.

PIONEER PARK (Colville NF)
14 units, trailers to 22', on Box Canyon Reservoir, fishing, elev. 2000', $8/night.
Cross the Pend Oreille River bridge on US 2, turn left and go 2 miles.

HUNTERS

CLOVER LEAF (Lake Roosevelt NRA)
6 tent sites, picnic area, drinking water, boat dock, swimming beach, $10/night.
Take State 25 north - located just south of Gifford.

DETILLON (Lake Roosevelt NRA)
12 campsites, boat-in only, boat dock, FREE.
Take State 20 south to its junction with the Spokane River and boat east 9 miles upriver to campground.

ENTERPRISE (Lake Roosevelt NRA)
13 campsites, boat-in only, FREE.
Located on the east bank of Lake Roosevelt; approximately 8 miles southwest of Hunters.

GIFFORD (Lake Roosevelt NRA)
47 units, trailers okay, picnic area, trailer waste disposal, boat ramp & dock, elev. 1249', $10/night.
Take State 25 north - located just south of Gifford.

HUNTERS (Lake Roosevelt NRA)
39 units plus 3 small group sites, trailers okay, picnic facilities, trailer waste disposal, swimming beach, boat ramp & dock, elev. 1233', $10/night.
Leave State 25 at Hunters and head west toward the water and campground.

JONES BAY (Lake Roosevelt NRA)
6 campsites, boat-in only, dock, elev. 1282', FREE.
Located on Lake Roosevelt, approximately 6 miles east of San Poil River's junction.

BRIDGEPORT

BIG RIVER RV PARK (Private) [A] [RV]
16 units w/full hookups, grassy tent area, reservations (509)686-2121, trailers to 40', showers, laundry, propane, on Columbia River, fishing, no pets, $7-14/night.
Located in Bridgeport, at 1415 Jefferson.

BRIDGEPORT (WA State Park) [A] [RV]
20 units w/hookups for water/elec. plus 14 tent sites, group area - reservations (509)686-7231, trailers to 45', flush toilets, showers, disabled access, community kitchen, trailer waste disposal, on Lake Rufus Woods, boat launch, fishing, open April thru Oct., $10-16/night.
Take State 173 northeast to State 17 and go north 1.5 miles.

WATERFRONT MARINA (City) [A] [RV]
18 units w/full hookups inc. cable, 4 w/water & elec., 1 handicap rv site plus 20 dry sites, reservations (509)686-4747, showers, covered picnic area, playground, trailer waste disposal, river, fishing, boat launch w/dock, pets okay, $11-16/night.
Located in Bridgeport, at Columbia and 7th St.

GRAND COULEE

COULEE PLAYLAND RESORT & RV PARK (Private) [A] [RV]
40 units w/hookups for water/elec./sewer, 13 w/water & elec., plus 12 tent sites, reservations (509)633-2671, showers, laundry, snack bar, groceries, playground, trailer waste disposal, on Banks Lake, swimming, fishing, boat launch & rental, pets okay, $16-18/night.
Follow State 155 west 1 mile to resort.

GRAND COULEE RV PARK (Private) [A] [RV]
10 units w/full hookups plus 16 tent sites, picnic area, showers, (509)633-0750, trailer waste disposal, pets okay, $9-15/night.
Follow State 174 northwest 2 miles.

KING'S COURT RV PARK (Private) [RV]
28 units w/full hookups, reservations (800)759-2608, trailers to 40', pull thrus, showers, wheelchair access, laundry, trailer waste disposal, store, pets okay, $15-20/night.
Located in Grand Coulee - right on State 174.

LAKEVIEW TERRACE RV PARK (Private) [A] [RV]
20 units w/hookups for water/elec./sewer plus group tent area, pull thrus, reservations (509)633-2169, showers, wheelchair access, laundry, picnic tables, playground, pets okay, $10 and up.
Take State 174 southeast 3 miles.

PLUM POINT (Lake Roosevelt NRA)
Tent campsites, boat-in or hike-in only, boat dock.
Located on lower end of Lake Roosevelt.

SPRING CANYON (Lake Roosevelt NRA)
78 units plus group area, trailers okay, picnic area, handicap
access, groceries, trailer & boat waste disposal, boat dock & ramp,
swimming, summer programs, pets okay, elev. 1234', $10/night.
Take State 174 southeast 5 miles to campground road, then head
1.1 miles north.

STEAMBOAT ROCK (WA State Park)
112 units w/hookups for water/elec./sewer, 82 tent & group
campsites, reservations (800) 452-5687, trailers to 60', flush toilets, showers, disabled access, snackbar, trailer waste disposal,
on Banks Lake, boat launch, fishing, water skiing, scuba diving
area, hiking & horse trails, pets okay, $11-16/night.
Take State 155 southwest 7.2 miles, and head northwest on
campground road.

SUN BANKS RESORT (Private)
250 units w/full hookups, tenters welcome, reservations
(509)633-3786, trailers to 70', pull thrus, showers, laundry,
wheelchair access, store, on Banks Lake, boat & jet ski rental,
boat launch/dock, swimming beach, fishing, hiking, horse corral,
trailer waste disposal, pets okay, $10-23/night.
Take State 155 south 3.5 miles.

FORT SPOKANE

CRYSTAL COVE (Lake Roosevelt NRA)
Tent campground, boat-in or hike-in only, on Spokane Arm of
Lake Roosevelt, FREE.
North of Fort Spokane; on Spokane River Arm.

FORT SPOKANE (Lake Roosevelt NRA)
67 units plus group area, trailers okay, handicap access, trailer
waste disposal, boat ramp, swimming, elev. 1247', $10/night.
Located just north of historic Fort Spokane on State 25.

PONDEROSA (Lake Roosevelt NRA)
Tent campground, boat-in or hike-in only, on spokane River Arm
of Lake Roosevelt, FREE.
Located north of Fort Spokane; on spokane River Arm of Lake
Roosevelt.

PORCUPINE BAY (Lake Roosevelt NRA)
31 units, trailers okay, trailer waste disposal, boat dock & ramp,
swimming, elev. 1238', $10/night.
Take State 25 south 8 miles, Porcupine Bay Rd. north 4.3 miles.

SEVEN BAYS MARINA (Private) 🔺 RV

36 units w/hookups for water/elec./sewer, 18 w/water, plus 40 tent sites, information (509)725-1676, trailers to 40', showers, laundry, wheelchair access, groceries, restaurant, propane, gas, on Lake Roosevelt, boat launch/moorage & dock, fishing, hiking, pets okay, open Easter thru Oct., $10-15/night.
Located south of Fort Spokane - follow signs off State 25.

WILBUR

BELLS RV/MOBILE HOME PARK (Private) 🔺 RV

30 sites w/full hookups plus grassy tent area, reservations (509)647-5888, showers, laundry, picnic area, pets okay, $10-14/night.
Located in Wilbur, one block off US 2, at east edge of town.

HALVORSON (BLM) 🔺

Campsites, boat-in or hike-in only, FREE.
Located north of Wilbur, on Lower Lake Roosevelt.

HAWK CREEK (Lake Roosevelt NRA) 🔺 RV

28 campsites, trailers okay, well water, on lake, fishing, boat launch & dock, pets okay, $10/night.
Take US 2 east to the town of Creston and go north 17 miles.

KELLER FERRY (Lake Roosevelt NRA) 🔺 RV

50 units, trailers okay, group sites - reservations (509)725-2751, trailer & boat waste disposal, boat ramp, swimming - lifeguard in summer, elev. 1229', $10-25/night.
Take State 21 14 miles north to Keller Ferry Landing.

PENIX CANYON (BLM) 🔺

Campsites, boat-in or hike-in only, boat ramp, FREE.
Located north of Wilbur, on Lower Lake Roosevelt.

THE RIVER RUE RV PARK (Private) 🔺 RV

25 units w/hookups for water/elec./sewer, 14 w/water & elec., plus 46 tent sites, reservations (509)647-2647, showers, wheelchair access, playfield, playground, groceries, snack bar, propane, trailer waste disposal, pets okay, $12-17/night.
Take State 21 north 14 miles.

SPOKANE

ALPINE MOTEL RV PARK (Private) 🔺 RV

22 pull thrus - 9 w/full hookups plus 9 w/water & elec., tents okay, reservations (509)928-2700, trailers to 50', showers, laundry, swimming pool, walk to restaurant & groceries, play area, pets okay, no water to sites Dec. thru Feb., $18-22/night.
Take I-90 east to exit #293 - located at 18815 Cataldo.

CEDAR VILLAGE RV PARK (Private)
7 units w/full hookups, no tents, reservations (509)838-8558, trailers to 35', cable tv, pets extra, $25/night.
Located in Spokane, 2 miles off the I-90 Airport/Business Loop, at W. 5415 Sunset Hwy.

DRAGOON CREEK (DNR)
22 campsites, drinking water, FREE.
Take US 395 north 9 miles.

FISHTRAP LAKE RESORT (Private)
20 units w/hookups for water & elec., tents okay, reservations (509)235-2284, trailers to 30', wheelchair access, groceries, ice, trailer waste disposal, swimming, fishing, boat launch & rental, pets okay, open mid April thru Sept., $10-12/night.
Take I-90 southwest 30 miles to exit #254 and Fishtrap Rd. southeast 3.5 miles to resort.

KOA OF SPOKANE (Private)
180 units w/full hookups plus 20 tent sites, reservations (509) 924-4722, trailers to 50', showers, laundry, wheelchair access, groceries, swimming pool, game room, playground, trailer waste disposal, pets okay, open March thru Oct., $20-26/night.
Take I-90 east to exit #293 and Barker Rd. north 1.3 miles.

LIBERTY LAKE PARK (County)
21 rv sites w/hookups for water & elec. plus tent area, information (509)456-4730, trailers to 35', showers, wheelchair access, playground, swimming, fishing, hiking, no pets, open mid April thru mid Oct., $7-10/night plus $2/person during summer
Take I-90 east to exit #296 and Liberty Lake Rd. south 4 miles.

LONG LAKE (DNR)
9 campsites, picnic shelter, handicap access, drinking water, boat launch, ancient Indian paintings, fishing, FREE.
Take State 291 to Long Lake; campground is 3 miles east of Long Lake Dam via Lapray Bridge Rd.

MALLARD BAY RESORT (Private)
50 units w/hookups for water & elec. plus tent area, reservations (509)299-3830, trailers to 40', pull thrus, showers, playground, trailer waste disposal, propane, Clear Lake, swimming, fishing, boat launch/dock & rental, pets okay, open April thru Sept., $14/night.
Take I-90 southwest to exit #264 and follow Salnaive Rd. north 2 miles to resort.

MOUNT SPOKANE (WA State Park)
12 units, trailers to 30', group area - reservations (509)456-4169, disabled access, picnic shelter, hiking, horse trails, $10/night.
Take US 2 northeast 10 mile and State 206 northeast 19 miles.

OVERLAND RV PARK (Private)
32 units w/hookups for water/elec./sewer plus tent area, reservations (509)747-1703, trailers to 65', pull thrus, showers operate April thru Sept., laundry, wheelchair access, groceries, playground, pets okay.
Leave I-90 at exit #272 and look for signs.

PARKLANE MOTEL & RV PARK (Private) RV
18 trailer sites w/hookups for water/elec./sewer, no tents, reservations (800)533-1626, free cont. breakfast, no restrooms, trailers to 45', laundry, ice, play area, pets okay, $21/night.
Leave I-90 at exit #283-B, go .8 mile to Havana St., north .03 mile to Sprague Ave., and east to 4412 Sprague Ave.

PICNIC PINES ON SILVER LAKE (Private)
30 units w/hookups for water/elec./sewer plus 12 tent sites, reservations (509)299-3223, trailers to 30', wheelchair accessible restrooms, restaurant/lounge, rec room, playground, swimming, fishing, boat launch & rental, pets okay, $13/night.
Take I-90 southwest to exit #270, the Medical Lake turnoff northwest 3.5 miles, and Silver Lake Rd. to campground.

RAINBOW COVE (Private)
4 units w/hookups for water/elec./sewer, 10 w/water & elec., 3 w/elec. only, plus 3 tent sites, reservations (509)299-3717, trailers to 36', showers, wheelchair access, picnic area, cafe, tackle shop, lake, boat launch/dock & rental, fishing, swimming, pets okay, open late April thru mid Oct., $14-15/night.
Take I-90 southwest to exit #270, the Medical Lake turnoff northwest 3.5 miles, and Clear Lake Rd. south 3 miles.

RIVERSIDE (WA State Park)
101 units, trailers to 45', flush toilets, showers, community kitchen, trailer waste disposal, on rivers, boat launch, fishing, horse trails & rental, ORV area, $10/night.
Located 6 miles northwest of Spokane.

RUBY'S ON SILVER LAKE (Private)
9 units w/water & elec., tents welcome, reservations (509)299-7829, trailers to 32', showers, wheelchair access, bait/tackle & camp supply store, trailer waste disposal, lake, swimming, fishing, row boat/kayak/canoe rentals, pets okay, open April thru Sept., $18/night.
Take I-90 southwest 7 miles to exit #270, the Medical Lake turnoff northwest 3.2 miles, and Four Lakes Rd. to resort.

SPOKANE TRAILER INNS (Private)
98 rv units w/full hookups plus 6 tent sites, reservations (800)659-4864, trailers to 65', pull thrus, showers, laundry, wheelchair access, tv room, playground, pets okay, $15-21/night.
Eastbound, leave I-90 at exit #285 and follow signs - located at 6021 East Fourth Ave. Westbound, take exit #287, turn left at

second light, right on Sprague Ave., left on Dollar Rd, take First 1 block, turn right to stop sign, and left on Fourth.

SUTTON BAY RESORT (Private) 🔺 RV
8 units w/hookups for water & elec. plus 12 tent sites, reservations (509)226-3660, trailers to 30', showers, wheelchair access, lots of room to play, on Newman Lake, boat launch/moorage & dock, fishing, boat/kayak/canoe rentals, hiking, small pets okay, open Mem. Day to Labor Day, $13-16/night.
Take I-90 east to exit #296 and head north 8 miles.

THE RESORT @ MT. SPOKANE (Private) 🔺 RV
21 units w/hookups for water & elec. plus 20 tent sites, reservations (509)238-9114, trailers to 40', showers, game room, playground, trailer waste disposal, groceries, restaurant/lounge, kids fishing area, horses & pets okay, $10-13/night.
Take US 2 northeast 10 miles and State 206 northeast 18 miles.

YOGI BEAR'S CAMP RESORT (Private) 🔺 RV
168 units w/full hookups plus 50 tent sites, reservations (800)494-7275, trailers to 60', pull thrus, showers, laundry, playground, trailer waste disposal, propane, miniature golf, basketball court, pets okay, $17-25/night.
Leave I-90 at exit #272, take Hallet Rd. east 1 mile and Mallon Rd. south .5 mile.

CHENEY

BUNKERS RESORT (Private) 🔺 RV
3 units w/full hookups plus 15 w/water & elec., reservations (509)235-5212, trailers to 35', showers, wheelchair access, groceries, cabins, trailer waste disposal, restaurant, on Williams Lake, boat launch & rental, fishing, swimming, hiking, pets okay, open April thru Sept., $10-20/night.
Take Cheney Plaza Rd. south 11.5 miles and Williams Lake Rd. west .5 mile.

PEACEFUL PINES RV PARK (Private) 🔺 RV
11 units w/full hookups, 14 w/water & elec., 14 w/out hookups, tents okay, reservations (509)235-4966, showers,trailer waste disposal, $12-17/night.
Located at 1231 W. 1st St.

WILLIAMS LAKE RESORT (Private) 🔺 RV
90 units w/full hookups, 50 w/water & elec. plus 10 tent sites, reservations (509)235-2391, trailers to 45', flush toilets, showers, wheelchair access, playground, propane, restaurant, groceries, trailer waste disposal, on lake, swimming, fishing, boat launch & rental, hiking, pets okay, $15-19/night.
Take Cheney Plaza Rd. south 11.5 miles and Williams Lake Rd. west 3.5 miles.

SPRAGUE

FOUR SEASONS CAMPGROUND (Private) 🏕 RV

24 units w/full hookups, 14 w/water or elec., plus grassy tent area, reservations (509)257-2332, trailers to 40', showers, wheelchair access, pool, groceries, trailer waste disposal, on Sprague Lake, boat launch/moorage/dock & rentals, fishing, pets okay, open mid March thru mid Oct., $13-18/night.
Go west towards Sprague Lake and follow signs to campground.

LAST ROUNDUP MOTEL/RV/CAMP (Private) 🏕 RV

13 units w/full hookups plus 10 tent sites, reservations (509)257-2583, showers, laundry, ice, playfield, pets okay, open April thru Sept., $12-16/night.
Located .5 mile east of I-90 Sprague exit #245.

SPRAGUE LAKE RESORT (Private) 🏕 RV

30 units w/full hookups plus 50 tent sites, reservations (509)257-2864, trailers to 40', pull thrus, showers, laundry, wheelchair access, ice, playground, trailer waste disposal, on lake, swimming, fishing, boat launch & rental, pets okay, open April thru Oct., $14-17/night.
Leave Sprague, and go west 2 miles to lake and resort.

WATERVILLE

DOUGLAS CREEK (BLM) 🏕

Dispersed camping, not recommended for trailers, fishing, hiking, birdwatching, swimming, orv, FREE.
Take State 2 east 8 miles, Road H SW down Slack Canyon and to Douglas Creek.

COULEE CITY

BLUE LAKE RESORT (Private) 🏕 RV

23 units w/water/elec./sewer, 33 w/water & elec., plus 44 tent sites, (509)632-5364, showers, groceries, playground, swimming, fishing, boat launch & rental, pets okay, $15/night.
Take US 2 west 2 miles and State 17 south 10 miles.

COULEE CITY PARK (City) 🏕 RV

34 units w/full hookups plus 106 tent sites, trailers to 24', reservations (509)632-5331, showers, playground, trailer waste disposal, on lake, swimming, fishing, boat launch, pets okay, $9-12/night.
Located in Coulee City, at north edge of town.

COULEE LODGE RESORT (Private) 🏕 RV

22 units w/full hookups, 11 w/water & elec., plus 19 tent sites, reservations (509)632-5565, disabled access, showers, laundry,

groceries, trailer waste disposal, on lake, swimming, fishing, boat launch, boat rental, pets okay, $13 and up.
Take US 2 west 2 miles and State 17 south 8 miles.

SUN VILLAGE RESORT (Private)
56 units w/full hookups, 40 w/water & elec., 28 tent sites, reservations (509)632-5664, pull thrus, showers, laundry, playground, rec room, store, propane, on lake, swimming, water skiing, boat launch/dock & rentals, fishing, hiking, pets okay, $16 and up.
Take US 2 west 2 miles, State 17 south 8 miles, and State Park Rd. east 1 mile to resort.

SUN LAKES PARK RESORT (Private)
59 units w/full hookups, tents okay, no fire pits, reservations (509)632-5291, showers, laundry, pool, playfield, groceries, propane, trailer waste disposal, on lake, swimming, fishing, boat launch & rental, golf, hiking, pets okay, $16 and up.
Take US 2 west 2 miles and State 17 south 7 miles.

SUN LAKES (WA State Park)
18 units w/full hookups, 175 standard sites, no fire pits, trailers to 50', group area, reservations (800)452-5687, flush toilets, showers, disabled access, groceries, trailer waste disposal, boat launch, fishing, swimming, boat & horse rental, horse trails, pets okay, $10-15/night.
Take US 2 west 2 miles and State 17 south 5 miles.

ODESSA

LAKEVIEW RANCH (BLM)
Campsites on 5300 acres, picnic area, fire grills, roads & trails in Channeled Scablands, horse corral & loading chute, wildlife viewing, geology, FREE.
Take State 21 north 2 miles and turn left on Lakeview Rd. for an additional mile.

REIMAN CITY PARK (City)
Campsites, flush toilets, drinking water.
Located at the corner of First Ave. and Second St.

HARRINGTON

TWIN LAKES (BLM)
Campsites on 15,000 acres, hiking & horse trails, mountain biking, boat launch, fishing, wildlife viewing, FREE.
Take Coffee Pot Rd. west 15 miles and Highline Rd. north 1.5 miles.

SOAP LAKE

SOAP LAKES SMOKIAM CAMPGROUND (City) 🅰 RV
52 units w/full hookups, tents okay, information (509)246-1211, showers, laundry, Soap Lake mud baths, playground, groceries, trailer waste disposal, swimming, fishing, pets okay, $7-10/night. Take State 17 north 3 miles to campground.

EPHRATA

OASIS PARK (Private) 🅰 RV
28 units w/full hookups, 41 w/water & elec., big tent area, reservations (509)754-5102, showers, laundry, wheelchair access, covered picnic area, playfield, pool, trailer waste disposal, groceries, mini golf, pond, fishing, hiking, pets okay, $10-16/night. On State 28, about 1 mile south of its junction with State 282.

QUINCY VALLEY GOLF & RV (Private) RV
5 units w/full hookups, no tents, reservations (509)787-3244, trailers to 40', golf course, pets okay, $15/night. Take State 28 south and west 16 miles to Quincy, turn south on State 281 and go 5 miles.

SHADY TREE RV PARK (Private) 🅰 RV
41 sites w/full hookups, tent area, reservations (509)785-2851, trailers to 40', showers, laundry, pets okay, restrooms closed Nov. thru April, $16-18/night. Take State 28 south 4 miles and State 283 southwest 15 miles - located near US 90.

STARS & STRIPES RV PARK (Private) 🅰 RV
73 units w/full hookups, 14 tent sites, reservations (509)787-1062, trailers to 40', 50 amp, showers, laundry, wheelchair access, heated pool, cabins, rv supply & grocery store, game room, game courts, playground, propane, trailer waste disposal, pets & horses okay, $16-18/night. Take State 28 south 5 miles to 5707 State Highway 28.

VILLAGER INN MOTEL/RV PARK (Private) RV
11 units w/full hookups, no tents, reservations (509)787-3515, no restrooms, trailers to 40', swimming pool, no pets, $19/night. Take State 28 south to Quincy - located at 711 Second Ave.

RITZVILLE

BEST WESTERN HERITAGE INN/RV PARK (Private) RV
30 units w/full hookups, reservations (509)659-1007, showers, laundry, wheelchair access, swimming & therapy pool, pets okay, $20/night. Located just off I-90 east at exit #221 – on frontage road.

ODESSA GOLF & RV PARK (Private)

12 units w/full hookups, reservations (509)982-0093, on golf course, pets okay, $10/night w/special rates to course golfers. Take I-90 west 14 miles, State 21 north 19 miles, and State 28 to the west end of Odessa and campground.

MOSES LAKE

BIG SUN RESORT & RV PARK (Private)

50 units w/full hookups plus 10 tent sites, reservations (509) 765-8294, showers, laundry, wheelchair access, playground, on Moses Lake, fishing, boat launch/rental, pets okay, $18/night. Leave I-90 at exit #176, take Broadway north .5 mile, and Marina Dr. west - located at 2300 W. Marina Dr.

MAR DON RESORT (Private)

160 sites w/full hookups, 55 w/water & elec., 135 dry sites, beach tent area, information (509)765-5061, flush toilets, showers, playground, cafe/lounge, groceries, propane, gas, on Potholes Reservoir, swimming beach, 2 boat launches, marina, moorage, fishing dock, boat & motor rental, hiking, pets okay - $5 fee, $16-19/night. Take State 17 southeast 10 miles and Potholes Reservoir Rd. west 8 miles.

PHEASANT RUN RV (Private)

10 units w/full hookups, no tents, restroom in store - wheelchair accessible, reservations (509)349-2514, trailers to 50', deli, pets okay, $15/night. Take State 17 south 12 miles and go east on State 170 toward Warden - located at 17005 State 170.

POTHOLES (WA State Park)

60 units w/full hookups plus 66 standard sites, trailers to 50', group area, reservations (800)452-5687, flush toilets, showers, wheelchair access - inc. trails, trailer waste disposal, on reservoir, boat launch, fishing, water skiing, pets okay, $11-16/night. Take State 17 southeast 10 miles and Potholes Reservoir Rd. west 13 miles.

SUN CREST RESORT (Private)

90 units w/full hookups, grassy tent area, reservations (509)765-0355, trailers to 52', pull thrus, showers, laundry, wheelchair access, pool, jacuzzi, game room, pets okay, $15-24/night. Take the Hansen Rd. exit off I-90 and go to 303 N. Hansen Rd.

WILLOWS TRAILER VILLAGE (Private)

38 units w/full hookups, 8 w/water & elec., plus large tent area, reservations (509)765-7531, showers, laundry, groceries, trailer waste disposal, pets okay, $13-17/night. Take State 17 south 2 miles and CR M southeast .3 mile.

OTHELLO

HUNTER HILL VINEYARD PARK (Private)
8 units w/hookups for water & elec. plus grassy tent area, reservations (509)346-2736, trailers to 37', showers, laundry, winery & tasting room, small store, trailer waste disposal, 60 nearby small lakes, pets okay, $10-16/night..
Head north out of Othello to McMananon Rd. - it's 9.5 miles to the vineyard park.

COLFAX

HILLTOP MOBILE HOME PARK (Private)
12 trailer sites w/full hookups, no tents, reservations (509)397-4029, trailers to 35', showers, laundry, wheelchair access, trailer waste disposal, small pets okay, $19/night.
Located on Highway 22, at the southwest edge of town.

TIFFANY'S RIVER INN @ BOYER PARK (Private)
14 units w/full hookups, 14 w/water & elec., tents okay, reservations (509)397-3208, trailers to 40', showers, laundry, wheelchair access, restaurant, trailer waste disposal, Snake River, swimming, fishing, marina, boat launch, hiking, pets okay, $14-16/night.
Take State 26 west and follow Almota Rd. to the park - located 23 miles south of Colfax.

PULLMAN

BOYER PARK & MARINA (Whitman County)
12 sites w/full hookups, 16 w/water & elec., picnic area, showers, snack bar, store, laundry, on north shore of Lower Granite Lake, swimming, pets okay, $12-17/night.
Located 2 miles west of Lower Granite Dam.

CITY OF PULLMAN RV PARK (City)
24 trailer sites w/full hookups, reservations (509)334-4555, nearby swimming pool, playfield, open April thru Nov., $12/night.
Take US 195 southeast 13 miles to Pullman, follow Grand Ave. 2 blocks northeast to Paradise St., go east to Spring St., and follow signs to City Playfield - located at south end of Playfield.

ILLIA LANDING (Corp)
Open camp area, trailers okay, picnic facilities, on Lower Granite Lake, boat ramp, pets okay, $7/night.
Located 3 miles west of Lower Granite Dam.

WAWAWAI COUNTY PARK (Whitman County)
9 units, trailers to 24', picnic area, handicap access, game area, on Lower Granite Lake, pets okay, $7/night.
Located 16 miles southwest of Pullman, on Wawawai Rd.

WAWAWAI LANDING (Corp)

Open camp area, trailers okay, picnic area, on Lower Granite Lake, boat ramp, $7/night.
Located 19 miles southwest of Pullman, on Wawawai Rd.

CONNELL

CONNELL PARK ESTATES (Private)

9 units w/full hookups, no tents, reservations (509)234-2222, trailers to 30', showers, laundry, wheelchair access, trailer waste disposal, small pets okay, $20/night.
Located in Connell, just off Highway 395, at 200 W. Hawthorne.

DEVILS BEACH (Corp)

Primitive camp area, on Snake River, boat ramp, $7/night.
Located 6 miles south of Kahlotus, WA, on Devil's Canyon Rd.

POMEROY

ALDER THICKET (Umatilla NF)

4 units, no potable water, elev. 5100', FREE.
Take State 128 south 9.1 miles, Mountain Rd. south 7.7 miles, and FSR 40 south 3.3 miles.

BIG SPRINGS (Umatilla NF)

8 units, picnic facilities, no potable water, elev. 5000', FREE.
Take State 128 southeast 9.1 miles, Mountain Rd. south 7.7 miles, FSR 40 south 8.8 miles to Clearwater Lookout, and FSR 42 3 miles to campground.

BLYTON LANDING (Corp)

Campsites, picnic facilities, on Lower Snake River - Granite Lake, boat ramp, pets okay, $7/night.
Located on North Shore Snake River Rd.

BOUNDARY (Umatilla NF)

5 units, trailers to 32', no potable water, elev. 4400', FREE.
Take State 128 south 9.1 miles, Mountain Rd. south 7.7 miles, and FSR 40 south .1 mile.

CENTRAL FERRY (WA State Park)

60 units w/full hookups, 9 dry sites, trailers to 45', group area, reservations (800)452-5687, flush toilets, showers, disabled access, picnic shelter, trailer & boat waste disposal, on Snake River, boat launch, fishing, water skiing, pets okay, $10-15/night.
Take US 12 northwest 13 miles and State 127 north 9 miles.

CHIEF TIMOTHY (WA State Park)

25 units w/full hookups, 8 w/water & elec., plus 33 standard sites, reservations (800)452-5687, trailers to 40', flush toilets,

showers, wheelchair access, groceries, picnic shelter, trailer waste disposal, on Lower Granite Lake, boat launch, docks for boat campers, fishing, water sports, interpretive center - Lewis & Clark Expedition - open Wed. thru Sun. 1-5:00 pm, $10-15/night.
Take US 12 east 22 miles.

LITTLE GOOSE LANDING (Corp)　　　　　🔺 RV
Open camp area, trailers okay, handicap access, on Snake River, boat ramp, $7/night.
Located 9 miles northeast of Starbuck, WA, on Little Goose Rd.

LYON'S FERRY (WA State Park)　　　　　🔺 RV
50 units - some will hold trailers to 45', flush toilets, showers, picnic shelter, disabled access, trailer waste disposal, historic site, at confluence of Snake & Palouse Rivers, boat launch, fishing, swimming, pets okay, open April thru Sept., $10/night.
US 12 northwest 22 miles, State 261 northwest 18 miles.

LYON'S FERRY MARINA & RV PARK (Port)　　🔺 RV
18 units w/full hookups plus 40 w/dry sites, tents okay, reservations (509)399-2001, trailers to 40', showers, wheelchair access, restaurant, store, propane, on river, boat ramp & rental, swimming, fishing, pets okay, $7-10/night.
US 12 northwest 22 miles, State 261 northwest 18 miles.

MISERY (Umatilla NF)　　　　　　　　　🔺
5 tent sites, no potable water, hiking, elev. 6000', FREE.
Take State 128 south 9.1 miles, Mountain Rd. south 7.7 miles, FSR 40 southeast 16.2 miles, and FSR 4030 south .5 mile.

NISQUALLY JOHN LANDING (Corp)　　　　🔺 RV
Open camp area, trailers okay, handicap access, on Snake River - Lower Granite Lake, boat ramp, pets okay, $7/night.
Located on North Shore Snake River Rd.

PALOUSE FALLS (WA State Park)　　　　　🔺 RV
10 units, trailers to 40', flush toilets, showers, picnic shelter, on Palouse River, 190' waterfall, hiking, open April thru Sept., $10/night.
US 12 northwest 22 miles, State 261 northwest 21 miles.

PANJAB (Umatilla NF)　　　　　　　　　🔺 RV
2 units, trailers to 18', no potable water, river, wilderness hiking, fishing in Tucannon River, elev. 3000', $3/night.
Take Geiger/Niebel Gulch Rd. southwest 17.6 miles, FSR 47/ Tucannon Rd. southwest 12.1 miles, and FSR 4713 south .2 mile.

PANJAB TRAILHEAD (Umatilla NF)　　　　🔺
7 tent sites, fishing, hiking, horse trails, elev. 3400', $3/night.
Take Geiger & Niebel Gulch Rds. southwest 17.6 miles, FSR 47/Tucannon Rd. southwest 12.1 miles, and FSR 4713 south 2.3 miles.

RIPARIA REC. AREA (Corp)
Primitive campground, picnic facilities, on Snake River, $7/night.
Located 3 miles west of Little Goose Dam, on North Shore Rd.

TEAL (Umatilla NF)
5 units, picnic facilities, no potable water, view of Wenaha-Tucannon Wilderness, hiking, nearby 4-wheel roads, elev. 5600', FREE.
Take State 128 south 9.1 miles, Mountain Rd. south 7.7 miles, and FSR 40 south 8.8 miles,and FSR 200 south .3 miles. Located just past Clearwater Lookout Tower.

TUCANNON (Umatilla NF)
13 units, trailers to 18', group picnic area, no potable water, river, nearby stocked fishing ponds, elev. 2600', FREE.
Take Geiger & Niebel Gulch Rds. southwest 17.6 miles, FSR 47/Tucannon Rd. southwest 8.1 miles, and FSR 160 south .2 mile.

WICKIUP (Umatilla NF)
3 units, primitive facilities, no potable water, elev. 5800', FREE.
Take State 128 south 9.1 miles, Mountain Rd. south 7.7 miles, and FSR 40 south 17 miles, and FSR 44 for 3 miles.

WILLOW LANDING (Corp)
Open camp area, picnic facilities, on Snake River, pets okay, $7/night.
Take US 12 northwest 13 miles, State 127 north 8 miles, Deadman Rd. east 4 miles, and Hasting Hill Rd. north 5 miles.

DAYTON

GODMAN (Umatilla NF)
8 tent sites, picnic area, no potable water, horse facilities, trails, elev. 6050', FREE.
Take North Fork Touchet River Rd. southeast 14.8 miles, and FSR 46 south 11 miles.

LEWIS & CLARK TRAIL (WA State Park)
30 units, some trailers to 28', group sites - reservations (509)337-6457, flush toilets, showers, community kitchen, trailer waste disposal, campfire programs in summer, fishing, $10/night.
Take US 12 southwest 5 miles.

TEEPEE (Umatilla NF)
7 units, trailers to 18', wilderness hiking, elev. 5700', $3/night.
Take North Fork Touchet River Rd. southeast 14.8 miles, FSR 46 south 11 miles, and FSR 4608 northeast 5 miles.

ASOTIN

FIELDS SPRING (WA State Park) 🏕️ RV
20 primitive sites, some trailers to 30', community kitchen, wheelchair access, trailer waste disposal, Puffer Butte trail, $7/night.
Take State 129 southwest 23.5 miles.

HELLER'S BAR (BLM) 🏕️ RV
10 sites, on Grande Ronde River, boat ramp, elev. 820', FREE.
Take State 129 south 17 miles.

RICHLAND

ARROWHEAD RV PARK (Private) 🏕️ RV
70 units w/full hookups, tents okay, reservations (509)545-8206, trailers to 50', pull thrus, showers, laundry, wheelchair access, pets extra, $22/night.
Located southeast of Richland, in Pasco, at 3120 Commercial.

AYER BOAT BASIN (Corps) 🏕️ RV
20 primitive sites, picnic shelter, on Snake River, boat ramp, pets okay, $7/night.
Take State 124 east 24 miles thru Clyde and Pleasant View to campground.

BEACH RV PARK (Private) RV
39 units w/full hookups, reservations (509) 588-5959, trailers to 40', pull thrus, showers, laundry, wheelchair access, Yakima River, fishing, pets okay, $18/night.
Take I-82 west 11 miles to the Benton City exit - located in Benton City, on Abby Ave.

BIG FLAT REC. AREA (Corps) 🏕️ RV
Primitive camp area, on Snake River, boat ramp, $7/night.
Take US 12 to Pasco-Kahlotus Rd., head east 11 miles and follow Dalton Rd. south 1 mile.

CHARBONNEAU PARK (Corps) 🏕️ RV
18 units w/full hookups plus 36 w/elec., tents okay, trailers to 60', pull thrus, showers, wheelchair access, playground, propane, gas, trailer waste disposal, on Lake Sacajawea, swimming, fishing, boat launch, limited facilities Nov. thru March, pets okay, $12-14/night.
I-82 east 5 miles, State 14 northeast 4 miles, US 12 south 3 miles, State 124 east 8 miles, and Sun Harbor Dr. north 2 miles.

COLUMBIA MOBILE VILLAGE (Private)
20 units w/full hookups, reservations (509)783-3314, pets okay, $15/night.
In Kennewick. Take State 14 and go 1.3 miles on Clearwater Ave.

COLUMBIA PARK (City)

18 sites w/water & elec., 82 tent/dry sites, reservations (509)585-4200, trailers to 70', showers, groceries, trailer waste disposal, on Lake Wallula, bike/hike trails, pets okay, open May thru Sept.
Take US 12 southeast to Columbia Center exit and follow signs.

DESERT GOLD TRAILER PARK/MOTEL (Private) RV

85 sites w/full hookups, no tents, reservations (509)627-1000, showers, laundry, groceries, pool, pets okay, $18/night.
Take US 12 southeast to Columbia Dr. and follow signs.

FISHHOOK PARK (Corps)

41 units w/water & elec., 20 tent sites, trailers to 45', pull thrus, showers, wheelchair access, playground, trailer waste disposal, on Lake Sacajawea, swimming, fishing, boat launch, elev. 4500', open April thru Sept., pets okay, $9-13/night.
I-82 east 5 miles, State 14 northeast 4 miles, US 12 south 3 miles, State 124 east 15 miles, and Page Rd. north 4 miles.

GREEN TREE RV PARK (Private) RV

50 rv sites w/full hookups, no restrooms, reservations (509)547-6220, trailers to 45', showers, laundry, pets okay, $18/night.
Leave I-82 east on exit #13 - park is just north, on 4th Ave.

HOOD PARK (Corps) A RV

69 units w/elec., tents okay, trailers to 60', pull thrus, showers, wheelchair access, playground, trailer waste disposal, on Lake Wallula, swimming, fishing, boat launch, elev. 3500', pets okay, open May thru Sept., $7-12/night.
I-82 east 5 miles, State 14 northeast 4 miles, and US 12 south 3 miles - located at junction with State 124.

LAKE EMMA REC. AREA (Corps) A RV

Primitive camp area, on Snake River, $7/night.
Take US 12 to Pasco-Kahlotus Hwy, follow this to Murphy Rd., head south 3 miles, and take Page Rd. south 1 mile.

MADAME DORION MEMORIAL PARK (Corps) A RV

15 units, picnic facilities, trailer waste disposal, on Lake Wallula, boat launch, pets okay, $10/night.
Located .7 mile south of Wallula, WA, on US 12.

MATTHEWS REC. AREA (Corps) A RV

Primitive area, on Snake River, boat ramp, pets okay, $7/night.
Take State 124 north 8.6 miles to Clyde, Lower Monumental Rd. for 15.2 miles, turn left 1 mile before the dam and drive east 1 miles to campground.

PLYMOUTH PARK (Corps) A RV

17 units w/full hookups plus 16 w/water & elec., trailers to 40', showers, wheelchair access, trailer waste disposal, lake, river,

swimming, fishing, boat launch, no hookups off season, $10-16/night.
Take I-82 south 29 miles - park is 1 mile west of Umatilla Bridge.

TRAILER CITY PARK (Private)   RV
60 sites w/full hookups, no tents, reservations (509)783-2513, no restrooms, trailers to 40', laundry, trailer waste disposal, small pets, $16/night.
In Kennewick, at 7120 W. Bonnie Ave.

WALKER REC. AREA (Corps)   A RV
Primitive camp area, on Snake River, $7/night.
Take State 124 north 8.6 miles to Clyde, Lower Monumental Rd. northwest 4 miles to Wooden Rd., and follow this 9.2 miles.

WINDUST PARK (Corps)   A RV
20 units, trailers to 70', wheelchair access, trailer waste disposal, on Lower Snake River, boat launch, fishing, pets okay, open year round - limited facilities Oct thru March, $7/night.
Take US 12 to Pasco/Kahlotus Hwy., head northeast 28 miles, and follow Burr Canyon Rd. south 6 miles.

WALLA WALLA

FORT WALLA WALLA CAMPGROUND (City)   A RV
25 sites w/full hookups plus 25 tent sites, reservations (509)527-4527, trailers to 50', showers, wheelchair access, playground, trailer waste disposal, 200 acre park w/museum, remote car & airplane track, nature trail, pets okay, open year round - no restrooms in winter, $10-15/night.
Follow State 125 southwest 4 miles, and Dalles Military Rd. west .7 mile.

GOLDEN WEST ESTATES (Private)   RV
8 rv sites w/full hookups inc. cable, no tents, adults only, reservations (509)529-4890, showers, laundry, wheelchair access, heated pool, club house w/game area, no pets, $12/night.
Take West Rose Pl. to Jasper - located at 1424 Jasper.

RV RESORT FOUR SEASONS (Private)   RV
90 rv sites w/full hookups, reservations (509)529-6072, trailers to 50', pull thrus, showers, laundry, wheelchair access, pets okay, $22/night.
Follow State 125 southwest 4 miles and Dalles Military Rd. west .7 mile.

INDEX

Cinder Hill - 122
Circle 5 Trailer Park - 114
Circle Creek Campground - 19
Circle W RV Park - 90
City Center Trailer Park - 29
Clackamas Lake - 103
Clark Creek Org. Camp - 73
Clay Creek - 33
Clear Creek Crossing - 109
Clear Lake - 103
Clearwater Falls - 79
Cleator Bend - 63
Cloud Cap Saddle - 100
Clyde Holliday - 155
Cobble Rock - 117
Coburg Hills RV Resort - 71
Coho Marina & RV Park - 36
Cold Springs - 114
Cold Springs Resort - 113
Coldwater Cove - 68
Collier State Park - 134
Columbia Gorge RV Village - 54
Columbia River Gorge Resort - 99
Condon MH/RV Park - 108
Contorta Point - 127
Coolwater Camp - 81
Corral Creek - 135
Corral Springs - 130
Cottage Grove Lake Primitive - 76
Cottonwood Rec. Area - 135
Cottonwood - 154
Cougar Rec. Area - 70
Country Campgrounds - 159
Country Hills Resort - 47
Cove Creek - 64
Cove Palisades State Park - 111
Cover - 85
Cow Camp Horse Camp - 115
Cow Creek Center RV Park - 85
Cow Meadow - 122
Coyote - 144
Coyote Rock RV Park - 27
Crane Prairie - 123
Crane Prairie Resort - 123
Crater Lake Motel/RV Park - 130
Crater Lake Resort - 133
Crater Lake RV Park - 133
Crescent - 155
Crescent Creek - 127
Crescent Lake - 127
Crescent RV Park - 127
Crook County RV Park - 117
Crooked River Ranch Park - 119
Crown Point RV Park - 56
Crown Villa RV Park - 120
Crystal Corral Park - 117
Crystal Crane Hot Springs - 161
Cultus Corral Horse Camp - 123
Cultus Lake - 123
Cushman Rv & Marina - 34
Cutsforth Park - 146

Cy Bingham Park - 128
Cypress Grove RV Park - 90
Cyrus Horse Camp - 111
Dairy Point - 131
Daley Creek - 92
Daphne Grove - 42
Darlings Resort - 34
Deadhorse Creek - 132
Deadhorse Lake - 132
Deep Creek - 117, 135
Deer Creek - 152
Delintment Lake - 162
Delta - 70
Depot Park - 155
Deschutes Bridge - 123
Deschutes River Resort - 111
Deschutes River State Park - 101
Desert Terrace - 119
Detroit Lake State Park - 64
Devil's Canyon - 109
Devil's Lake State Park - 27
Devils Flat - 86
Devils Half Acre - 103
Devils Lake - 120
Dewitt's Town & Country RV - 47
Dexter Shores RV Park - 73
Diamond Lake - 83
Diamond Lake RV Park - 83
Diamond Mill - 23
Digit Point - 130
Discovery Point Resort - 37
Dixie - 155
Dixon Greenvalley Campers - 88
Doe Point - 92
Dolly Varden - 73
Dougherty Springs - 144
Dove Creek - 148
Dovre - 25
Drift Creek Landing - 31
Drift Fence - 149
Driftwood - 115
Driftwood II - 34
Driftwood RV Park - 40, 48
Dry Creek Horse Camp - 117
Duck Lake - 151
Dufur City Park - 105
Dumont Creek - 85
Duncan Reservoir - 131
Dusty Spring - 141
Eagle Creek - 99
Eagle Forks - 152
Eagle Rock - 78
Eagle Valley RV/MH Park - 152
East Bay - 131
East Davis Lake - 128
East Lake - 123
East Lake Resort & RV Park - 123
East Lemolo - 84
East Shore Recreation Site - 37
Ecola State Park - 20
Edson Creek - 44

Sugar Pine - 96
Summer Lake Hot Springs - 133
Summit Lake - 104, 129
Sumpter Pine RV Park - 153
Sundowner Mobile Park - 147
Sunlake Marina RV - 39
Sunnyside Park - 67
Sunset - 137
Sunset Bay Stae Park - 40
Sunset Cove - 129
Sunset Lake Resort - 19
Sunset Landing - 28
Sunstrip - 60
Surfwood Campground - 38
Surveyor - 138
Susan Creek - 79
Suttle Lake Resort - 116
Sutton Campground - 36
Swamp Wells - 122
Swedes Landing - 152
Sweet Home/Foster L. KOA - 67
Tahkenitch Campground - 38
Tahkenitch Landing - 38
Tamarack - 148
Target Meadows - 142
Taylor's Travel Park - 72
Taylors Landing - 32
Ten Mile Creek - 32
Thief Valley Campground - 148
Thielsen View - 84
Thompson Reservoir - 131
Three Creek Lake - 116
Three Creek Meadow - 116
Threehorn - 86
Tillicum Beach - 32
Tilly Jane - 101
Timber River RV Park - 79
Time And A Half - 147
Timothy Springs - 142
Timpanogas Lake - 76
Tin Can - 90
Tingley Lake Estates - 138
Tipsu Tyee Camp - 95
Todd Lake - 122
Toketee Lake - 80
Toll Bridge Park - 101
Tollbridge - 150
Tollgate - 105
Tomichi Village - 26
Topsy - 138
Town & Country RV Park - 56
Trail Bridge - 69
Trailer Park Village - 63
Trails End Campground - 48
Trails West RV Park - 112
Trapper Creek - 129
Trask Park - 24
Trask River Mobile Park - 24
Trees of Oregon RV/B&B - 80
Triangle Lake Horse Camp - 61
Trillium Lake - 104

Trout Creek - 67, 112
Trout Farm - 157
Troy Wilderness Lodge Park - 145
Trucke's RV Park - 20
Tucker Flat - 86
Tucker Park - 100
Tugman State Park - 38
Tumalo - 122
Tunnel Launch - 152
Twin Cedars Mobile Park - 65
Twin Lakes - 151
Twin Lakes Resort - 126
Twin Rivers Vacation Park - 82
Twin Springs - 161
Two Color - 148
Two Pan - 144
Tyee - 36, 80
Ukiah-Dale Forest - 149
Umatilla Forks - 143
Umatilla Marina & RV Park - 141
Umpqua Lighthouse Park - 38
Umpqua Safari RV Park - 82
Union Creek - 87, 153
Unity Lake - 158
Unity Motel & RV Park - 158
Upper Arm - 65
Upper Buck - 131
Upper Jones - 133
Valley Falls Store Camp - 136
Valley Of The Rogue -91
Van Duzer Forest - 27
Venice RV Park - 20
Vermillion Bar - 148
Viento State Park - 100
Vigne - 145
Village Green RV Park - 77
Village RV Park - 162
Vincent Creek - 38
Wahtum Lake - 101
Waldport/Newport KOA - 32
Wallowa Lake - 146
Walt's Cozy Camp - 134
Walton Lake - 118
Wandamere Campground - 30
Wandering Spirit RV Park - 28
Wapinitia - 110
Warehouse Beach Rec. Area - 141
Wasco County Fairgrounds - 106
Washburne State Park - 33
Water Wheel Campground - 134
Waterloo Campground - 65
Watkins - 95
Waxmyrtle (Siltcoos) - 36
Wayside RV & Mobile Park - 36
Webb Park - 26
Welch Creek - 150
Well Springs - 96
West Cultus - 127
West Davis Lake - 129
West South Twin Lake - 127
Westerner RV Park - 161

311

DISCOVER THE PACIFIC NORTHWEST'S BEST VACATION GETAWAYS

KiKi Canniff has spent the last 25 years exploring the Pacific Northwest. During that time she has written nearly a dozen books, including *Oregon Free, Washington in Your Pocket, THE Campground Guide, Northwest Free,* and *Great Vacations in Oregon & Washington.*

Her straight-forward style, and dependable information have made her a long-standing favorite with local residents. She has explored every corner of Oregon & Washington, and catalogued thousands of fun family attractions.

GREAT VACATIONS IN OREGON & WASHINGTON; A Travel Writer's Favorite Vacation Getaways was written to answer the three questions she's most often asked: "Where do you take your family when you go on vacation?, Can you recommend a good place to stay?, and, Please share some of your favorite places with us."

Each of the book's ten vacation regions has its own chapter, with enough information to plan several weekend getaways or a complete vacation. You'll learn about the area's history and scenic attractions, where to find the best trails, wildlife viewing, special attractions, local festivals, and much, much more.

At the end of each chapter you'll discover listings of area bed & breakfasts, resorts, motels, youth hostels, rv parks and campgrounds. Something for every budget!

Whether you're looking for a coastal getaway, mountain escape, old-growth retreat or desert journey, KiKi will show you how to have a great time in the Pacific Northwest's best vacation areas!

ORDER FORM

Please send:

___THE Campground Guide;
     Oregon/Washington Edition

$16.50 ea. _____

___Great Vacations in Oregon &
     Washington; A Travel Writer's
     Favorite Vacation Getaways

$18.50 ea. _____

Shipping __2.00*__

Total amount due _____

Ship to:

Name _____

Address _____

City/State/Zip _____

Bill to:

Credit Card # _____

Exp. date/phone number _____

Name on Credit Card _____

Signature _____

Mail to:

Ki^2 Enterprises
1214 Wallace Rd. NW #165
Salem, OR 97304

These books are also available from your favorite bookseller!

C99